ALEXANDRIA

Alexandria

City of Memory

Michael Haag

YALE UNIVERSITY PRESS

New Haven and London

For information about this and other Yale University Press publications, please contact:
U.S. Office: sales.press@yale.edu   yalebooks.com
Europe Office: sales@yaleup.co.uk   www.yalebooks.co.uk

Set in Minion by SNP Best-set Typesetter, Hong Kong
Printed in the United Kingdom at the University Press, Cambridge

ISBN 0–300–10415–4

Library of Congress Catalog Control Number 2004107532

A catalogue record for this book is available from the British Library.

10 9 8 7 6 5 4 3 2 1

To Loutfia
το όνομα του αγαθού δαίμονος

Capitally, what is this city of ours? What is resumed in the word Alexandria?

Lawrence Durrell, *The Alexandria Quartet*

CONTENTS

ILLUSTRATIONS

Credits

1, 19, 21, 23, 61, 66, 69, 84: Photograph by Michael Haag; 2, 3, 8, 12, 16, 27, 28, 29, 31, 33, 34, 41, 42, 43, 44, 46, 47, 48, 49, 50, 52, 53, 54, 56, 76: Private Collection; 4, 22, 25: Roger-Viollet, Paris; 5, 9, 10, 11, 13, 15, 18, 24, 32, 58: Michael Haag Collection; 6, 7, 14: King's College, Cambridge; 17, 39: Samuel Lock Collection; 20: Benaki Museum, Athens; 35, 36, 38, 45: Jacques Mawas Collection; 37, 74, 79, 80: Eric Vincendon Collection; 40: Marta Loria Fuller Collection; 51, 68, 75: Penelope Durrell Hope Collection; 55: Jackie Rolo Collection; 57: Mary Bentley Honor Collection; 59: Sandro Manzoni Collection; 60, 62, 64, 82: Eve Cohen Durrell Collection; 63, 65, 71, 77, 78: Paul Gotch Collection; 67: Gaston Zananiri Collection; 70, 81: Bernard de Zogheb Collection; 72, 73: Frances Fedden Collection; 83: Diana Forde Mitchell Collection

SOURCES, SUGGESTED READING
AND ACKNOWLEDGEMENTS

A great amount of the information in this book comes from people who have known cosmopolitan Alexandria and have talked or written to me about it or whose diaries, letters, photographs, etc., have been made available to me by themselves, their friends or their families. Their names are found among the list of persons acknowledged below. They are also mentioned by name when quoted in the text, though in most cases spoken material has not been footnoted, only written sources. My visits to Alexandria with Eve Durrell, who relived her memories of the city *in situ* have added considerably to the value of this book, as have my excursions with my friend Bernard de Zogheb, who was truly the last of the Alexandrians.

The footnotes may be scoured for books and other published sources of particular interest. For the reader wanting general accounts of the city, however, and of Durrell, Forster and Cavafy, the following remarks may prove helpful.

Little has been published on the history of modern cosmopolitan Alexandria beyond the essays in *Alexandrie entre deux mondes*, edited by Robert Ilbert (Aix-en-Provence 1988), and *Alexandrie 1860–1960*, edited by Robert Ilbert and Ilios Yannakakis (Paris 1992). A few books have been written in the guise of memoirs, but while these can convey an atmosphere they too often rely on invention and thus cannot be taken as historical or biographical records. One of these is André Aciman's fictionalised memoir *Out of Egypt* (New York 1994).

The ancient city is wonderfully served by Peter M. Fraser's *Ptolemaic Alexandria* (Oxford 1972), Alfred J. Butler's *The Arab Conquest of Egypt*, second edition, edited by Peter M. Fraser (Oxford 1978), and Jean-Yves Empereur's *Alexandria Rediscovered* (London 1998), while the ancient history and topography of the Lake Mareotis region and the Western Desert is recorded in Anthony de Cosson's *Mareotis* (London 1935). I am indebted to these works for much information on the ancient city and its surroundings.

There are two biographies of Forster, P. N. Furbank's magisterial *E. M. Forster: A Life* (Oxford 1979) and Nicola Beauman's *Morgan: A Biography of E. M. Forster* (London 1993), which introduces some new material. Forster's *Alexandria: A History and a Guide* was originally published in Alexandria in 1922, and a second edition was published there in 1938; they are as gold dust. The first edition was republished in New York in 1961, and again in London in 1982, with an introduction by Lawrence Durrell, then again with revised notes in 1986; these are scarce. A combined edition of *Alexandria: A History and a Guide* and Forster's *Pharos and Pharillon*, edited by Miriam Allott, was published in London in 2004.

There are also two biographies of Durrell, Gordon Bowker's tendentious *Through the Dark Labyrinth* (London 1996) and Ian MacNiven's far better researched *Lawrence Durrell: A Biography* (London 1998). A curiosity of both these Durrell biographies, however, is that they betray very little knowledge of Durrell's life in Alexandria and of how he came to write *Justine*, *Balthazar*, *Mountolive* and *Clea*, the novels comprising *The Alexandria Quartet* (London 1962).

Robert Liddell's *Cavafy: A Critical Biography* (London 1974), has the virtue of being written by someone who knew Alexandria and providing a portrait of both the city and the poet. The best translation of Cavafy's poetry is Edmund Keeley and Philip Sherrard's *C. P. Cavafy: Collected Poems* (London 1975).

During the journey of writing this book, and even before I knew that the journey had begun, I benefited from the information, clues, encouragement and assistance provided by a great many people, to whom I give my thanks: Mayssa Abaza, Khaled El Adm, Hajj Ahmed, Miriam Allott, Naomi 'Moughee' Athanassian, Mohammed Awad, Mohammed Badr, Zeinab Niazi Badr, Ralph Bagnold, Nicola Beauman, Morris Bierbrier, John Bodley, Joseph Boulad, John Cromer Braun, Reverend Robert Braun, Alice Brinton, John Brinton, Josie Brinton, Jon Buller, Adriana Butta-Calice, Lisa Chaney, William Cleveland, Mario Colucci, Artemis Cooper, Jacqueline Klat Cooper, Mariangela Corteza, Robert Crisp, Lucienne Dalil, Jamie Darke, Eve Cohen Durrell, Lawrence Durrell, Roger Evans, Frances Fedden, Patrick Leigh Fermor, Elizabeth Wace French, Marta Loria Fuller, Ronald Fuller, P. N. Furbank, Béatrice Gasche, Robert Gasche, Paul Gotch, Mary Mollo Hadkinson, Hala Halim, Yussef Halim, Denise Harvey, Mary Bentley Honor, Penelope Durrell Hope, Gabriel Josipovici, Edmund Keeley, Sir Frank Kermode, Françoise Kestsman, George Kypreos, George Kyriakides, Caroline Lassalle, Maria Leoncavallo, Canon Howard Levitt, Robert Liddell, Samuel Lock, Ian MacNiven, Jackie Magar, Sybil Magar, Sandro Manzoni, Alfonso De Martino, Lina Mattatia, Jacques Mawas, Nicolette Pinto Mawas, Tawfik Megalli, Anahide Merametdjian, Diana Forde Mitchell, Mia Monasterly, Anthea Morton-Saner, Adel 'Roby' Moursi, Thalia Nakeeb, Emin Niazi, Ann O'Leary, Herta Pappo, Mavis Phocas, Frank Pike, Richard Pine, Father Pierre Riches, Samir Rifaat, John Rodenbeck, Leslie Rofe, Jackie Rolo, Sir Steven Runciman, Jack Sarfatti, Amr Shadi, Jean Shamas, Philip Sherrard, Waghida Sidahmed, Mohammed Sirry, Yana Sistovaris, Alan G. Thomas, Victoria Thompson, Donatienne Tortillia, Molly Tuby, Eric Vincendon, Gwyn Williams, Nevine Yusri, Adel Abou Zahra, Nadim Zaidan, Gaston Zananiri, Bernard de Zogheb, Ali Zulficar.

I would also like to thank Faber and Faber, Duckworth, Princeton University Press, the estate of Lawrence Durrell, the British Library and King's College, Cambridge.

MAPS

Map 1 The country round Alexandria
from Alamein to Aboukir

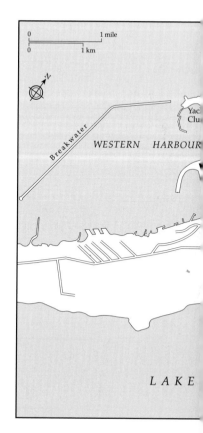

Map 2 Alexandria and Ramleh in the
1910s and 1920s

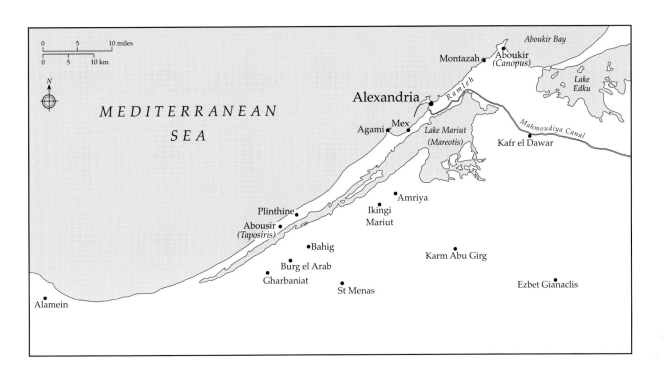

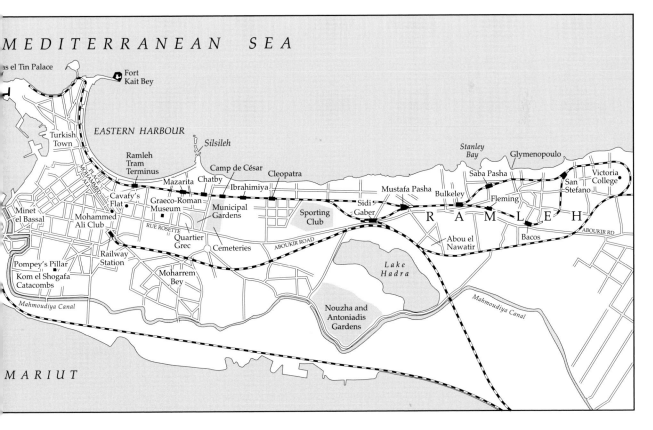

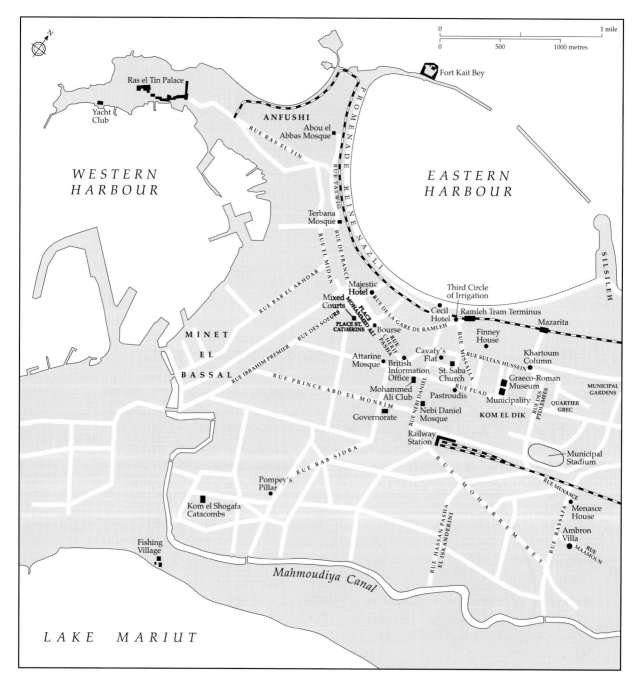

WESTERN
HARBOUR

EASTERN
HARBOUR

0   1 mile

0   500   1000 metres

Fort Kait Bey

Ras el Tin Palace

Yacht
Club

ANFUSHI

Abou el
Abbas Mosque

RUE RAS EL TIN

RUE TATWIG

RUE DE FRANCE

PROMENADE REINE NAZLI

SILSILEH

Terbana
Mosque

RUE EL MIDAN

RUE BAB EL AKHDAR

Majestic
Hotel

Third Circle
of Irrigation

Cecil
Hotel

Ramleh Tram Terminus

Mazarita

MINET

EL

BASSAL

Mixed
Courts

PLACE
MOHAMMED
ALI

PLACE ST.
CATHERINE

Bourse

RUE DES SOEURS

RUE CHERIF PACHA

RUE DE LA GARE DE RAMLEH

Finney
House

RUE MISSALLA

RUE SULTAN HUSSEIN

Khartoum
Column

Attarine
Mosque

British
Information
Office

Cavafy's
Flat

St. Saba
Church

RUE FUAD

Graeco-Roman
Museum

MUNICIPAL
GARDENS

RUE IBRAHIM PREMIER

RUE PRINCE ABD EL MONEIM

Mohammed
Ali Club

RUE NEBI DANIEL

Pastroudis

Municipality

KOM EL DIK

RUE DES PTOLEMEES

QUARTIER
GREC

Governorate

Nebi Daniel
Mosque

Railway
Station

RUE BAB SIDRA

Pompey's
Pillar

RUE MOHARREM BEY

Municipal
Stadium

RUE MENASCE

Kom el Shogafa
Catacombs

RUE HASSAN PASHA
EL ISKANDERINI

RUE RASSAFA

Menasce
House

Ambron
Villa

RUE
MAAMOUN

Fishing
Village

Mahmoudiya Canal

LAKE   MARIUT

Map 3 Alexandra in the 1930s and 1940s

The Capital of Memory

You tell yourself: I'll be gone
To some other land, some other sea,
To a city lovelier far than this
Could ever have been or hoped to be...

There's no new land, my friend, no
New sea; for the city will follow you,
In the same streets you'll wander endlessly.

Constantine Cavafy, 'The City', translated by Lawrence Durrell[1]

In October 1977 Lawrence Durrell returned to Alexandria and checked in at the old familiar Hotel Cecil on the Corniche, the vast gilt mirrors in its lobby reflecting the blowing palms outside, and listened to the sea wind sweeping under his door. Even during the war cosmopolitan Alexandria had been a rising wave on an ebbing tide, the days of its foreign communities numbered. Their expulsion began a decade later and Durrell feared that Nasser's puritanical socialist revolution had destroyed the city he had known.

He was twenty-nine in spring 1941 when the Germans overran Greece and he escaped with his wife Nancy and their infant daughter to Egypt. Then Alexandria had been 'five races, five languages, a dozen creeds: five fleets turning through their greasy reflections behind the harbour bar'.[2] Now, a lifetime later, he faced Alexandria with apprehension, as a man abandoned to exile by the passage of time.

In July 1942, when Rommel threatened Egypt and stood at Alamein, Nancy and the child were evacuated to Palestine; the Durrells' marriage was already under strain and Nancy did not return. The following year in Alexandria Durrell met Eve Cohen, who became his second wife, 'a strange, smashing, dark-eyed woman, with every response right',[3] to whom he dedicated *Justine* – 'To Eve, these memorials of her native city'.[4] He finished this first volume of *The Alexandria Quartet* on Cyprus in 1956: 'It's a sort of prose poem', Durrell wrote to his friend Henry Miller, 'to one of the great capitals of the heart, the Capital of Memory, and it carries a series of sharp cartoons of the women of Alexandria, certainly the loveliest and most world-weary women in the world.'[5] But now the only memories awaiting him were of old haunts, old friends and old loves long vanished.

Durrell would not have come back at all had he not been persuaded by the BBC to make a film called *Spirit of Place*. His task was to lead the crew round the city he had so lusciously described – or had he invented it? – and this too filled him with anxiety. In the days that followed, at first aimlessly, then picking up the threads of his habitual routes, Durrell walked through the streets of Alexandria. The city seemed to him listless and spiritless, its harbour a mere cemetery, its famous cafés, Pastroudis and Baudrot, no longer twinkling with music and lights. 'Foreign posters and advertisements have vanished, everything is in Arabic; in our time film posters were billed in several languages with Arabic subtitles, so to speak.'[6] His favourite bookshop, Cité du Livre on the Rue Fuad, had gone, and in others – 'They used to be full of La Pléiade editions'[7] – he found a lamentable stock. All about him lay 'Iskandariya', the uncomprehended Arabic of its inhabitants translating only into emptiness.

'Alexandria, princess and whore. The royal city and the *anus mundi*. She would never change so long as the races continued to seethe here like must in a vat.'[8] Instead the camera pointed at palatial villas overgrown with bougainvillaea 'where Nessim and Justine gave their parties',[9] abandoned or confiscated or left to rot by their impoverished owners, their rusting gates opening onto wild and unkempt gardens where marble fountains and crumbling statuary testified to a glory since departed.

He was drinking heavily, a 'lonely, sad figure slumped over the bar' at the Cecil,[10] observed Peter Adam, who was directing the film. 'It sounds silly', Durrell said to him, 'but I am extremely incurious, and my real life seems to pass either in books or in dreams.'[11] His mood brightened momentarily when two enormous prostitutes walked by in leather mini-skirts: 'Thank you, thank you, Egypt! What magnetism, what magical wobble!'[12]

The film crew followed Durrell as Nessim and Darley (Durrell's all but namesake) had once followed Justine into what used to be called the native quarter, the old town dating from the Turkish period, though the entire city was native now, among the 'smashed and unlimbered houses' behind Tatwig Street. 'The scene on which we intruded was ferociously original. . . . It was a house of child prostitutes, and there in the dimness, clad in ludicrous biblical nightshirts, with rouged lips, arch bead fringes and cheap rings, stood a dozen fuzzy-haired girls who could not have been above ten years of age; the peculiar innocence of childhood which shone out from under the fancy-dress was in startling contrast to the barbaric adult figure of the French sailor who stood in the centre of the room' – here Justine had come to search for her kidnapped daughter.[13] The theme of daughters lost runs through Durrell's life, and in his writings the theme of incest too, the childhood rape of his heroine Justine carrying suggestions of events in Eve's own life.

Near the crossroads of what had been the European city, Durrell turned into a narrow street called Sharia Sharm el Sheikh, in commemoration of the town at the mouth of the

1 Rue Lepsius. Constantine Cavafy lived in the flat with the balcony at 10 Rue Lepsius from 1907 until his death in 1933, the years of his poetic maturity. 'Where could I live better?' Cavafy said. 'Below, the brothel caters for the flesh. And there is the church which forgives sin. And there is the hospital where we die.'

Gulf of Aqaba lost to Israel in the Six Day War of 1967, but previously known as the Rue Lepsius, after the German Egyptologist Karl Richard Lepsius (1810–84). E. M. Forster knew it well; here the literary apotheosis of Alexandria began: at number 10 (now number 4), on the second floor, above a brothel, lived Constantine Cavafy for the last twenty-five years of his life, from late 1907 to early 1933, the period of his poetic maturity.

Forster met Cavafy during the First World War while working for the Red Cross in Alexandria: 'It never occurred to him that I might like his work or even understand it...

and I remember the delight to us both, one dusky evening in his flat, when it appeared that I was "following". When he was pleased he'd jump and light a candle, and then another candle and he would cut cigarettes in half and light them and bring offerings of mastica with little bits of bread and cheese, and his talk would sway over the Mediterranean world and over much of the world within.'[14] From then on, Forster did more than anyone to promote Cavafy's work, years later remarking, 'I did a little to spread his fame. It was about the best thing I did.'[15]

In 1977 Durrell found that Cavafy's flat had become 'a small pension of the kind described in many Middle Eastern novels, modest and somewhat seedy'.[16] This was the Pension Amir, which in its shabbiness preserved something of the shadows and mystery that gave one of Cavafy's callers the impression of a flat inhabited by 'the hero of a fantastic tale of Hoffmann'.[17] In his novels Durrell gave its tenancy to Balthazar, its 'worm-eaten room with the cane chair which creaked all night, and where once the old poet of the city had recited *The Barbarians*';[18] and he gave him too the same wide-ranging conversation that Forster described in his early meeting with the poet: 'Balthazar talked discursively (half asleep) of the Vineyard of Ammon, the Kings of the Harpoon Kingdom and their battles, or of the Mareotic wine to which, not history, but the gossiping Horace once attributed Cleopatra's distempers of mind.'[19] Recently the flat has been taken over by the cultural section of the Greek Consulate and with noble intention made into a museum, though you must look at the old photographs there to recover the atmospheric Arabo-Byzantine clutter it enjoyed during Cavafy's lifetime. Its originally green, red and mauve walls have been repainted white or in pale pastels; his desk, his bed and a few pieces of his furniture are stood neatly about in the wrong rooms; and his death mask, like a prize cabbage at a farmers' fair, is propped upon a cushion.

Cavafy reserved the small red salon leading onto the balcony for special visitors, and it was here one evening that Forster, drawing on scraps of his public-school Greek, 'followed' 'The God Abandons Antony'. The poem, which would become the centrepiece of Forster's *Alexandria: A History and a Guide*, recalls Plutarch's story that the night before Antony's final battle against Octavian 'a marvellous sound of music' was heard passing 'through the middle of the city towards the outer gate, which led to the enemy's camp'.[20] It was the god Dionysus who was loved by Antony and who loved him, passing along the Canopic Way towards the Gate of the Sun. In his poem Cavafy replaces Dionysus, or Hercules in Shakespeare's *Antony and Cleopatra*, with Alexandria, suggesting that the city has always had the 'godlike power to move the minds of mortals with poetic conceptions of itself'.[21]

Now Durrell followed the departing music of the city eastwards along that same ancient thoroughfare, known to him as the Rue Fuad, to Cavafy and Forster as the Rue Rosette, while under Nasser its identity changed again, to Sharia Horreya (Liberty Street), and soon they came to Pastroudis, a café where in the *Quartet* Darley, Nessim and Balthazar would sometimes go for an arak. Here in 1943 Durrell and Eve began their affair: 'I felt as if I was possessed', remembered Eve. 'That's the way I can say it; that my self was not my own anymore; that I had no say in the matter. It was physical, and Larry had it too; it was mutual. And that's *le coup de foudre*.'

A bit farther on at 63 Sharia Horreya, opposite the Municipality, Durrell led the BBC crew past the handsome block of flats where another woman in his life had lived throughout his time in the city, though they never met in Alexandria;[22] instead ten years were to pass after the war before they would first meet on Cyprus when he was still working on *Justine*. 'I had fallen into a bad patch of distress and apathy after Eve left with the child, which I miss', he wrote to Miller in 1956, 'and by a stroke of luck a lovely young Alexandrian tumbled into my arms and gave me enough spark to settle down and demolish the book.'[23]

This was Claude Vincendon, his third and 'best wife I've had',[24] a member of one of the wealthiest and most distinguished families of Alexandria. Together in their imaginations they journeyed through the city he had once shared with Eve, but through Claude he entered the realm of rediscovery, as she helped him rewrite both the city and his life – 'You see, Darley, I wanted to sort of recompose the city for you so that you could walk back into the painting from another angle and feel quite at home.'[25]

From Cyprus they went to live in France, where her inspiration lay behind his completion of the *Quartet* – *Justine*, published in 1957, *Balthazar* and *Mountolive*, published in 1958, and finally *Clea*, published in 1960. As he had put much of Eve into Justine, so in Clea there is much of Claude, to whom he also offered a dedication: hers is 'the name of the guardian spirit', 'το όνομα του αγαθού δαίμονος', that appears as an epigraph to the third volume, *Mountolive*.[26] At Christmas time in 1966 Claude was taken to hospital with what the doctors diagnosed as a curable bacterial infection; on New Year's Day she was dead, from pulmonary cancer, leaving Durrell by his own account 'wandering about in a tremendous vagueness',[27] his family fearful for his state of mind.

Two months before coming back to Alexandria in 1977, Durrell had divorced his fourth wife, Ghislaine de Boysson, a French fashion model; the marriage had been brief, Durrell acknowledging that it had been a mismatch from the start, but it worked on his mood: 'I've had a bad year. The divorce and all that.'[28] Sixty-five and alone, Durrell had returned to the city that framed his life, 'The City' that was his favourite of Cavafy's poems,[29] which he had translated and placed at the end of *Justine*.

Peter Adam especially wanted Durrell to find the house where he had lived during the war, and although he had forgotten the address the way through the streets was familiar enough. Before getting as far as the vanished Gate of the Sun, Durrell turned right into the Rue Neroutsos, then round the stadium and under the mainline track to Cairo, where, entering the familiar neighbourhood of Moharrem Bey in the south of the city, he eventually stumbled upon his old house at 17 (now 19) Rue Maamoun.

Durrell was transformed with delight as all at once the years fell away: 'Here we sat for dinner', he shouted, rushing up the stairs, 'and there', looking across the garden, 'is the studio of the woman who owned the place, the studio where Clea worked',[30] recalling Amelia Ambron and their mutual friend Clea Badaro, the painter who was another

2   Cleopatra's Needle, *c.* 1860s. Almost nothing of the past survives in Alexandria. Cleopatra's Needles, two obelisks marking the site of the Caesareum, a shrine begun by Cleopatra in honour of Julius Caesar or Mark Antony, were given away by Egypt's ruler, Mohammed Ali, in the nineteenth century to London and New York.

model for the Clea of his novels. 'It is certainly the weirdest feeling to find myself after nearly forty years in this strange garden belonging to an old Italian architect; and in this garden and in the little tower that I fixed up on the roof of the house I wrote *Prospero's Cell* and some rather good poems for *Personal Landscape* and lived out two and one half years of great, extravagant and colourful life in wartime Alexandria. It was a good writing period in a sense, though of course the war was an exhausting moment to think about writing because there was no future attached to anything one did. But perhaps it was a good thing in a way because it compressed up life and forced one to do what one should always do, namely not think about tomorrow, live entirely for today.'[31]

The memories came tumbling out that day, as they would when he opened his pocket scrapbooks full of leaves, photographs, wrappers, cinema tickets, an image captured in a line or two ('boabs', the concierges of Egypt, 'like sightless mushrooms on their stools'):[32] 'An old garbage heap of stuff, a bus ticket or an entry to the Alexandria museum stuck in a book is full of radium and even years afterwards flipping through it you suddenly remember whole sections of things which come in useful in writing.'[33] The present tenant, Effat Nagui ('stunningly beautiful', thought Peter Adam, 'a mix of Anaïs Nin and Isak Dinesen'),[34] invited them to a gathering that evening, her drawing room filled with paintings, her own and some by Clea, who had died of breast cancer, she told Durrell, in 1968.

Soon the word went round Alexandria that the famous Lawrence Durrell was in town. At another dinner, given by Adham Nakeeb and his English wife Thalia at their villa opposite the Sporting Club, Peter Adam observed that 'Larry is very flirtatious, and much taken by the voluptuous and elegant ladies of French, Greek and Jewish origins, real products of Alexandria, the sort of people who inhabit the *Quartet*.'[35] Their consuming interest was to learn from the author who was who in his novels. 'They're all tremendously composite', though Durrell confessed that the range was not very wide. 'The amount of people one meets in a lifetime really isn't all that numerous – people who mark you, I mean.'[36] Then fixing on a young woman with dark chestnut hair and lively, fiery eyes, Lucienne Dalil, of Graeco-Armenian extraction, he added her to the composition, pronouncing her the very image of Justine.

But Durrell, who hated social events, left an impression of indifference. He was 'not a particularly pleasant man', recalled Thalia, 'not as pleasant as Peter Adam and the others with him', while afterwards Durrell said to Adam, 'The beauty of these women is their low IQ. It's like making love to crème Chantilly.'[37] He was returning to an old theme, as when during the war he told Miller that there was nothing 'lovelier and emptier than an Alexandrian girl. Their very emptiness is a caress. Imagine making love to a vacuum.'[38] But then his attitude to women, like his response to Alexandria, was always ambivalent, and his remarks spoke less of the moment, more about his lifetime's disappointment in women, leaving him or dying on him, letting him down.

In 1982, five years after his return to the city, Durrell wrote in his introduction to the first British edition of Forster's *Alexandria: A History and a Guide* that 'once again Alexandria has sunk into oblivion, and I must be forgiven for finding that the present town is depressing beyond endurance'.[39] Yet while he was there, it seemed to him that Alexandria flickered still. After meeting Lucienne he wrote to Miller that Alexandria 'had the grace to put me up one young Justine, just to prove that the old rose tree is not dead'.[40] And on the back of a picture postcard of the Cecil he wrote to his oldest friend, Alan Thomas, in London, 'Much to my surprise very little has changed here and the Cavafian city still has all its luciferian charm – sizzling with sex like a rasher of bacon – we film in the abandoned garden of the Ambrons where I spent the last two war years – a strange poetic beauty like that of the Villa Cleobolus in Rhodes. How very treacherous memory is! I had forgotten so much by the act of writing it down!'[41]

Not only Durrell but also Cavafy and Forster were equivocal in their response to Alexandria. Yet the city haunted each of them, that cosmopolitan Alexandria refounded on the fragile memory-traces of its past. Unlike Rome or Athens with their monuments extant, Alexandria is all intimation: here (some spot) is where Alexander lay entombed; here Cleopatra and Antony loved; here the Library, the Serapeum, and so on – and there is almost nothing physically there. If more of the city survived it would haunt you less, but the imagination is left to dream, and the dream for some becomes palpable, sensual and 'real' – 'The city, half-imagined (yet wholly real), begins and ends in us, roots lodged in our memory.'[42]

The roots are those of Western civilisation itself, for Alexandria was once the centre of the Hellenistic world, the resort of artists, poets and scholars from all over the Mediterranean, attracted by the royal patronage of the Ptolemies and a lively cosmopolitan milieu of Greeks and Hellenised Jews and Egyptians. There was often a playfulness about their art, its images worn now but original then: 'Darts and hearts, sighs and eyes, breasts and chests, all originated in Alexandria', Forster discovered, as in the decorative and mythologically allusive couplet ascribed to one of the early Librarians:

> Who sculptured Love and set him by the pool,
> thinking with water such fire to cool?[43]

The Library preserved the literary heritage of Greece and gave employment to the greatest poets of the Hellenistic age: Theocritus, honoured by his successors as the Homer of the Alexandrian drawing room, whose Fifteenth Idyll with vivid incident and a modern ring describes daily life in the city; Apollonius of Rhodes, who served as a model for the Roman Virgil; and Callimachus, famous for the polish and wit of his epigrams, and also for some of the most moving poems written in Greek.

The Museion, of which the Library was a part, was the great intellectual accomplishment of the Ptolemies, a vast complex of lecture halls, laboratories, observatories, a dining hall, a park and a zoo. It was like a university, except that the scholars, scientists and literary men it supported were under no obligation to teach. Among its mathematicians and scientists were Euclid, who in his theories of numbers and plane and solid geometry demonstrated how knowledge can be derived from rational methods alone; Eratosthenes, who determined the earth's diameter; Aristarchus of Samos, who, anticipating Copernicus by eighteen hundred years, was the author of the heliocentric theory; and Erasistratus, who came close to discovering the circulation of blood and first made the distinction between motor and sensory nerves.

Later, in Roman times, philosophy flourished too, so that here, between desert and sea, men enquired into the problems of the universe in a way unknown before in Egypt, though unlike some of their predecessors in Greece never doubting the existence of God: much of the theological basis of early Christianity, the attempt to link the human and divine intellectually through Platonism, spiritually through love, was developed in Alexandria.

3   The Mahmoudiya Canal. Alexandria's population had declined to five thousand by the time Mohammed Ali became ruler of Egypt in 1805, but his Mahmoudiya Canal, completed in 1820, re-connected the city to the Nile so that almost the entire trade between Europe and Egypt passed through its Western Harbour. Mohammed Ali encouraged Greeks, Italians and others to settle in the city, which by the early twentieth century rivalled in size and population the Alexandria of Cleopatra.

Wider and earlier forces than the Arab invasion of Egypt in 640–2 helped destroy the vitality of the city, but certainly over the following twelve hundred years the city declined, becoming the miserable village of five thousand inhabitants that Napoleon found when he landed nearby in 1798. What brought Alexandria back to life was the construction of the Mahmoudiya Canal in 1820 by Mohammed Ali, an ambitious and westernising Ottoman adventurer from northern Greece who made himself master of the country after Nelson forced Napoleon's withdrawal. The canal, which linked the Nile with the city's Western Harbour, gave Alexandria access to the reorganised potential of the Egyptian hinterland and brought Egypt again face to face with the sea. With the aim of attracting foreign capital and expertise, Mohammed Ali also granted land for settlement to the Greek, English, French, Armenian and other communities in the centre of his new city, whose Western Harbour he enlarged, making it the largest in the Mediterranean. Within a century Alexandria's population grew to nearly half a million, about what it had been in Cleopatra's time, and many foreigners, mostly Greeks and Italians, but also Jews, Syro-Lebanese and others, had planted their family roots there, so that all of what is now central Alexandria and the coast eastwards towards Montazah became a cosmopolitan town.

British and French investment in the construction of the Suez Canal, which opened in 1869, greatly increased foreign interest in the country, especially that of Britain, which was concerned for its route to India. In 1882 Colonel Ahmed Arabi,[44] a native Egyptian and Minister of War, led a nationalist revolt against his own government, which he opposed for its Turkish and European leanings. Riots broke out in Alexandria, where over 150 Europeans were killed. This was met by the bombardment of Alexandria's harbour defences by the British fleet, which in turn incited further riots during which much of the European city was burnt to the ground. The British then landed forces in Egypt, Arabi was defeated, and the country, though notionally governed by Egyptians – or rather principally by the descendants of Mohammed Ali and his followers, the Turco-Circassian aristocracy – became subject to Britain's 'special interest', which was given greater authority soon after the outbreak of war in 1914, when Egypt was declared a Protectorate. With Britain's abolition of the Protectorate in 1922, Egypt was granted limited sovereignty but did not become wholly independent until 1936, and even then a British military presence continued under the guise of a twenty-year alliance. The half-century between 1882 and 1936 was the heyday of cosmopolitan Alexandria, its lease extended, the times given stimulus, by the Second World War.

Cavafy died before the end, though the falling note of his poetry assumed it; Forster thought that its future 'like that of other great commercial cities is dubious';[45] by the time Durrell completed *The Alexandria Quartet* it was gone. 'I stepped laughing out into the street once more to make a circuit of the quarter which still hummed with the derisive, concrete life of men and women . . . I began to walk slowly, deeply bemused, and to describe to myself in words this whole quarter of Alexandria for I knew that soon it would be forgotten and revisited only by those whose memories had been appropriated by the fevered city, clinging to the minds of old men like traces of perfume upon a sleeve: Alexandria, the capital of Memory.'[46]

Cavafy, Forster and Durrell all knew that perfume: 'I inhaled the warm summer perfume of her dress and skin – a perfume which was called, I don't know why, *Jamais de la vie*'[47] – the phrase means 'never'. Haunted by failure and haunted by glory, for a while there was a resonance between the modern cosmopolitan city and the one that Alexander founded long ago on this African shore.

Now that cosmopolitan city is also gone and has left no formal history, its documents some poems, some novels, some guidebooks and memoirs and academic monographs. But there are letters too, and diaries, and the oral testimony of the city's surviving witnesses, and there are the streets and trams and the crumbling architecture of the city itself, all recalling what has passed.

CHAPTER 1

A Tram with a View

We came to Alexandria at the same time, but it was two years before our friendship was settled. I noticed you first in the spring of 1916 when I stopped with Furness at Abou el Nawatir. You were on the Bacos tram which has the blue label. I looking up from the ground as you went past, thought 'nice', and the morning was fresh and sunny.

E. M. Forster, 'letter' to Mohammed el Adl, 1922–9[1]

For most of the First World War E. M. Forster was in Alexandria, an out-planting of European civilisation growing luxuriantly on the coast of Africa. It was for him 'something suspiciously like a funk-hole',[2] but he brought to the city a mind informed on the deepest currents of his age, and he met there a Greek poet, 'very wise, very civilised',[3] a man for whom history was the atmosphere of his imagination, and in time Alexandria became for Forster not a funk-hole but a fulcrum, the means to prise open the moment and in the midst of the calamity overwhelming Europe take the longer view. 'I apprehended the magic and the antiquity and the complexity of the city, and determined to write about her. A guidebook suggested itself.'[4] No ordinary guidebook, but a guide to learning about the way we love. And probably it would never have been written had not Forster found for the first time in his life sex and love in Alexandria.

Edward Morgan Forster was thirty-six when he landed at Port Said on 20 November 1915 and went immediately to Alexandria by train, travelling via Zagazig and Tanta across the breadth of the Nile Delta. He had been curious to see Egypt but his first response was disappointment. The landscape seemed 'at one moment an ordinary Cambridgeshire/Surrey effect of crops and ditches and trees, at the next vignettes from the Arabian nights. . . . To one who has been to India, it is almost irritating – the "real East" seems always vanishing round the corner, fluttering the hem of a garment on the phantom of a smell.'[5]

Forster had visited India three years before, calling his five-month tour of the country the most expensive, comfortable and enjoyable in his life. Then he had travelled eagerly and was open to sensations, for the way had been prepared by Syed Ross Masood, a warm and expansive young man whom he had met in England in 1906. Masood had been waiting to go up to Oxford, and Forster was engaged to tutor him in Latin. Instead it was the student who regaled his teacher with the splendours of the Mogul past. 'He woke me up out of my suburban and academic life', Forster recalled, 'showed me new horizons and a new civilisation, and helped me towards the understanding of a continent.'[6] His awakening was coupled with feelings of love towards Masood, though the certainty of their being unrequited was confirmed only in January 1913 when they met again in India, Forster writing in his diary, 'Aie-aie-aie – growing after tears'.[7]

A string of successful novels had preceded his Indian visit – *Where Angels Fear to Tread* in 1905, *The Longest Journey* in 1907, *A Room with a View* in 1908 and *Howards End*, the book that established his reputation and made him famous, published in 1910. But then came a period of creative sterility. A clue to its cause is provided by the thoughts Forster confided to his diary on 1 November 1911: 'Last night, alone, I had a Satanic fit of rage against mother for her grumbling and fault finding, and figured a scene in which I swept the mantelpiece with my arm and then rushed out of doors or cut my throat. I was all red and trembling after. I write it down partly in the hope that I shall see its absurdity and so refuse it admittance again.'[8] He made one small attempt at explanation early in the following year, when next to his entry of the previous November he noted a date he claimed never to have known: 'Discover, some months later, that October 31 is the anniversary of my father's death.' Within two years of Forster's birth on 1 January 1879 his father had died of consumption at Bournemouth, leaving a comfortably-off widow of twenty-five who looked to her only son for emotional support. This was the foundation of a mutual dependence that was to play a central role in Forster's life.

The oriental novel that Forster began soon after his disappointed return from the sub-continent, and that would emerge as *A Passage to India* only in 1924, had faltered by the end of 1913. He turned instead to writing *Maurice*, his plea for the acceptance of homosexual love. Defending the character of Maurice to a critical friend, Forster wrote, 'The man in my book is, roughly speaking, good, but Society nearly destroys him, he nearly slinks through his life furtive and afraid, and burdened with a sense of sin. . . . Blame Society not Maurice, and be thankful even in a novel when a man is left to lead the best life he is capable of leading! . . . My defence at any Last Judgement would be "I was trying to connect up and use all the fragments I was born with." '[9] But his hope that by writing *Maurice* he could prime his creative flow was checked by the realisation that it could not be published 'until my death or England's'.[10]

Not long after, Germany invaded Belgium and on 4 August 1914 England declared war. As the military historian John Terraine has written, 'All the protestations of peace-loving, all the search for security, all the liberal dreams had crashed; in August 1914 the First World War began, and with it the most drastic, swift and terrifying processes of change yet known to Man.'[11]

'Don't indulge in Romance', Forster wrote to a friend a few months into the war, 'or suppose that an era of jolly little nationalities is dawning', for whoever won, he predicted, the outcome would be a defeat for civilisation in Europe. All the same, he

4   The French Gardens between Mohammed Ali Square and the Eastern Harbour, and the Majestic Hotel. During his early months in Alexandria E. M. Forster stayed at the Majestic Hotel, the building on the right with the two cupolas. His first impression of the city was dismissive: 'just a clean cosmopolitan town by some blue water', he wrote to his mother.

admitted, 'I am sure we could not have kept out of this war', for he saw that the German attack on France through Belgium directly menaced the security of England and was convinced it was right to send 'plenty of trained troops' across the Channel.[12]

His was the liberal dream that had crashed, but it need not have come to this, he believed. Four years before in *Howards End* Forster had written that if certain remarks were repeated often enough they could be self-fulfilling, as 'the remark "England and Germany are bound to fight" renders war a little more likely each time that it is made'[13] – so that when war did come he despaired of it as a victory for mindlessness. There was no conscription as yet and Forster would not volunteer, denying that he counted his life above that of the average man but saying he would not lend himself to the mood of hysteria and conformism that trampled personal values beneath the instincts of the herd. But unlike many of his Cambridge and Bloomsbury friends who were passionately opposed to the war and protested that it had nothing to do with them, Forster felt implicated, on 4 August writing in his diary, 'Feel the war exists on my account. If I died it would stop, but it is here to give me experiences if I choose to receive them.'[14] In answer to the sense of failure that hung over the world he had known, as it hung over his personal and writing life, he was determined at least to make himself useful and obtained a post as cataloguer and occasional night fire-watcher at the National Gallery. The more valuable paintings were being put in store: if he were killed by bombs, he told his friends, he would die, appropriately, among second-rate masterpieces.

He was half-dead already: 'I am leading the life of a little girl so long as I am tied to home', he wrote of his existence at his mother's home in Surrey in August 1915. 'It isn't even as if I make mother happy by stopping – she is always wanting me to be five years old again, so happiness is obviously impossible for her.'[15]

The war fever in England, at once pious and bloodthirsty, made Forster depressed and would eventually, he was sure, drive him out of his mind. Deciding that 'all one can do in this world of maniacs is to pick up the poor tortured broken people and try to mend them',[16] he thought of joining a volunteer ambulance brigade in Italy, but his mother worried at the danger. Instead he got himself posted to Alexandria as a Red Cross 'searcher', questioning wounded soldiers for news of their missing comrades.

Though a civilian, Forster wore the khaki uniform and bore the status of an officer and was expected to arrange his own accommodation. He took a room at the newly built Majestic Hotel overlooking the French Gardens which extended north from the Place Mohammed Ali at the centre of town: 'Every modern comfort and luxury', says a guidebook of the time.[17] The Majestic was entered from the Rue de l'Eglise Ecossaise, which ran along the east side of the gardens past the Presbyterian Church of St Andrew and the French Consulate to the Eastern Harbour, while at the northeast corner of the hotel was the Rue Temple Menasce, named for its synagogue built in 1873 by the financier Yaqub Levi Menasce. Soon after settling in, Forster wrote to his mother for a supply of Kolynos tooth powder, adding, 'one can't dislike Alex . . . because it is impossible to dislike either the sea or stones. But it consists of nothing else as far as I can gather: just a clean cosmopolitan town by some blue water.'[18]

The names of the streets have changed, and the gardens, 'a pleasant strip'[19] in Forster's time, are now Midan Arabi, planted with a tram terminus. The hotel, no longer majestic in name or appearance, has been converted to commercial offices, its unlit rubbish-strewn entranceway the resort of idle characters in galabiyyas, and behind them a broken lift like a gibbet, permanently suspended between floors. Ascending the broad flights of worn stone steps rising through storeys of towering corridors, glassed-off lounges and voluminous rooms, it is pointless explaining your curiosity to the shrouded young secretaries wearing the hejab, that veil covering their heads, necks and shoulders, and revealing only their faces, who despite the evidence around them deny that the building could ever have been a hotel at all. Nor can they comprehend your wish to step onto a balcony for the view. A great sea change has washed over Alexandria and its populace inhabits a history disconnected from the city's past.

Forster intended to remain only three months in Alexandria but in the event stayed more than three years, far longer than his pre- and post-war visits to India put together. Like the *ci-devant* Majestic, enough survives of Forster's city that you can follow his

5   A postcard showing Mohammed Ali Square, at the centre of the city. To the right of the equestrian statue of Mohammed Ali are the Mixed Courts, at the far end the Cotton Exchange and the Bourse, and on the left behind the trees the Anglican Church of St Mark.

progress through Alexandria today, though it is hardly a conventional tour. 'Tut, tut! Miss Lucy!' he had written nearly a decade earlier in *A Room with a View*, 'I hope we shall soon emancipate you from Baedeker. He does but touch the surface of things.'[20] To travel without Baedeker was not only to risk not recognising a Giotto when you saw one but to chance unfamiliar social and cultural encounters, and this in fact was the essence of Forster's idea of 'a view'. With luck, you might even meet someone disreputable, or someone you might love though you were not meant to, and these both happened to Forster in Alexandria.

Forster's first impression of Alexandria as related to his mother was at once guarded and charitable when read against a 1909 survey. 'All considerations of science, art and archaeology are choked by the city's strenuous commercial activity', it states frankly. 'Affairs of commerce, the state of trade, the movements in stocks and shares form the staple of the daily round of conversation in the clubs, in the streets, on the wharves, on the trams, in the trains, in short everywhere in this city once famous as the battleground of various religions and sects at deadly enmity one with another, now wholly and wholeheartedly given to the worship of the modern deity Mammon, who exacts the most exclusive devotion from his followers.'[21]

Tourists famously gave Alexandria short shrift. 'They arrive in the Western Harbour, land, and rush off to Cairo, where there is more sunshine and less rain, also more to see and less commercial talk. They do not remain in Alexandria to study Graeco-Egyptian art; and after a day spent in Chérif Pasha Street travel south as quickly as they can. Owing to this, Alexandria is dull in winter – the tourist season proper for Egypt. But during the summer, when the heat of Cairo is considered to be unbearable, thousands of holiday-makers of certain defined classes from the capital spend two or three months on the Mediterranean seashore. This is consequently the season of such gaiety as Alexandria enjoys. But whereas tourists spend freely, the class of people who stay at Alexandria, being acquainted with current prices, spend little. The summer visitors consist almost entirely of faded officials on a few days' leave from Cairo, businessmen from the capital unable to get over to Europe and a certain class of Levantine who invariably return to Cairo richer than they left.' Even then there was a dearth of amusements, so that 'sea-bathing constitutes the chief recreation'.

If there was hope for release from this philistinism and tedium, the survey desperately suggested, it lay in unearthing the remains of the past. At the turn of the century the ground had given way beneath a grazing donkey near Pompey's Pillar, revealing the unsuspected catacombs of Kom el Shogafa, where weird sculptures mutely testify to the merging and melting of classical and ancient Egyptian beliefs. Thanks to such discoveries as these, 'it is possible that within a few years Alexandria's renaissance will no longer be purely commercial, but archaeological and perhaps artistic as well'.[22]

In fact the Alexandrians were content enough to be bypassed by tourists and to feel themselves not quite part of Egypt. They might have to visit Cairo on business or matters of policy, but they looked down on the intrigue, the place-seeking and the parvenu atmosphere of the capital. Alexandria had neither been founded by the Arabs nor was it the seat of British rule; in all their ethnic and religious diversity, Alexandria's foreign communities had built the city themselves, their families had in many cases been settled there for generations and towards it they felt the special pride that citizens have for their city-state. 'As regards the social constitution and general aspects of life in Alexandria', the same 1909 survey continued, 'the population is very mixed. Among the lower classes the Egyptian and foreign elements mingle as they would never dream of doing in Cairo; also in the upper classes they manage to live side by side in harmony – a gratifying state of things which may be attributed largely to the existence of a Municipality' – Alexandria was the first self-governing city in the Middle East, its Municipality founded in 1890, whereas local government came to Cairo only in 1947 – 'and to the absence of an army of government officials. Politics, owing to the same probable reasons, play a relatively small role in the daily life.'[23]

During the First World War, when Egypt's population was nearly thirteen million (compared to over seventy million today), about two hundred thousand of the country's inhabitants were foreign nationals. In total, Alexandria's population approached half a million while Cairo's was double that, yet it was the smaller city that was home to nearly half of all foreigners living in Egypt. About thirty thousand of these were Greek and twenty thousand Italian, and these gave the port city its distinctive Mediterranean atmosphere.

But citizenship and ethnic origin did not always coincide. About twenty-five per cent of all those who considered themselves ethnically Greek, for example, were not Greek citizens. With the outbreak of war, numbers of inhabitants who had been Ottoman subjects, including ethnic Greeks, Armenians, Syro-Lebanese and Jews, now found themselves stateless or were counted as Russians, Bulgarians, Persians, North Africans or Egyptians. Some foreign powers, the French especially in an effort to increase their influence in Egypt, sold or otherwise granted citizenship papers, while many British citizens were Maltese, Gibraltarians and Cypriots. Certainly in Alexandria the number of those who were not ethnically Egyptian was greater than the official citizenship figures indicated and amounted to something like a quarter to a third of the population.

In religion the city was no less varied. Christians were represented by the Greek Orthodox, Syrian Greek Orthodox, Coptic Orthodox and Armenian Churches, by the Roman Catholic Church and, in communion with Rome, the Maronite, Greek Catholic, Coptic Catholic, Armenian Catholic and Chaldean Catholic Churches, while Protestants adhered to the Presbyterian, Anglican and other denominational Churches. Almost all Egypt's Jews, sixty thousand at the time of the First World War, lived in the two metropolises, about twenty-five thousand in Alexandria and thirty thousand in Cairo. A third of Jews were Egyptian citizens and about a fifth foreign citizens (most often Italian, especially the upper-class Sephardic Jews of Alexandria, but also French and British), while nearly half were stateless. Christians, Jews and Muslims each had their churches, synagogues and mosques in the city.

'One might be inclined to believe that such a variety of races, languages, religions and manners could not constitute a town whose essential qualities are precisely tolerance and reciprocal respect', wrote Evaristo Breccia, director of the Graeco-Roman Museum, in his guide to the ancient and modern city, *Alexandrea ad Aegyptum*, first published in French just before the war in 1914 and appearing in an English translation in 1922. 'Alexandria, however, is a proof that much prejudice and racial hatred, much chauvinism, much religious fanaticism may grow milder, and may even disappear, when a race or a nationality has occasion to live in daily contact with other races and other nationalities. . . . Each retains his political, social and moral ideal, but they all respect that of others, and no one insists that his is the best or the finest and that it ought to govern the world.'[24]

In the hinterland beyond the waters of Lake Mariut, the ancient Mareotis, lay Egypt, from which the cosmopolitan city stood isolated. Alexandria, as the title of Breccia's guide reminded his readers, was *ad* and not *in* Aegyptum, at Egypt but not in it, a distinction that applied as much to the modern as to the ancient city. Its foreign communities learnt only enough 'kitchen Arabic' to give instructions to their cooks and servants, while from the Place Mohammed Ali and along the Rue Chérif Pasha at the centre of town, and eastwards along the Rue Rosette past the elegant enclave of the Quartier Grec and on out through the suburban villas of Ramleh there might be the occasional Egyptian laundry but hardly one Egyptian shop.

Excepting the minority of westernised and better-off Egyptians, the poorer native population, preponderant in numbers, generally lived to the west of the Place Mohammed Ali in the warren of the old Turkish town or cheek by jowl with lower-class Europeans in the narrow tenemented streets towards Pompey's Pillar to the southwest, the site of Rhakotis, that Egyptian settlement of coastguards and goatherds known to Alexander the Great when he founded his metropolis on this African shore in 331 BC. As in the ancient Hellenistic city, so in the refounded Alexandria of the nineteenth and early twentieth centuries, the 'foreign' population were the simpler Egyptians, immigrants off the land who were drawn to the city by the economic activity of its overseas founders whose culture they hardly shared.

Alexandria's gaze was seawards and the city belonged as much to the Mediterranean world as Naples, Genoa, Marseilles or Athens. French became its lingua franca early in the twentieth century, and English to some extent later on, but as you can see on the old tombstones in the foreign cemeteries Italian had previously been the common tongue, and still today 'robe vecchie! bottiglie!' ('old clothes! bottles!') is the street-cry of the Alexandrian rag-and-bone man.

The Greeks constituted the largest proportion of Alexandria's Europeans, dominating by their commercial energy the grocery trade, food processing, the manufacture of soft drinks, spirits and cigarettes, and the ginning and export of cotton. But the builders of the city were Italians, who more than any other community were the architects and engineers of modern Alexandria. 'The streets between the harbour and the railway station might have been imported from Naples', wrote the traveller Douglas Sladen in 1910, describing the city reborn from the incendiary riots and the British bombardment of 1882 – in fact the streets were almost literally imported, the cobblestones laid by labourers from Sicily and southern Italy. 'Alexandria has two ports divided by a spit of land, which was the Heptastadion of the Ptolemies. The eastern port is the beautiful circular bay round which a new Alexandria is growing up – another Bay of Naples. The western port, the Eunostos, or safe harbourage of the [ancient] Greeks, is a busy commercial port after the style of Genoa, with hardly more Eastern life on its waters than an Italian port would have',[25] while along the Mahmoudiya Canal skirting the south of the city 'the decaying villas give the effect of one of those delightful back-canals of Venice, which have palaces with gardens, if only Venice had mosques'.[26] In sum, thought Sladen, 'Alexandria is an Italian city: its vegetation is almost Italian; it has wild flowers. Its climate is almost Italian; it has wind and rain as well as fierce blue skies. Its streets are almost entirely Italian; and Italian is its staple language. Even its ruins are Roman. If it were not for the mosque of Kait Bey, where the Pharos ought to be, and a few minarets in the strip of old Alexandria between the two forts, you would not believe that you were in a city of Islam.'[27]

Yet palpable reminders of the historical city that had once stood at the centre of Western civilisation were almost wholly absent, and instead the past lodged itself in the Alexandrian imagination to an unusual degree. Rome and Constantinople, its ancient rivals, have been continuously inhabited since antiquity and preserve in their monuments a tangible historical memory. But Ptolemaic Alexandria was overbuilt by the Romans and Byzantines and again in its years of decline by the Arabs, a great recycling of materials involved in the process, layers of debris mounting over the centuries, before the site was entirely abandoned except for the Turkish town on the silted-up Heptastadion where there was nothing of ancient interest either to obliterate or preserve. Where once the streets had so dazzled with marble that the Arab cavalrymen of Amr Ibn al-As had to shield their eyes as they entered the city in 642, Napoleon found only Pompey's Pillar, the obelisks of the Caesareum ('Cleopatra's Needles'), some columns that may have formed part of the ancient Gymnasium and a section of Roman wall on the eastern shore remaining above the level of the ground, so that Alexandria seemed an immense and silent cemetery.

Rapid development followed the refounding of the city, and Breccia had to admit in his guide that 'the Alexandrians of today have been accused of ignoring or neglecting the remains of their city's glorious past, for their feverish activity in levelling and building causes many precious monuments to be broken or covered up, perhaps forever'.[28] Many of the finds made while digging foundations were consequently fortuitous, but in any case, as Breccia makes clear, there were few precise indications on which to base systematic excavations: 'As far as the complete destruction of its edifices and as the uncertainty of its topography are concerned, Alexandria, unfortunately, takes precedence over every other great city of the ancient world.'[29] There are contemporary descriptions, the most celebrated and detailed being that of Strabo, who visited the city in 24 BC, but despite the temples, monuments and palaces described, it has been almost always impossible to determine their exact site, so that to the present day even the famous Museion and Library, as well as the Soma, Alexander's tomb, have eluded excavators, their whereabouts remaining matters of conjecture.

And yet no other city in the world has such an unmistakable and enduring form: two limestone ridges running parallel to the coast, the inner ridge holding Alexandria fixed against the shifting alluvium of Egypt, the outer breaking the waves and giving Alexandria its harbours. It is a unique and timeless feature in Egypt, which Alexander, if he could return, would still recognise. Plutarch tells the story that Alexander was led to the site in a dream, in which a grey-haired man of venerable appearance stood by his side, reciting from book IV of *The Odyssey*:

There is an island in the surging sea, which they call Pharos, lying off Egypt.[30]

Alexander rose the next morning and immediately visited Pharos. When he saw the natural advantages the place possessed he declared that Homer, besides his other admirable qualities, was also a far-seeing architect, and he ordered that a great and populous Greek city be founded there, the first to bear the name of Alexander.

The sensation of inhabiting a present that has been given form by the past continues as you walk along the main thoroughfare of the city, conscious as the land falls gently away to the Eastern Harbour that you are following the spine of the inner ridge along the ancient road, the Canopic Way. Indeed, the most systematic research carried out in the nineteenth century, such as that of Mahmoud el Falaki and Dr Tassos Neroutsos, concerned the street plan of the ancient city and its correspondence to the modern, so that when Breccia asked in his introduction to his guide what has become of 'the noisy city where no one was idle, where artists, poets, philosophers and critics had exercised their refined intelligence, where the love of gain was equalled only by the love of pleasure, and where women were as beautiful as they were frail',[31] you suspect that he thought it could be rediscovered about him in the streets of the cosmopolitan city.

For Forster, who arrived at the tail end of a calamity, such thoughts were a long way from his own. In April 1915 Alexandria had become the centre of operations for the ill-fated Gallipoli campaign, meant to wrest control of the Dardanelles from the Turks and threaten Constantinople. But from the first British and Anzac (Australian and New Zealand) landings on the Gallipoli peninsula to their final withdrawal at the end of the year, a returning stream of soldiers, wounded and mutilated, all but overwhelmed Alexandria's hospitals.

The Majestic was perfectly suited to Forster's first months as a searcher with the Red Cross, whose headquarters were a few minutes' walk east in St Mark's Buildings on the corner of the Rue St Marc and the Rue de l'Ancienne Bourse. From there he would set out at about ten each morning to make his hospital rounds, returning to the hotel for lunch, then to the hospitals again and finishing up at about seven. In the evenings he wrote his reports, which ultimately found their way to the War Office in London from where they were forwarded to the soldiers' relatives. It could be depressing work, for if he did get news about the missing, it was usually bad news. But there was pleasure in making himself useful to the wounded soldiers in various unofficial ways, lending them books, writing their letters, getting their watches mended, and he found them charming and grateful.

Unexpectedly, Forster also found himself in a faintly heroic mood, for contrary to his reassurances to his mother a Turkish invasion was threatened, and though a civilian he could soon be in the line of battle. The Gallipoli campaign had been a response to the Turkish attempt to capture the Suez Canal and invade Egypt early in 1915, and the Turks remained a continuing threat in Sinai throughout the following year, while in the Libyan Desert Turkish and German agents persuaded the Senussi, a Bedouin people, to attack Egypt's western frontier. Yet Alexandria was strangely insulated from events by the imposition of strict press censorship, an English resident of the city describing how 'blankness enveloped us, like a fog that leaves near objects clear and blots out the rest of the world with baffling completeness'.[32]

6 E. M. Forster in Alexandria, 1917. This is the only known photograph of Forster in Alexandria.

But the view neither near nor far was obscured for Forster, who as soon as he arrived called on Robin Furness, an old King's College acquaintance who had become head of the Press Censorship Department, its headquarters in Alexandria rather than Cairo, the better to intercept communications with abroad. Within months of coming down from King's, Furness had entered the Egyptian Civil Service, where he began his career as far as imaginable from an ivory tower. 'I have long been a policeman or inspector of police in this disorderly town', he wrote from Alexandria to his friend John Maynard Keynes in 1907. 'Daily I feed my disgusted eyes on drunken Welsh governesses and stabbed Circassian whores; I peer into the anus of catamites; I hold inquests upon beggars who die and are eaten by worms.'[33] He was just as intimately acquainted with the curiosa of *The Greek Anthology*, a thousand years of sometimes erotic poetry from Hellenistic to

Byzantine times, and made free with the Alexandria police press to print his transla-tions of the ancient poets of the city. While a man of 'exquisite literary taste', recalled Laurence Grafftey-Smith, vice-consul in Alexandria during the war, 'his tastes on other levels were comprehensively catholic, and we shared some strange excursions'.[34]

Furness (later Sir Robin) was to spend the whole of his professional life in Egypt, in the 1920s serving as Oriental Secretary at the British High Commission in Cairo while continuing to devote himself to literary scholarship: his *Poems of Callimachus* and *Trans-lations from the Greek Anthology* were published in London in 1931 and 1932 and have endured, remaining among the handful of regularly cited texts. From 1936 to 1944 he was professor of English at Fuad (later Cairo) University and during the Second World War also resumed his old job as head of Censorship.

In Alexandria Furness was devoted to Aida Borchgrevink, a woman in her late fifties and the widow since 1910 of the Norwegian procurer-general at the Mixed Courts of Egypt. An American by birth, the daughter of a Midwest corn king, she had trained as an opera singer before her marriage, changing her name from Ada to Aida after attending a performance of Verdi's opera during her honeymoon. Furness, who had the look of 'a cerebral and ruffled heron',[35] knew her as an ebullient and romantic woman who drove through the city singing Wagner at the top of her voice. The communion between them was platonic but nevertheless intense: she took him in hand and inspir-ited him, and throughout his early career he relied on her guidance – in particular it was Aida Borchgrevink who recruited most of the cosmopolite staff of his Censorship Department, among whom were Pericles Anastassiades, a longtime friend of Constantine Cavafy, and the young and debonair George Antonius, both soon to become part of Forster's circle.

'I don't know how long I shall be here', Forster wrote to Masood on 29 December 1915, adding of Egyptians, 'I feel as instinctively not at home among them as I feel instinc-tively at home among Indians.' Despite Masood's rejection of Forster's advances nearly three years before, the two remained friends and, particularly until he found another object for his affections, Forster used the correspondence to compare Egypt unfavourably with India. 'The only non-English person of whom I see anything here is a Syrian – a very nice and amusing fellow. I am dining with him tomorrow and – discarding my uniform – shall then plunge in his company into the Bazaar, to see whatever may be seen, but understand that is not much.'[36]

The 'Syrian' was George Antonius, then twenty-five, an Alexandrian of Palestinian family, British citizenship and Greek Orthodox faith, at ease in English, French, Italian and Arabic, who after attending Victoria College, the English-run public school for boys in the eastern suburb of Ramleh, had gone like Forster and Furness before him to King's College, Cambridge. Antonius' work at the Censorship Department was the prelude to a remarkable career in Middle Eastern affairs, first with the British, for which he received a CBE, then from 1930 in the cause of an Arab Palestine. In 1939 he came to London as secretary-general to the Arab delegation at the Round Table Conference on Palestine, having made his name the previous year as the author of *The Arab Awakening*, which Edward Said has called 'the finest Arab study of the struggle for independence'.[37]

In 1915 Antonius, along with many Arabs outside Egypt, saw the war in a hopeful light, with Britain as their ally in their desire to free themselves from the Ottoman Empire. But Forster, surveying the world he had known beyond Alexandria, saw only disintegration: 'All that I cared for in civilisation has gone forever',[38] he wrote in that same December letter to Masood as he awaited his excursion the following day with Antonius into the native town. Though Forster had been in the city for more than a month, and though the bazaar was hardly farther west from the Majestic than the Red Cross headquarters were to the east, Forster had evidently not ventured beyond the Place Mohammed Ali which lay between them.

'The Square', as the English called the Place Mohammed Ali, was at the very heart of the city's affairs, with the Bourse containing the cotton and stock exchanges at its eastern end, the Anglican Church of St Mark nearby (of which St Mark's Buildings behind were a dependency), the Mixed Courts on its south side,[39] a bronze equestrian statue of Mohammed Ali himself in the middle (though unidentified by an inscription in deference to the Islamic prohibition against representing human or animal forms) and smart cafés, restaurants and shops all round. The Square was also a reminder of that summer of 1882 around which Alexandrians arranged their history as 'before the events' and 'after the events'. Off to the south ran the interminable Rue des Soeurs where the rioting had begun, its name owed to its Roman Catholic convent and school though more infamous then and since for its services to sailors, while a month later in the Square itself the last insurrectionists were buried beneath the trees to which they had been tied and then shot.

If Forster possessed a copy of Baedeker, he would have read that beyond the Square ('embellished with trees') the native quarter presented 'interesting scenes of oriental life',[40] though it could think of nothing specific to see. More helpful was Breccia's *Alexandrea ad Aegyptum*, which Forster might not yet have acquired, though he later relied on it heavily. Instead his cicerone during his early months in Alexandria was Antonius, whom Forster, when he came to write his own guide to the city, would list first among those to whom he owed thanks, 'for his assistance with those interesting but little known buildings, the Alexandria Mosques'.[41]

But that was later: Forster began writing his *Alexandria: A History and a Guide* in October 1918, a month before the end of the war and three months before his departure from Egypt, and he did not correct the final proofs until February 1922. The excursion with Antonius was Forster's first encounter with native Egypt, and for a long time he did not like what he saw, writing in August 1916, for example, that 'in ten months I've acquired an instinctive dislike to the Arab voice, the Arab figure, the Arab way of looking or walking or pump shitting or eating or laughing or anything'. But his reaction disturbed him: 'Exactly the emotion that I censured in the Anglo-Indian towards the native there. . . . It's damnable and disgraceful, and it's in me.'[42]

Forster's aesthetic distaste was compounded by the repugnance he felt at the behaviour of an Egyptian acquaintance in the police administration who invited him to visit a hashish den run by a one-eyed Maltese. 'We push in, and find a small and well mannered company smoking the drug, quiet and languorous. There was also an Arab girl, barefoot, very young and tired, and some boy attendants, playing cards together – not to speak of odd noises in unopened rooms.' Three dapper young men in straw hats with the look of Italian shop assistants also came in, but seeing Forster and his companion from the police drew once or twice on the pipe and went away, 'as if this was all they had come for'.[43] Forster found the company all very pleasant and would have smoked himself had he been alone. He was sickened when the Egyptian told him a few days later that he had reported the Maltese to the police. 'It was my duty. I am private gentleman in the evening but a member of the administration by day. I keep the two apart.' That he did not keep the two apart was to Forster a betrayal of trust and a muddying of the moral waters: 'He is considered the pick of the natives here, and he performed an act of pure mud.'[44]

Forster's response to Alexandria was the antithesis to his feelings about India. When he visited India before the war, he had gone there to make friends among its people and through them to open his imagination to the country. The subcontinent was fairly calm and the Raj seemed secure. Politics did not press on him and he was content to share the opinion of his travelling companions Robert Trevelyan and Goldsworthy Lowes Dickinson and of his other Liberal friends that the home-rule movement was more noise than substance and independence only a distant ideal.[45] When Forster left India in 1913 the impressions he took with him were wholly romantic: 'No doubt it is ridiculous to have fallen in love with a continent . . . but apparently this is what I've done.'[46]

India was the romance of the entire nation, a match that had been sealed in 1877, two years before Forster's birth, when Queen Victoria was proclaimed Empress of India through the agency of her prime minister Benjamin Disraeli. Disraeli was a Conservative and his act served to mute the opposition Liberals, who saw the empire not as an asset but as a liability. Critics, Disraeli said, were at fault for 'viewing everything in a financial aspect, and totally passing by those moral and political considerations which make nations great, and by the influence of which alone men are distinguished from animals. . . . England will have to decide between national and cosmopolitan principles. The issue is not a mean one. It is whether you will be content to be a comfortable England, modelled and moulded upon Continental principles and meeting in due course an inevitable fate, or whether you will be a great country – an Imperial country – a country where your sons, when they rise, rise to paramount positions, and obtain not merely the esteem of their countrymen, but command the respect of the world.'[47]

By the time Forster first went to India the Liberals too had accepted the empire as part of the order of things, not least because, as Disraeli understood, it appealed to the English thirst for romance that during the nineteenth century had combined with a sense of national mission to bring the benefits of enlightenment and progress to the world. In the words of Lord Curzon, viceroy during the early years of the twentieth century, India was 'the biggest thing that the British are doing anywhere'.[48] To withdraw would be both a betrayal of India and a renunciation of England's own idealistic conception of itself.

True, in *Howards End* Forster had written that 'the Imperialist is not what he thinks or seems. He is a destroyer',[49] but he was referring to a type and still believed in a better world in which Englishmen had an improving role to play, and he took it lightly when shortly before he left India a friend of Masood's, Saeed Mirza, with whom Forster was out riding, had 'burst out against the English. "It may be fifty or five hundred years but we shall turn you out."'[50] Ten years later those words are heard again in the cry of failure and loss that concludes *A Passage to India*, but in *Howards End* the fault of the imperialist lay less in oppression than in deracination, and here Forster took exception to Disraeli's version of the romance: the imperialist 'prepares the way for cosmopolitanism, and though his ambitions may be fulfilled the earth that he inherits will be grey'.[51]

And so his mother would have grasped his meaning when Forster wrote to her that Alexandria was just a clean cosmopolitan town: the city offered nothing that would separate him from her. His values and emotions were tied to Rooksnest, the house in Hertfordshire where they had lived from his fifth to his fifteenth year and which was the direct model for Howards End:

> Here had lived an elder race, to which we look back with disquietude. The country, which we visit at week-ends, was really a home to it, and the graver sides of life, the deaths, the partings, the yearnings for love, have their deepest expression in the hearts of the fields. All was not sadness. The sun was shining without. The thrush sang his two syllables on the budding guelder rose. Some children were playing uproariously in heaps of golden straw. . . . In these English farms, if anywhere, one might see life steadily and see it whole, group in one vision its transitoriness and its eternal youth, connect – connect without bitterness until all men were brothers.[52]

Opposed to this vision of wholeness and love was the city: 'I hate this continual flux of London. It is an epitome of us at our worst – eternal formlessness; all the qualities, good, bad and indifferent, streaming away – streaming, streaming for ever.'[53] Imperialism, cosmopolitanism and the city were all leading to one conclusion, as when Helen pointed to London creeping across the meadows towards Howards End and said to Margaret, 'London is only part of something else, I'm afraid. Life's going to be melted down, all over the world.'[54]

> London was but a foretaste of this nomadic civilisation which is altering human nature so profoundly, and throws upon personal relations a stress greater than they have ever borne before. Under cosmopolitanism, if it comes, we shall receive no help from the earth. Trees and meadows and mountains will only be a spectacle, and the

binding force that they once exercised on a character must be entrusted to Love alone. May Love be equal to the task![55]

Though from the Majestic Forster could comfortably get about central Alexandria on foot or by horse-drawn calèche, his visits to the eastern suburbs of Ramleh made travelling by tram a necessity – journeys that must have carried a certain frisson: 'She wanted something big, and she believed that it would have come to her on the windswept platform of an electric tram',[56] as he had written of Lucy in *A Room with a View*. Red Cross flags flew over a number of Ramleh villas, Victoria College had been converted to a military hospital, and farther out at Montazah, the summer resort of the Egyptian ruling family, the Selamlik (the men's quarters built early in the century by Khedive Abbas II in a style intended to please his Austrian mistress) had become the troops' favourite convalescent home. Forster's first visit to Montazah was on 9 January 1916, not long after his thirty-seventh birthday; at its western gate, he noticed with pleasure, was a faded sign left over from the time of the khedive's residency: 'No admission this way even if the fence has fallen down.'[57] Here and elsewhere on his rounds he did 'the motherly to Tommies',[58] and over the coming months, apart from his searching, he read aloud scenes from Dickens, Hardy and Tolstoy.

'I consort only with Tommies and others who have no interest in, or illusions about, bloodshed.' He liked the soldiers for their dignity and lack of self-pity, and hated, even more than the wounds and mutilations they suffered, war's 'inward death', its displacement of 'all the old healthy growths – love, joy, thought, despair – deluding men by its semblance of vitality'.[59] The censorship outraged him, and he was angered by the distorted official accounts of the fighting against the Turks along the Suez Canal. He read to the soldiers because he believed that great literature 'helps us to abstain from fear, from hatred, from tribal religion'; that books portray 'a world of greatness, the world of the spirit, that helps us to endure danger and ingratitude and answer a lie with a truth'.[60]

Already in January he had decided to stay on in Alexandria; he was enjoying his work and the mood of the city – 'The weather is perfect, the tennis courts of the Sporting Club thronged by day, the brothels by night'[61] – while his journeys out to the hospitals began to take on a romance. 'Come here Mustafa Pasha, come here Sidi Bishr', shouted the fat tram official at the Ramleh terminus as though evoking jinns. 'Yes yes come here Bulkeley and Glymenopoulo',[62] he roared, as Forster obediently boarded the magical conveyance. He had begun giving lectures to the soldiers on ancient and modern Alexandria, and if space had become a military zone he could tour freely by the trams through time. 'The first half mile of the tram lines traverses ground of immense historical fame', he would write in his guidebook, describing the journey from the terminus out to Ramleh. 'Every inch was once sacred or royal. On the football fields to the left were the Ptolemaic Palaces . . . The walls of the Museion, too, are said to have extended into the area, but we know no details and can only be certain that the Ancient World never surpassed the splendour of the scene. On the right, from the higher ground, the Theatre overlooked it, and the dramas of Aeschylus and Euripides could be performed against the background of a newer and a greater Greece. No eye will see that achievement again, no mind can imagine it. Grit and gravel have taken its place today.'[63] The stations click by in Forster's guide. Mazarita: 'The original Church of St Mark, where the evangelist was buried, must have stood on the shore. There is nothing to see today.' Chatby: 'Traces of ancient roads and drains have been found here.' Camp de César: 'Caesar never camped here.' Cleopatra: 'Cleopatra never lived here. . . . Left from the station, at the base of a cliff by the edge of the sea, is a Ptolemaic tomb with painted walls, but even while one describes such things they are being destroyed.' Sidi Gaber: 'Mosque of a beneficent local saint, who flies about at night, looks after children, etc.' Mustafa Pasha: 'Right, up the road, is the hill of Abou el Nawatir, the highest near Alexandria; exquisite view.'[64]

The name Abou el Nawatir has all but fallen out of use and even the hill is hardly noticeable from the tram line for the high buildings all around. During the First World War, recalled Grafftey-Smith, the little house which was the summer residence of the high commissioner stood at the top and only 'a few select villas shared with us an aristocratic eminence'.[65] The area is now called Rushdi, and as you ascend its slopes you pass villa after villa, but often their gardens have been sold off to make room for modern apartment blocks so that like the British Residency, built soon after Forster's time, they no longer have a view.

'I imagine it is here that civilisation will expire', Forster wrote to Virginia Woolf on 15 April 1916. 'It is already dead in Cairo, which has war correspondents and 119 Generals and clubs of perturbed and earnest men. But in Alexandria it seems still possible to read books and bathe.'[66] He was writing from the garden of Furness' villa on the hill of Abou el Nawatir, where an artillery piece, a British relic from 1882, lay nearby in the sand, but from where the European war seemed a long way off: shops were still boasting that they had supplied the Crown Princess of Württemberg and the trams were advertising 'Schutz für junge Mädchen' (refuge for young girls); Forster had a vague scheme for a book about Alexander the Great (like *Maurice*, however, 'unpublishable') and Furness was translating the *Anthologia Palatina*; and sometimes there was a party in a rich Levantine's house. 'How long will it last? Booh! bumble!'[67]

Some among his broadening circle of friends were taking him in charge. 'I am entirely living on Furness', who since early April had relieved him of the expense of living at the Majestic – Forster's Red Cross salary was insignificant and he had to rely on what private income he could ship out from England – 'and am teaching English for £4 a month to a well-pleased Greek', he explained in his letter to Virginia Woolf.[68] The Greek was Pericles Anastassiades, who had been raised and educated in England; any help he received with his English could not have amounted to more than polish, his need for lessons as much a disguised form of patronage.

Anastassiades was a cotton broker who lived on the corner of the Rue Rosette and the Rue Young, just west of the Graeco-Roman Museum; an amateur painter with intellectual interests, he had been a close friend of Constantine Cavafy's since at least 1889 and something of a patron to him as well, lending him books, paying for his first visit to Greece in 1901 and probably guiding him in the small speculations he made on the Bourse which supplemented his income as a government clerk. It was he who introduced Furness to Cavafy, the two men discovering that they had much in common, Cavafy later recalling a conversation about *The Greek Anthology* and 'its wonderful succinct expressions' and describing Furness as 'a most cultivated man with first-class artistic originality'.[69]

The meeting between Cavafy and Forster, when it came, was to be of primary importance to twentieth-century literature – 'I often think of my good fortune and the opportunity, which the chance of a horrible war gave me, to meet one of the great poets of our time', Forster later wrote[70] – and so not surprisingly various claims have been made as to who was the intermediary. According to Antonius family tradition it was George Antonius who introduced Forster to Cavafy. Other sources say it was Anastassiades, while Forster, many years later, said, 'Furness took me to see him in 1916–17'.[71]

Whoever it was, Anastassiades was clearly the central link, and he was probably among the party of Greeks with whom Forster dined on 7 March 1916 when he was first introduced to Cavafy. The occasion took place at the Mohammed Ali Club at 2 Rue Rosette,[72] a ten-minute walk from the Majestic where Forster was still in residence. Furness and his friends were members, and soon Forster was put up for membership too. Smart and cosmopolitan, the club was the haunt of bankers, cotton brokers and *rentiers* who would sit on its verandah admiring the stylish women out shopping along the Rue Chérif Pasha, while inside were comfortable lounges, a library, reading and music rooms and gaming tables at which there was high play.

Literary evenings with his new Greek acquaintances followed, but Forster's friendship with Cavafy and his appreciation of his peculiar poetic imagination took some time to mature. Six months passed before he was describing Cavafy as 'the really first class member of that group',[73] though even after almost a year Forster was uncertain what to make of him, writing to Goldsworthy Lowes Dickinson on 10 January 1917 that he found Cavafy 'sensitive, scholarly and acute – not at all devoid of creative power but devoting it to rearranging and resuscitating the past'.[74]

Meanwhile, Forster, attempting to exorcise his own past, was determinedly pursuing his personal liberation in the Alexandrian present. A month or so after being introduced to the poet at the Mohammed Ali Club and while he was staying with Furness at Abou el Nawatir, Forster first set eyes ('and the morning was fresh and sunny') on Mohammed el Adl, a young tram conductor. On following mornings at the same hour Forster would wait hopefully at the Mustafa Pasha stop for the Bacos tram, identified by its blue label,[75] and was sometimes successful in finding Mohammed aboard, the only conductor, he noticed, who moved between passengers without treading on their feet. Once when Forster was travelling with Furness they saw Mohammed laughing with a soldier, and then, when the tram had reached the Ramleh terminus in town, touching one button

7   Mohammed el Adl, 1917. This photograph was taken shortly after Forster had succeeded in parting with 'Respectability'.

on his uniform after another in a goodbye caress. They found it charming and smiled: 'That boy has some African-Negro-blood',[76] said Forster, and Furness agreed.

But Mohammed's gesture towards the soldier only reminded Forster of how trapped he felt within his own sexual frustration. A week after arriving at Furness' villa, Forster had written to a friend, 'This physical loneliness has gone on for too many months. . . . I am sure that some of the decent people I see daily would be willing to save me if they knew, but they don't know, can't know. . . . I sit leaning over them for a bit and there it ends – except for images that burn into my sleep.' He was referring to the soldiers he met at the hospitals: 'It's awful to live with an unsatisfied craving, now and then smothering it but never killing it or even wanting to.'[77]

Britain had probably the finest imperial gendarmerie since Rome, but the scale of the present conflict made wholly new demands. Even when it became clear by the end of 1914 that millions of men would be needed to fight the war, recruitment to the first

8 Ramleh trams, *c*. First World War–early 1920s. Banks of sand line the tram route between town and Ramleh. A Bacos tram is on the left; Mohammed el Adl was a conductor on the Bacos route.

mass army in British history remained voluntary. Forster believed he had settled his obligations by joining the Red Cross, but in January 1916 Parliament passed an act introducing conscription, and in June the Red Cross decided to release its able-bodied personnel for military service. Forster's 'Booh! bumble!' mood of April was shattered. Telling the head of the Red Cross in Egypt that taking another human life was the most horrible thing he could do, he was grudgingly given permission to return to England where he could present his case as a conscientious objector before a tribunal. But meanwhile, his 'amazingly competent and sympathetic friends'[78] intervened with the army, which informed the Red Cross that it did not want him: 'I am quite shameless over this wirepulling', he wrote to his mother. 'If I can't keep out of the army by fair means then hey for foul! Let alone that there conscience.'[79]

'I am an artist', he wrote on 2 July to Florence Barger, the wife of an undergraduate friend from his days at King's College, in whom he was discovering a confidante, '– after a week of stress like this one has the right to utter that discredited word – and the artist must (yes! I am actually going to say this too!) live his life.' But then came the whisper: 'I mention [this] to you because I oughtn't to mother – there is no occasion for her to know of such subsidiary soul stirrings.'[80]

Alexandria was a 'towsled unsmartened sort of place' and in its environs he found 'a magic'.[81] From Abou el Nawatir he would descend southwards to Lake Hadra lying against the Nouzha Gardens, once the suburb of Eleusis where Callimachus had lived. He had read Callimachus at Cambridge, but that could not compare with walking the ancient ground and going over the poet's lines with Furness *in situ*:

> Someone told me, Heracleitus, of your end;
> and I wept, and thought how often you and I
> sunk the sun with talking. Well! and now you lie
> antiquated ashes somewhere, Carian friend.
> But your nightingales, your songs, are living still;
> them the death that clutches all things cannot kill.[82]

Skirting the lake and the gardens to the south was the Mahmoudiya Canal, that artery by which Mohammed Ali had brought Alexandria back to life, and where it curled along the southern flank of the modern town it probably followed the course of the ancient canal to Canopus, 'whither the Alexandrians used to go out in barges, to enjoy themselves and to worship Serapis'.[83] Here Forster would dine at 'mild restaurants'[84] and then follow the canal bank westwards, the waters of Mariut off to his left, to a lakeside neighbourhood of palms, bananas and vegetable gardens not far from Kom el Shogafa and Gabbari station, where he found a fishing village built on a tiny creek, in appearance, he thought, quite Japanese.

He also went for long walks along the Mediterranean shore, which in those days lay within sight of the Ramleh tram. Built between 1860 and 1879, the Ramleh light railway was transformed in 1904 into an electric tram line. But even after the coming of the tram the Ramleh sands here and there came down to the sea. In winter the landscape was covered with ice-plants, crocuses and wild flowers, so that the sand ('ramleh' in Arabic) was set with bright-hued blossoms and shone like enamelled gold. From spring to autumn there was swimming along the coves and sandy beaches running for nine miles from the Eastern Harbour to Montazah, and even as near town as Cleopatra Forster found it was possible to go bathing without a costume. 'The coast walk from Alexandria to Ramleh is rarely taken but is charming – low crumbly cliffs, sandy beaches, flat rocks, and vestiges of ancient houses and tombs that help one realise how the whole site of the city has sunk.' Cape Lochias, where the Ptolemies had built their royal palace to catch the freshening sea breezes, was now mostly under water, its vestige the narrow point of Silsileh, where in Arab times a beacon was raised, the diminutive Pharillon no more than a flickering reminder of the marvellous Pharos that once had towered on the opposite arm of the harbour. 'There is no road east of Silsileh. The scheme for a grandiose "Corniche" drive has fortunately failed, and the scenery has escaped the standardised dulness that environs most big towns.'[85]

Forster would go for a swim before breakfast, call in at St Mark's Buildings later in the morning and afterwards 'crawl to a nice cool little Italian restaurant and then tram on to the hospital'.[86] Montazah, as he wrote to Dickinson on 28 July, offered a glimpse of earthly paradise: 'Amongst its tamarisk groves and avenues of flowering oleander, on its reefs and fantastic promontories of rocks and sands, hundreds of young men . . . go about bare chested and bare legged, the blue of their linen shorts and the pale mauve of their shirts accenting the brown splendour of their bodies, and down by the sea many of them spend half their days naked and unrebuked and unashamed [the last two words were crossed out]. . . . It makes me very happy yet very sad – they came from the unspeakable, all these young gods, and in a fortnight at the latest return to it: the beauty on the crest of a wave. . . . I come away from that place each time thinking "Why not more of this? Why not? What would it injure? Why not a world like this – its beauty of course impaired by death and old age and poverty and disease, but a world that should not torture itself by organised and artificial horrors?" It's evidently not to be in our day, nor while nationality lives.'[87]

It was probably at Montazah that he had sex with a soldier on the beach. 'Yesterday', he wrote to Florence Barger on 16 October, 'for the first time in my life I parted with respectability.' He had felt the moment coming for many months and when it happened found it neither glamorous nor squalid; instead it left him feeling curiously sad. There was nothing intimate in the act, nothing human, nothing beyond the satisfaction of physical hunger, and this seemed to confirm that he was 'tethered to the life of the spirit', tethered by the habits of his thirty-seven years, from which his free will or aspirations could not release him. There was 'this enormous torrent in me that never stops' but which found no outlet: 'My life . . . has been too damn lop sided for words and physically damn lonely.' But the letter is insistent: 'Well, my dear, this is odd news for a Matron to receive, but you've got to receive it because you're the only person in the world I want to tell it to.'[88]

But there was something else about his confidante, apart from her tolerance and his relief in knowing that 'you like me to tell you things'.[89] Florence Barger was also a friend of his mother's and lived only five miles from her home in Weybridge, Surrey, the two women, at Forster's invitation, showing one another his letters – except those he intended for Florence's eyes only, which must have carried the thrill of defiance.

Sometime in late spring or early summer Aida Borchgrevink found Forster rooms with her former maid, Irene, an impetuous if greying Greek from Corfu where Italian had been the lingua franca until 1848, as it was only just ceasing to be in Alexandria. Irene owned two properties, one at Saba Pasha not far from Aida's, the other at Camp de César closer to town, and she seemed always to be moving between the two. 'Lo porto con me', she would say, dragging him along and making him feel, he said, like a doll. She amused him, and he enjoyed her fussings and would eat more just to please her, and welcomed her kindness, once saying, 'I almost forgot I am in exile.'[90]

If Irene was an eccentric version of home, Aida Borchgrevink was an extravagant free spirit who soared above convention. Forster was drawn by her charm, her intellectual curiosity and her sympathetic understanding; she was among those who took a passion-ate interest in him during his conscription troubles. Her comfortable book-filled house was perched on the cliffs above Stanley Bay in the heart of Ramleh ('the straggling suburb where the British and other foreigners live', as he later wrote in his guide: 'Lovely private gardens, the best in Egypt')[91] and was near the Saba Pasha stop for the red-labelled Victoria tram which followed the more direct coastal route taken by Forster when going to Montazah. He often broke his journeys there to take lunch in her enormous garden, afterwards walking down to the bay where he taught himself to swim, a routine, he was later to say, that introduced him to the rhythm of the city, 'the slow Levantine dégringolade',[92] though he was probably referring as much to the way he began unravelling under Aida's attentions. His dishevelled appearance and his habit of standing on one leg and winding the other around it made her think him shy, but he would surprise her with his subtle quips and unforeseen remarks, and now he also confided to her something of his sexual yearnings.

In her own playful and perhaps goading, even warning, reading of his character she insisted on calling him Rickie after the protagonist of *The Longest Journey*, which in so many details and themes was a re-creation of Forster's own life. Decades later he called the novel 'the one I am most glad to have written'; it had come upon him 'without my knowledge' and with 'the magic sense of being visited'.[93]

'The cow is there' – so begins *The Longest Journey*, with an argument among undergraduates in Rickie's rooms at Cambridge. 'It was philosophy. They were discussing the existence of objects. Do they exist only when there is someone to look at them? or have they a real existence of their own? It is all very interesting, but at the same time it is difficult. Hence the cow. She seemed to make things easier. She was so familiar, so solid, that surely the truths that she illustrated would in time become familiar and solid also. Is the cow there or not? This was better than deciding between objectivity and subjectivity.'[94]

But in Forster's first diary entry for *The Longest Journey* the cow is not yet there: 'An idea for an entire novel – that of a man who discovers that he has an illegitimate brother.'[95] That was in 1904, but over the next three years he explored the ethical choices presented by his theme: Rickie discovers the truth about Stephen, who does not know of their relation, and decides he 'must be told such a real thing'.[96] Rickie's wife objects, she wants her husband entirely for herself. Neither of them likes the uncouth Stephen, but Rickie presses his case: 'It seems to me that here and there in life we meet with a person or incident that is symbolical. It's nothing in itself, yet for the moment it stands for some eternal principle. We accept it, at whatever cost, and we have accepted life. But if we are frightened and reject it, the moment, so to speak, passes; the symbol is never offered again' – 'But at the back of his soul he knew that the woman had conquered.'[97]

In failing to accept Stephen as his brother – 'Our duty to acknowledge each man accurately, however vile he is'[98] – Rickie suffers the moral consequence of failing to face reality. *The Longest Journey* ends with Rickie saving his brother's life at the cost of sacrificing his own. For the reader it is a strange and unsatisfying act of self-annihilation. But for Forster it carried an autobiographical truth: the supremacy of personal relationships had been encouraged at Cambridge, but Forster despaired that the love of 'brothers' could ever be possible for him, and in London, for instance, he had been driven to cruising Hyde Park and loitering in public toilets. This or the arid life of the spirit were the extremes by which he was trapped – in fact until 1909 when he was thirty it was even worse than that: only then, having already published three novels, did he fully understand how sexual intercourse took place. 'Only connect!' he wrote in *Howards End* soon after making this discovery, '. . . and human love will be seen at its highest. Live in fragments no longer. Only connect, and the beast and the monk, robbed of the isolation that is life to either, will die.'[99] But in the autumn of 1916, after having sex with the soldier, he feared that his fate was forever to inhabit the isolated extremes of his own fragmentation, and for weeks he sank into depression and spread gloom among his friends.

Early in November he collapsed – 'Quite the fashionable thing to do on a first visit', he wrote lightly to Florence Barger. He was at the home of Charles Leveaux at 11 Rue des Abbassides in the Quartier Grec, a wealthy European area off the Rue Rosette towards the vanished Gate of the Sun. Leveaux was British and practised law at the Mixed Courts; he was also a Jew and the guiding spirit behind Alexandria's Theosophical Society. The gathering had been talking creeds and literature and 'in the spirit of the Helleno-Christian city' had found the doctrine of the Incarnation in *Howards End*. 'There is plenty of interest and of tolerance in the mixed communities out here', Forster told Florence, though also it was a city of 'ingenious muddlements' where the religiously minded were in their element, leaving no room for 'what Cambridge knew as thought'. Put to bed and richly pampered at Leveaux's – 'hot baths and three Arab servants to wait upon me'[100] – Forster reflected on how Athanasius, the fourth-century theologian and patriarch of Alexandria, had destroyed the old Hellenic harmony of the city with the dogma and self-abnegation of Christian orthodoxy, which Forster saw as the wrong turning taken by Western civilisation.

Two weeks after visiting Leveaux he vomited, and though Irene tendered tisanes made from Corfiot herbs the vomiting continued. Taken to an English doctor, he was diagnosed as having jaundice and despatched to a military hospital overlooking Lake Mariut, where 'so amiable is my mind that during the orange dawn and the whiteness of trees succeeding, it sometimes pretends to me that I am in India'.[101] He confessed his gladness at having to do no work; he had liked it, but his year in Alexandria – almost to the day – had left him feeling caught in a rut. Soon he was transferred to Montazah where he enjoyed a growingly 'festive'[102] convalescence.

On 1 January 1917, his thirty-eighth birthday, he returned to his lodgings and copied out from Walter Pater's novel *Marius the Epicurean* a passage in which Marcus Aurelius longs for the Ideal City but feels it lies even farther from his grasp than it had from Plato's, because, unlike Plato, Marcus Aurelius 'conceived of it as including tenderness and pity; virtue, wisdom and beauty were not enough'.[103]

Within days he began his pursuit of the tram conductor Mohammed el Adl, and through him Alexandria would become Forster's Ideal City.

9   A postcard showing Sidi Gaber Mosque. Forster described Sidi Gaber as the 'mosque of a beneficent local saint, who flies about at night, looks after children, etc'. From the nearby tram stop, Forster stumbled home in the dark, erotically excited that Mohammed had agreed to meet him.

Returning to Irene's late one January evening in 1917, Forster caught the Bacos tram and sat where Mohammed kept his coat. The night was cold, and Mohammed asked him to rise so that he might get it. They had not spoken before; Forster was delighted with the discovery that he knew English and in the exchange each took a liking to the other's manner. Afterwards if they happened to see one another at the Ramleh terminus, Mohammed would greet him with a half salute. Then in March, as Forster offered his fare, Mohammed declared, 'You shall never pay',[104] reminding him of the incident of the coat and saying how his courtesy had given him pleasure.

The next night Forster was back at the Ramleh terminus carrying a copy of *Punch* meant as a gift. At some point he had made a note of Mohammed's badge number, eighty-six on a little oval plaque of white and blue, but he knew neither his name nor schedule and tarried in vain. On a luckier occasion he found Mohammed's tram but then made a mess of it. He offered Mohammed a cigarette, which he refused, saying he seldom smoked as 'my Ministry of Finance does not permit me'.[105] Forster took this as a hint for a tip and proffered more than the fare, saying he should keep the change, but Mohammed closed his hand in a fist and let the coins fall to the floor. Only the ludicrous sight of Forster scrabbling about after them on his knees persuaded Mohammed to accept. In turn Mohammed's reluctance must have pleased him; at about this time Forster visited the house of an acquaintance: 'His mistress was there, as was the mistress of one of his friends – an intelligent girl with whom I talked Dostoieffsky. I envied their security, but not their relationship. It was all coyness and flattery, and the basis commercial: which I find – not wrong but profoundly anti-aphrodisiac.'[106]

The courting continued into April and May, Forster spending 'God knows how many hours' waiting for the desired tram, the desired conductor, while all the time contriving to make their meetings seem accidental. Then once as Forster was bound for the hospital at Montazah, Mohammed said, 'I want to ask you a question about Mohammedans, which please answer truly, sir.' But there was no time to reply, and saying that he would catch him on the journey back, Forster got Mohammed to tell him his hours. The question was why did the English so much dislike Muslims. 'They don't', said Forster. 'They do, because I heard one soldier say to the other in the tram "That's a mosque for fucking (I beg your pardon) Mohammedans."' Forster protested, saying one of his greatest friends was a Muslim and that he had been to India to see him. Mohammed thought the money could have been better spent: 'If I was rich I should build first an eye hospital, then a mosque.'[107] Only then would he spend the rest on himself and like Forster travel to see the world.

Now that he knew Mohammed's hours, Forster abandoned the pretence of accidental meetings and to avoid argument no longer attempted to pay the fare; instead during their frequent journeys together they spent the time happily chatting. But 'the reprehensible habit of joy rides' brought their relationship to a crisis when an inspector caught Forster without a ticket and rather than challenge a European turned angrily on Mohammed. When Forster asked Mohammed what had happened, he said, 'I am to get the sack.' Forster was appalled – 'This is too awful' – but Mohammed replied, 'Why so? I have performed a good action', and tried to change the subject, asking how many miles it was to India. 'I don't know or care!' Forster cried, 'Whenever shall I see you again?'[108]

Early the next morning Forster went to see Furness, who called on the stationmaster and returned with the news that all was well. Though sympathetic, he urged Forster to be careful – 'general conditions, onlookers, etc' – and advised him to give Mohammed's tram a miss for the present. Forster ignored the advice: 'This is rather unlike me. I just went ahead, and it is the thing I am proudest of in all my life.' Mohammed told him that the matter had been dropped and asked if he had been to the stationmaster. Forster said no, but when he asked in return if they could meet, Mohammed answered with gratitude, 'Any time any place any hour.'[109]

Mohammed was only about seventeen when Forster first saw him in the spring of 1916 while staying with Furness, and he was no more than eighteen when their affair began. They would last meet in February 1922, when Forster passed through Egypt on his way back from his second visit to India. In England a few months later Forster pressed open a hardcover notebook and started his 'letter' to Mohammed, continuing with it every now and again over the next seven years. Finally, on 27 December 1929, he inscribed it:

To Mohammed el Adl:

who died at Mansourah shortly after the 8th of May, 1922, aged about twenty three: of consumption; his mother, father, brother and son died before him; his daughter has died since, his widow is said to have married again:

and to my love for him.

In his 'letter' Forster looked back to that night in May 1917 when Mohammed had said, 'Any time any place any hour': 'Tonight I have to write sensually, even if I have to tear the pages out of the letter later on. I must always have loved you in that way too, but how the sensuality has come and gone! It came violently when you first agreed to meet me. I got off your tram at Sidi Gaber and stumbled home in the dark.'[110]

Sidi Gaber was not the stop at which Forster ought to have got off the tram. From there it was a long walk to Irene's, whether back to Camp de César or on to Saba Pasha (where he was probably still living at the time), and perhaps, recalling Furness' warning that morning, Forster was afflicted as much by caution as by violent passion in stumbling home from where he did. The inhibiting and distorting effects of caution and fear were much on Forster's mind. Amid the Great War raging beyond Alexandria, he was fighting a personal battle, and he saw the two as connected: he was no less a soldier but was fighting against the depersonalising aspects of war, fighting in the cause of private emotions and relationships.

There was fear in Forster's ardent pursuit of Mohammed, as he admitted when he broached the relationship to Florence on 29 May 1917: 'I have plunged into an anxious but very beautiful affair.' But, he argued with himself, there was no harm in feeling frightened, for 'fear is an emotion' to be confronted honestly; what was corrupting was the pressure of habit and social convention trying to make him behave falsely.[111] That was the world he had known in England, his mother's world in which he had been kept a child, but three days later, referring again to Mohammed, he announced to Florence his passage into a new dimension: 'I first feel a grown up man.'[112]

His longing to outgrow that world of social and emotional constraint had been pursued in his novels, but with *Howards End* he hit a wall, as he had recognised when he wrote from India after the incident with Masood, 'I want something beyond the field of action and behaviour: the waters of the river that rises from the middle of the earth to join the Ganges and the Jumna where they join'[113] – that is, something beyond the contrivances a novelist can command, a benediction, for the Ganges and the Jumna are said to be joined at their confluence by the Saraswati, invisible except to the eye of faith. Here Hindu pilgrims come to bathe to purify themselves from karma, the sum total of their past actions. But though Forster could grant happiness to the Schlegel sisters in the form of their implicit homosexual marriage in *Howards End*, his own search for fulfilment remained disguised and frustrated; nor could he confer grace upon himself by writing *Maurice*, his overtly homosexual novel.

In Alexandria Forster was determined to connect the emotional and the physical and in Mohammed el Adl he found the benediction he was looking for. On that May night when Forster had stumbled home from the tram at Sidi Gaber, they had agreed to meet at a place Mohammed called 'Chatby Gardens':[114] he did not know their real name, Mohammed explained, but the gardens were near Chatby and he gave everything a name. A tram ticket Forster kept among his mementoes identifies the rendezvous: on the back of it he scrawled, 'Mazarita not Ramleh, up the road by the column'.[115]

Like his stumbling home from Sidi Gaber, this note betrays his anxiety and caution: by Ramleh he does not mean the eastern suburbs but the Ramleh tram terminus in town. They are not to attract attention by meeting there; instead, one stop along is Mazarita and up the road from it were the Municipal Gardens (now the Shallalat Gardens). In his guide, Forster describes the gardens as following the line of the Arab walls and intersecting the course of the old Farkha canal that until the beginning of the twentieth century connected the Mahmoudiya Canal and the sea: 'Both these features have been utilised; the fortifications have turned into picturesque hillocks or survive as masses of masonry, which, though of little merit in themselves, have been cleverly grouped and look mediaeval by moonlight; while the water of the canal has been preserved in an artificial pool, the abode of ducks. The gardens should be thoroughly explored.'[116]

Even from the tram stop at Mazarita the column can be seen rising at the west end of the gardens. It is Ptolemaic, a monolithic shaft of pink Aswan granite, probably from a great building of the royal quarter hereabouts. Flanked by statues of Sekhmet, the lion-headed goddess of war, the column was erected to commemorate the retaking of Khartoum by General Kitchener on 2 September 1898, thirteen years after its fall to the Mahdi and the death of General Gordon.

Here in May 1917 Mohammed and Forster had their first rendezvous, the Egyptian smartly dressed and self-assured, the Englishman with an offering of sticky cakes. They sat on a bench, perhaps with a view of the ducks. 'I do not care for cakes. What did you pay for them? How many centuries ago did you buy them?' (He later told Forster he had thought they might be drugged.) Then suddenly he said, 'Would you like to see my Home of Misery? It will be *dreadful*,[117] and walking back down the road to Mazarita they took the tram to Bacos, Mohammed amusing himself by handing the cakes round among the passengers.

Bacos is now overcrowded and poor, but then it was a quiet, lower-middle-class area, and Mohammed's house stood in a garden with a flowering jacaranda tree. (A typical example of a modest house of the time in Bacos, and perhaps not unlike the one in which Mohammed lived, is that at 12 Sharia Kannawaty, south off Sharia Mustafa Pasha: here on 15 January 1918 was born Gamal Abdel Nasser, the son of a postmaster and the future ruler of Egypt.) Mohammed could be humorously self-deprecating and 'Home of Misery' was probably something of an exaggeration; all the same he lived very simply, in a single room which seemed to Forster very poor and bare – Mohammed opened his

10 A postcard showing the Municipal Gardens. Forster and Mohammed had their first rendezvous at the Municipal Gardens, landscaped to make picturesque use of an old canal and the remains of the city's Arab walls.

trunk containing the whole of his belongings and flung them out, saying, 'not much but all clean; now I have shown you all there is to show'.[118] They sat on the bed with food between them and chatted, and for the first time Mohammed told Forster his name and spoke about his background. He had come to Alexandria less than two years before from Mansourah in the eastern Delta, where he had learnt to read, write and speak English at the American missionary school. His family had remained at Mansourah, but 'I have always ate apart and lived apart and thought apart. Perhaps I am not my father's son.' Forster had felt uneasy about Mohammed's lack of years but was reassured by his maturity, independence and grace, writing to Florence, 'I can scarcely believe him the son of Egypt, for there is no Nile mud either in his body or his mind.'[119] Mohammed in turn was touched that the Englishman had come into his home, saying as they were parting, 'This is the very happiest evening of my life.'[120]

Soon Forster returned to Mohammed's room and was introduced to some of his friends, a Syrian midwife and a young Egyptian who ran a matrimonial agency, with whom he conversed in Italian, but his attention was for Mohammed: 'I was so fascinated by your character and talk', he later wrote in his 'letter'; and looking for signs that his own sensual feelings were reciprocated, 'I noticed that you always kept your hand in your pocket for a minute or two when we met.'[121] Only now did he tell Mohammed his name, but not what he did for a living.

Their third meeting – the moment of benediction – was in Forster's room at Irene's in Ramleh around the middle of June, and now 'the caresses started'. In his 'letter' Forster recalled how they played chess and then lay on the bed: 'I touched your knee – you incline towards me. I stretch and touch your hair, you say "short hair but crisp", you touch mine and say "beautiful hair" and as my head sinks beside yours on the pillow, your left arm goes under it. Our first kiss follows. . . . For the rest, the evening was a muddle. Seeing the lump on your trousers, I unbuttoned them, also my own, first saying, "How fond of me are you?" Perhaps this put you off for you said "What do you mean?" and muttered "Hm" when you saw my condition although it was your own. Something had bored you. When I touched you again you defended yourself and hurt my hand. You didn't get off my bed, but wouldn't let me come near you and by accident I scratched your face. That sobered us. We went to the washstand and staunched the blood, I thought you were superstitious and would reckon it against me that I had hurt you, but no, next day on the tram we laughed about it.'[122] Forster himself used the word 'blessed' in describing to Florence what happened, its meaning a gift, yet Mohammed had to defend himself against Forster's forcefulness. Once famously described as looking like 'the man who came to wind the clocks',[123] in fact Forster was a man used to getting his way while finding the words to make it seem otherwise, though in another sense of the word his use of 'blessed' was entirely accurate, its original meaning being to make sacred by marking with blood or sacrifice.

To Goldsworthy Lowes Dickinson he wrote at the end of June, 'I don't know how it'll end. But how does anything end? One should act as if things last.'[124]

> It wouldn't have lasted long anyway –
> years of experience make that clear.

As in these and the following lines from 'In the Evening', published in 1917 and written the previous year, a sense of loss pervades Cavafy's poetry. What he salvages is remembered sensation, which mingles with the life of the city:

> An echo from my days of indulgence,
> an echo from those days came back to me,
> something from the fire of the young life we shared:
> I picked up a letter again,
> read it over and over till the light faded.

Then, sad, I went out on to the balcony,
went out to change my thoughts at last by seeing
something of this city I love,
a little movement in the streets, in the shops.[125]

Cavafy was fifty-four in 1917 when Forster got to know him well and had been an active homosexual for over thirty years. Now he dyed his hair and took special care of his skin and fell back increasingly on his memories. Yet even in his younger days in Alexandria he seems never to have had a sexual relationship with a social equal, nor is he known to have had a sustained affair with anyone at all. Instead Cavafy paid for sex:

The room was cheap and sordid,
hidden above the suspect taverna.

. . .

And there on that ordinary, plain bed
I had love's body . . .

'One Night' (published in 1915)[126]

When Cavafy was still in his twenties and thirties and living with his mother in the Rue de la Gare de Ramleh, he would bribe the servant to ruffle up his bed so that he would seem to have spent the night at home and then slip away to the Attarine quarter or beyond the rabbit warren of the Genenah to the Rue Anastasi, parallel to the Rue des Soeurs. Here on the squalid fringes of the European city, young Greeks, often immigrants from their impoverished country, endured long and ill-paid hours as workmen, grocers' boys and taverna waiters seven days a week, their one day off throughout the year at Sham el Nessim, a national spring holiday going back to pharaonic times, which coincided with Easter Monday in the Orthodox Church. 'All that work and movement makes their bodies light and symmetrical', observed Cavafy. 'They're nearly always slender. Their faces – white when they work in shops and sunburnt when they work outdoors – have a pleasant, poetical colour.' Yet he was not indifferent to their social condition, which he contrasted with that of 'rich young men who are sick and psychologically dirty, or fat and greasy from all their food and drink and soft beds'.[127] He was touched by the beauty of these poor young men and saw it as a compensation for all they lacked – though if he did not see himself as exploiting them, he was certainly attracted by their affordability. From the upper rooms at night came the cries and screams of the bordellos, where girls and boys catered for every taste: here for a handful of piastres the young men of Cavafy's poems offered him their exhausted bodies:

In the evenings, after the shop closed,
if there was something he longed for especially,

···
a beautiful blue shirt in some store window,
he'd sell his body for a half-crown or two.

I ask myself if the great Alexandria
of ancient times could boast of a boy
more exquisite, more perfect . . .
. . . we don't have a statue or painting of him;
thrust into that poor ironmonger's shop,
overworked, harassed, given to cheap debauchery,
he was soon used up.

'Days of 1909, '10 and '11' (published in 1928)[128]

In the ancient city, says Cavafy in this poem, beauty would have been honoured in marble. But also in contrasting the present with the past, Cavafy is suggesting something more: in today's Alexandria homosexuality is seen as depraved, but in the great Alexandria of ancient times homosexual love was normal, indeed celebrated by sculptors and painters, and acclaimed by the poets of *The Greek Anthology* as the most Hellenic form of eroticism. And if then, why not now? It is an argument that weaves its way through Cavafy's poetry, here unusually within a single poem but more often in the correspondences he creates between one poem and another and between the past and the present.

And yet, as Cavafy must have known (he is elsewhere in his poetry too meticulous in his attention to historical detail not to have known), homosexuality did not have this standing in ancient Alexandria. Callimachus, to whom Forster compared him, though he freely circulated his homo-erotic poetry, was nevertheless probably something of an outcast for being exclusively homosexual, having 'the disease of loving boys' as he put it in one of his epigrams. What the ancients celebrated was physical beauty, and they were not surprised that men might wish to caress and penetrate other beautiful men, but this was within the context of bisexuality, especially as practised among youths in the years between puberty and their acceptance of manhood's social responsibilities. Homosexuality when practised exclusively was repugnant for two reasons: there was the need to maintain the population in a world where the mortality rate was high, and for free men, on whom the entire weight of civic responsibility in a highly ordered hierarchical society lay, to maintain their position of dominance with regard to women and slaves. To allow oneself to be penetrated by another man was to place oneself in the position of a woman, sexually and socially. In consequence, male prostitutes ran the risk of heavier legal and social sanctions than females, and were additionally detested for their compensatory rapacity and venality. Callimachus often lamented the loss of virtue in a world where richer men could outbid him for gratification, and being short of purse would become long on elevated disdain: 'I hate a boy whom any man can have, nor do

11   In his twenties and thirties Cavafy lived with his mother in the Rue de la Gare de Ramleh, which was respectable enough by day but thronged at night with female prostitutes parading along one side of the street and male prostitutes along the other.

I drink from a public fountain; all common things disgust me.' Cavafy was fortunate that in modern Alexandria boys came so cheap, but he also knew with Callimachus the loneliness of the homosexual who was not approved of by society, just as he must also have known that the Alexandria of his poetry, his Ideal City, was a sad sleight of hand.

In January 1917 Forster had remarked disparagingly that Cavafy's creative powers were devoted to revising and reviving the past, an observation likely to have been based on conversation only, for he had not yet, it seems, read any of Cavafy's poetry. Nor is it likely that they yet, if ever, shared the intimate details of their lives; nor, given their very different pursuits (the Greek paid cash, the Englishman transacted in a currency he called love), could they have offered each other any practical advice, at most only general encouragement. Theirs was always to be a literary friendship, and even that was only just beginning, but finally it would alter Forster's view of history.

'As an escape from the war Alexandria is matchless: or rather escapes', Forster wrote to Robert Trevelyan in August 1917. 'The Syrians dance. The Bedouins lay eggs. The French give lectures on Kultur to the French. The Italians build il nostro Consolato, nostro Consolato nuovo, ricco, grandioso, forte come il nostro Cadorna, profondo come il nostro mare, alto come il nostro cielo che muove l'altre stelle, e tutto vicino al terminus Ramleh Tramways. The English have witnessed "Candida" or "Vice Detected".'[129]

But his preferred escape was the Greek, 'for the Greeks are the only community here that attempt to understand what they are talking about, and to be with them is to reenter, however imperfectly, the Academic world. They are the only important people east of Ventimiglia –: dirty, dishonest, unaristocratic, roving, and warped by Hellenic and Byzantine dreams – but they do effervesce intellectually, they do have creative desires, and one comes round to them in the end.' Of the Greeks he singled out Cavafy: 'with much help I have read one or two [of his poems] and thought them beautiful'.[130]

Forster's acquaintance with Cavafy had moved on from meetings at the Mohammed Ali Club and literary evenings in the Quartier Grec. He tells of hearing his name proclaimed in the street near the centre of town and turning to see 'a Greek gentleman in a straw hat, standing absolutely motionless at a slight angle to the universe'. It was Cavafy who if he was on his way to his office would vanish with a slight gesture of despair. But if he was returning from the office to his flat he might be persuaded to begin an immense and complicated yet shapely sentence, 'a sentence that moves with logic to its foreseen end, yet to an end that is always more vivid and thrilling than one foresaw'. Delivered with equal ease in Greek, French or English, the sentence might sometimes carry its listener all the way back to the flat: 'It deals with the tricky behaviour of the Emperor Alexius Comnenus in 1096, or with olives, their possibilities and price, or with the fortunes of friends, or George Eliot, or the dialects of the interior of Asia Minor.' In it Forster found something which went beyond what Cambridge knew as thought, for 'despite its intellectual richness and human outlook, despite the matured charity of its judgements, one feels that it too stands at a slight angle to the universe: it is the sentence of a poet'.[131]

Now Forster, taken there first by Furness, began visiting the 'dusky family-furnished flat'[132] in the Rue Lepsius where the poet lived for the last twenty-five years of his life, from late 1907 to early 1933. He had never meant to stay there so long, and even in 1925 he was saying to a friend, 'Shall I leave, or shall I put in electric light?'[133] Cavafy was generally at home between five and seven to any friends who cared to call, hours when his rooms looking east out over the street to the gardens of the Greek Hospital and the Church of St Saba beyond were deep in shadow: 'our meetings', said Forster, 'are rather dim'.[134]

Nor were they illuminated by Cavafy's poetry, which had not yet been translated out of Greek, indeed had hardly been published in the conventional sense. Occasionally his poems would appear in *Nea Zoe* or *Grammata*, the principal Greek literary journals of the city, but more often Cavafy had each poem separately and privately printed, the sheets then put into folders and circulated among his select audience of readers. 'To be understood in Alexandria and tolerated in Athens was the extent of his ambition',[135] said Forster, whose literary empire extended to wherever English was read round the world, though the condescension was Cavafy's, who spoke of Shakespeare as having lived 'outside the walls of the city of Greek speech'.[136] Forster, too, stood without the walls, but Cavafy was speaking as much of history, experience and sensibility as of language when he said, 'You could never understand my poetry, my dear Forster, never.'[137]

12   A native quarter café. For the longest time, and despite his love for Mohammed, Forster compared native Egypt unfavourably with India, only much later recalling Alexandria's native quarter as 'picturesque, and, especially at evening, full of gentle charm. The best way of seeing it is to wander aimlessly about.'

Then one evening at the Rue Lepsius 'a poem is produced – "The God Abandons Antony" – and I detect some coincidences between its Greek and public-school Greek. Cavafy is amazed. "Oh, but this is good, my dear Forster, this is very good indeed", and he raises his hand, takes over, and leads me through. It was not my knowledge that touched him but my desire to know and to receive'.[138]

> When at the hour of midnight
> an invisible choir is suddenly heard passing
> with exquisite music, with voices –
> Do not lament your fortune that at last subsides,
> your life's work that has failed, your schemes that have proved illusions.
> But like a man prepared, like a brave man,
> bid farewell to her, to Alexandria who is departing.

Above all, do not delude yourself, do not say that it is a dream,
that your ear was mistaken.
Do not condescend to such empty hopes.
Like a man for long prepared, like a brave man,
like to the man who was worthy of such a city,
go to the window firmly,
and listen with emotion,
but not with the prayers and complaints of the coward
(Ah! supreme rapture!)
listen to the notes, to the exquisite instruments of the mystic choir,
and bid farewell to her, to Alexandria whom you are losing.[139]

Alexandria was the capital of Cavafy's imagination – 'Queen of the Greek world, / genius of all knowledge, of every art' ('The Glory of the Ptolemies') – and though the settings of his historical poems range throughout the Greek diaspora, from Italy through Greece to Asia Minor, to Syria and into Persia, ancient Alexandria claims the greatest number. It is 'Alexandria, a godly city' ('If Actually Dead') where 'you'll see palaces and monuments that will amaze you' ('Exiles'), and where 'all are brilliant, / glorious, mighty, benevolent; everything they undertake is full of wisdom' ('Caesarion') – yet in each of these poems the theme is failure.[140]

In 'Alexandrian Kings', for example, published in 1912, the populace turns out in force at the Donations of Alexandria, a great festival arranged by Cleopatra and Antony, where their children were proclaimed kings of Armenia, Media, Parthia, Cilicia, Syria and Phoenicia, and where Cleopatra's eldest, Caesarion, her son and heir by Julius Caesar, was proclaimed King of Kings:

> . . . the day was warm and exquisite,
> the sky clear and blue,
> the Gymnasium of Alexandria a triumph of art,
> the courtiers' apparel magnificent,
> Caesarion full of grace and beauty
> . . .
> and the Alexandrians ran to see the show
> and grew enthusiastic, and applauded
> in Greek, in Egyptian, and some in Hebrew,
> bewitched with the beautiful spectacle,
> though they knew perfectly well how worthless,
> what empty words, were these king-makings.[141]

In historical fact the Donations were neither empty words nor meaningless pomp; they were part of Antony's realisable, if ambitiously far-reaching, design for a new Hellenistic empire based on Alexandria. All the same, we know that things did not work out that way, that Cleopatra and Antony were defeated at Actium three years later in 31 BC, that they took their lives the following year and that the victorious Octavian, addressing the same throng in the same Gymnasium, promised the Alexandrians leniency because their city was so splendid, because Alexander was its founder – and then had Caesarion put to death ('It is bad to have too many Caesars').[142] Yet for all their willing delight in spectacle and their pleasure in playing along with dreams, Cavafy's Alexandrians also *know*: 'It wouldn't have lasted long anyway / years of experience make that clear' – three thousand years of experience in which Greek cities and kingdoms and empires and dreams have fallen again and again to the ironies of history.

When Forster came to Alexandria he thought the war would bring an end to the civilisation he had known, but he was determined at least to fight against its 'inward death'. Now he found that Cavafy, standing on his balcony, was already surveying a wider wreckage. His exemplar was not Alexander, who had founded the city, but Antony, who bade it farewell; fallen to Rome, fallen to the Arabs, Cavafy saw failure and loss as the central Alexandrian experience, his native city the capital of the repeatedly wounded world of Hellenism, which as he spoke could seem to connote the entire civilisation of humankind. Like the populace in 'Alexandrian Kings', he snatched what he could from the moment.

Forster and Mohammed met every other week at one or the other's room – Mohammed's long hours on the trams prevented them from meeting more often – and enjoyed what Forster called a physical understanding if not yet an agreement. But even these infrequent meetings were interrupted around the middle of July by a letter from Mohammed saying his mother had died and he had gone to Mansourah for the funeral. Forster was thrown into turmoil by his absence, and at the end of July he had to confess to Florence that he had somewhat anticipated the nature of their affair: 'I told you – many weeks back – we had parted with Respectability. Well, we hadn't entirely, and I wish to – it indeed seems right to me that we should, and I thought his objections trivial, and beat against them. He has made me see that I must not do this. . . . Am a bit bewildered for the moment – it is getting so very big', so that Mohammed had to calm him with talk of tenderness and affection: 'As soon as he can give more he will give it. . . . I realise he will help me.'[143]

In August their opportunities for intimacy were diminished further when Mohammed's half-brother came from Mansourah to stay with him at Bacos (where he 'squats blinking in the corner of the room that would otherwise be ours'),[144] while in Ramleh Irene had grown suspicious. Instead he and Mohammed would spend a couple of hours together each week at public resorts, meeting and parting there and never travelling together on the trams. One Sunday morning they visited Pompey's Pillar and the Kom el Shogafa catacombs, on another they went out to the Nouzha Gardens, or sometimes of an evening they would return to the ducks at the Municipal Gardens in the middle of town.

22. - ALEXANDRIA
Pompey Column and Sphynx

13   A postcard showing Pompey's Pillar. In fact dedicated to Diocletian in about AD 300, Pompey's Pillar may originally have been part of the portico of the Ptolemaic Serapeum. It is the largest column in the Graeco-Roman world and the only ancient monument still standing in Alexandria.

'As regards arrangements, precautions, his sweetness and good sense are extraordinary. I am ashamed, ashamed, to have to ask him to behave as I do.'[145] In return Mohammed kept up a show of pride: his work left him with little leisure – 'I am continually in a temper which is bad for my health',[146] he would say – and making an exception of Forster he told him, 'I want only to have no more friends. What I have are quite enough.'[147] But occasionally his remarks were touched with bitterness, or perhaps there was an ironic recognition that acceptance and endurance were his fate and beyond Forster's knowing. 'I find a certain amount of lies necessary to life'[148] was his maxim, but with Forster he was as straight as his pursuer would allow. Flattered and touched by Forster's warmth and interest, he gave him, without drama, his deep affection.

Their outings were made enjoyable by Mohammed's foolery and charm, but beneath this there was a directness and maturity that especially appealed to Forster. At first he took it as an impertinency when Mohammed called him 'Forster', but on reflection he decided approvingly that it was designed to break down all financial and social barriers.

In the same way he was delighted when Mohammed ragged him about his appearance: 'You know, Forster, though I am poorer than you I would never be seen in such a coat. I am not blaming you – no, I praise – but I would never be seen, and your hat has a hole and your boot has a hole and your socks have a hole.'[149]

At the best of times Forster looked a shabby and awkward figure, but for him the peculiarity lay elsewhere. Mohammed always wore a fez and had one good suit that he would wear on their outings; otherwise when they were together in Bacos he wore 'a long and rather unpleasing nightgown over which you button a sort of frock coat: bare feet in clogs'. But no matter where they were 'our juxtaposition is noticeable': to Florence he described Mohammed as 'unfortunately black. . . . It was thoughtless of him to have been born that colour, and only the will of Allah prevented his mother from tattooing little blue birds at the corners of his eyes. Blobs on his wrist have sufficed her.'[150] Of course the juxtapositions were part of the appeal, and to Forster they seemed liberating. Their affair, he said, had 'none of the solemnity which Christianity has thought essential to Romance. . . . One's never afraid of doing the wrong thing.'[151] But Mohammed, after listening to Forster philosophise on right and wrong, wrote to him, 'Be sure your religious opinions do not put me off you as well as you respect mine as I do yours. I told you before that God knows what happened, what happens, and is will be happened. He knew that some of the human beings will have evil thoughts therefore He created them, but he did not order you to behave in them.'[152]

It was as though Forster had gone out of his way to find all that was seemingly irreconcilable to prove that reconciliation was possible. What is more, he provided himself with an audience for this – but not in Alexandria, where, whatever was known of his proclivities, nothing was known of his continuing relationship with Mohammed (Furness thought the matter had died down, Aida Borchgrevink seems not to have known at the time, while others, including Cavafy, were probably never told). Forster's audience was in England, where he wrote of his affair to several homosexual friends, not regularly nor in the confiding detail he reserved for Florence Barger, but in celebration all the same. Among his readership were Goldsworthy Lowes Dickinson (a shoe fetishist and passionate though unrequited lover of young men), Edward Carpenter (author of *The Intermediate Sex* and an inspiration for *Maurice*) and Lytton Strachey (the flamboyantly homosexual doyen of the Bloomsbury Group who just then was completing his *Eminent Victorians*). Strachey, whose private opinion of Forster's novels was that they were 'second rate',[153] wrote back saying, 'Your situation sounds all that could be wished, though I suppose you may suppress the drawbacks. And perhaps you exaggerate the Romance – for my benefit – or your own.'[154]

'The half moon, with beautiful blue markings on its primrose, stands looking at the sunset. The sparrows – chattering as they never do in England – go to bed in the Square below.' This was towards the end of August 1917 and Forster was writing to Florence Barger from the verandah of the Khedivial Club at the Bourse. 'Natives, especially of the lower city class, are dirty in body and mind, incapable of fineness, and only out for what they can get. That is the theory to which, after some reluctance, I had fully subscribed, and like all theories it has broken down.' His relationship with Mohammed was 'such a triumph over nonsense and artificial difficulties. . . . When I am with him, smoking or talking quietly ahead, or whatever it may be, I see, beyond my own happiness and intimacy, occasional glimpses of the happiness of thousands of others whose names I shall never hear, and know that there is a great unrecorded history. I have never had anything like this in my life – much friendliness and tolerance, but never this.'[155]

Forster, through his love of Mohammed, wanted to love all humanity. In an abstract way he could, as he could also happily fill the moment with the alien chatter of sparrows, but the truth was that, Mohammed excepted, his feelings towards Egyptians had not broken down at all. That same month while visiting Furness at the Governorate between the Rue Attarine and the Rue des Soeurs, Forster wrote on a sheet of official Censorship paper to Florence: 'Ramadan ended an hour ago and all the sheep that the Egyptians have been fattening in place and out of place for the feast will soon be killed. But I cannot tell you how little I am interested in the Egyptians. Yesterday evening I dressed in civies, and walked, as I do almost once a month, through the prostitutional and other quarters of the native town. It's such a meagre vapid attenuated East – nothing solid, no colour: non-European clothes and food, and non-European jabber: that's all. Sometimes I wonder if it's me (or the war) who's to blame, but I don't think so: I am alive enough to other things still.'[156]

It was the same a month later when he wrote to Masood. 'I am weary beyond expression of Alexandria, its trams and its streets. One is as far from the East here as in London. All is so colourless and banal.' He had met one Egyptian he greatly liked, 'who sometimes reminds me of you', but 'on the whole I dislike the Egyptians'.[157]

Though Forster had found good friends and stimulation in the cosmopolitan city, especially among the Greeks, the war on the one hand and his frustrated attempts to find something worthy in its native inhabitants on the other left him feeling trapped in Alexandria. Cavafy had made the city his world, linking the present with the past, the squalid with the exalted, and imbuing the whole with feeling, but he did so by keeping within his own Greek culture. He spoke no Arabic, never visited an Egyptian house, dismissed ancient Egypt with the remark 'I don't understand those big immobile things',[158] barely acknowledged the Muslim conquest and did not if he could help it go to natives for sex. When Cavafy listened to the music of the city what he heard was the god's mystic choir; Forster, going out one evening with Mohammed to hear some native music, found it 'such bald bad stuff played on the oudh (a kind of guitar) – and a silly little drum. These people are most uninventive and puerile.'[159]

In fact the social, cultural and racial differences between Forster and Mohammed were never far from the front of either's mind and made each one cautious with the other. Only in September did Forster get round to telling Mohammed that he worked for the Red Cross, and in turn Mohammed told him, 'I must be independent – if I do not want to meet you, I must say "I do not", if I am not sure, I must be able to say "perhaps", you must respect me as I respect you.'[160] Forster liked this reply, once again taking it as the triumph of respect and trust over the barriers of race and class, but Mohammed was less certain of the bargain: 'Do you never consider that your wish has led you to know a tram conductor? And do you not think that a pity for you and a disgrace?' This last remark was made at the end of September, when Forster again pressed him for sex. Mohammed refused, saying, 'Never! Never!'[161]

During the summer of 1917 the chance came for Forster to leave the city. In July the Red Cross told him that searchers were needed in Thessaloniki in northern Greece; without hesitation he refused, 'from personal and public reasons'.[162] But in August, as though hungry for a dilemma, he beset himself with thoughts of taking home leave: his mother, who was nursing her closest friend through her final illness, would 'grieve'[163] if he was not there, and even after the friend died in September he still felt drawn. But the danger was that in going home he might be conscripted. He took his problem to his friends, but they were disinclined to agonise over his self-inflicted predicament: Furness and Antonius strongly advised him against going, as probably Aida did too, and when he discussed with Mohammed the worry that the threat of conscription might cause his mother, he too said, 'do not go, for she will only be unhappy in case they make you a soldier'.[164]

To Florence he wrote ambiguously in September, 'For the third time since I have been in Egypt my "daimonion" seems whispering "do the bigger, the risky, thing"'.[165] He denied to Florence that his relationship with Mohammed came into it: 'this, oddly enough, doesn't the least weigh';[166] nor would he admit to defiance of his mother; but it does seem that on the streets of Alexandria he heard a whisper that he should live.

The workings of Forster's mind are suggested by 'Our Diversions: *Diana's Dilemma*', an article he wrote around this time for a Sunday newspaper, the *Egyptian Mail*. The article begins with Forster reading a cinema poster: Diana has had a shady past and feels unworthy of the man she loves; she throws herself into Lake Como, but he saves her and they happily marry. Forster has previously seen posters advertising the Dilemmas of Myra, Lydia, Juliette, Scava, Silvia and Grazia: 'I somehow felt that Diana's would land me in nothing new.' Only the backdrops would change from film to film, oblivion sought variously in Niagara, Windermere or the Grand Canal.

Forster then recalls how after emerging from one of these showings he noticed a fruit shop: 'It rose from the darkness as a square of light, no larger than a cinema-screen, but oranges and cucumbers, bananas and apricots glowed in it, like jewels, or piled in the foreground stood in black relief against the radiance where an Arab moved like a magician. . . . Diana's dilemma is so dull. That is its greatest defect. It is duller than life. It is incidentally false but fundamentally dull. A fruit shop beats it as poetry, just as the sea, murmuring against the embankment opposite, tells of more passion than all the waters of Como, sacred though they be to expensive and adulterous love.'

14　Forster carried Mohammed's worn photograph around with him for years. It was only saved from worse damage by the tram ticket he pasted to the back, 'Alexandrie à Cléopâtre', a memento of their love affair.

This means more when you know that at the beginning of the article Forster says he has been reading the poster for *Diana's Dilemma* while waiting for his tram at the Ramleh terminus, and that he approaches the end of his article by saying the film he has seen is 'not as lovely or romantic as the commonplace street, down which I was walking to the tram. It was now night, certainly, and night knows a magic beyond the reach of art or day. Yet the whole world of ordinary experiences seemed to be crying:- "The diversion mankind seeks is not to be found in any cinema, it is here, here."' He is standing again at the Ramleh terminus, 'a fruit shop was opposite',[167] but its radiance, you suspect, was more a reflection of Forster's mood as he awaited the tram that murmured of passion and poetry, and its conductor who moved like a magician.

On 8 October Forster wrote to Florence, 'I cable today I am not coming. The restlessness seems to have passed. I should not have come (if I had come) purely for mother. It would have been too much of a burden for her mind, that. My longing to see her was part of a general feeling that I had grown out of touch, useless, stale, and that life, whether in peace or war, can only be lived once, and that we are all two years older; and at the bottom of my mind is the belief that the war never will end and that to save oneself up against a better time is to save up a mummy' – an interesting choice of word.

In that same letter, but seven paragraphs further down, Forster offered another reason for his restlessness passing. A few days earlier he and Mohammed had managed to find some time to themselves at the Home of Misery: 'Respectability has been parted with, and in the simplest most inevitable way, just as you hoped. I am so happy – not for the actual pleasure but because the last barrier has fallen; and no doubt it has much to do with my sudden placidness.'[168]

In other ways, too, that October was a time of partings – 'Everything seems breaking here.'[169] Furness was posted to the High Commission in Cairo, where he was to become Oriental Secretary, and Forster was able to prevail upon him for a favour. For some time he had been trying to find Mohammed a better paid job as a government clerk. Instead Furness found him an opening with the military on the Suez Canal, where he was to do some low-level intelligence work; 'to be a spy',[170] as Mohammed bluntly expressed it – or more bluntly, being paid by the British to inform on his people, pure mud. But Forster did not quite see it that way. 'He and I both think it rather beastly, but not very. Anyhow it's more interesting as well as more lucrative than his present work, and like all these people he has no feeling for truth except when he is dealing with a friend. It won't "harm" him in the least. And I, who have seen him battered and hustled and wearied in his present job have lost my high moral values and want him to have a little money and, through it, occasional leisure.' Their parting would be a wrench, but as Forster had been dithering over his own future he felt he could hardly object, and now that they had finally made love 'our relationship is too deep and firm to fear separation'.

One other barrier fell when Mohammed at last consented to having his photograph taken. Forster sent a print to Florence, pointing out that 'the fly whisk once was mine';[171] he gave it to Mohammed as a keepsake and made him pose with it – 'You say that it is valuable but I think ivory is not yet included amongst the precious stones',[172] was Mohammed's remark, but it carried valued associations for Forster, who had brought it from India. 'Mohammed el Adl, c.1917. With whisk', Forster later wrote on the reverse of his copy of the photograph. By then the photograph was cracked and worn – Forster seems to have carried it around with him for years – and was preserved against worse damage only by the tram ticket he had pasted to the back, a summary history of his affair with Mohammed and of the ancient city: 'Alexandrie à Cléopâtre'.[173]

Mohammed left for the Canal on 11 October, calling as the train slid out of the station, 'Don't forget me, don't –'. To Forster, left behind in Alexandria, it felt like the fall of a curtain; 'So much for Adl',[174] he remarked, not knowing if they would ever meet again.

CHAPTER 2

Alexandria from the Inside

His material as a poet, then, begins with his own experiences and sensations: his interest in courage and cowardice and bodily pleasure, and so on. He begins from within. But he never makes a cult of himself or of what he feels. All the time he is being beckoned to and being called by history, particularly by the history of his own race.

E. M. Forster, 'The Complete Poems of C. P. Cavafy',
in *Two Cheers for Democracy*, 1951

In the aftermath of Mohammed's departure and with winter coming on, Forster found Alexandria 'a grim stony place with nothing to divert one into the tourist for an hour except Pompey's Pillar'.[1] Moreover, with Furness gone to Cairo he felt increasingly out of touch with English concerns. Even letter writing became difficult – the world beyond began to seem unreal. The wartime contrast between Alexandria and England contributed to his mood, 'the luxury here, the misery there', and for a while he refused invitations to dinner – 'I could not bear the festal side of it'[2] – but it was a whim, he admitted, not a principle, and he would go to dinners again as soon as it passed. Meanwhile, he ate simply in his room at Camp de César and played Chopin, Franck, Verdi, Schumann and Beethoven on the piano. The Beethoven especially was played in a spirit of protest ever since he had been to a party in Ramleh where someone had asked for the *Moonlight Sonata* but the hostess had demurred, saying 'Hun music' might compromise them. 'No, it's all right', a young officer piped up, 'a chap who knows about those things from the inside told me Beethoven's definitely Belgian.'[3]

'You will have seen from my little articles', he wrote to Florence in February 1918, 'how cheerful and alert my Egyptian mind is, and how inapplicable to England',[4] for at this moment, when externally he had every reason to feel lonely and marooned, inwardly he was coming alive. With Mohammed he had known a private magic, an emotional release that had largely relied on his ability to romanticise their relationship. Now Mohammed was gone but his muse remained, and Forster took up his pen to write about the city he was making his own.[5]

In the articles he wrote for the *Egyptian Mail* under the name of Pharos he commented on the city's features, its people and its history. In mid-December 1917, at the invitation of Anastassiades, he visited the floor of the Cotton Exchange at the Bourse, where he compared the howling and frantically gesturing brokers to the tormented souls of Dante's Inferno: 'Cotton shirts and cotton wool and reels of cotton would not come to us if merchants did not suffer in Alexandria. Nay, Alexandria herself could not have re-arisen from the waves, there would be no French gardens, no English church at Bulkeley, possibly not even any drains.'[6]

But Forster's facetiousness disguised a deeper intent, the rescue of the poetry of the ancient city from the jaws of the new. The Corniche, or New Quay as it was then called, had been built in 1906 round the Eastern Harbour. It was 'a colossal work', Breccia wrote in his guide to the city, 'which has enriched the town by its splendid promenade, to be ornamented later on with palaces, edifices and statues which, let us hope, will constitute a worthy homage to art and to aesthetics'.[7] In 'The New Quay', published in December 1917, Forster wrote:

> It is interesting when a great public work fails to touch the popular imagination. Were our citizen asked what is the most remarkable object in the district he would reply, 'Pompey's Pillar', or more cheerfully, 'The Cosmograph', and never give a thought to the curve of stone behind him. . . . But the New Quay is so fine, while historically it is the successor of the old Ptolemies' causeway that once divided the two harbours. It does not deserve obscurity. Seen from the south, when there is mist in the morning, its beauty is fairy like; seen from the northern extremity it forms a complete ring round a circle of blue water. I admire it so much that I have the right to mention its faults. They are two in number. It splashes and it stinks. . . . Much the Quay cares. If men have developed clothes and noses that is their affair. Fish carry on without either. It was not built to pamper perishable flesh. To stretch right and left in an exquisite parabola and attain poetry through mathematics – that is its only aim, and an aim not unbecoming to the city of Eratosthenes and Euclid.[8]

Alexandria, he wrote in an article of March 1918, 'Alexandria Vignettes: Between the Sun and the Moon', was 'a city of the soul'. He was not referring to the modern town whose principal thoroughfare yearned to be merely genteel and smart. Rather the Rue Rosette had once been the ancient Canopic Way, which began at the Gate of the Sun (by the Municipal Gardens) and traversed the city until it reached the Western Harbour (near the cotton shoonas or warehouses of Minet el Bassal), 'and here stood the Gate of the Moon, to close what the Sun had begun'. The Canopic Way 'presented throughout its length scenes of extraordinary splendour. . . . The street was lined with marble colonnades from end to end, as was the Rue Nebi Daniel, and the point of their intersection (where now one stands in hopeless expectation of a tram) was one of the most glorious crossways of the ancient world. . . . There (beneath the Mosque of Nebi Daniel) is the body of Alexander the Great. There he lies, lapped in gold and laid in a coffin of glass. . . . And of this glory all that tangibly remains is a road: the alignment of the Rue Rosette. Christian and Arab destroyed the rest, but they could not destroy the direction of the road.'[9]

But to have any vision of the city of the soul it helped if one was not an Englishman. In 'Alexandria Vignettes: Handel in Egypt', published on 6 January, he describes his attendance at a performance of the *Messiah* at St Mark's in Mohammed Ali Square. Few Englishmen could listen unmoved to Handel's music, he wrote: 'it awakes in us so many memories, tender and absurd' that 'we forget that Handel was not an Englishman'. Also forgotten here in St Mark's was the organ blower, who 'through no fault of his own was an Arab. . . . Being merry by nature he kept grinning in the hope that one of us would lighten his labours by grinning back, which we were too respectable to do. . . . But in his person Egypt and the East were represented in that church – the East that generated Handel's religion and now receives it back in an inexplosive form. The gospel according to Handel is so homely. "And he shall feed his sheep" ring the sweet voices, sweeter than ever in exile. There is nothing mystic here.'[10]

With whatever irony and facetiousness, Forster was distancing himself in his articles from his own native people, from those of them anyway who were false in their sentiments, false in their vision, from those who likewise closed their eyes to the reality of Egypt. And beneath it all there was anger: once there was 'an older and friendlier civilisation',[11] as he wrote in his article about the ancient road that traversed his city of the soul.

Forster was finding himself to be more comfortable among Alexandria's Levantines, who could claim to be part of the regional fauna, as he explained in 'A Musician in Egypt', published on 21 October 1917:

The civilisations of Egypt are, roughly speaking, three in number. There is Egypt of the Pharaohs which still moves tourists and popular novelists, but which means nothing to the resident, nothing at all. Then there is Arab Egypt in which we more or less live and less or more have our being – a real civilisation this, but static and incomprehensible. And thirdly, there is Egypt of the Levant – the coastal strip on which since the days of Herodotus European influences have rained. A European personally, I feel kindly toward this coastal strip. It raises my interest and even a sense of romance. It is so small in area, yet first and last it has produced so much that is good. It always has been and always must be a civilisation of eclecticism and of exiles. But despite these defects it has managed to carry on century after century, buried at times by the sands of the south, yet always reappearing. There is a certain little bird – I forget its name but its destiny is to accompany the rhinoceros about and to perform for him various duties that he is too unwieldy to perform for himself. Well, coastal Egypt is just such a little bird, perched lively and alert upon the hide of that huge pachyderm Africa. It may not be an eagle or a swan. But unlike the rhinoceros its host it can flit through the blue air. And now and then it sings.

15   A postcard showing Anglican Church of St Mark. This church was built in the middle of the nineteenth century on land granted to the English community by Mohammed Ali. Its form is based on early Christian churches, but its façade is adorned with Arab architectural elements.

'The above remarks', he continued, 'are suggested by some music that has recently been performed at San Stefano, Alexandria: a symphonic poem by a local composer named Enrico Terni' – not an Egyptian musician but a musician in Egypt, for like Alexandrian artists before him from Ptolemaic to Byzantine times 'there is always this straining of the eyes beyond the sea, always this turning away from Africa, the vast, the formless, the helpless and unhelpful, the pachyderm. Of this coastal civilisation the music of Signor Terni is the most recent product. It is, in its very tenderness and yearning, the music of exile.'[12]

Enrico Terni, of Italian-Jewish descent and born in Alexandria, was exactly Forster's age; he and his wife, the journalist and novelist Fausta Cialente, would continue to make an important contribution to the city's cultural life until the 1950s, when they left for Italy. The two men probably met in the spring of 1916, when Forster was organising classical concerts for the troops at Montazah; this was at the time that he was staying with Furness at Abou el Nawatir and quite likely they were introduced by Terni's neighbour, the operatic Aida Borchgrevink. By summer they were friends, and Forster would go to stay with him near Stanley Bay, where they would swim and sing Wagnerian leitmotifs to each other under the water.

After the article was published, the two met for lunch and Terni told Forster of a recent incident at his bank where he observed that a customer had carelessly left several hundred pounds in notes on the counter. Running after the man, he returned the money and was warmly thanked, but Terni buttonholed him: 'You are doubtless aware that I am entitled by section 193 to a remuneration of ten per cent on the sum.' 'I am aware of it', the customer replied, 'but I respect your character and your artistic attainments too highly to put the law in motion.' 'I do not share your scruples', answered Terni, who was now, he told Forster, pursuing the percentage in court. The incident seemed typical of Alexandria where, as though in accord with its low-lying landscape, no moral high ground was claimed, but as there was no precipice, so there was no 'danger, courage or beauty'[13] entailed in going too near the edge.

The exception was Cavafy, for whom, Forster wrote, 'either life entails courage or it ceases to be life',[14] but courage neither 'in an ordinary nor a reputable form'.[15] In a skit sent to Robert Trevelyan in the summer of 1918 called 'Pericles in Heaven', Forster has Anastassiades standing on a staircase which stretches infinitely in either direction. 'Someone must come along soon', he says, 'then I shall know which way to go. One assumes it will be up, but these places are very tricky.' Then Cavafy appears, but from above. Why is he going the wrong way? 'A regrettable tendency, my dear Perry, a regrettable tendency.' 'But surely the show's upstair', Anastassiades protests, but Cavafy replies, 'Perhaps regrettably perhaps not regrettably I descend I descend', and he vanishes below. 'Now what's one to make of a chap like that? Now there's a chap of acknowledged talent, and yet he goes down', says Anastassiades. ''Pon my word I believe Cavafy would know. Besides I'm an artist myself. I'll risk it', and he runs down the stairs after Cavafy but collides with Terni who is coming up. 'Accidente! zizift!' cries Terni, but Anastassiades shrieks at him, 'You call yourself an artist! Well, you ought to go down not up down not up!'[16]

In those days, during the first two decades of the twentieth century, Alexandria was the seat of Greek letters, while Athens was no more than a provincial town doing labour as the capital of a newfound nationalism. Mounting the steps to Cavafy's flat at 10 Rue Lepsius came many of the best and most innovative writers, poets, actors, musicians and artists, with whom he shared his literary and historical interests, also Greek, French and British diplomats, and friends like the cotton baron and art collector Antony Benachi, whose sister, the writer Penelope Delta, kept Cavafy supplied with his favourite mastica liqueur from Chios. Anybody might drop in and bring their friends, though he was discriminating with his hospitality, reserving his best whisky for those he esteemed and offering others, if he suffered them at all, what he called his 'Palamas whisky', after the leading Athenian poet of those years, whom he regarded as second-rate.

Before they could ascend the two flights of stairs visitors had to run a gauntlet of whores who called to passers-by from the windows of the brothel on the ground floor, so that among Alexandrian wags the street became known as the Rue Clapsius. 'Poor things!' Cavafy would say of the girls downstairs, 'One must be sorry for them. They

16　The Minet el Bassal shoonas. Cotton was cleaned and pressed into bales at Minet el Bassal near the Western Harbour where it was stored in these shoonas, or warehouses, awaiting export.

receive some disgusting people, some monsters, but' – and here his voice took on a deep, ardent tone – 'they receive some angels, some angels!'[17]

Forster makes no mention of the prostitutes, who perhaps only moved in after the First World War, and says almost nothing about his visits to the flat or about Cavafy's predilections. But there is the testimony of others at that time and later. Now renumbered and renamed 4 Sharia Sharm el Sheikh, the building and its street are merely broken down and lacking in either vice or charm, but in the 1920s and early 1930s, as Gaston Zananiri remembered, 'towards twilight, towards evening', he would join Cavafy on his balcony and their view would be over the gardens of the Greek Hospital, today filled with mechanics' workshops and garages, and to the Patriarchal Church of St Saba beyond. With glasses of zabib in hand, they would sometimes talk about Byzantine civilisation, 'this model', in Zananiri's words, 'of poetry, sentiment and sex'. 'Where could I live better?' Cavafy said to him. 'Below, the brothel caters for the flesh. And there is the church which forgives sin. And there is the hospital where we die.'[18]

Twilight was Cavafy's favourite time of day for receiving visitors, and then he would open or close his shutters and curtains, adjusting the fall of light on his guests, and when a beautiful face came into the room he would illuminate it with a candle or two while he kept to the shadows all but unseen. On one such visit Timos Malanos, a young man during the war, later a leading authority on Cavafy, came to show him his poetry: 'I had stayed late in his salon. Then, for one moment, I felt, I remember, his whole soul concentrated in his glance and the touch of his hand, ready to hazard in my direction a movement as of a carnivorous plant.'[19] It is one of the very few recorded instances of Cavafy not attempting to pay his way; Malanos felt physically repelled and nothing came of it. Instead, as Zananiri recalled, he and Cavafy would 'frequent the cabarets. He used to go spend the nights there and look at the young lads. And when he returned home he used to scribble notes about his impressions. You will see in some of his poems where he says old men lean on their memories.' At the time, Zananiri was a young *homme de lettres*, just twenty-two when he met Cavafy in 1926; seventy years later he was living as a Dominican friar in Paris on the Rue Faubourg St Honoré, and when asked what else besides poetry passed between him and Cavafy, he replied, 'Poetry was the only thing I talked about with Cavafy. Oh really, you say! My relations with Cavafy were essentially artistic – poetry and the Byzantine spirit. Cavafy never occurred to me as anything else but a poet.' And so Cavafy when he was feeling lonely at night would go down into the streets and search the bars and cafés for hard-up young men like Spyros or George, two names that are mentioned, or his favourite, a motor mechanic called Toto, and 'tip' them to come up to his flat.

With good reason, historical associations came readily, even inescapably, to Alexandrians, and above all to the poet of the city, Forster putting it quite literally when he said that 'kings, emperors, patriarchs have trodden the ground between his office and his flat'.[20]

Cavafy worked for the Irrigation Department, a division of the Ministry of Public Works, whose 'Third Circle'[21] had offices in a building near the tram terminus at the eastern end of the Rue de la Gare de Ramleh.[22] He would have remembered the two obelisks that in his youth had stood close by the shore, one standing, the other prone and half buried in the sand. They marked the site of the Caesareum, a shrine begun by Cleopatra in honour of Julius Caesar or Mark Antony but completed for the worship of Augustus, as Octavian styled himself after he conquered Egypt. The Caesareum was built on a magnificent scale, beautiful all over with gold and silver, and was surrounded by porticoes, libraries and consecrated groves. Later it became the patriarchal church, but in time only the obelisks remained. Then in the nineteenth century 'Cleopatra's Needles' were given away, the fallen obelisk erected on London's Embankment, the standing obelisk in New York's Central Park. Now, as Cavafy made his way home along the Rue Missalla ('missalla' the Arabic for obelisk), he could remember when the obelisk that had gone to New York had stood exactly on the site of the Third Circle of Irrigation.

There were other associations for Cavafy as he approached the Rue Lepsius, where history and his sense of communion with the Greek world made St Saba's as potent as any, for as the seat of the Greek Orthodox Patriarch of Alexandria, Libya, Pentapolis, Ethiopia and all Egypt it is the direct descendant of the Caesareum.[23] St Saba's was built in 1687,[24] on the site of an ancient church founded in 615, and it represents the Church that stayed loyal to Byzantium and the emperor at the Council of Chalcedon in 451, when Egypt's native Christians, the Copts, turned towards monophysitism. The patriarch remains autocephalous, as he has always been, beholden to no higher ecclesiastical authority, and in the worldwide hierarchy ranks second only to the Oecumenical Patriarch of Constantinople.

Though Cavafy thought all religions were 'cooked',[25] he would attend St Saba's on Good Fridays, standing among the faithful as the touching and beautiful funeral procession of Christ emerged from the patriarchate:

> When I go there, into a church of the Greeks,
> with its aroma of incense,
> its liturgical chanting and harmony,
> the majestic presence of the priests,
> dazzling in their ornate vestments,
> the solemn rhythm of their gestures –
> my thoughts turn to the great glories of our race,
> to the splendour of our Byzantine heritage.

'In Church' (written in 1892, published in 1912)[26]

The Greek Hospital similarly yielded the almost inevitable associations when prior to its construction in 1880 the ground was excavated, revealing the massive foundations of an ancient building adorned with marble statues, thought to have been the palace of the Emperor Hadrian who visited Egypt in AD 130. Elsewhere in the vicinity more statues were found, including a colossal figure of Marcus Aurelius and a Hellenistic statue of Hercules. A dedicatory inscription to Isis Plusia uncovered at the corner of the Rue Nebi Daniel and the Rue de l'Hôpital Grec indicated a temple to the goddess which perhaps extended beneath Cavafy's house on the Rue Lepsius.

17 Constantine Cavafy, photographed here in about 1903, though he continued to circulate this and other photographs of himself for years after they were taken. Once when the publisher of *Grammata* asked for something more up to date, Cavafy told him rather to alter the caption to 'Cavafy years ago'.

These finds and others, including the tracing of the ancient street plan of Alexandria, suggested that here had been the heart of the ancient city. The Museion and Library, thought Breccia, must have stood between the Rue Missalla, the Rue de l'Hôpital Grec and the Rues Nebi Daniel, Rosette and Chérif Pasha. In *Alexandrea ad Aegyptum*, Breccia also identified the Rue Rosette with the Canopic Way and the Rue Nebi Daniel with the Street of the Soma, placing Alexander's tomb (soma) somewhere near these crossroads – that is, a few footsteps from the Rue Lepsius.

Coming home along the Rue Missalla Cavafy would pass two of his favourite haunts, the Café Al Salam and the Billiards Palace,[27] the latter living up to its name with marble-topped café tables at the front and young men passing back and forth between the street and sixteen snooker tables and four French billiards tables in the halls behind. At such places he would sometimes pass the hours drinking port or raki and nibbling at dates, his thoughts suspended somewhere between reverie and lust:

He must be barely twenty-two years old –
yet I'm certain just about that long ago
I enjoyed the very same body.

. . .

There, now that he's sitting down at the next table,
I recognise every motion he makes – and under his clothes
I see again the limbs that I loved, naked.

'The Next Table' (written in January 1918)[28]

For Cavafy that 'long ago' when he had 'enjoyed the very same body' was also history
of a sort, intensely personal and charged with sensation, those café Adonises no less part
of that spectral pageant of patriarchs and kings. Here most likely, along the Rue Missalla,
Forster encountered Cavafy 'standing at a slight angle to the universe' and prevailed
upon him to deliver one of those immense and complicated sentences, 'the sentence of
a poet',[29] that before it was done might carry them both back to the Rue Lepsius. There,
like Cavafy and Zananiri a decade later, they would have talked about poetry and the
past and, as Zananiri said, about 'Alexandria not again but still'.[30]

Though Cavafy worked as a government clerk at the Third Circle of Irrigation, he never
forgot that he had been born a rich man's son. But his circumstances and the rise and
fall of his family's fortune were also part of a greater story, the long and precarious
history of the diaspora Greeks in which he took a cultural pride. He professed that he
was not a Greek ('ο Ελλεν', a Hellene); rather he called himself Greek ('ελλενικοζ',
Hellenic) in the adjectival sense, expressing his attachment to a heritage less pure but
possessed of grandeur all the same. From Marseilles to India and from the Caspian Sea
to the Cataracts of the upper Nile stretched the *oecumene*, as the ancients called it, the
universe, where Greek language and culture were the common possession of all civilised
men. This had been the Hellenistic world bequeathed by Alexander, its inhabitants
Greek in mind and manner if not in blood, a world not of nations but international
and cosmopolitan. Through his feeling for history and through place and language
Cavafy laid claim to this inheritance for himself and for his city:

Well, we're nearly there, Hermippos.
Day after tomorrow, it seems – that's what the captain said.
At least we're sailing our seas,
the waters of our own countries – Cyprus, Syria, Egypt –
waters we know and love.
Why so silent? Ask your heart:
didn't you too feel happier
the further we got from Greece?

What's the point of fooling ourselves?
That wouldn't be properly Greek, would it?

'Returning from Greece' (written in 1914)[31]

Born in Alexandria in 1863, Constantine Cavafy was the youngest of seven sons of parents who had been established for generations in the prosperous Greek community of Constantinople. Both sides of his family could claim eminent ancestors, a Moldavian governor and an Antiochan archpriest in the paternal line, an archbishop of Caesarea in the maternal. His mother's family also liked to claim descent from the Byzantine imperial house of Ducas; the Cavafys on the other hand are thought to have originated on the Armenian-Persian frontier, where they acquired their name, derived from 'ayakkabici', Turkish for shoemaker.

Cavafy's father Peter followed his older brother to England, where in 1849 they founded Cavafy Brothers, an import-export company based in London that traded in Egyptian cotton and Manchester textiles. In that same year, on a visit to Constantinople, Peter married Haricleia, the daughter of a diamond merchant, and on returning with her to England in 1850 he acquired British citizenship. Five years later Peter took his family to Alexandria where he established P. J. Cavafy and Company, trading in cotton and grain, with branches in Cairo, London and Liverpool. Benefiting first from the Crimean War, which drove up the price of grain, and then from the American Civil War, which forced English mills to turn to Egypt for their supplies of cotton, Peter soon became one of the leading merchants in Alexandria. Wealthy, lively and cultivated, he moved in the highest circles, and counted the khedives Said and Ismail among his friends.

Constantine Cavafy was born at the height of the cotton boom in the elegant Rue Chérif Pasha – the year 1863 a dividing line, for the Greek families who came to Alexandria before that date, the founders of Greek commerce and banking in the city, continued to enjoy social precedence over those who came after the accession of Ismail and the rise of European, especially British, influence and capital. But Peter died suddenly in 1870, leaving his business but little real property to his family, his eldest but inexperienced sons taking up senior positions with the company in Alexandria, Liverpool and London, and Haricleia with her youngest son in tow living in each city in turn. By 1876 the firm had failed and the family's fortune was lost, and in the following year they returned to Alexandria, Cavafy's brothers taking what jobs they could as clerks and managers with other Greek companies.

His father's death and the loss of the family's capital marked Cavafy, but so did his years of education in England, its literature, language and manners continuing to influence him throughout his life. To his dying day he spoke Greek with an English accent, and he may have first 'thought' some of his poems in English before writing them in Greek. Nor could the events of 1882, when he was nineteen, have failed to make an

24   ALEXANDRIA. — *Mosque of Prophet Daniel.* — **LL.**

18   A postcard showing Nebi Daniel Mosque. The Mosque of Nebi Daniel, wrote Forster, 'stands on the site of Alexander's tomb.... The cellars have never been explored, and there is a gossipy story that Alexander still lies in one of them, intact.'

impression. On 5 June that year, even before the Rue des Soeurs riot, an Alexandrian friend wrote to Cavafy from England, 'I see in the papers that all the Europeans are running away from Egypt, and I cannot help roaring when I imagine you . . . running away with an umbrella in one hand and a sac in the other and with a couple of hundred barbarians after you. . . . Is that fool Arabi Pasha kicking up such a row as they say? Confounded cheek of him, he wants his head smacked, and I can't make out Gladstone who keeps on saying that it is impossible to do something, or some rot of that kind. If Disraeli were here he would manage it tambour battant [with beating drum].'[32] This was very much the view of Egyptian Greeks generally and it would be surprising if it was not one that Cavafy shared. Reluctantly the Cavafys were among the last to leave, sailing for Constantinople less than a week before the bombardment.

   In 1885 Cavafy and his mother returned once again to Alexandria where he lived with her until her death in 1899. She could be possessive, and as she grew older became increasingly afraid of being alone, which was another reason why he waited for her to go to sleep before he would slip out at night and make for the Attarine. One of her older sons said, 'All her life was anormale and we had to compromise with this abnormality or she would have died!' But though Constantine complained that it was almost impossible for him to make an appointment or accept an invitation lest her demands made him cancel his plans at the last moment, he was devoted to her: 'I think the only one who will weep for me if I die is Costaki', she said of her youngest.[33]

At a time when better-off families were starting to move away from the centre of town to the Quartier Grec or Moharrem Bey or farther out to Ramleh, the Cavafys lived first in the Rue Tewfik, parallel to though not quite up to the style of the Rue Chérif Pasha, and then in the Rue de la Gare de Ramleh, the latter respectable enough by day but lively at night with prostitutes of both sexes, the females parading along one side of the street, the males along the other.

But though the Cavafys' means were limited, their social credit held good, and soon mother and sons were caught up in the swirl of Alexandrian society, attending the khedivial court at Ras el Tin Palace, going to the races at the Sporting Club, to entertainments at the San Stefano Casino, and being invited to balls and parties at the splendid villas of Greeks and other Levantines. Once a week Haricleia was 'at home' to callers, and her guest list shows the wealthy and cosmopolitan circle in which her family moved: several French and English families, among them the Carvers and Aldersons; the Syro-Lebanese Debbanes and Zoghebs;[34] and the Greek Benachis, Choremis, Antoniades, Sinadinos, Zizinias and Zervoudachis. Wealth was a great leveller in Alexandrian society and was countered by a cult of snobbery, its accoutrements sometimes a purchased title, an art collection, almost always an English nanny. But if the Cavafys were not *riche*s, nor were they *nouveaux*, Cavafy's brother John writing in verse with deprecating irony of a family who were both: 'The Zervoudachis have some while / Been here, I meet them pretty often: / I bow – and their grim faces soften / In what is meant to be a smile.'[35]

The Benachis had offered Cavafy a job with their cotton export firm Choremi Benachi and Company, but he refused, perhaps because he did not want to be beholden to fellow Greeks. He could better preserve his independence, and indeed his anonymity, as a minor civil servant, a British citizen (only sometime later, the date is unknown, did he take Greek nationality) working under British directors at the Third Circle of Irrigation, where he supervised the English-language correspondence. His superiors at the Irrigation treated him with respect and were charmed by his erudition, often asking him into their offices and getting him to talk at length about historical matters. 'I have two capacities', he once said, 'to write poetry or to write history',[36] and though he never wrote history his passion for historical detail brought the past alive, and he would delight his English managers with his talk of the personages of the ancient city as though he was gossiping about some currently scandalous intrigue in the Alexandrian world outside.

He began at the Irrigation in 1889 and owed his position to George Zananiri Pasha, of Syrian Christian descent but likewise a British citizen, who was influential in the city's financial and administrative circles, and to Michael Zananiri, the pasha's brother, who was chief accountant at the Irrigation (Gaston Zananiri was the pasha's son and Michael's nephew). Though Cavafy's salary never amounted to much, his leaves were generous and his hours not onerous. He was meant to start at eight in the morning, but he never arrived before half past nine (his English bosses arrived even later), and he had only to stay until one o'clock when the office closed for the day, leaving him free to spend the occasional afternoon supplementing his income with some small brokering on the Exchange. Even these brief hours were not devoted entirely to matters of irrigation: 'Cavafy was very cunning', remembered Ibrahim el Kayar, who worked under him. 'He covered his desk with folders, opened them and scattered them about to give the impression that he was overwhelmed with work. "I am very busy", he constantly replied on the telephone. Sometimes my colleague and I looked through the keyhole. We saw him lift up his hands like an actor, and put on a strange expression as if in ecstasy, then he would bend down to write something. It was the moment of inspiration. Naturally we found it funny and we giggled.'[37]

Forster and Cavafy were often joined at the Rue Lepsius by George Valassopoulos, a lawyer and yet another King's College man who lived at 9 Rue des Fatimites in the Quartier Grec. Valassopoulos more than Cavafy himself led Forster through the poems in their original Greek and also provided him with elegant and, Cavafy felt, faithful translations. Valassopoulos became their chosen instrument for rendering the poems into English so that Forster could introduce them to the English-speaking world.[38] But Valassopoulos worked slowly: even by the end of the 1920s and despite all Forster's cajolings barely more than a dozen of Cavafy's poems had been published in England. It later transpired that Valassopoulos' pace was related to his distaste for the 'lurid'[39] poems, which he refused to translate, saying they would only damage Cavafy's reputation. Nor, it seems, did he speak of them to Forster.

But it would have been hard for Forster to have been unaware of Cavafy's homo-erotic poetry, certainly after February 1918 when Greek literary society in Alexandria was scandalised by a lecture on Cavafy given by Alexander Singopoulos, a young friend of Cavafy's and later his literary executor, a lecture written in fact by Cavafy himself. Cavafy had been publishing his erotic poems since 1912, but it was possible not to think of them as homosexual or even as self-revealing. This was because the personal pronoun is not mandatory in Greek and was often omitted by him, so that the sex of the loved one could remain ambiguous, and because he sometimes distanced himself by using the third instead of the first person: 'He swears every now and then to begin a better life. / But when night comes . . . / he returns, lost, to the same fatal pleasure' ('He Swears', published in 1915). But the lecture, by using the device 'It may be – I can't say definitely – Cavafy's opinion that . . .', amounted, as Robert Liddell, his biographer, later wrote, to 'a frank declaration of Cavafy's hedonism: there could no longer be any doubt about the poet's identification with his work, or that the poems analysed were autobiographical – and most people must have known that they were homosexual'.[40]

Numerous homo-erotic poems by Cavafy also appeared in *Grammata* during the war. *Grammata* was published by Stephen Pargas, alias Nikos Zelitas, who ran the Grammata

19   The Billiards Palace playing tables. One of Cavafy's favourite haunts was the Billiards Palace on the Rue Missala. The café at the front was frequented by writers and journalists, and Cavafy was fond of its 'literary cat', but he would also go into the adjoining billiards room to pick up young men for sex.

bookshop in the Rue Debbane running north off the Rue Chérif Pasha. Cavafy sometimes went there late at night with a poem he had just finished: 'I brought it to you now, Niko, so that I can go to sleep in peace'; and on another occasion: 'Take it, Niko, it's burning my fingers.'[41] In particular Forster was likely to have noticed the essay on Rupert Brooke sent from Cairo by Furness in the October 1917 issue, which also contained three of Cavafy's erotic poems, 'Understanding', 'Tomb of Lanis' and 'Body, Remember . . .' ('Body, remember not only how much you were loved, / not only the beds you lay on, / but also those desires glowing openly / in eyes that looked at you, / trembling for you in voices – / only some chance obstacle frustrated them').[42] Of course the poems were in Greek, as was the lecture by Singopoulos, but that should not have prevented Forster from learning of their drift. Yet if Forster knew about Cavafy's erotic poetry, he seems not to have been very much interested and may not have discussed it with Cavafy either.[43] The evidence is that it was not Cavafy's hedonism that excited Forster but his view of history.

'By now I've got used to Alexandria', Cavafy had written in 1907, the year he moved into his flat in the Rue Lepsius, 'and it's very likely that even if I were rich I'd stay here. But in spite of this, how the place disturbs me. What trouble, what a burden, small cities are – what a lack of freedom. I'd stay here (then again I'm not entirely certain that I'd stay) because it is like a native country for me, because it is related to my life's memories. But how much a man like me – so different – needs a large city. London, let's say.'[44] But as in these last few lines of 'The City', drafted in 1894 and published in 1910, he had come to understand that escape was useless:

> You'll always end up in this city. Don't hope for
> things elsewhere:
> there's no ship for you, there's no road.
> Now that you've wasted your life here, in this small corner,
> you've destroyed it everywhere in the world.[45]

For Cavafy, looking back in 'Days of 1896' (written in 1925), Alexandrian society before the First World War had been 'totally narrow-minded',[46] but it was not only a homosexual's complaint. In his youth he also wrote of hating the city for 'all this futility':[47] the place could seem superficial and boring, its cultural environment limited, and indeed it was probably not until the war, when he began making friends among Englishmen and Frenchmen stationed in the city, that he regularly shared the company of his intellectual equals. But meanwhile, Cavafy had overcome his ambivalent love-hate relationship with Alexandria. In an early draft of 'The City' he had written, 'I hate the people here and they hate me, / here where I've lived half my life',[48] but in the published version of the poem he replaced these lines with 'Wherever I turn, wherever I look, / I see the black ruins of my life': there is no escape in blaming Alexandria for your misfortunes; the city is what you make it, as you would make any city. And so taking command of time and space, Cavafy made Alexandria the capital of his art.

This development in his thinking became clear in 1917 when he gathered his published poems into a bound booklet to circulate among his friends: the collection began with 'The City'. And though subsequent collections were enlarged and their contents rearranged, so that past and present, reflection and sensation, were rewoven into an evolving pattern, 'The City' always came first, as though by entering its walls you entered Cavafy's world. Indeed, Cavafy's progression through life was marked by his feelings for his city: in 1929, three years before his death, he published 'In the Same Space', in which the 'black ruins' were transformed into a personal landscape of his own triumphant creation:

> The setting of houses, cafés, the neighbourhood
> that I've seen and walked through years on end:
> I created you while I was happy, while I was sad,
> with so many incidents, so many details.
> And, for me, the whole of you has been transformed into feeling.[49]

'The City' is hardly a heroic poem, yet there are resonances with 'The God Abandons Antony'. In both cases your life is in ruins, escape is impossible; what is left to you is the courage to live fully, in one case in this moment, in the other in this city. For Cavafy the moment and the city are as good as one, you have arrived at them both through history. His hero was Antony, who like a brave man stood at the window and listened with emotion to the Alexandria he was losing. 'Above all, do not delude yourself, do not say that it is a dream': words that applied as much to Cavafy as he went out on to his balcony in the evening:

> It was soon over, that wonderful life.
> Yet how strong the scents were,
> what a magnificent bed we lay in,
> what pleasures we gave our bodies.[50]

As Masood had once introduced Forster to the civilisation of another continent, so Cavafy introduced him to another version of a civilisation he thought he had known. The West teaches of victories within the narrow limits of Greece during a brief classical Golden Age – Marathon, Salamis, Plataea – and then loses interest. Cavafy writes of defeats – Thermopylae, Cynoscephalae, Magnesia, Pydna, Corinth at the time of the Achaean League, Actium, Constantinople and again and again Alexandria – yet in doing so covers a far longer term and a wider world than schoolbook Greece.

In Cavafy Forster heard a voice that spoke across the centuries and from across another civilisation, the civilisation of the Greeks so often defeated, but in his person, in this far exile, neither broken nor extinguished. 'Racial purity bored him, so did political idealism. . . . The civilisation he respected was a bastardy in which the Greek strain prevailed, and into which, age after age, outsiders would push, to modify and be modified. If the strain died out – never mind: it had done its work.'[51]

To Forster, the troubled Englishman disaffected by the homely gospel of his countrymen, the Greek gentleman in a straw hat stood history at an angle. In 1918, as if asking his eternal question – how will it end, how does it always end? – Cavafy, half humorously, half seriously, challenged Forster with what seemed at the time an impossible thought: 'Never forget about the Greeks that we are bankrupt. That is the difference between us and ancient Greeks, and, my dear Forster, between us and yourselves. Pray, my dear Forster, that you – you English with your capacity for adventure – never lose your capital, otherwise you will resemble us, restless, shifty, liars.'[52]

In November 1917 Forster read T. S. Eliot's *Prufrock and Other Observations*, published that year, and later wrote, 'The author was irritated by tea-parties, and not afraid to say so. . . . Here was a protest, and a feeble one, and the more congenial for being feeble. For what, in that world of gigantic horror, was tolerable except the slighter gestures of dissent? He who measured himself against the war, who drew himself to his full height, as it were, and said to Armadillo-Armageddon "Avaunt!" collapsed at once into a pinch of dust. But he who could turn aside to complain of ladies and drawing-rooms preserved a tiny drop of our self-respect, he carried on the human heritage.'

Forster's reading of Eliot's poems that autumn coincided with his developing view that the Alexandrian way of life, seemingly idle, sensuous and disreputable, was preferable to, indeed could be the only human response to, the conformism, hysteria and hatred that fuelled the war. The poems were 'not epicurean; still they were innocent of public-spiritedness',[53] and for Forster 'The Love Song of J. Alfred Prufrock' (in which 'the women come and go / Talking of Michelangelo') was an 'Alexandrian' poem.[54] In this he might have been thinking of Theocritus' Fifteenth Idyll, describing life in the Greek quarter of third-century-BC Alexandria, its dialogue between Gorgo and her friend Praxinoë as likely to 'be heard today in any of the little drawing rooms of Camp de César or Ibrahimieh', as he was to write in his history and guide. 'History is too much an affair of armies and kings. The Fifteenth Idyll corrects the error. Only through literature can the past be recovered and here Theocritus, wielding the double spell of realism and poetry, has evoked an entire city from the dead and filled its streets with men. As Praxinoë remarks of the draperies, "Why the figures seem to stand up and to move, they're not patterns, they are alive." '[55]

Forster himself was never a man to be daunted by a tea party, nor, as he had written to Florence, did he have any principled objections to evenings out to dinner. He might think of the wartime misery of England, its air raids and food queues, but he was not averse to the ease and luxuriousness of Alexandria. It was all in keeping with his profound belief, as he was writing to Siegfried Sassoon in the spring and summer of 1918, of being at war with the world: 'defensive warfare', he called it, and 'conscious shirking'.[56] He had two hopes for the future, he told Sassoon, one for 'a league of nations', the other for 'general apathy and fatigue' as 'all vigour is these days misdirected'.[57]

Though Forster says little about Alexandrian society, he could hardly have avoided visiting the great houses of the city's cotton and banking barons in the company of such friends as Furness, Terni, Antonius, Anastassiades, Valassopoulos – and Cavafy himself. Timos Malanos recalled how Cavafy took pride in his social connections, announcing, 'Tomorrow evening I'm invited to Antony Benachi's', and would 'positively flash with happiness' when he was in the company of smart society. At those moments, Malanos said, 'we the rank and file of his friends had the impression that these people entirely robbed us of him, and forever'.[58]

As Cavafy appreciated as well as anyone, that sumptuous world of Meissen and Sèvres, of Persian carpets and French paintings, was founded almost entirely on cotton. Within decades of its introduction by Mohammed Ali early in the nineteenth century, cotton became the key sector in Egypt's agricultural and export economy and throughout the first half of the twentieth century annually represented between seventy and eight-five per cent of Egypt's total value of exports. Excepting Liverpool, nowhere handled a greater trade in cotton than the Alexandria Cotton Exchange, and much of Egypt's infrastructure was financed from cotton profits – indeed, directly or indirectly the whole of Alexandria. 'White gold', they called it, and for both Egypt and the great cotton barons of Alexandria it earned a tremendous wealth.

The Egyptian peasantry, the fellahin, picked the cotton and baled it, but most non-manual functions were performed by Europeans, among whom the Greeks were predominant, in the provinces as landowners, middlemen and cotton ginners, in Alexandria as insurers, brokers, bankers and exporters. In wealth and culture the upper-class Greeks of Alexandria were a world apart from the Greek clerks and grocers, teachers and journalists, municipal officials, tobacco workers and keepers of cheap hotels in the city, and though they maintained close links with Greece and usually spent the summer months there, among them it was almost a point of honour to speak, even at home, the French or English they had learnt from their nannies – so explaining why Greek never became the Alexandrian lingua franca. (Moreover, their names were generally rendered in French, as was usual among upper-class Alexandrians by this time – hence, for example, Antoine Benachi, Michel Salvagos, Jean Choremi and so on.) Greek was confined to the middle and working classes and to the intellectuals, among them Constantine Cavafy, who might also have turned from his native tongue had his father not made a fortune in cotton and had his sons not lost it.

These wealthy Greeks, if they did not live in Ramleh, where in any case they were likely to have second homes, had from the end of the nineteenth century built their handsome villas at the eastern end of the city inside the curve of the ninth-century Arab walls, whose remnants could be traced, better then than now, from the main railway station round to the Municipal Gardens, their apex at the ancient city's vanished Gate of the Sun, where the Rue Rosette departed from town as the Aboukir road. Though not only Greeks lived in this exclusive quarter, so many did that it became known as the Quartier Grec, while the English called it 'the Peloponnese'.

In fact they came from almost anywhere but the backward Peloponnese (whose emigrant peasantry went mostly to America) and were cosmopolitans long before they came to Alexandria. Here in the Quartier Grec members of George Averoff's family still lived. Averoff had come from Metsovo, now little more than a large mountain village in northern Greece, but from the seventeenth to nineteenth centuries, when it enjoyed special privileges from the Porte, it had been the home of many rich Christian merchant families. Having made his fortune in Alexandria, Averoff returned to Greece before his death in 1899. There he donated an enormous sum for the restoration of the ancient stadium in Athens, where the first modern Olympic games were held in 1896, and gave the Greek navy its first battleship. John Casulli's family came from Rhodes. A cotton merchant who possessed a priceless collection of Rhodian-Iznik ware and ran a model farm near Aboukir, where a herd of buffalo provided excellent milk and butter to selected clients, Casulli directed his wealth, until he went bankrupt in the crash of 1929, to the freeing of his ancestral island and the rest of the Dodecanese from Italian rule. The Benachis, Choremis and Salvagos (the three most powerful Greek families in Alexandria, interrelated and all dealing in cotton) were refugees from Chios, respectively via Syros, England and Marseilles – their families perhaps of Genoese extraction (most suggested by the closeness of Benachi to Bonaccio), for Chios, scene of the 1822 Turkish atrocities that shocked Europe and led Delacroix to paint his famous if insufficiently grisly *Massacres of Scio*, had long been held by the Genoese. These, like several other notable Greek families in Alexandria – the Sinadinos, bankers from Trieste though originally also from Chios; the Cassavetis from Zagora; the Tossizas from Metsovo via Mohammed Ali's birthplace of Kavalla, whose Alexandrian mansion, after they returned to Greece later in the nineteenth century, became the Bourse in Mohammed Ali Square; the Cavafys from Constantinople via Manchester, Liverpool and London – had come from important Greek commercial centres under Turkish rule, where they were part of the mercantile bourgeoisie trading between the Ottoman Empire and Europe. They were the remnants of Byzantium.

But as Forster knew, there was more going on at the glittering gatherings at the great Alexandrian houses than the fainéantism he pretended and wished for. The Greek War of Independence of the 1820s had transformed a one-time peripheral province of the Ottoman Empire into the nation-state of Greece, but one with aspirations to restore territories in Asia Minor to Greek rule, particularly Smyrna on the Aegean coast and its hinterland, and also Constantinople, once centres of the ancient Greek and Byzantine worlds and where two million Greeks still lived. For many the dream was a sacred cause. Cavafy's friends, the Benachis, were at the heart of the issue that filled the drawing rooms and cafés of the Greeks of the city – the 'Μεγάλη Ιδέα', the Great Idea.

The Great Idea was especially advanced by the charismatic Eleftherios Venizelos, the Liberal prime minister of Greece. During the Dardanelles campaign the British had sought Greek help, offering territory in Asia Minor if Greece would enter the war. Venizelos agreed but was dismissed by the pro-German king. A month later, in April 1915, Venizelos came to Alexandria, seeking influential expatriate support.

Alexandria gave Venizelos a rapturous reception. The entire city seemed dressed in the blue and white colours of the Greek flag, and twenty-five thousand cheering Greeks thronged his route as he travelled in an open car from the port to the Greek Club at the centre of town. Many of Venizelos' countrymen had come to Egypt to escape the illiberal and backward environment of Greece, while a third had come from areas long inhabited by Greeks but still under Ottoman domination. Here in Alexandria cotton barons and shopkeepers alike had found scope for their entrepreneurial abilities, and living under the British Protectorate they generally favoured Venizelos' policy of alliance. They also held to the Great Idea, which sat well with their sense of a civilising mission and their invocation of the glorious past to justify their presence in Egypt. And if further proof of the legitimacy and continuity of the Greek presence was needed, they had only to look around them: modern Alexandria stood on the site of the ancient city founded by Alexander the Great.

The elderly president of the Greek community, Michael Sinadinos of a wealthy cotton exporting family with close business and kinship links to the Choremi-Benachi empire, was too overcome with emotion to deliver his welcoming speech. The Greek Club was

20   The Greek statesman Eleftherios Venizelos (left) came to Alexandria in 1915 to gain the support of its wealthy Greeks, among them Antony Benachi (right), who was a close friend of Cavafy's. Venizelos was the leading exponent of the Great Idea, the dream of establishing a Greater Greece on both the European and Asian shores of the Aegean. But the dream ended amid flames and massacre at Smyrna in 1922, an event which set alarm bells ringing among the Greeks of Alexandria.

on the Rue Rosette near the Greek Orthodox Patriarchate, only a short walk from the Rue Lepsius, and perhaps Cavafy was there with his friend Antony Benachi, whose father Emmanuel had previously been the community's president. Old Benachi was one of the richest men in Alexandria, one of the richest men in the Greek diaspora, and had already made a huge personal donation to the National Bank of Greece. Venizelos met with Emmanuel Benachi privately and persuaded him to settle in Athens, where he soon became mayor, backing the Venizelist cause in the struggle against the king, and other leading Greeks of Alexandria followed. You can imagine Cavafy at the club listening to Venizelos proclaim his dream of a 'Great Greece, a Greece of five seas and two continents',[59] and thinking of Antony's sons by Cleopatra, of horizons not yet conquered, and of the kingships of Asia with which they were bestowed.

Venizelos was again elected prime minister in June 1915, and this time he fought his campaign on the specific issues of an alliance with Britain and its allies Italy, France and Russia and the fulfilment of the age-old dream of a New Byzantium, so that when once more his policy was obstructed, Venizelos charged the king with unconstitutional behaviour. Now a schism ran through the country, culminating in October 1916 with

Venizelos' declaration of a provisional government at Salonika (Thessaloniki), recognised by the allies two months later when British and French troops landed in the city.

Forster followed these events closely and echoed them in letters, as when he wrote to Trevelyan of the Greeks of Alexandria being 'warped by Hellenic and Byzantine dreams'.[60] A month later, in September 1917, his article 'Our Diversions: Sunday Music' appeared in the *Mail*, in which he described the Levantine audience at a Beethoven concert as Syrian, French, Jewish, Italian, Armenian and – instead of Greek – Royalist and Venizelist. The facetiousness, as often in Forster, pointed to a matter that touched him deeply.

He had been to Greece once, in 1903, and the cruise took him also to Cnidus in Asia Minor where, rather than within the boundaries of modern Greece itself, the ancient Greek world came alive for him. Here were the remains of a shrine to the goddess Demeter, whose statue had been removed to the British Museum where it had already become something of a cult with him: 'Demeter alone among gods has true immortality', he wrote a year later, 'to her, all over the world, rise prayers of idolatry from suffering men as well as suffering women, for she has transcended sex.' Through the British Museum's matronly Demeter, 'warm and comfortable', though 'she cannot be touched',[61] Greece was for Forster a unity, transcending place and time. But now to attempt to materialise that spiritual idea of Greece by conflict at home and in Asia Minor was divisive, disturbing and dangerous. In Alexandria itself not all were for the Great Idea, and Cavafy, who had friends on both sides and at least one brother outspokenly opposed, maintained an ambivalent silence.

This was probably one of the reasons, not unrelated to his feelings towards the war in general and towards his mother and Mohammed, why Forster refused 'from personal and public reasons'[62] the request of the Red Cross in the summer of 1917 that he should go to the Venizelist stronghold of Thessaloniki.

That November the British advanced against the Turks as far as Jaffa, and in December General Allenby entered Jerusalem. Those Alexandrian Greeks who were supporters of the Great Idea followed the Palestine campaign eagerly and saw the British entry into the Holy Land as a harbinger for their own ambitions in Asia Minor. With Greece in the war, and following the defeat of Germany and the Ottoman Empire at the end of 1918, Venizelos was given the opportunity he had been looking for. In May 1919, under cover of the guns of British, French and American warships the Greek army landed at Smyrna. It was the beginning of a catastrophe for the Greeks that would send tremors through Alexandria.

CHAPTER 3

If Love is Eternal

I should be delighted if the distinguished society of which you are President should republish my Alexandria: it is a book for which I have always had an affection, for the writing of it helped me through some difficult days, and I should like to see it in print.

E. M. Forster to Jasper Yeates Brinton, president of the Royal
Archaeological Society of Alexandria, 5 February 1936[1]

'Alexandria, though so cosmopolitan, lies on the verge of civilisation.' These words open the chapter in Forster's guidebook dealing with Lake Mariut, its western arm reaching out into the Libyan Desert. His walks between Mex and Amriya offered 'the best day's tramp near Alexandria', while continuing round the southern shore to a spot called Ikingi Mariut he found that 'the local flora is one of the finest in the world'.[2] During his three successive Alexandrian springtimes Forster explored the fragile landscape round this western arm of the lake, going as far west as Abousir, the ancient Taposiris Magna, with its Ptolemaic temple of Osiris and its contemporary lighthouse (since medieval times called Burg el Arab, Tower of the Arabs), modelled on the Pharos but one-tenth its size. Here there had been no refounding of a city, and the lakeside landscape became for him a lesson of how things can vanish completely.

The main basin of Mariut spreads blue and vast to the south of Alexandria, its surface broken by islands of reeds. Five thousand years ago this was the home of the Harpoon Kingdom conquered by Narmer, also called Menes, the first pharaoh of a united Egypt, and despite the encroachment of factories since Forster's time it still can seem primordial: reed huts stand along its shores, small villages hide beneath the horizon line of vegetation, and fishermen pole their boats across its shallow and melancholy waters. Westwards extends an arm of the lake between two parallel rises, one the limestone coastal ridge, the other a low range of inland hills. Though containing 'accredited oriental ingredients' such as Bedouins and camels, the country here, 'delicate and august', reminded Forster of a Scottish moor: 'the whole district has a marked tendency to go purple, especially in its hollows – into that sombre brownish purple that may be caused by moorland growths'.[3] In autumn, numberless duck, geese and quail would gather in the marshes running out to mudflats and mirages that expired in the desert sands halfway between Alexandria and Alamein.

But in Ptolemaic times Mareotis, as the Greeks called it, was linked by a canal to the Nile near Canopus and the cornucopia of Egypt poured through its harbour, which handled a greater tonnage than Alexandria's two sea harbours combined, while the western arm of the lake, better watered than now, supported a flourishing lacustrine civilisation comparable to the Swiss and Italian lakes of today. Plantations of papyrus and of the giant water bean, ten feet high with great cup-shaped leaves, stood in the shallows, vineyards and olive groves and orchards of figs patterned the surrounding shores, while amid the farms were the gardens and summer houses of wealthy Alexandrians. The vine especially was intensively cultivated and cuttings were imported in their tens of thousands from across the Mediterranean, their grapes producing a wine of the highest quality – indeed, according to Athenaeus, writing in the second century AD but drawing on an earlier source, the vineyards were no more than a re-import, for it was at Plinthine, immediately east of Taposiris Magna, that the vine was first discovered.

Cleopatra herself kept a garden here and would sail on the lake waters in her pleasure barge, her mind, said Horace, propagandising on Octavian's behalf, 'disordered by Mareotic wine'.[4] But then Octavian, said Forster, was 'one of the most odious of the world's successful men and to his cold mind the career of Cleopatra could appear as nothing but a vulgar debauch. Vice, in his opinion, should be furtive.'[5]

The dynasty of the Ptolemies had been established for three hundred years, and in that time 'the Egyptians, who lived under it, were more tolerant', for its greatness lay, said Forster, in representing the complex country that it ruled: 'In Upper Egypt it carried on the tradition of the Pharaohs: on the coast it was Hellenistic and in touch with Mediterranean culture.'[6] Certainly, when it came to justifying their authority and concentrating it in their dynastic line the Ptolemies found it convenient to break with Greek practice and follow the example of the pharaohs, who like Osiris and Isis were not only husband and wife but also brother and sister – 'keeping the business in the family by keeping the family in the business',[7] as one historian has said. 'In flesh', Forster noted, 'as in spirit, the dynasty claimed to be apart from common men', appearing as successive divine emanations 'in pairs of male and female.'[8] And so it happened that the last of the Ptolemies, Cleopatra VII, was the brilliant product of generations of incest.

As Cleopatra's consort, Antony was identified with the god Osiris, whom the Greeks equated with Dionysus, the inventor of wine, and it was to the god's temple across the lake at Taposiris that pilgrims made their way on feast days, when this western reach of Mareotis became the happy resort of the people of the city. Sailing from island to island they would refresh themselves with beer and wine beneath trellises of vines at little tavernas, before drifting off to make merry in the shade and seclusion of the great bean leaves close to shore. Then as evening fell the glow of lanterns and singing voices travelled across the dark waters as the boats stirred homewards to Alexandria.

21   The ancient Tower of the Arabs (Burg el Arab). On the limestone ridge at Abusir a Ptolemaic lighthouse overlooks the western arm of Lake Mariut on one side and the Mediterranean on the other. It was probably modelled on the Pharos at Alexandria but is only one-tenth its size. Since medieval times it has been known as Burg el Arab, the Tower of the Arabs, and after the First World War its name was also given to Bramly's desert settlement nearby.

But in 'Alexandria Vignettes: The Solitary Place', printed in the *Mail* in March 1918, Forster found that Mareotis 'has beat a general retreat from civilisation, and the spirit of the place, without being savage, is singularly austere'. It was relieved only by the wildflowers that came all in a rush in January, February and March – purple and white anemones, scarlet and yellow ranunculus, coltsfoot and dwarf orange marigolds, poppies, nettles, henbane, mallows, celandine, convolvulus and mignonette. It was nothing like the ordered progress of an English spring; instead, all was confusion and hurry. 'The pageant passes like the waving of a handkerchief. . . . As it came, so it goes. It has been more like a ray of coloured light playing on the earth than the work of the earth herself, and if one had not picked a few of the flowers and entombed them in vases upon an Alexandrian mantlepiece, they could seem afterwards like the growths of a dream.' And so he has worked round from the idyll to the elegy: 'Year after year she has given this extraordinary show to a few Bedouins, has covered the Mareotic civilisation with dust and raised flowers from its shards. Will she do the same to our own tins and barbed wire? Probably not, for man has now got so far ahead of other forms of life that he will scarcely permit the flowers to grow over his works again. His old tins will be buried under new tins. This is the triumph of civilisation, I suppose, the final imprint of the human upon this devoted planet, which should exhibit in its apotheosis a solid crust of machinery and graves.'

In February 1918 Forster had written to Florence that Mohammed was 'the most wonderful thing that's ever happened to me',[9] but there was no one in Alexandria he could speak to about him and he worried about the tremendous solitude of his feelings. Now in March they were to see each other again, and this time, Forster kept telling himself, when Mohammed came to Alexandria he must stay with him at Irene's. Yet even as the fighting receded farther from Egypt, its effects came closer to home for ordinary Egyptians and merged Forster's love for Mohammed with his hatred of the war.

Forster had noted a marked change in the Egyptians since the beginning of the year. Before they had been invariably friendly towards the British, but now he was met with silence. The Turks were holding on in the hill country of Galilee and the campaign, directed at Damascus, was dragging on. The British army was provisioned from Egypt, while the fellahin with their beasts of burden were pressed into service to carry supplies to the front, but the pay was no compensation for the fields they left unploughed at home. Now as Forster waited for Mohammed and walked through the native quarters of the city, he heard only a plaintive street song:

> My native town, oh my native town!
> The military authorities have taken my boy.

Such was Forster's state of anticipation that when Mohammed wrote from the Canal that he was ill and would not be coming, Forster snapped and accused him of lying. He had come down with some minor ailment and was sent to hospital where he caught a fever that nearly killed him, but the story, thought Forster, was an excuse to save his feelings, and Mohammed had spent his holiday at Mansourah instead. 'What lies have you picked up from my letter?' Mohammed replied, 'I remember that I did not tell you any in my letter. I think that this news annoyed me too much. Please write very soon', adding that he was suffering a recurrence of his illness and would probably have to go back to hospital.[10]

It took some time for Forster to believe Mohammed, and then he blamed the British, deciding that their attitude towards the Egyptians, whether those provisioning the army in Palestine or those working on the Canal, was that they were never ill, but if ill were certain to die, so that it hardly mattered if they were sent to ill-run hospitals which were centres of infection. When Mohammed told him how he had to bribe an orderly even for a bed, while others around him were dying unattended, Forster reacted bitterly: 'The army just shovels them about like dirt.'[11] He wanted to see Mohammed, but as typhus was rife along the Canal five days had to be spent in quarantine before returning, which his job would not allow. 'I feel as you do', came a letter from Mohammed, 'We shall never meet again'. Forster felt helpless and was cast into despair, and to Florence he wrote towards the end of March, 'The shadow of tragedy seems very close now.'[12]

But by May Mohammed was well enough and spent a few days' leave in Alexandria. It was no longer true that his work as a spy for the British along the Canal was merely a 'beastly' expedient that 'won't "harm" him in the least'.[13] There was not a trace of Nile mud in him, yet the British had treated him like dirt, and Forster began feeling nostalgia for the Home of Misery which 'led us to know and trust each other absolutely'.[14] He wrote to Furness to see if he could find a job for Mohammed in Alexandria and meanwhile promised to give him an allowance, but Mohammed refused: 'Two days have passed like two minutes, yet I think perhaps it is best so, for if I walk with the same friend every day I have sometimes wanted another. Now we shall again be anxious for one another for six months and then have this time of happiness.' It was the sort of remark that Forster loved Mohammed for; he always found in him simplicity and affection, maturity and realism, not thinking that perhaps the weight of their relationship was overbalanced on his own side. At the same time, recalling Irene's reaction the year before, he felt he could not after all take Mohammed into his rooms: 'When a perfect person turns odd and huffed you have noticed it',[15] he wrote of Irene to Florence, who asked him why then did he not move. Instead they spent the brief visit together at Bacos in the home of Mohammed's friend, the matrimonial agent, or sat on the limestone ridge above Mex with views along the western arm of Mareotis.

'Above all', Forster wrote when thanking his various Alexandrian friends for their help with his guidebook, 'Mr G. H. Ludolf, to whose suggestion this book is due, and without whose help it would never have been completed.'[16] Ludolf was an elderly man, 'beautiful in body and mind', a post office official and part-time searcher who lived with his 'hard, good managing wife'[17] at Glymenopoulo, one tram stop along from Saba Pasha. Little is known of the Ludolfs, but they seem to have known better days – Mrs Ludolf had for a friend in Egypt Lady Anne King-Noel Blunt, Baroness Wentworth, a granddaughter of Lord Byron and the estranged wife of Wilfrid Scawen Blunt, the poet and traveller who had been an outspoken champion of Arabi Pasha and Egyptian nationalism, while for Ludolf the post office job seems to have been a fairly recent necessity. He knew the city well and introduced Forster to many of its more curious and inaccessible sights; moreover, although he was British he had a German father, so that Forster, who was terribly fond of him, would have taken his German background as another opportunity to win a private victory in the midst of the war, and for this reason too perhaps he dedicated to 'GHL' the first edition of *Alexandria: A History and a Guide*.

'But what a funny task to set yourself', D. H. Lawrence wrote to Forster in 1923, soon after the guidebook's publication, 'though I always remember the thrill you got out of that National Gallery catalogue.'[18] Forster's work there had been something of a remedy against the outbreak of war, as now towards war's end was *Alexandria*, Forster writing to Trevelyan in August 1918: 'No doubt truth was suppressed in previous wars, but there was not so copious a supply of the official substitutes. It's these that weigh one down like masses of decaying flesh, and drive one for cleanliness to fancy or the past.'[19] But this was no catalogue nor was he half-dead; on the contrary he was in love, he had come alive, and he was regaining possession of his creative powers. Early in November, a month after beginning *Alexandria*, he wrote happily to his mother, 'I never thought to write another book, and the mere fact of being able to concentrate is a pleasure.'[20]

Yet his decision to write a guidebook at all was peculiar, as Breccia's excellent *Alexandrea ad Aegyptum*, largely historical though reviewing the principal features of the modern town, had been in print, albeit it French, since 1914, and Forster must have known that an English edition was imminent; indeed, the translation had been completed early in 1917 and publication was intended as soon as the war was over. What is more, as Breccia was director of the Graeco-Roman Museum, his was in a sense the official guidebook to the city, its market guaranteed.

In fact, concealed behind Forster's graceful acknowledgement of Ludolf's 'suggestion' was his determination and need to express his personal experience of Alexandria. That experience was a double one, sensual on the one hand, intellectual and spiritual on the other, and though Cavafy was an influence, especially on the latter, it was the sexual stimulus of his romanticised affair with Mohammed that released his capacity for tenderness and love. The result, in the words of Lawrence Durrell, who with a copy of Forster's book in hand followed in his footsteps a generation later, was 'a small work of art, for it contains some of Forster's best prose, as well as felicities of touch such as only a novelist of major talent could command. The author who was marooned here during the First World War must (one feels it) have been deeply happy, perhaps deeply in love, for his joie de vivre rings out in every affectionate line. . . . Paradoxically, if that is the word, the book is also saturated with the feeling of loneliness, that of a cultivated man talking to himself, walking by himself.'[21]

That a guidebook could convey so much is only partly attributable to Forster's handling of prose. Where *Alexandria* differs entirely from *Alexandrea ad Aegyptum* is in its approach, which subverts the Baedeker convention of describing what anyone can see for himself by presenting a vision of the unseen, its pages ringing with such phrases as 'featureless spot', 'little remains', 'must be hunted for patiently', 'wrongly supposed to have stood on this site', 'has disappeared', 'nothing to see'. But here in cosmopolitan Alexandria he had loved, and as he went about in trams or bathed in the delicious sea, the city rose before him in visions. At the crossroads near Cavafy's flat he would erect the tomb of Alexander the Great, and while waiting for a tram at the Ramleh terminus, with the Caesareum looming in his mind's eye nearby, he would look across the harbour and multiply the height of Fort Kait Bey by four, envisaging the Pharos that had once stood on the spot.

Though his book is almost equally divided between History and Guide, the Guide, says Forster, has little value, for 'the "sights" of Alexandria are in themselves not interesting, but they fascinate when we approach them through the past'.[22] Forster's *Alexandria*, with time in one section, place in the other, and its many invitations to flip between the two, confuses the categories with lucid effect. Alexandria begins to unfold, as Forster tells us Cleopatra unfolded before Antony: 'She never bored him, and since grossness means monotony she sharpened his mind to those more delicate delights, where sense verges into spirit. Her infinite variety lay in that.'[23] What Forster is leading you through is that process of love that brought him to his visionary city: 'When you are in love with one of its inhabitants', as Durrell wrote in *The Alexandria Quartet*, 'a city can become a world.'[24]

During the second weekend of July 1918 Forster went to Mansourah to visit Mohammed. His father had recently died and now his brother, seized by a cramp, had drowned in the Nile. Forster found Mohammed terribly grave, borne down by sorrow and the weight of new responsibilities. He had inherited the family house along a narrow lane by the station in what Forster described as very nearly a slum – 'O my dear the sanitation!'[25] he wrote to Florence – and during much of the visit their conversation turned on the possibility that Mohammed might marry his brother's widow and raise their child, of whom he was fond. Forster was not jealous at all; it was enough that Mohammed was his when he wanted, and at least this softened the answer to his question of long ago, 'How will it end?', if indeed it had to end. On the contrary, Forster encouraged the prospect and did what he could to cheer him up.

Mohammed showed him round Mansourah, which was a thriving emporium for cotton and other products of the eastern Delta, whose crowded native quarter was gradually giving way to tree-lined avenues and elegant houses built in the European style. There were several consulates, a branch of the Mixed Courts, a theatre and the American Mission, where Mohammed had received his education. Forster especially liked Mansourah for its relaxed riverside corniche and cafés where they talked for hours. He was also favourably impressed by Mohammed's friends, several of whom spoke both French and English, the uncle of one of them a doctor educated at the University of London. To none of them had Mohammed admitted that in Alexandria he had been a tram conductor.

The problem of a job for Mohammed had become acute. He could no longer afford to absent himself for long from Mansourah but if he re-enlisted for work on the Canal the terms were now that it must be for the duration, and with the Germans still threatening Paris no one could say when the war would end. Forster was deeply hurt by Furness' failure to find Mohammed a more suitable position or even to mention the subject again. Once more he pressed Mohammed to accept an allowance while looking for work in Alexandria, and this time he agreed to come the following month. By their last evening together Mohammed's mood had brightened, making Forster feel 'so proud

13 Gare de Ramleh Alexandrie

22   The Gare de Ramleh. Since the beginning of his affair with Mohammed, Forster had visions of the ancient city. 'On this featureless spot', he wrote of the Ramleh tram terminus, 'once arose a stupendous temple, the Caesareum, and a pair of obelisks, Cleopatra's Needles.'

and happy', and that night in bed they laughingly ragged and grabbed one another – 'Morgan I will hurt you', 'Edward I will kill you' – until they fell asleep. They had never, Forster told Florence, enjoyed such perfect conditions before, and over the course of the weekend, he felt, there had been a 'deepening of emotion'. Aboard the train to Alexandria Forster reflected pleasurably on his adaptability at entering a little into native life, not only in Mansourah but while travelling there and back: 'To put the lid on it', he told Florence, 'I travelled 3rd.'[26]

This too, travelling third class, was something of a protest against the war, an insistence on seeing ordinary life, the lives of the powerless, in a world, as he wrote to Siegfried Sassoon a fortnight after returning from Mansourah, where 'war and the cosmogony of strife steal into one's inmost recesses'.[27] Forster's correspondents while he was in Alexandria read like a list of anti-war opinion at the highest echelons of British society. Most he had known before, such as Bertrand Russell, whose *Principia Mathematica*, published between 1910 and 1913, won him the reputation of being the greatest logician since Aristotle, but who was jailed early in 1918 for a pacifist article judged to be seditious, Forster writing to him in prison 'to send you my love'.[28] Since spring he had also been writing to Sassoon, scion of a London banking family, whose service at the front roused in him a hatred of war. Sassoon had just been reading *Howards End* and hoped to meet Forster for the first time when the ship carrying his unit from Palestine to France put in at Alexandria harbour in May. Unable to disembark, Sassoon had written from shipboard, his poem 'Convoy to Marseilles' showing the influence of Forster's reply: 'Give a man power over other men' – Forster was referring to the officer class – 'and he deteriorates at once'; the troops are decent and charming, he went on, contradicting Sassoon, 'not because they suffer but because they are powerless – And the devil who rules this planet has contrived that those who are powerless shall suffer.'[29]

As though in remedy to the domination and herd instinct of the war Forster announced, 'Very often I'm happy, and for good reasons. Ancient Alexandria – to mention one – is proving a most amusing companion. I'm constructing by archaeological and other reading an immense ghost city. How quite to fit into it Euclid, Plotinus, and Timothy the Cat I don't yet see, but they were all here, though not at the same moment. Here Hypatia was slain and Cleopatra loved and died, please.'[30] Here in one place, though from different times and with different views and lives, he would bring them together in his cosmopolis.

At about this time Forster was preparing to give a lecture at the Theosophical Society on 'The Philosophers and Philosophies of Ancient Alexandria'. Since his illness at Leveaux's in the Quartier Grec over a year and a half before, he had continued to attend the society's meetings and was to mention it in his guidebook when describing the recent discovery of what appeared to be a sunken prehistoric harbour off Ras el Tin (the one-time island of Pharos), saying, 'Theosophists, with more zeal than probability, have annexed it to the vanished civilisation of Atlantis.'[31] Despite his wry scepticism, the Theosophists interested Forster on several counts. Their high priestess was the British-born socialist Annie Besant, who for some years had been living in India where the Theosophical Society had its headquarters. In 1916 she founded the Home Rule for India League and from 1917 to 1923 was president of the Indian National Congress. When Edwin Montagu, the British secretary of state for India met her in New Delhi in 1917 he described her in his diary, along with Gandhi and Jinnah, the future founder of Pakistan, as one of 'the real giants of the Indian political world'.[32] More important to Forster was the influential role played by the Theosophical Society in spreading ideas about Eastern religion, especially Hinduism and Buddhism, in the West. Theosophy promotes universal brotherhood and teaches that all religions are versions of one esoteric truth realised by the individual's direct apprehension of the divine.

The substance of Forster's lecture to the society would find its way into *Alexandria*, in the preface to which he explains that in the manner of a pageant his History attempts to marshal the activities of Alexandria since its founding. The History is arranged into periods – Graeco-Egyptian, Christian, Arab and Modern – but after the Christian period is an interlude, 'The Spiritual City', which considers Alexandrian philosophy and religion, both pagan and Christian: 'It seemed better to segregate these subjects, partly because they interrupt the main historical procession, partly because many readers are not interested in them.'[33] But they interested Forster more than anything else about Alexandria.

The Ptolemies had adorned their city with architecture, science, scholarship and poetry, but once Alexandria had been reduced to a provincial capital of the Roman Empire, what remained of its glory? These are not the measure of a city's vitality, was Forster's reply. 'There is a splendour that kings do not give and cannot take away, and just when she lost her outward independence she was recompensed by discovering the kingdom that lies within.'[34] Not unlike the modern city, the Alexandria of the first to fourth centuries AD had been a cosmopolis not only of people but of ideas, though then it was the intellectual capital of the Graeco-Roman world and became the fountainhead of Western thought for two millennia to come. Here in the ancient city where Jews, pagans and Christians lived and taught side by side, Platonism was raised to mystical heights, here it was combined with the Hebrew scriptures, and here, drawing on both, Christianity acquired its philosophical and doctrinal underpinnings.

And so the earlier city's interest to Forster was that through it he could critically trace the shaping of modern civilisation's values. We 'stand upon money as we stand upon islands', Forster had Margaret say in *Howards End*. 'It's so firm beneath our feet that we forget its very existence. . . . Last night, when we were talking up here round the fire, I began to think that the very soul of the world is economic, and that the lowest abyss is not the absence of love, but the absence of coin. . . . Most of the others are down below the surface of the sea. . . . What's a joke up here is down there a reality.'[35] Forster had wanted to preserve that Howards End world, though he was not blind to the privilege that supported its values. The values, founded on love and the inner life, were worthwhile, but as Margaret knew, 'Logically, they had no right to be alive. One's hope was in the weakness of logic'[36] – by which Forster meant the power of love, and this, he believed, had been the central theme in the spiritual life of the ancient city. 'She did cling to the idea of Love, and much philosophic absurdity, much theological aridity, must be pardoned to those who maintain that the best thing on earth is likely to be the best in heaven.'[37]

Among the philosophers of whom Forster spoke when addressing the mixed religions, races and nationalities gathered at Leveaux's was Plotinus, whose vision appealed to him most and was not so different from that of the Theosophists themselves. Plotinus, as he later repeated in *Alexandria*, was probably born in Upper Egypt, but no one could be certain because he was reticent about it, saying that 'the descent of his soul into his body had been a great misfortune, which he did not desire to discuss'.[38] Whatever his origins, certainly his culture was Greek, and he came as a youth to Alexandria in the early years of the third century AD to study under the Neoplatonist Ammonius Saccas, a former dockhand who had abandoned the Christian faith, and whose students included the pagan philosopher Longinus and the Christian theologian Origen.

Plotinus believed in God, whose highest manifestation he called the One. The One is unity – which is the One. There is nothing more to say. But the One emanates, rather as light streams from the sun or as a fountain overflows, and its emanations descend through stages until the lowest of realities is reached, the one in which we live. Yet the One is not diminished by this outpouring, rather it embraces all, and as in a tremendous arc of emanation and redemption, everything including our souls yearns to flow back to the One.

This descent of his soul into corporeal form – this separation from God, this deprivation of union – was why Plotinus was so distressed at being born. But regrettable though it is to inhabit this universe of the senses, we find in it beauty that recalls to our souls the more perfect beauty of the higher realms. Here Plotinus often used the language of sensual love: the lover, overwhelmingly amazed and excited by a beautiful face, a beautiful body, has a memory of the greater beauty beyond; the lover devours the loved one with his senses but only truly loves when he has impressed the beauty of the loved one on his soul: 'How lies the path? How come to vision of the inaccessible Beauty?' asks Plotinus, who then teaches how the vision can be obtained:

> 'Let us flee to the beloved Fatherland.' This is the soundest counsel. But what is the flight? How are we to gain the open sea?
> The Fatherland is There whence we have come, and There is the Father.
> What then is our course, what the manner of our flight? This is not a journey for the feet; the feet bring us only from land to land; all this order of things you must set aside and refuse to see; you must close the eyes and call instead upon another vision which is to be waked within you, a vision the birthright of all, which few can see.
> . . .
> Withdraw into yourself and look. . . . you are now become very vision; now call up all your confidence, strike forward yet a step – you need a guide no longer – strain and see.[39]

Perhaps on the quays of Alexandria Plotinus talked with Hindu merchants, thought Forster, who saw parallels between his system and the religious writings of India. In Plotinus the gulf between man and God can be crossed by looking within ourselves because each of us is a microcosm of the universe, each of us is God. Forster wrote of Plotinus with an obvious sympathy and quoted the passages above, and more; and perhaps smiling at the words 'you need a guide no longer', he quoted him also on the title page of his *Alexandria*: 'To any vision must be brought an eye adapted to what is to be seen.'

When Forster wrote in his guidebook that Alexandria lies on the verge of civilisation, the desert stretching away behind, he added that 'the very existence of this desert is forgotten by most of the dwellers in the city, but it has played a great part in her history,

23   Deir el Suriani in the Wadi Natrun. Forster travelled by train and camel into the desert beyond Alexandria to visit Deir el Suriani and the other early Christian monasteries in the Wadi Natrun. The desert had played a great part in Alexandria's history, he observed, especially in Christian times.

especially in Christian times, and no one who would understand her career can ignore it'.[40] The moment when Forster could no longer ignore the desert came in June 1918, when he went out of his way to make the long journey by train and camel to the Wadi Natrun.

Here, during the early decades of the fourth century, were founded the world's first Christian monasteries, and even today the four that survive and continue to be inhabited can seem to belong to another world. Their high walls, raised in the ninth century to protect them from Bedouin raids, create the impression of diluvial arks bearing the faithful upon a desert sea, but the original communities, at one time about fifty in all, were much humbler foundations. A fourth-century pilgrim described his visit: 'The way to it is to be found or shown by no track and no landmarks of earth, but one journeys by the signs and courses of the stars. Water is hard to find. . . . Here therefore are men made perfect in holiness (for so terrible a spot could be endured by none save those of austere resolve and supreme constancy), yet their chief concern is the love which they show to one another and towards such as by chance reach that spot.'[41]

The monasteries are astonishing, for their setting, even for their meagre but often beautiful decorations, and above all for their history. Nowhere in the Roman Empire had the persecution of Christians been so terrible as in Egypt during the third and early fourth centuries. 'They paid no heed to torture in all its terrifying forms', wrote Eusebius, an eyewitness to the awful climax initiated by the Emperor Diocletian in 303, 'but undaunted spoke boldly of their devotion to the God of the universe and with joy, laughter and gaiety received the final sentence of death.'[42]

A few sought refuge in the desert, but it was only after Constantine's Edict of Toleration of 313, when the need to flee had passed, that the great exodus began. Martyrdom had offered a direct route to God; now the way would be found in the desert. This was a peculiarly Egyptian response, for the first solitaries and monks were natives nearly to a man (and so it marks the beginning of the Coptic, that is Egyptian, Church). In an astonishing act of anarchy, Egyptians in their tens of thousands deserted the towns and cultivation for the barren wilderness with the aim of shedding all worldly posses- sions and distinctions, wishing if possible even to shed their sense of self, the better to unite with God.

Forster would have preferred that the monks had kept their certainties to themselves and themselves to the desert, and in particular their conception of love, founded on their rejection of this world. Plotinus had believed that this world emanated from God, and that love provided the means of reverting to him; this was the lesson that Hypatia, the last of the Neoplatonists, taught at the Museion in Alexandria. For this reason, as much as because Alexandria was 'foreign', the monks of the Wadi Natrun hated the city and made it their enemy.

In the late fourth century, when Christianity was made compulsory throughout the Roman Empire, the monks burst into Alexandria and destroyed the Serapeum, the stronghold of paganism, along with its library, 'Daughter' to the great 'Mother' Library closer to the Eastern Harbour, installing a monastery on its site. 'Nationality did not exist in the modern sense', Forster wrote, 'it was a religious not a patriotic age. But under the cloak of religion racial passions could shelter.' During another irruption in 415, 'anxious to perform some crowning piety before they retired to their monasteries', they murdered Hypatia at the Caesareum: 'With her the Greece that is a spirit expired – the Greece that tried to discover truth and create beauty and that created Alexandria.'[43]

This for Forster was the mortal wound. Before the last half of the third century there was no dominant strain of Christianity, no overweening orthodoxy that could accuse others of heresy. Just as Plotinus had studied alongside Origen, an Early Father of the Church, and both were students of Ammonius Saccas, who had himself converted from Christianity to paganism, so the majority of Christians held a variety of heterodox beliefs. Forster allowed that the early orthodox assertion that Christ was the link between God and man was 'a humanising belief; the work of the Greek scholars who had subtilised and universalised the simpler faith of Palestine, and had imparted into it doctrines taught by Paganism',[44] but in an appendix he also quoted approvingly from several uncanonical gospels, as when Christ is asked by a woman when the Last Judgement shall come, and he answers, 'Whenever ye put off the garment of shame, when the two become one, and the male with the female, there being neither male nor female.'[45]

But with the growing power of orthodoxy, Forster wrote in his section on 'The Spiritual City', 'We must now watch [Christianity] harden and transform.'[46] Once Christianity was tolerated by the state early in the fourth century and then made the state religion towards the century's end, domination not only by Christianity over paganism but by one Christian group over the others became a realisable ambition and attracted the energies of the politically adept. There was Athanasius, for example, a 'street type',[47] said Forster, who through intellectual ability, vitriolic abuse, physical violence and unstoppable determination saw his argument against Arius over the nature of Christ enshrined in the Nicene Creed,[48] one of the defining documents for Christians to this day. For three centuries and more, in one form or another, Christ's nature served as a battleground within Alexandria, or between Alexandria and Constantinople, engendering hatred among Christians and between Egyptians and Greeks.

And so it came almost as a relief when the Arabs entered the city in 642. 'It is not easy to see why Alexandria did fall. There was no physical reason for it. One is almost driven to say that she fell because she had no soul.'[49] Against the conflicting certainties of the embattled Christians they offered one simpler certainty of their own: 'There is no God but God, and Mohammed is his Prophet.' As the god had departed from Antony in Cavafy's poem, so love had departed from Alexandria, and 'Islam, strong through its abjuration of Love',[50] entered the city unopposed. Little had been ruined so far, Forster continued, and as Amr's horsemen rode through the Gate of the Sun, marble colonnades still ran the length of the Canopic Way and across the harbour the Pharos was yet a towering wonder. 'I have taken a city', Amr wrote to the caliph in Arabia, 'of which I can only say that it contains 4,000 palaces, 4,000 baths, 400 theatres, 1,200 greengrocers and 40,000 Jews.'[51] 'There was nothing studied in this indifference',[52] remarked Forster, for 'the Arabs could not realise the value of their prize. They knew that Allah had given them a large and strong city. They could not know that there was no other like it in the world, that the science of Greece had planned it, that it had been the intellectual birthplace of Christianity. Legends of a dim Alexander, a dimmer Cleopatra, might move in their minds, but they had not the historical sense, they could never realise what had happened on this spot. . . . And so though they had no intention of destroying her, they destroyed her, as a child might a watch. She never functioned again for over 1,000 years.'[53]

Mohammed did not come to Alexandria in August. Instead he wrote to Forster that he was ill. He was spitting blood and losing weight, and was fairly sure that he had consumption. 'I do not trouble much about my illness', he wrote despairingly, 'I believe that only the death is my relief from this troublesome world.' Along with the house, he had inherited some money, and soon after Forster had left Mansourah Mohammed had decided to set himself up in the cotton business, hoping to benefit from its doubling in price since the beginning of the war by buying from the outlying villages and selling to dealers. But financial anxieties and fatigue from working long hours had helped undermine his appetite and his health. Forster sent him money for extra meat and milk to build up his strength, ran various business errands for him in Alexandria and followed Mohammed's moods as they fluctuated between depression and expectation. Though the plan to marry his brother's widow had fallen through, he had quickly made another match and was looking forward to 'living as a happy man in my own paternal home'.[54]

Meanwhile, the weekend in July that Forster went to Mansourah proved to be the final turning point in the war. The German offensive in the second battle of the Marne had been repulsed and by the beginning of October the French and British, joined by the Americans, who had entered the war in April 1917, were relentlessly pushing back the German front. The story was the same against the Turks, and at the beginning of October Damascus was taken. Just over a month later, on 11 November, the Great War was over. Even the news from Mansourah was good, Mohammed writing to Forster on 2 October, 'Yesterday was the first day of marriage – a happy day was it and I believe it was only two hours – happy hours pass quickly.'[55]

Also by October Forster had found a publisher for his intended History and Guide. They were Whitehead Morris Limited at 15 Rue Chérif Pasha, whose normal business was not publishing at all; rather they announced themselves as 'printers and stationers, engravers and account book makers' – account-book making was big business in Alexandria. They were a branch of a London firm and their local manager was a Mr Mann. He was 'a straw complexioned and rather jumpy man . . . he had little idea of what he was in for, and no idea at all of galley proofs and page proofs'.[56] Mr Mann drew up the agreement, 'a curious document',[57] as Forster later called it, by which he would receive a not unreasonable advance. But what mattered more to him at the time was to write a book and see it go into print, his first since *Howards End* in 1910.

During this month, with the war winding down and the hospitals gradually emptying, Forster now began to write *Alexandria* in the evenings after returning from work. 'There is not much to see here', he wrote to his aunt, 'but there is very much to think about.'[58] Over recent months his journalism had continued to be a preparation. He had written a series of ironic articles about the personages of the ancient city: there was Alexander's journey to the oasis of Siwa, where the misheard or mispronounced greetings of a priest at the temple of Ammon caused the young conqueror to be declared a god; misbehaviour at the Ptolemaic court contributing to the dynasty's decline; the philosopher Philo's anxious trip to Rome to explain why his fellow Jews could not worship Caligula as a god, only to find that the man who posed as god-emperor of the Roman Empire was completely mad; and Athanasius' rise from being a delinquent urchin to becoming the hammer of Christian orthodoxy – each article in one way or

24 The Attarine Mosque. This mosque occupies part of the site of a great fourth-century church on the north side of the Canopic Way dedicated to St Athanasias. Forster regarded Athanasias as a spiritual thug who destroyed the old Hellenic harmony of Alexandria and perverted the course of Western civilisation.

another revolving around claims to power, truth and divinity but reducing them to fit subjects for a gossip column in the *Mail*. He also reviewed *Modern Sons of the Pharaohs*, S. H. Leeder's study of the Copts, and read Plutarch, Dryden and Shakespeare on Antony and Cleopatra. He was writing, he said, 'a superior sort of guide book with a good deal of history to it. . . . The spirit of a procession is to inform it.'[59]

Also with the end of the war drawing near Forster had to tell Mohammed that he would soon be leaving Alexandria. This threw him into a new bout of depression, and he replied, 'I feel very feeble. . . . I believe I am growing thinner and thinner. . . . I am not looking forward to my future nor to my career. Your miserable friend, Moh. el Adl.'[60]

Around the middle of November, soon after the armistice, Forster went to Mansourah for a week where he found things better than he had feared. Though Mohammed was worried about money and his health, he was putting on weight and enjoying marriage, saying that before 'he had not been in the world'.[61] Forster caught glimpses of his bride, Gamila, 'very young, simple, and charming', he told Florence, 'and I loved hearing them laugh together. She is like some tame and pretty country animal, and he will be kind to her as all.' He was touched at his welcome, for it was against custom to have a European to stay in a married household: 'He has made more sacrifices for me than I ever have for him.' Yet even now Forster was blind to how far Mohammed had extended himself beyond courtesies, reluctantly acceding to Forster's sexual demands and making himself cheerful in his presence despite his illness and financial troubles. Occasionally he let slip a note of bitterness, as when Forster asked him to help find some country pipes that he could take back to England as presents and Mohammed, referring to himself and his wife, said, 'Why do you not take them costlier gifts? Why not take them a pair of Egyptians?' They arranged to meet once again in January – 'I find it very necessary to see him occasionally as absence raises chimeras'[62] – and before departing from Man- sourah, Forster, after much pressing, succeeded in lending Mohammed seventy pounds for his business, telling Florence he would make a present of it when he sailed. This was about the sum Forster would receive from Whitehead Morris – quite literally he was writing *Alexandria* for Mohammed.

Forster had arrived at Alexandria at the age of thirty-six, a man without experience of sex or love, a captive child in his mother's house, which as much as the war was the reason he had left England. Now on 1 January 1919 Forster turned forty, and though he was never entirely to escape from the dependence he and his mother had on one another, he had found a home for his emotions in an Alexandria he had made his own.

Sometime towards the middle of January he went to see Mohammed again and found him fatter and heavier. He had not spat blood for months, nor was he suffering any longer from the desolating feeling of fatigue, though for a while, as he put it, he had been 'just on the verge'. 'What a relief all this is', Forster wrote to Florence. 'I had expected to sail amid rending anxieties, and I leave him on his feet and don't deny myself the sat- isfaction of thinking that I helped to place him on them.' On their last morning he and Mohammed went for a long walk across the fields, and as when he had first crossed the Delta from Port Said to Alexandria more than three years earlier, its landscape seemed 'awfully like Cambridge – flat with ditches and in the distance misty farms and trees'.[63] But this time, instead of rejecting Egypt for not being India, he was seeing it through the eyes of love.

By the sixteenth Forster was back in Alexandria, where on the same day he went round to the Rue Chérif Pasha and signed the publishing agreement with Whitehead Morris. On 21 January, after making his farewells to Cavafy, Valassopoulos, Ludolf, Anastassiades,

Antonius, Terni, Aida Borchgrevink, Irene and all the others who had filled his world, he sailed for Marseilles and on the last day of the month was back in England.

Five weeks later, on 8 March 1919, Egypt rose in revolt. Throughout 1918 the allied powers had been making promises to the subject peoples of Europe and of the Ottoman Empire. First in January that year President Woodrow Wilson of the United States announced his Fourteen Points embodying the principle of national self-determination; then in July the British government assured a group of nationalist Syrians with whom it met in Cairo that the sovereign independence of all areas liberated from the Turks by Arab arms would be recognised; and finally in November an Anglo-French declaration affirmed that the formation of indigenous governments in Syria and Mesopotamia would be encouraged. 'Syria' was then normally taken to mean the historical region of Greater Syria, including all that was to become Syria, Jordan, Lebanon and Palestine; these and Iraq and the Arabian peninsula all received assurances of self-rule. Egypt was not mentioned, but the Egyptians assumed that their own nationalist ambitions, going back to Arabi's revolt in 1882, would be fulfilled. They felt their expectations were justified by the contribution they had made to the war effort, at least as great as that of the Syrians or of the Arabs of the Hejaz, and also because their infrastructure and political institutions were far more developed than anywhere else in the Middle East.

On 13 November 1918, two days after the armistice, Saad Zaghloul, at the head of a delegation (or wafd) composed of several of his fellow elected members of the legislative assembly that had been suspended at the outbreak of war, called on Sir Reginald Wingate, the British high commissioner in Cairo, and presented the nationalist case for independence. All were moderate men with a realistic understanding of Britain's interests and strategic concerns. Their programme, Wingate noted, was for the complete autonomy of Egypt while reserving to Britain the supervision of the country's debt and special facilities regarding the Suez Canal. They also undertook to make a perpetual treaty of friendship with Britain which they regarded as Egypt's closest ally, and meanwhile looked to an early end to martial law and to press censorship. Wingate heard the delegation sympathetically and referred the matter to London.

But the Wafd, though it represented nationalist opinion, was not the Egyptian government, which, Wingate rightly guessed, had nevertheless approved of Zaghloul's approach. The government was in a delicate position, for it had the three-way task of being pliable towards the British, being answerable to Sultan Fuad and yet needing to command the respect of ordinary Egyptians.[64] Though the centuries-old distinction between native Egyptians and the Turco-Circassian ascendancy had become increasingly blurred since Mohammed Ali's time through intermarriage, education and the advancement of Egyptians to high positions in the army and government, the prime minister and his cabinet were, like the dynasty they served, Turco-Circassians (except for an obligatory Copt), foreign-educated and cosmopolitan in outlook. In contrast, Saad Zaghloul, like Arabi, was of fellah stock, though from his Mongolian countenance you might guess that he too carried something alien in his make-up from the thousand years when Egypt was ruled by peoples of Kurdish, Turkic and Central Asian extraction. Born in 1860, Zaghloul's intelligence and industry carried him from a village school to the Muslim University of Al Azhar in Cairo, where he took a law degree and went on to become a judge in the Native Court of Appeal. As Egyptian law was based on the *Code Napoléon*, he set out to learn French, gossip saying that he acquired much of his facility in the course of a long-running affair with Princess Nazli Fazil, a niece of the Khedive Ismail. Marriage to the daughter of the then prime minister brought Zaghloul to the attention of Lord Cromer, the consul-general and in all but name viceroy of Egypt, who had him appointed minister of education in 1907, remarking, 'Due to his capacity, sincerity, straight-forwardness and courage, if I am not mistaken, I predict that Saad Pasha will have a brilliant future.'[65]

But it was Zaghloul's image as a simple son of the Nile that made him a darling of the people, who called him simply 'the Egyptian'. The government could not act without him, and Zaghloul had indeed called on Wingate with the foreknowledge of the sultan and the cabinet. The subject of independence having been broached in this way to the British, Rushdi Pasha, the prime minister, proposed to Wingate that he and one of his ministers, Adly Pasha, should go to London to present their case at the highest level, but insisted that he could carry nationalist opinion only if Zaghloul and his delegation came too. Wingate now cabled to Arthur Balfour, the foreign secretary, recommending that both parties be invited to London.

Two weeks later the answer came: Wingate was told that his reception of the 'extremist' and 'anti-British'[66] Wafd had been unfortunate, and that they must not be permitted to leave Egypt. Rushdi and Adly might be seen some time in the following year, but just now His Majesty's Government was far too busy preparing for the Paris Peace Conference opening in December. Indeed Lloyd George, the prime minister, and Balfour would be going there to meet aspirations and settle the peace among the thirty-nine countries represented. But Egypt was not one of them, nor could Anglo-Egyptian affairs be considered an international matter, as the view in London was that Egypt should become part of the British Empire, though with some degree of self-government.

London's contemptuous reply was a slap in the face to all concerned. Over the following months both Wingate and Rushdi resigned, had their resignations refused and resigned again, while against the din of nationalist outrage the sultan found it impossible to form a new government and grew fearful for his throne. During the night of 7 March 1919 the commander of British troops in Egypt arrested Zaghloul and deported him with three of his colleagues to Malta. The following morning the country awoke to cries of revolt. Students called for strikes and demonstrations; Coptic priests carried the call to the mosques and imams preached it in the churches. Huge processions filled the streets calling for independence, calling for Zaghloul. Railway and telegraph communications were cut and Cairo and Alexandria were isolated. In the countryside the bitterness of the fellahin over their forced conscription during the war as navvies and camel drivers erupted into violence, with mobs storming stranded trains and murdering soldiers and civilians on board.

The bloody phase of the Egyptian revolution was brief. By the time General Allenby, the liberator of Jerusalem, arrived as special high commissioner at the end of March the army had done its work: against forty British dead, nearly a thousand Egyptians were killed. To calm the country Zaghloul was released from Malta on 7 April, but negotiations and disorders were to continue for the next three years, during which Zaghloul was again shipped off, again released. His returns were triumphs, vast crowds lining the railway between Alexandria and Cairo. In Alexandria today, at what Forster described as 'this featureless spot' close by the Ramleh tram terminus, a statue of Saad Zaghloul looks out upon the sea of his captivity.

Forster followed these events with anxious involvement, and on 29 March had a letter published in the *Manchester Guardian* in which he described the forcible conscription of the fellahin during the war, their disgraceful treatment by the army and, retailing what he had learnt from Mohammed, the appalling conditions in the hospitals. British victories in Palestine, he wrote, had been 'victories to which, according to all accounts, the work of our Egyptian auxiliaries substantially contributed. . . . We can never replace the fellahin whom we have so needlessly destroyed, but we can perhaps enter into the feelings of the survivors and realise why the present disturbances have occurred quite as much in country as in the towns.'[67]

Two weeks later from the Punjab came news of the Amritsar massacre, where following a period of Sikh insurrection a crowd of five thousand or so gathered in defiance of a martial law proclamation. The occasion was a religious festival, but known rebels were among them and to the British officer in command the crowd seemed hostile; two Englishwomen had been brutally attacked only days before and the British were panicky. The officer ordered the crowd to disperse, not realising that the Jallianwallah Bagh in which they had gathered, an open space surrounded by walls, had only one exit. 'I took thirty seconds to make up my mind',[68] he said, and then opened up with 1,500 rounds, killing 379 unarmed Indians. Towards the end of May Forster expressed his feelings about the unfolding situation in an ironical letter to the *Daily Herald*: 'Europe is starving. In Egypt the native population is being arrested wholesale. Similarly in India. In Russia our troops are being employed on some unknown adventure. At home prices are rising, unrest is increasing, our homes are full of the wreckage of war. Are we downhearted?'[69]

At about this same time Forster was thrown into turmoil by news from Egypt that Mohammed had been sent to prison. Though he had very few details of Mohammed's offence, his guess that it had something to do with the uprising in March fuelled his anger against Britain and bound India and Egypt together in his emotions. At moments he attempted to resume work on *A Passage to India*, which had barely reached seventy pages when he put it aside before the war, but by the end of June he had not got beyond another two or three pages, writing to Sassoon, 'While trying to write my novel, I wanted to scream aloud like a maniac.'[70]

Meanwhile, Forster pressed on with *Alexandria*, raising memories of his passage through the city. Retracing that first 'plunge' with Antonius into the native town ('to see whatever may be seen, but understand that is not much,'[71] as he had written to Masood), he turned his mind's eye to Alexandria's recycled past, a prayer hall supported by antique columns, a sculpture of the lion-headed goddess Sekhmet built into a wall, and a stone fragment, covered with hieroglyphs, used as an upside-down seat. In his memory the old quarter became 'picturesque, and, especially at evening, full of gentle charm. The best way of seeing it is to wander aimlessly about.'[72] But through the rest of the city he made its tram routes the organising principle of his guidebook. Turning his readers' gaze from the vanished Caesareum towards the Ramleh terminus, there is excitement in his cry 'We now take the tram'[73] as he sets out on his journey through time and wakening love from 'Alexandrie à Cléopâtre' and beyond. Even the Anglican Church of St Mark, merely 'a tolerable building,'[74] its only historical associations the plaques inside commemorating the fighting against Arabi, is tenderly recommended for its churchyard trees where 'multitudinous sparrows gather at sunset, and fill the Square with their chatter,'[75] recalling that moment two years before when, sitting on the verandah of the Khedivial Club, he had written to Florence of the intimacy and happiness he had found with Mohammed.

All this time he was plying Ludolf for help, receiving from him a 'magnificent map of the Serapeum'[76] and requesting copies of the *Egyptian Gazette* for 'familiar news' – 'pick me out a spicy number'.[77] But back in England the familiar was slipping away. 'The class to which you and I belong', he wrote to Ludolf, 'is sliding into the abyss. . . . I can't feel it much matters, but a certain amount of precious stuff, a certain tradition of behaviour and culture will perish.' Without enthusiasm he would vote for Labour, because 'for the wrong reasons, it wants some of the right things', but as it was he felt like 'the last little flower of a vanishing civilisation'.[78]

At last in November he heard from Mohammed, who over a number of letters told what had happened. During the rebellion in March he and a friend, taking advantage of the railway strike and the local shortage of food, had sailed up to Cairo and bought a boat-load of beans to sell at a handsome profit on the streets of Mansourah. 'I thought the time after looking at me always cross began to smile,'[79] he wrote, but their travels during the height of the rebellion attracted the attention of a pair of Australian soldiers who put their suspicions to the test by offering to sell them an army revolver. The friend haggled for a bit until Mohammed sent them away, but a while later the soldiers returned with an order for their arrest on the charge of attempting to buy firearms. Brought before a military court, his friend admitted the charge and was sentenced to four months' hard labour, but Mohammed, who denied there had been any talk of a gun and said the soldiers had accosted them for baksheesh, was given hard labour for six months instead. In prison they had humiliated him, had shaved his head and bullied him, and

25 The Rue Chérif Pasha. This was the Bond Street of Alexandria. Cavafy was born here, though that was in the days before it became shoppy. Whitehead Morris, the publishers of Forster's guidebook, had their establishment in this street.

had served him up inedible meals so that he would have starved had he not spent his savings bribing the guard to bring provisions from home. Protesting his innocence at the trial, he said that he had known an Englishman who had told him that the English were just, and he had believed him. Now, he told Forster, he hated the British.

Forster had been anticipating something like this, and after months of falling prey to bouts of nervousness and bad temper, the anguish he had suffered in waiting for certain news erupted in anger. As Forster saw it, those politicians and officers whom the war had made arrogant and irresponsible were the men running the British Empire, and in Mohammed he saw the epitome of all those in India and Egypt who suffered under their injustice. As when the war broke out and Forster felt it existed on his account, now he felt complicit in imperial sins. But what most immediately worried him was Mohammed's health, which he feared had been fatally undermined in prison. He admitted to Ludolf, without saying why, that through these months his own health had been poor, and now briefly he took to bed with influenza, recording in his diary at the end of the year that he had been 'really wrecked'[80] by Mohammed's imprisonment.

But his stamina had held up long enough that by early October he had finished *Alexandria*. Mr Mann was on a visit to London, and as there was a national railway strike

Forster bicycled up from his mother's house in Surrey – 'quite thrilling'[81] – to the Tower Hill headquarters of Whitehead Morris, where he delivered the manuscript into Mr Mann's hands and was given a cheque for the advance on royalties. But their conversation left Forster feeling uneasy, for Mann argued that the illustrations and a large coloured map, though allowed for in the estimate, would prove too expensive. Reluctantly, Forster gave way on the illustrations but became all the more anxious that the maps be well drawn and that the book proceed quickly. On the tenth of the month he wrote to Ludolf, saying he should see Mann the moment he returned to Alexandria and press him to set the manuscript up in print and insist that the proofs of maps and text should be sent to him, 'And soon.'[82]

In fact Forster had not quite finished the book, for he also asked Ludolf to have a look at the distribution of objects in Room 12 of the Graeco-Roman Museum, where he remembered having seen the marble head of a goddess with 'beautiful hair' (the phrase Mohammed had used about Forster's own) as well as two heads of Berenice, one 'with elaborate curls'.[83]

Berenice was queen to Ptolemy Euergetes who came to the throne in 246 BC and was still only a young bride when a year later he went off to war in Syria. Sorrowing at his absence she promised the goddess Aphrodite at her temple near Canopus that if the king returned safely she would make a votive offering of a lock of her hair. Berenice was soon able to make good her promise – but then calamity: her hair went missing from the temple. The palace called upon the resources of Alexandrian science and art, and happily Conon, the court astronomer, quickly discovered the lock as a constellation of seven faint stars near the tail of Leo, between Acturus and the Great Bear. Callimachus, the poet laureate, soon composed a lament in which the ravished lock, though appreciative of its heavenly honour, says it would have preferred to have remained on Berenice's head to enjoy 'the scent of myrrh of a married woman's hair, having enjoyed the simpler perfumes used by her while still a maiden'.[84]

The story is typical of the way, as Forster described, 'the delights of study, the delights of love'[85] lightly decorated the surface of the Alexandrian universe, though its subject matter of hair touched him at a deeper and powerfully erotic level. The story runs as a motif throughout the History and the Guide, where it is interwoven with another theme, the essential immutability of Alexandria's geography. Forster's maps, which so concerned him, emphasise the point, the ancient harbours and streets overlaid by the modern, and if there was 'nothing to see', the outline and contours of the city were still determined by the limestone ridges that forever set Alexandria apart from Egypt and fixed its gaze upon the sea, 'and at night the constellation of Berenice's Hair still shines as brightly as when it caught the attention of Conon the astronomer'.[86]

This was Forster's Alexandria the eternal, a city he had placed out of the reach of time, but these words come only at the conclusion to his History, which probably he had not written yet or was perhaps to alter much later, two and a half years later, when he

26   This aerial photograph of Alexandria taken after the First World War (*c.* 1922) shows how the modern city follows the outline of the old. Running westwards through the centre is the Rue Rosette, renamed the Rue Fuad in 1922, which traces the route of the ancient Canopic Way from the Gate of the Sun to the Gate of the Moon. In the distance is the Western Harbour, and on the right is the Eastern Harbour Corniche, not built up as yet. In Alexander's plan, the harbours were divided by the Heptastadion; over the centuries it silted up and formed the neck of land on which the Turkish town was built. In the foreground are the Municipal Gardens which follow the curve of the Arab walls. Between the Rue Fuad and the curve of the gardens on the right is the Quartier Grec. A part of the Christian and Jewish cemeteries can be seen in the lower right of the photograph.

returned briefly to Egypt and made the final corrections to his proofs on the bed where Mohammed lay dying.

Mohammed's letters about his imprisonment came hard on the heels of reports in the *Egyptian Gazette*, sent by Ludolf, of furious rioting in Alexandria in October 1919 directed against the imminent arrival of a commission of inquiry headed by the colonial secretary, Lord Milner. The commission's terms of reference were 'To enquire into the cause of the late disorders in Egypt and to report on the existing situation in the country and the form of the Constitution which, under the Protectorate, will be best calculated to promote its peace and prosperity, the progressive development of self governing institutions, and the protection of foreign interests.'[87] The offending phrase was 'under the Protectorate', for the previous April the Egyptians had been disabused of President Wilson's high-flown sentiments about self-determination when at the Paris

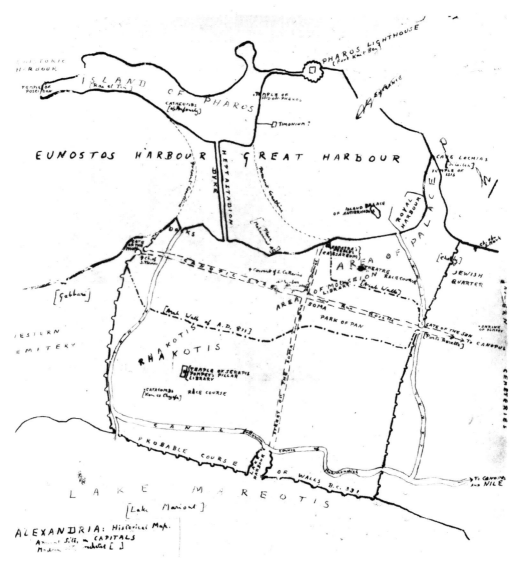

27   Forster's own hand-drawn map of ancient Alexandria indicates the modern coastline and identifies the Street of the Soma with the Rue Nebi Daniel and the Canopic Way with the Rue Rosette.

Peace Conference the American government recognised the British Protectorate over Egypt. The Milner Commission, it seemed, was nothing more than an imperial stitch-up, and no one in Egypt apart from the sultan and his ministers, and in Alexandria representatives of the Mixed Courts and the European chambers of commerce, was prepared to meet its members. The boycott led by the Wafd was almost totally effective.

Forster was 'full of excitement' as *The Times* was running a series of articles saying that the Egyptians must be given self-government – 'Quite amazing' – and Andreas

Cameron, until recently Grafftey-Smith's superior as British consul at Alexandria, 'chips in with a revolutionary letter saying that we had better make Zaghloul Prime Minister'. Meanwhile, 'old Furness keeps silence'.[88] Forster was looking for someone in Egypt who would act as his agent in doling out money to Mohammed; Ludolf was 'a dear fellow, but so totally uncomprehending that I could not tell him about M', he wrote to Florence, while 'Furness' behaviour has perhaps rather shaken my nerve for asking favours. Not a line since I detailed the case in August.' Aida Borchgrevink had recently been in England and had asked Forster if he had heard anything from Furness on the matter, saying she had not either – which suggests he had taken her into his confidence, though why she could not have been his agent is not clear. And so when amid this frustration Leonard Woolf asked Forster to contribute to a Labour Research Department pamphlet on Egypt he agreed, 'for the sake of Mohammed and his sufferings'[89] – among these the death at about this time of Mohammed's infant son whose middle name was Morgan.

To the pamphlet, called *The Government of Egypt*, Forster contributed the historical summary. Of the bombardment of Alexandria and the defeat of Arabi he wrote, 'Thus perished a moment which, if treated sympathetically, might have set Egypt upon the path of constitutional liberty.' As for recent events, 'The mild and cheerful Egyptians seemed – especially to one who had known Indians – an easy people to live with',[90] but they had been alienated by British high-handedness. Yet Forster could not bring himself to recommend independence; rather he seemed more concerned to strike at England and, resorting to displacing the empire with a paternalism that was more comfortably woolly, he came down in favour of a League of Nations mandate.

But by the time the pamphlet was published in the summer of 1920, the Milner Commission had gone far beyond its own brief, concluding that Egypt's independence should be recognised, though qualified by an Anglo-Egyptian treaty of alliance. The treaty was to provide for British troops to be stationed at an agreed place on Egyptian soil for the purpose of defending the country and Britain's imperial communications (that is, air routes and the Suez Canal), and also for Britain to retain a measure of control over legislation and administration in order to safeguard the position of foreigners. But over the next two years Britain's attempts at securing agreement for the Milner proposals were bedevilled by the continuing split between the Egyptian government and the nationalists. Though these were nearly enough the terms Zaghloul himself had proposed back in 1918, his position had hardened since his deportation and the uprising that followed. Behind the visage of high-minded rectitude was the man of party fearful of criticism should he abandon his perfectionist slogan of complete independence. In an off-the-record interview with an Egyptian journalist, Zaghloul was asked what he thought of the Milner proposals and answered, 'As an Egyptian, I am surprised and delighted. As President of the Wafd, I find the recommendations unacceptable.'[91]

In the meantime Forster's public foray into politics was disturbing his vision of Alexandria. Antonius 'lost his hair' over the Egyptian pamphlet, saying it was inaccurate and misleading, while Ludolf wrote to disagree, saying Antonius was a sinister figure who might put a word in the right places to ensure that Forster would not be allowed to return to Egypt. 'Antonius is very pleasant and clever', Forster wrote to Florence in November, 'but a born intriguer, and fully aware that his job, whether as censor or anything else, would disappear if the Milner report – let alone my Pamphlet! – was adopted. The Syrians in Egypt, like the Armenians there, only retain their footing as jackals to the British: when we go they will go, and with less dignity. Ludolf – who dislikes them and likes the Egyptians – was illuminating and copious on this point, which I had only apprehended dimly. He says they live by making mischief and are greatly responsible for our unpopularity. . . . If the Report passes Parliament [Antonius] will be dumped back in to Syria, where he doesn't want to be for nuts. God damn those Oriental Christians! I understand why the Turks cut their throats.'[92]

The truth was that Alexandria no longer held its old appeal for an increasingly politicised Forster. Even his History and Guide seemed bound for oblivion; a year and a half had passed between his giving the manuscript to Mr Mann and the letter he now wrote to Cavafy on 15 March 1921: 'As for my book on Alexandria, I have lost all interest in it. The MS remains in Chérif Pacha Street and for ever will remain there as far as I can see. . . . What is the use of any MS? And what, above all, is the use of Chérif Pacha Street? I would wish, next time you walk down it, you would ask, in those tones of yours, that question.' The letter was written aboard ship as Forster was steaming towards the Suez Canal, 'as near as I can hope to get to the Rue Lepsius for the present'.[93] He was bound once again for India, where he had been offered a temporary post as private secretary to the Hindu maharajah of Dewas, and had written to Mohammed that they should meet at Port Said.

No sooner had the ship arrived than Mohammed bribed his way on board with expensive cigarettes from a pack he had bought as a gift for Forster. The night was cold, and Mohammed was wearing a great coat, one of Forster's cast-offs, and knitted gloves with which he repeatedly clasped his hands, saying, 'How are you, friend, how are you?' For Mohammed things were not well at all; he had lost weight, he had no job and his father-in-law had gone bankrupt, but with just four hours together while the ship took on coal they agreed to talk of only happy things. It was like a dream, said Forster, and Mohammed too said it was a dream, and after he had shown him round the 'glories of 2nd class P & O' they went ashore and drank Turkish coffee – 'I always make him pay', Forster told Florence – and walked to the statue of Ferdinand de Lesseps on the mole and looked at its toes, the upper regions invisible in the darkness. Then strolling along the beach on the Mediterranean shore, but keeping back from the sea 'lest the coast guard mistook us for importers of haschish',[94] they sat down for a while on the sand. 'It was the last time you had your full vigour', Forster later wrote in his 'letter' to Mohammed. 'I hadn't seen you for two years and took joy in touching your stiffened flesh again. You said "foolish": I: "All have their foolishness and this is mine." '[95]

As though describing a voyage through an inner geography Forster told Florence that his mother had 'been in my mind whenever I go up a stair – except when M is in my mind, as he has been almost without pause for the last 3 days! . . . Now we pound down the Gulf of Suez, and tomorrow I hope to think about India.'[96] In England he had been feeling 'awfully East-sick'[97] and for several months tore against his mother's attempts to hold him – 'I must try to be a brave mammy and keep cheerful', reads a letter she left for him on the eve of his departure, 'and look forward to your return.'[98] And so he had set off, not least with the intention of seeking sexual gratification (there had been none in England), but this time it was not an escape from war but a deliberate break from home and a plunge into a politically charged situation. Gandhi, with the backing of both Hindus and Muslims, had begun his civil disobedience campaign against the British, and the overriding issue in the country had become the contest for power.

Forster's service to the maharajah, whose irresponsible extravagance he vainly attempted to curtail, seemed pointless and his time misused, while in his private life force not sympathy towards Indians was gaining the upper hand. Forster had revealed himself as a homosexual to the maharajah, who promptly procured for him a pretty young man called Kanaya, who in his guise as the palace barber would come bidden to Forster's quarters to serve as his catamite. This was Forster's first experience of regular sex; 'he was always merry and improved my health', he recalled in a private memoir the following year, but 'I couldn't get from Kanaya the emotional response of an Egyptian, because he had the body and soul of a slave'. Thwarted in combining his lust with his ideal of the supremacy of personal relationships, Forster grew violent and angry towards the Indian, beating him and buggering him 'with the desire to inflict pain'.[99]

Whether having the flies flicked off him by the chuprassi or dismissing the chauffeur ('He was dumb')[100] or bending Kanaya to his sexual desires, Forster discovered that he possessed a capacity for indifference, even cruelty, in the exercise of power – and that for the moment he did not care. 'I wasn't trying to punish him', he wrote of Kanaya, 'I knew his silly little soul was incurable. I just felt he was a slave, without rights, and I a despot whom no one could call to account.'[101] Publicly he expressed the malady of the Raj rather differently, referring to the English in India in an article published in the *Athenaeum* in January 1922 as being 'associated with a system that supported rudeness in railway carriages', and concluding, 'Never in history did ill-breeding contribute so much towards the dissolution of an Empire.'[102]

With trams if not railway carriages in mind, he confided his sexual exploits to Mohammed, who replied reprovingly, 'I got nothing to say except that you are so silly. I am very sad for that game and I have just understood why the (what you call them bad) people oppose you. . . . I am looking forward to see you and to blame you about your foolish deeds, foolish deeds.'[103] But Forster was looking for more than reproval and was already dreaming of Mohammed doing to him something of what he had done to Kanaya: 'I promised myself that on my return I would get you to penetrate me behind, however much it hurt and although it must decrease your respect for me.'[104] Meanwhile, he had got nowhere with his novel, but at last Whitehead Morris had sent him proofs of *Alexandria*. Once again he wrote to Mohammed saying to meet him at Port Said, and on 14 January he sailed longingly for Egypt.

Sailing up the Red Sea and into the Suez Canal, Forster wrote to his mother: 'The atmosphere, temperature and colours have been so exquisite and fresh; compared to India, where all is aged and complex, it is like a world in its morning. . . . We reach Port Said a day earlier than expected so I don't know whether Mohammed, who says he will meet me, will succeed' – Forster had told his mother only that Mohammed was a friend. 'I am anxious to see something of Egyptians, so don't want to get entangled in Alexandria too much, except of course – always excepting! – dear Ludolf, and would also like to stay a day or two with Irene.'[105] There was no mention of Cavafy and indeed there is no indication that in the whole of his month's stay in Egypt, ten days of it spent in Alexandria, he went round to the Rue Lepsius. Whatever Cavafy meant to him intellectually, this was a visit of the heart.

Landing at Port Said on 23 January 1922, Forster was met by a letter from Mohammed saying he had collapsed from consumption a fortnight earlier. He went immediately to Mansourah, where, he told Florence, 'though he is rallying from this particular attack I know that I see him for the last time', adding 'I am quite well and keeping my head.'[106] He would return to see Mohammed again and if he had gained the strength to travel he would take him to a doctor in Cairo and perhaps on to Helwan, a health resort south of the city. Then, after two days in Mansourah, Forster made the familiar journey across the Delta to Alexandria.

Word of his arrival was quickly spread by Irene, who had shrieked with excitement when she saw him out walking with Ludolf, kissing his hand, invoking heaven and calling him her son, so that a few days later, while sitting with the Ludolfs in their garden at Glymenopoulo, Furness and Aida Borchgrevink came riding across the sands and leaning from their horses called animated greetings over the wall. But when Furness asked him to stay with him for a while in Cairo, and Aida also asked him to be her guest, he refused both invitations. Forster had been opening up a little about Mohammed to Ludolf, whose sympathetic response made him think that here after all was the agent he needed to remit monthly allowances, for he feared that if he paid over a lump sum to Mohammed the doctors would have it off him at once. He was uncertain, in any case, how long he would remain in Egypt. A month earlier Anglo-Egyptian negotiations over the Milner proposals had broken down; Zaghloul had been deported a second time and once more the country was on the brink of rebellion. To Dickinson he wrote at the end of the month, 'I can look no Egyptian in the face. Their hostility is obvious, and they obstruct one in various little ways, and would do more if they dared. It is odious being in this country. India absolutely different, for there we have committed no comprehensive wrong.'[107]

Meanwhile Forster was revising his *Alexandria*: 'Rue Sidi Abou el Abbas leads to the square of that name – the most considerable in the Turkish town; here, by evening light,

28   The court house and carpet factory at Burg el Arab. These buildings formed the desert settlement founded for the Bedouins by Wilfred Jennings Bramly. However, Egyptian nationalists condemned it as an unpatriotic gesture towards the Bedouins, who were traditionally Egypt's enemies, and in 1924 Bramly abandoned his plans, leaving what Forster called 'this austere beautiful town' standing silent and empty.

one sometimes has the illusion of oriental romance; here (1922) is the rallying point of the Nationalist demonstrations.'[108] He seems also to have made another journey around Lake Mariut, where the flowers were just starting to rush into blossom, for in his Guide he describes a place that had hardly come into existence when he left Alexandria in January 1919. This was Burg el Arab, not the ancient lighthouse with which he was already familiar on the ridge between the Mediterranean and the lake at Taposiris, but an incipient settlement nearby. It could be made out from a distance 'by the tower of the new carpet factory', where work was being given to widowed Senussi Bedouin women whose husbands had been killed in the war and round which was growing the headquarters of the Eastern District of the Western Desert Province Frontier Districts Administration: 'It is being planned and executed with great taste, thanks mainly to the genius of the Officer Commanding, W. E. Jennings Bramly, MC. . . . Other buildings are rising, including a small walled town. It is all most interesting, and one of the few pieces of modern creative work to be seen in these parts.'[109] Forster most likely owed his introduction to Burg el Arab to the Ludolfs, who probably came to know Bramly through Lady Anne Blunt when he was the Blunts' neighbour in Cairo in the 1890s, where in the former palace gardens of the Khedive Ismail at Giza Bramly was establishing the city's famous zoo.

Perhaps Burg el Arab especially appealed to Forster because it spoke against his fears that the Mareotic landscape he had loved would one day be covered, as he had written in 'The Solitary Place', by a solid crust of tins and barbed wire. Not confining his enthusiasm to his Guide, to Forster it seemed 'A Birth in the Desert', the title of his article in the November 1924 issue of the *Athenaeum*: 'In harmony with the scenery and its inhabitants rise these puzzling buildings, abrupt, visible for miles, yet spiritually at home. . . . Did the Bedouins put them up? Impossible. Bedouins don't build, but if they did they would build like this. Something has evidently happened; some influence has passed over the desert, and the latent architectural capabilities of a race have been stirred.'[110]

On 6 February Forster was in Cairo with Mohammed where they consulted the city's leading physician, who diagnosed the tuberculosis as well advanced and pronounced the case hopeless. Going on to Helwan they shared a hotel room for five days; there Forster continued to proofread *Alexandria*, still making changes as he went along. Sometimes he would 'massage' Mohammed, who as Forster did so would think of women. Forster arranged for Gamila to come up to Helwan and lodged her and Mohammed in a guest house over the weekend, encouraging him to make love to her: 'It killed you, probably, but made you happy.'[111]

On the twentieth Forster sailed for England and from shipboard described to Florence their parting: 'He saw me off at Cairo. . . . He sat by me in the railway carriage and said "My love to you there is nothing else to say" which is exactly the truth.'[112]

Eight days later while Forster was still at sea, Britain unilaterally conceded Egyptian independence, though it reserved four points until such time as they could mutually be agreed: the security of the communications of the British Empire in Egypt; the defence of Egypt against all foreign aggression or interference, direct or indirect; the protection of foreign interests in Egypt and the protection of minorities; and Britain's continued role in governing the Sudan.

Back in England Forster wrote or rewrote the final version of his conclusion to Alexandria's history. 'Links with the past have been wantonly broken – for example the name of the Rue Rosette has been altered' (to Rue Fuad Premier: on 1 March 1922 Sultan Fuad took the title of king) 'and the exquisite Covered Bazaar near the Rue de France destroyed. . . . Only the climate, only the north wind and the sea remain as pure as when Menelaus, the first visitor, landed upon Ras el Tin, three thousand years ago.' This reference to book IV of *The Odyssey* is a nod to Cavafy, through whom Forster came to see the diaspora Greeks almost as a force of nature: 'Politically she is now more closely connected with the rest of Egypt than ever in the past, but the old foreign elements remain, and it is to the oldest of them, the Greek, that she owes such modern culture as is to be found in her.'[113] Except through hints Forster was silent about Mohammed, but through him he found himself standing at a slight angle to England: Cavafy was the history lesson, but Mohammed was the emotional lever. Durrell, who was born in India, later wrote, comparing his experience of Alexandria with Forster's, 'It was lucky that I was rootless by background and inheritance – a colonial. It is remarkable that Forster, who had good English roots, should have responded to his own exile in such a positive fashion, putting down new roots in this unfamiliar soil.'[114] In fact something rather different happened to Forster through his experience of Alexandria, as he explained years later: 'I don't feel of any where. I wish I did. It is not that I am deraciné. It is that the soil is being washed away.'[115]

To his friends in England, Forster's passage to India and back seemed like a failure, Virginia Woolf remarking that he was 'depressed to the verge of inanition'. She had thought when he left that he would never return, 'He will become a mystic, sit by the roadside and forget Europe', but now 'to come back to Weybridge, to come back to an ugly house a mile from the station, an old, fussy, exacting mother. . . .'[116] He spoke to them about India, about rowing on the lake at Dewas, about the sparrows flying about the palace, but his thoughts were with Mohammed in Mansourah. Letters came: 'I think we shall meet each other if not in the world it will be in the heaven',[117] Mohammed wrote in March. Forster could hardly wait for Mohammed to get there, confiding to his diary, 'I want him to tell me that he is dead, and so set me free to make an image of him. Latterly my great love prevents my feeling he is real'; and then trying to free himself from guilt: 'Determined my life should contain one success I have concealed from myself and others M's frequent coldness to me. And his occasional warmth may be due to politeness, gratitude, or pity. The prospect of his death gives me no pain.'[118]

On 8 May he wrote to Dickinson that he was writing a bit but would become so bored with his Indian novel that he could spit on the paper instead of inking it. 'I am bored not only by my creative impotence, but by the tiresomeness and conventionalities of fiction-form: eg the convention that one must view the action through the mind of one of the characters; and say of the others "perhaps they thought", or at all events adopt their viewpoint for a moment only. If you can pretend you can get inside one character, why not pretend it about all the characters? I see why. The illusion of life may vanish, and the creator degenerate into the showman. Yet some change of the sort must be made.'[119] He had been reading Proust on the voyage back from Egypt and must also have been thinking of his recently completed attempt at an Alexandrian pageant, and how he had devised his History and Guide so that nevertheless it shuffled time – how, like Cavafy, he could gain mastery over the oppressive personal dimensions of his universe.

A few days later he heard from Mohammed again, first a letter dated 6 May:

> Dear Morgan
> I am sending you the photograph

I am very bad
I got nothing more to say
The family are good. My compliments to mother
My love to you
My love to you
My love to you
do not forget your ever friend
Moh el adl[120]

Then a letter dated two days later:

Dear Morgan
I got the mony today from you and thank you very much for it.
I am absolutely bad I don't go out I can't stand
I am very weak
How are you no more today
My love to you
My love to you[121]

By the time Forster received these letters Mohammed was dead. Confirmation came on 17 May in a letter from his brother; Mohammed had bequeathed Forster his ring and when he received it he would put it on once a day. Those were during his private moments; publicly he was making his rounds, to London to stay with the Woolfs, to Oxfordshire to stay with Strachey and making an excursion from there on the last Sunday of the month to nearby Garsington Manor, the country residence of Lady Ottoline Morrell and the scene of lavish weekend gatherings of the literary and artistic avant-garde. Here he met Lord David Cecil, later the author of an elegant and sensitive biography of Lord Melbourne, 'a rabbity nervous undergraduate, very intelligent and polite. We got on quite well and he vows he will come out next Sunday for further conversation. Then Lady O shunted me on to another undergraduate, neither as high born nor as nice as the Lord, being an Alexandrian Jew who knew Cavafy.'[122] The needlessness of this remark to his mother betrays an irritation that goes beyond the impressions of a slight encounter; Jean de Menasce knew Cavafy independently of Forster and was set to promote the poet's work while he was at Oxford, publishing with Cavafy's approval four of Valassopoulos' translations in *Oxford Outlook* in 1924. Perhaps Forster felt a trespass upon his personal Cavafy that afternoon at Garsington; at any rate, within the next few weeks he renewed his campaign to get Cavafy in print and was urging Valassopoulos on with his translations.

In his *Alexandria*, between the History and the Guide, Forster had placed Cavafy's 'The God Abandons Antony', his tribute to the poet who embodied the city's past and present. But despite a number of 'stingers'[123] to Mr Mann there was still no sign of the book emerging from the bowels of Whitehead Morris. And so he agreed with Leonard Woolf that his Hogarth Press should publish *Pharos and Pharillon*, a collection of twelve of his Alexandrian articles (sometimes combined or in otherwise altered form) together with four additional pieces, among them 'The Poetry of C. P. Cavafy', which he hoped might make a wider impression here than it had when it appeared in the *Athenaeum* in 1919.

Forster dedicated the book in Greek to 'Ἑρμῆ ψυχοπομπῷ', Hermes Psychopompos, a veiled reference at once witty and sad to Mohammed the tram conductor, for 'psychopompos' means 'conductor of souls', a task associated with the god Hermes. This was as public as he would be about Mohammed. But in his secret moments 'Hermes' filled his thoughts: the god was associated with fertility and rebirth and was sometimes represented with an erection.

In July Forster wrote to Ludolf, 'I am working at my old Indian novel (don't tell anyone this – secrecy conveniences me)',[124] and on the fifth of the following month he began with greater secrecy still his 'letter' to Mohammed: 'Tonight I must write sensually, even if I have to tear the pages out of the letter later on. I must always have loved you.' In November he continued: 'Mohammed I try to keep this real, but my own words get in the way, and you are decayed to terrible things by this time – dead six months. I do not mind that, but I fear you becoming unreal, so that all our talks and the occasional nights we have slept in one bed will seem to belong to other people. . . . Dear boy, I want those memories to be of you, not stained by me. I do not want to prate of perfect love, only to write to you as if you are real. So I try to think of your putrescence in your grave sometimes. It is real, and contemporary with me, it leads me back to the real you.'[125]

In Alexandria they had watched over the past three years as the Greek adventure in Asia Minor moved towards its fatal conclusion. By May 1919, when the Greek army made its triumphant landing at Smyrna under the protection of British and American naval guns, hundreds of thousands of Greeks had been intermittently under arms for seven years, since the start of the Balkan wars in 1912. In a land of peasant farmers, whose families' fortunes, even their subsistence, was threatened by the prolonged absence of their husbands and sons, there was a growing mood for demobilisation, successfully exploited by the Royalists in the November 1920 election. At Venizelos' defeat the British withdrew their financial support, but the Royalists, instead of demobilising as they had promised, or even concentrating their army around Smyrna, were themselves fatefully seduced by the sacred cause and ordered a general offensive. Its effect was to galvanise the Turks into action.

By August 1921 the Greeks had pushed east almost to Ankara, but with their lines over-extended, their men ill-equipped and their officer corps demoralised by political divisions, they were halted in twenty-two days of bloody fighting at the banks of the Sangarios River by the reorganised Turkish army under Mustafa Kemal (the future Kemal Atatürk), the victor of Gallipoli. In August the following year it was the turn of the Turks to go on the offensive, and rallying to Kemal's cry 'To the Mediterranean!' within two weeks they drove the Greeks, both their army and their population, into Smyrna. By the evening of 13 September 1922 the city was in flames; one and a half million refugees fled by sea across the Aegean; tens of thousands more who could not escape met their deaths in fire and massacre. So ended the Great Idea and with it three thousand years of Hellenism in Asia Minor.

Cavafy told a friend that he had been deeply moved by the Balkan wars of 1912–13, when the Greek state acquired the ancient Hellenic territories of Epirus, Macedonia and the cities of Thessaloniki (the birthplace of Kemal Atatürk) and Kavalla (the birthplace of Mohammed Ali), but which side he took, if either, when Greece was divided between the Royalist and the Venizelist camps is unknown, and on the Smyrna disaster he was silent, except to remark that for Greek writers it meant the loss of a market for their books.

But in February 1922 Cavafy did write and publish 'Those Who Fought for the Achaean League', its final couplet filled with a bitter and perhaps double irony:

> Brave men you who fought and died so nobly,
> never afraid of those who were winning every battle.
> You weren't to blame if Diaios and Kritolaos were at fault.
> When Greeks are in a mood to boast, they'll say
> 'It's men like those our nation breeds.'
> That's how great their praise will be.
>
> Written by an Achaean in Alexandria
> during the seventh year of Ptolemy Lathyros' reign.[126]

The Achaean League, led by the unworthy generals Diaios and Kritolaos, was defeated by the Romans in 146 BC, and the independence of Greece was extinguished. An Achaean, perhaps a veteran of the battle, looks back on that day but also looks towards a redeeming future. He has written the lines in Alexandria and dates them by the conventional method. But Lathyros, too, turned out to be unworthy: a year or two after the seventh of his reign a dynastic quarrel forced him to flee from Alexandria. Far from being a bulwark against the power of Rome across the sea, he borrowed money from the Romans to regain his throne, bringing nearer the day when they would make Ptolemaic Egypt their own.

To those who saw a direct correspondence between the poem and the unfolding disaster in Asia Minor, Cavafy answered with an indignant denial: his poems describe an interior dimension, their true subject memory, feeling and association, the point of any one moment not its topicality but its universal extension. All the same, that does not mean that Cavafy's contemporary environment did not enter his historical poems, but perhaps one should look closer to home than Smyrna, especially as he was engaged in

29   The Rue Fuad, *c.* First World War–early 1920s. The Rue Rosette, or the Rue Fuad as it became in 1922, follows the course of the Canopic Way but is much narrower than the ancient road.

making Alexandria a universal capital and was himself its presiding genius. It is interesting, for example, that if the Achaean had come to Alexandria immediately after the league's defeat, then by the seventh year of Lathyros' reign he had been in the city for thirty-seven years; and that Cavafy had returned to Alexandria in 1885, following the bombardment: by 1922 he too was looking back on thirty-seven years in the city, and perhaps he saw in the fate of Smyrna the eventual fate of Alexandria.

Not that Cavafy had to look as far as Smyrna, for in Alexandria the foreign communities were beginning to feel as vulnerable as they had been in 1882. But now the British, instead of bringing their gunboats to bear, seemed to be looking the other way. Like other foreigners, the Greeks had originally been invited to Egypt by Mohammed Ali, where they enjoyed the benefits and protection of the Capitulations,[127] which had their basis in international law. But at the Paris Peace Conference in 1919 the British had argued that Egypt was their domestic concern, and thereafter it had become Britain's growing opinion that the Capitulations were politically embarassing and morally indefensible, and that further, as long as the Capitulations remained, the foreign element in the country might engage with immunity in anti-British intrigues. Egypt's nationalists were ambivalent: they were less anti-foreign than anti-British and were not keen to see the Capitulations abolished if that meant Britain would assume yet more power by making itself, as Milner proposed, responsible for the foreign communities. Not that the British were free to abolish the Capitulations; under international law that was a matter for negotiation and agreement among all the Capitulatory powers, and the Americans, Italians and French in particular, in jealous pursuit of their own interests, were unwilling to see British power augmented.

The Greek government under Venizelos took a different view, however: embroiled in its Asia Minor ambitions and dependent on British help, in September 1920 it agreed in principle to surrender its Capitulatory rights on such terms and at such a time as the British should decide. That two months later Venizelos was out of power and Britain had withdrawn its financial backing from his Asia Minor venture did not augur well for the future of the Greek community in Egypt, and indeed the fears of Alexandria's Greeks were realised when in May 1921 a nationalist demonstration exploded into a three-day riot.

The trouble broke out in the Hamamil quarter, that same neighbourhood inhabited by Egyptians and poor Europeans south of Mohammed Ali Square along the Rue des Soeurs where the events of 1882 had begun. At first the British were disinclined to intervene, and when they did they sent out a force of three armoured cars and three hundred men, many of them kitchen staff. By the time they had restored order, forty-three Egyptians, twelve Greeks and three other Europeans were dead and many more injured, and a hundred shops, ninety of them Greek, had been looted or burned. 'Anarchy and Fear in Alexandria – Many Victims Massacred' ran the headline in *Tachidromos*, the daily newspaper read by Cavafy, who then would have turned to the leader inside:

This is no longer a question of victims of the sudden eruption of a mob, to be forgotten in time like the victims of a natural disaster. Nor is it a question of material damage to be restored by compensation. It is rather a question of the continuing presence of the European population of this country which has been exposed to the wild passions and rapacious instincts of a native mob, ready to rise up at the prompting of any chance demagogue or at the first nod from those in power. Yesterday we lost something more valuable than the blood of our fellow Greeks and the property of our ruined merchants. We lost all faith in the nominal [Egyptian] and actual [British] authorities and in the assurances of hospitality given to us by politicians and notables.

The government does not have the power, even if it had the will, to protect us. The Power [Britain] which protects this country stood by and allowed the government to admit its inability to maintain order so that it could intervene to protect the very interests it claimed to be protecting when it occupied Egypt in the first place![128]

A few days after the riot, Michael Salvagos, president of the Greek community in Alexandria, wrote to Allenby, thanking him for the intervention of his forces which had prevented the loss of 'thousands of lives', and to express the hope that the 'protection of His Britannic Majesty's forces, which is the only secure safeguard for the lives and property of foreign subjects, will be continued in the future'[129] – a hope not widely shared among his fellow Greeks.

These events, brought to pass once Venizelos had mortgaged his cause to the British, hung heavily in the Alexandrian air as Cavafy wrote of Ptolemy Lathyros. Moving with uncharacteristic speed, Cavafy apparently wrote and published 'Those Who Fought for the Achaean League' within the first two days of February 1922. On 28 February Britain publicly and unilaterally proclaimed the end of the Protectorate, but Allenby had already decided to recommend this course on 12 January and threatened to resign if it was not adopted. 'His thinking was known to many',[130] remarked Grafftey-Smith, and given Cavafy's connections he might very well have been among those who knew well before the public pronouncement. The Greeks, the largest foreign community in Egypt, had already placed their security in Britain's hands; now Britain, though reserving to itself the protection of foreigners, was initiating a handover of power to the Egyptians. A sense of anxiety stole into the lives of the foreign communities, for they guessed that in any future negotiations the British would be willing to sacrifice the interests of foreigners and minorities if the Egyptians would concede in return the two reserved points that were of genuine stategic importance – the security of imperial communications and the defence of Egypt against foreign aggression – as indeed was to happen in 1936.

Those 'fools' Whitehead Morris at last published *Alexandria* in Egypt in December 1922, Forster lambasting them three months later: '[I] doubt whether the book will ever reach a second edition. It does not, and cannot, sell. The publisher will not let people who are not booksellers have it because they are not booksellers, and he will not let booksellers have it because booksellers are dishonest.'[131] He thought he knew much about publishers, he later wrote to Ludolf, 'toujours excepté Monsieur Homme [Mr Mann]'.[132] In compensation *Pharos and Pharillon* was published in England in May to enthusiastic reviews. As Forster had hoped, the essay on Cavafy attracted particular attention, John Middleton Murry, the former editor of the *Athenaeum*, writing in *The Times Literary Supplement*: 'In Alexandria Mr Forster has found a spiritual home. Being a dubious character, he goes off to a dubious city, to that portion of the inhabited world where there is most obviously a bend in the spiritual dimension, where the atmosphere is preternaturally keen and there is a lucid confusion of the categories. At this point a spinning eddy marks the convergence of two worlds, and in the vortex contradictions are reconciled. It is nothing less than a crack in the human universe. Mr Forster wanders off to put his ear to it. He finds Mr Cavafy already engaged in the enterprise.'[133] 'The review has got us rather well', Forster wrote to Cavafy while admonishing him ('You are a bad poet')[134] for not answering letters or getting Valassopoulos to translate and send

30 Constantine Cavafy,
photographed in about
1925 in his flat on the
Rue Lepsius.

more poems. As well as wanting to place the poems in journals, Forster was keen to have
them published in volume form. But when he heard from Cavafy at all, his letters were
hardly the warm replies of personal friendship, but rather polite expressions of gratitude for Forster's efforts on his behalf – and still the translations failed to arrive or did
so only sporadically. There was Valassopoulos' unwillingness to translate the erotic
poems, but as Forster realised decades later, 'Deep behind it all is Cavafy.'[135] As work in
progress, his poetry could never be complete within his lifetime, and Cavafy would
hardly want his poems collected in England – outside the walls – when he was still
writing, arranging and rearranging the Greek originals in the light of his evolving personal experience.

But for Forster too the story was still in progress as he struggled in vain against visions of Mohammed: 'You are dead, Mohammed, and Morgan is alive and thinks more about himself and less of you every word he writes. You called out my name at Beebit el Hagar station after we had seen that ruined temple about two miles from it that no one but us seems to have seen. It was dark and I heard an Egyptian shouting who had lost his friend: Margan, Margan – you calling me and I felt we belonged to each other, you had made me an Egyptian.'[136]

Forster was also struggling with *A Passage to India*, not blaming any decline in his creative powers, rather saying 'my patience with ordinary people has given out',[137] as though exasperated that he could no longer convincingly make his characters do what he wanted them to do. In *Howards End*, in the face of a world that he already sensed was disintegrating, he had made his characters love one another, be with one another. Now he could make nothing hold together: 'The upheavals in society and psychology and physics (all at the same time) are too much for a form of art which assumed a certain amount of stability in all three.'[138]

He was helped through the last months of his book by reading *The Seven Pillars of Wisdom*. He had met T. E. Lawrence two years earlier when Antonius, then on the staff of the Emir Feisal, the leader of the wartime Arab Revolt against the Turks, asked Forster to join the three of them for lunch at a London hotel. Lawrence had excited Forster then, and now reading *Seven Pillars* he found his own romantic passion for the East evoked 'with almost intolerable violence'.[139] In this mood he drove his novel to its end. Like Cavafy's Antony, like his own struggle to see Mohammed for the putrescence he had become, he concluded *A Passage to India* with Aziz and Fielding echoing the world's cry of failure and loss:

'If it's fifty-five hundred years we shall get rid of you, yes, we shall drive every blasted Englishman into the sea, and then' – he rode against him furiously – 'and then', he concluded, half kissing him, 'you and I shall be friends'.

'Why can't we be friends now?' said the other, holding him affectionately. 'It's what I want. It's what you want.'

But the horses didn't want it – they swerved apart; the earth didn't want it, sending up rocks through which riders must pass single file; the temples, the tank, the jail, the palace, the birds, the carrion, the Guest House, that came into view as they issued from the gap and saw Mau beneath: they didn't want it, they said in their hundred voices, 'No, not yet', and the sky said, 'No, not there'.[140]

On 21 January 1924 Forster told Leonard Woolf, 'I have this moment written the last words of my novel and who but Virginia and yourself should be told about it first?'[141] But first of all there had been Mohammed: as well as the ring, Forster had as a keepsake a pencil that had once been his; at ' "No, not yet", and the sky said, "No, not there" ', he laid down his pen and with Mohammed's pencil inscribed in his diary that he had completed *A Passage to India.*

Later that year he wrote to a friend, 'I have acquired the feeling that people must go away from each other (spiritually) every now and then, and improve themselves if the relationship is to develop or even endure. *A Passage to India* describes such a going away – preparatory to the next advance, which I am not capable of describing.'[142]

Early in 1928 Forster received a regretful letter from Whitehead Morris informing him that there had been a fire in the warehouse and that their languishing copies of *Alexandria*, two hundred and forty-six out of the original thousand, had been burnt. Fortunately, they said, the books had been insured, and they enclosed a generous cheque in compensation.[143] But this was not the end of the story, as Forster later recalled. 'Soon after I received a further letter from Alexandria with more regrettable news. The books had not been burnt at all. They were in a cellar which had escaped the flames, and this, as the publishers pointed out, placed us in a difficult position, for we had taken the insurance money. They had given some thought and had decided that the only thing to do was to burn the books artificially, and this they had done. *Alexandria: A History and a Guide* perished in personal flames. I don't know whether this was the right course. I only know that this fantastic enterprise is all of a piece.'[144]

And so the copy of *Alexandria* that Forster gave to T. E. Lawrence in June 1929 already had the value of being rare. This was a few days before Forster set sail with the Bargers on a cruise round the Cape, calling at South Africa, Rhodesia and Kenya. Feeling aimless at the time, he had allowed himself to be persuaded to join the voyage, but he almost immediately regretted his decision: the cruise had been organised by the British Association and involved several hundred scientists; he would feel out of place and expected to 'be shown everything and see nothing'.[145]

From Rhodesia he wrote to his friend Sebastian Sprott, an academic who was a familiar face at Garsington and one of Maynard Keynes' lovers, 'My relation to [Florence Barger] is queer. I told her all about myself up to 1921 – ie the year Mohammed died, and she has made something sacred and permanent for herself out of this, which fresh confidences would disturb.'[146] Apart from misrepresenting the date of Mohammed's death, which was burnt into his mind, he had been confiding to Florence his feelings about Mohammed until at least the end of 1926, when he told her, 'Was re-reading Mohammed's letters today – the later ones. They have more affection and depth than those he wrote earlier, and gave me a good deal of comfort. I knew I minimised his worries at the end of his life but didn't realise how clearly he saw this too.'[147]

Forster could be very good at not seeing the obvious when convenient, and the inaccuracies in his remark to Sprott served to conceal that it was Forster who had made something 'sacred and permanent' out of his relationship with Mohammed. Now he was trying to free himself, but precisely because he had so long and entirely shared

Mohammed with Florence he felt that she was an encumbrance. Nevertheless and mother-like, she was with him that mid-September day when they stepped off the train at Alexandria, where they immediately got lost, for the station had moved.

In the six and a half years since his last visit to Alexandria, Forster found that it had 'developed a great deal'; there was much new building and the general standard of living had risen, but 'this progress had not changed the individual character of the city'.[148] His tour round Africa had depressed him, he wrote to Joe Ackerley, later the author of *Hindoo Holiday*: 'Most of the African peoples seem simply heart-broken; they wander about as if their lives were lost; trade and Christianity together have done them in.'[149] In contrast, 'Egypt after the British Empire is more wonderful, beautiful and amusing than can well be imagined',[150] and the experience made him feel only half his age. He stayed in Alexandria about a week, the guest of Valassopoulos in the Quartier Grec, and called on Cavafy in the Rue Lepsius. 'Your stay here was too short', Cavafy afterwards wrote, 'The hours we were together were too few: our friendship required more. At least during these few hours I had the opportunity to express to you fully my admiration for that beautiful book *A Passage to India*, to explain the reasons for my admiration. They have become, ever since 1924, companions of mine: – Mrs Moore, Fielding, Aziz, Adela, Heaslop, the Nawab Bahadur, MacBryde.'[151]

But the main purpose of his visit to Alexandria, of the entire roundabout journey, was to lay Mohammed's ghost, and with Florence in tow he boarded the Bacos tram to return to the Home of Misery. Back in England three months later he opened the hard-cover notebook in which he had been writing his 'letter' and spoke to Mohammed for the last time:

This letter shall be finished tonight. It is over seven years since it was begun, and time it was signed. I promised you I would never return to Egypt after your death, the remark did not interest you and I have broken my promise and taken Florence to see the H of M. It is still standing, with rebuilding all around it, and, what I hadn't remembered, there is a large flowering tree in the garden behind it – pole purple. Am glad I went back to Alexandria, I was happy there, and often thought of you, which I don't do now for months at a time, not even when I wear your ring. You have sunk into a grande passion – I knew you would, but you still float about the Egyptians for me – the complexion here, the stoop of the head there. It appears to me, looking back, that you were not deeply attached to me, excited and flattered at first, grateful after-wards – that's all. But if I am wrong, and if lovers can meet after death, and go on with their love, call to me and I'll come. I am close on 51 and I can never love anyone so much, and if there is the unlikely arrangement of a personal and pleasurable eter-nity, I would like to share it with you. I never have the sense that there is one, or that you are waiting for me, and I don't care for love as I did – my needs for the moment are lust and friendship, preferably but not necessarily directed towards the same person. It is just the chance, the faint chance: I am still just able to write 'you' instead of 'him'. Tomorrow you must join my dead, I think, tonight I'll wear your ring. I did love you and if love is eternal I may start again. Only it's for you to start me and to beckon. So much has happened to me since that I may not recognise you and am pretty certain not to think of you when I die. I knew how it would be from the first, yet shouldn't have been so happy in Egypt this autumn but for you,

Mohammed el Adl –

my love,

Morgan

December 27th, 1929[152]

Four months later in London Forster met Bob Buckingham, a policeman. Not long afterwards, Bob married, and after some initial stormy scenes by his wife the three settled into a lifetime of mutual devotion. Forster died at their home in 1970.

Meanwhile memories of Mohammed did not go away. In 1958 Forster wrote to his friend and – though he did not know it then – future biographer P. N. Furbank, 'I am destroying or rearranging letters, and came across those from Mohammed el Adl – I may not have mentioned his name to you, he was a tram conductor whom I met in Alexandria 1917–1919, and again saw in 1922, soon before his death. I assumed the letters would be nothing much, but gave a glance before destroying them and was amazed – all the things I most adore glimmering in them. . . . They have given me the oddest feeling, and one which I am very fortunate to have. (Something like 100 letters). I was an awful nuisance to one or two friends at the time, and no wonder. If I talk about him to you, you will anyhow not have to find him a job.'[153] And five years later he wrote to William Plomer, then Forster's intended biographer, 'A big matter – Mohammed el Adl – has occurred to me. I think you know that the scraps surviving from him are gathered in a box, together with some "memories" of him, shymaking and threnodic. With one exception – and that a tremendous one – he has been the greatest thing in my life.'[154]

But long before that, in 1936, still during the heyday of cosmopolitan Alexandria, the ghosts of the city were reawakened by the unlikely figure of a Philadelphia judge. To Leonard Woolf on 24 May that year Forster wrote enthusiastically, 'My Alexandria Guide is being reprinted. The local archaeological society there has taken it up, and a fussy and polite but seemingly competent American judge called Jasper G. [*sic*] Brinton writes me endlessly. The president of the society was unluckily an Italian, and dead against le Forster, since a guide by an Italian already exists. The strife was transferred to the Municipal Council, where after a heated debate the Anglo Saxons and their allies were completely victorious, and the Municipality voted no less than £200 to the expenses. Nor did Judge Jasper G. B. rest there. Going on to the newly established le tourisme bureau, he received from the Bey in charge a promise of £100 more. The local Whitehead Morris is in ecstasy.'[155]

CHAPTER 4
High Society: A History and a Guide

> It was a very European city, very cultivated, artistic and musical. I don't want to pick an argument with that gentleman [Lawrence Durrell], but I thought it very wrong of him to describe it as a degenerate city. The people were aristocrats, behaved themselves; just as well behaved as the elegant society of old Philadelphia.
>
> Jasper Yeates Brinton, interviewed for the *Philadelphia Bulletin*, 1972[1]

Forster's mock-dramatic account to Leonard Woolf of the 'heated debate' and 'strife' between Anglo-Saxons and Italians over the republication of his *Alexandria* entirely misrepresented the situation, as Forster himself knew well enough. The president of the Royal Archaeological Society of Alexandria was the American Jasper Brinton and his predecessor had been British; no president had ever been Italian. If any Italian voice was raised it was probably that of Achille Adriani, who from 1932 was Evaristo Breccia's successor as director of the Graeco-Roman Museum. As he was also a member of the society he may have spoken up for Breccia's *Alexandrea ad Aegyptum*, but if he did, Brinton had settled the matter before writing to Forster. The real difficulties lay with Whitehead Morris.

By 1935, when Judge Jasper Brinton was 'gently insinuated' into the office of president of the Archaeological Society, it had become 'a dignified if somewhat somnolent organisation whose principal activity was the publication of an annual Bulletin. The possibilities for expanded activities were large, and I decided to put a little new life into an old body.'[2] One of his first acts was to write to Forster on 27 December that year proposing the republication of his History and Guide, but a reply was slow in coming. Forster had been in a nursing home recovering from a prostate operation that he had thought might kill him; now about to go under the knife again he replied on 5 February 1936, apologising for the delay but full of enthusiasm.

Brinton immediately put the matter to Whitehead Morris, saying that if they reprinted the guidebook the Archaeological Society would take five hundred copies, but they replied, 'Our past experience in selling these copies has been such as not to justify ourselves in locking up any capital at the present time.'[3] Undaunted, Brinton set about ways of financing the book, and by the beginning of May had convinced the Tourism Bureau that they should pay LE100 for five hundred copies, bringing the print-run up to one thousand in all. Meanwhile, Brinton began recruiting friends to update the book, asking its author for his approval but receiving an acknowledgement from Bob Buckingham, saying that Forster was 'recovering from a severe operation' but would reply shortly.[4] Eventually on 24 March Forster was well enough 'to answer your two kind letters with a "Yes"',[5] happy to leave Brinton to the all too familiar Alexandrian toils.

Forster had other matters on his mind. Within months of Hitler coming to power in 1933, Germany had withdrawn from the League of Nations and had embarked on a programme of massive rearmament. Then in October 1935 Mussolini invaded Ethiopia, and now at the beginning of March 1936 Hitler marched his troops into the demilitarised Rhineland. Three days after saying yes to Brinton, Forster was writing to Leonard Woolf, from whom he had heard that there were some in their circle who were talking of fleeing England at the threat of another war. 'Various things which cannot be removed from England hold me to it', Forster told Woolf, 'so that I could never emigrate myself, but if I was married or had children to be saved I should think of it, certainly.'[6]

Among the things that held him were his mother and Bob Buckingham, in his devotion to whom he characteristically sought his solution to the wider crisis, writing in the *Spectator* in November 1935, 'The desire to devote oneself to another person or persons seems to be as innate as the desire for personal liberty. If the two desires could combine, the menace to freedom from within, the fundamental menace, might disappear, and the political evils now filling all the foreground of our lives would be deprived of the poison which nourishes them. . . . There is the Beloved Republic to dream about and to work for through our dreams; the better polity which once seemed to be approaching on greased wheels, the City of God.'[7]

Work on revising Forster's guidebook began in the spring of 1936, when two friends of Brinton's, Anthony de Cosson and J. M. (John) Marshall, both members of the Archaeological Society, produced twenty-nine typewritten pages of commentary on the first edition. The notes on the Western Desert were those of de Cosson, who was the director of the Desert Railways, as were possibly those on Montazah and east to Rosetta. But the notes on Alexandria itself seem to have been entirely the work of Marshall, whom Brinton described to Forster as 'a more or less retired and retiring banker – a great authority on Alexandrian history and topography'.[8]

'Forster wrote, I suppose, in 1919–20', Marshall's commentary began.[9] 'Since then the population of Alexandria has increased very much and naturally a great deal of building has been necessary to accommodate the newcomers.' Not only had many empty spaces been filled in, but 'many large blocks of flats have taken the place, both in town and in Ramleh, of self-contained houses, and the result in Ramleh is naturally a decrease in the number of gardens'. The hill of Abou el Nawatir was now largely built over and

31   Stanley Bay, 1930s. In the early 1930s the seasonal beach cabins at Stanley Bay were replaced by tiers of concrete boxes, a transformation that coincided with the extension of the Corniche from the Eastern Harbour all the way out through Ramleh.

Lake Hadra had been drained, while along the Mahmoudiya Canal, 'where in Forster's day were old, ruined or at least decaying houses and large neglected gardens, there are now factories or store houses, for the road has become the chief industrial quarter of Alexandria'.

If Alexandria had greatly changed in the last fifteen years or so, 'this change is nothing compared with the metamorphosis of Ramleh, and it must be very difficult for one who has not seen it during that time to form any picture of what it is like today'. The motor car and the bus and 'the great extension of the bathing habit' had contributed to the changes and were promoted in turn by the construction of the new Corniche road running twelve miles along the Mediterranean seafront from the Eastern Harbour to Montazah. Where Forster had written that apart from the grandiose Italian Consulate 'the fine New Quays are attracting no buildings to their curve', there were now some Venetian-style buildings on one side, the Hotel Cecil on the other, and indeed the entire sweep of the Eastern Harbour was handsomely built up. 'From Silsileh onwards, between the road and the sea, except in a few places where the rocks make bathing impossible,

32   This aerial view of Alexandria in the 1930s shows new buildings, including the Hotel Cecil, along the Eastern Harbour Corniche. Large warships of Britain's Mediterranean Fleet can be seen in the Western Harbour.

are rows of bath cabins. The Municipality has completely civilised Stanley Bay. It is now an amphitheatre of ledges of cement, on which are placed rows of standardised bathing boxes painted in appropriate shades of green and white. I do not know how many hundreds (or thousands) of boxes there are at Stanley Bay alone', while here and elsewhere along the Corniche were 'restaurants, cafés, boîtes de nuit'.

Almost everywhere that Marshall made some statement of fact correcting a topographical description, Forster would approve the change, often simply writing 'yes' in the margin of Marshall's notes. But wherever the point was a historical one, Forster almost always resisted. 'Was Callimachus ever Librarian?' Marshall questioned, citing a papyrus from which 'it seems definitely confirmed that Callimachus was never Librarian', against which Forster wrote 'no', meaning that he would allow no alteration, though in this he was almost certainly wrong. Nor was Forster accommodating when it came to the Mosque of Nebi Daniel, which he had said stood 'on the site of Alexander's tomb', though 'the cellars have never been explored, and there is a gossipy story that Alexander still lies in one of them, intact'.[10] Now with Marshall telling him that Breccia had since explored the cellars but 'unfortunately with no result', Forster reported the outcome of Breccia's search but nevertheless repeated both the gossipy story and his bald assertion that the mosque marked Alexander's burial place. In a rare exception Forster allowed the date for the Arab walls, which he had put at AD 811, to be altered to 881, when Marshall demonstrated that Forster had obtained his date from Baedeker, who had in turn, Marshall discovered, used a German-drawn map of the ancient city, a copy of which was in the Graeco-Roman Museum, but had misprinted the date. 'Alter 811 to 881', wrote Forster in the margin, 'I think I was trapped by Baedeker!'

Forster explained himself in a letter to Brinton. Concerning topographical corrections, 'All these I accept – only stipulating that no expressions of opinion should be introduced.' As for historical corrections, 'After some thought I am rejecting almost all of these, and must justify my attitude. Mr Marshall, and others, who are helping, must not think that it arises from discourtesy or conceit! I have no claim to be a scholar and I know how limited my work for the book was. I am sure it is full of errors. At the same time it is to be reissued in my name, and I don't see that I can accept matter which I haven't personally verified. I should have to examine the authorities on which the historical corrections are based, and in many cases rival authorities also, and I have neither the health nor the leisure to do this.'[11]

Yet it does not seem to have been only that. 'The following year Amr entered in triumph. . . . Little had been ruined so far',[12] wrote Marshall, quoting Forster's account of the Arab conquest of the city back to him, then commenting, 'This seems impossible to believe. Ever since the Roman occupation, Egypt had been squeezed in every possible way: and all the money extracted from the country and all the grain sent to Rome and Constantinople were sheer loss, as going out without any return: as a result the fellahin of the day were in a miserable condition. Apart from this Alexandria had been the scene of perpetual revolts and riots: the Bruchion [the royal quarter] had been destroyed by Aurelian in the repression of one revolt and the whole city by Diocletian after another. There was also continual strife between Christians and Jews or Christians and pagans or Christians among themselves. We know that churches were built on the ruins of the Serapeum and the Caesareum: and it is very probable that these had been in their turn destroyed by the Persians. The description in the text is, I imagine, mainly based on Butler, but Butler . . . has allowed himself to be carried away by the tales of the Arab historians and contradicts what he has written in other parts of his book. That Alexandria, even in ruins should be a wonderful sight to desert Arabs is not surprising, but Breccia is much more likely to be correct in saying, "In spite of an uninterrupted succession of disasters, the town still retained traces of its former magnificence. At any rate the Arab historians speak of it with enthusiasm". On this view the Arabs cannot be accused of destroying Alexandria "as a child might a watch". The destruction was more than half completed.'[13] To which Forster wrote in the margin, 'No'.

No, because Forster was less interested in tracing the course of external events than in describing the internal drama of a civilisation. The literature that had grown up in the Museion, he had written in his History, 'developed when the heroic age of Greece was over, when liberty was lost and possibly honour too', but 'it had strength of a kind, for it saw that out of the wreck of traditional hopes three good things remained – namely the decorative surface of the universe, the delights of study, and the delights of love, and that of these three the best was love'.[14] In his guidebook Forster has the theme of love continued by Plotinus, the Gnostics and the Early Christians – that is, for as long as something of the Hellenistic world survived – but as he was to repeat in the second edition, 'Islam, strong through its abjuration of Love, was the one system that the city could not handle. . . . The physical decay that crept on her in the 7th century had its counterpart in a spiritual decay'[15] – that last sentence being Forster's point: in our own civilisation, he is saying, as in that of ancient Alexandria, the ultimate struggle turns on love. 'Amr and his Arabs were not fanatics or barbarians and they were about to start near Cairo a new Egypt of their own. But they instinctively shrank from Alexandria; she seemed to them idolatrous and foolish; and a thousand years of silence succeeded them.'[16] But Forster is also talking of his own unalterable experience of Alexandria, and in that word 'foolish' especially you can almost hear Mohammed el Adl chiding him for his attentions, but Forster's version of the city spoke otherwise: 'Love as a cruel and wanton boy flits through the literature of Alexandria.'[17]

And then when Marshall quoted Forster's conclusion to his History back to him – 'It is to the oldest of them, the Greek, that she owes such modern culture as is to be found in her'[18] – and commented bluntly, 'Don't agree at all', Forster left the margin empty.

Topographically Brinton and his friends brought the city up to date, but more than that had changed since Forster's passage from India in January 1922, when he saw Mohammed in Egypt for the last time.

In the early morning of a winter's day shortly before Christmas 1921 Jasper Brinton saw for the first time the low white line of the Egyptian coast emerging on the horizon. He was to see the same sight many times in the years to come and always with a pleasantly increased feeling of homecoming. But now, as his ship slid quietly past the lighthouse and the breakwater into the Western Harbour and past the long façade of the royal palace of Ras el Tin, he saw before him in the fascinating panorama of Alexandria only the strangeness of an unknown future.

Within moments of drawing alongside the howling quayside rabble of porters and hangers-on, two swarthy French-speaking emissaries in blue uniforms and red fezzes presented themselves at his cabin with a letter from the secretary of the Mixed Courts saying they were at his service, while a burly fellow in a yellow uniform took charge of his possessions. With an air of authority they led him briskly through the customs hall and proceeded grandly through the city, pausing as he chose a hotel on the waterfront where his young son could amuse himself with fishing in the company of 'numerous local Izaac Waltons'.[19] Then they conducted Brinton to an imposing building on Mohammed Ali Square. Above the granite pillars that framed its entrance he saw the

33   The judges of the Court of Appeal of the Mixed Courts. Judge Jasper Brinton is seen in profile, just
behind and to the left of the judge wearing a fez. Brinton was also president of the Royal Archaeological
Society of Alexandria, where his enthusiasm for Forster's *Alexandria: A History and a Guide* led to the
publication of a new edition, which became a bible for Lawrence Durrell during the Second World War.

inscription, in Italian, French and Arabic, 'Palace of Justice', and above this, in Arabic,
the legend 'Justice is the Foundation of the State'.[20]

Brinton had arrived at the Court of Appeal of the Mixed Courts, where he was presented with his insignia of office, a gold-fringed green silk sash to which was attached
a gold medallion, and was fitted out with his official costume, the high-collared frock
coat called a stamboulin and a crimson fez. Here he would serve, he thought, for the
next two or three years: public service and moral rectitude were his family watchwords,
but it was to escape Philadelphia's conception of the latter that he had come for a while
to Alexandria.

Jasper Yeates Brinton was born forty-three years earlier into a Philadelphia family
whose roots he could trace deep into America's colonial past. One ancestor had founded
the University of Pennsylvania at the urging of Benjamin Franklin and became its first
provost; others occupied themselves with the law, medicine and the ministry. From
generation to generation sons inscribed the virtues of their fathers in the family Bible,
Brinton's father writing of his own in turn, 'He had lived as he desired a life of purity

and in dying has left behind him a reputation blameless and without reproach – May I do the same.'[21]

At the turn of the century, Jasper Brinton was completing his studies in classics and law and was venturing into Philadelphia society, then still compact and homogeneous: 'as to who belonged and who did not', he recalled, 'the question answered itself'.[22] Debutantes' balls, dinner parties and twice-weekly visits to the opera filled the season; but society, though lavish and gay, was rigorous in its observance of social conventions: 'You forgot at your peril, after dining out, to leave your card on your hostess within two or three days.'[23]

Following America's entry into the Great War, Brinton was appointed Judge Advocate in charge of the port of Bordeaux. Two million American troops in France required a juridical presence, and Brinton presided over cases ranging from drunkenness, larceny and graft to desertion, mutiny and murder, as well as instances of property damage to the town and surrounding countryside, involving considerable sums in compensation. His services and tact were greatly appreciated by the French government, which at war's end made him a Chevalier of the Legion of Honour.

After his two years abroad Brinton returned to a foundering marriage, and the prospect of divorce meant that his re-entry into Philadelphia society would not be easy. When colleagues suggested that he accept the position of Justice of the Court of Appeal of the Mixed Courts of Egypt, it seemed a useful solution. His three-year-old daughter remained with her mother, who three years later discreetly divorced him in Paris, and to Egypt he came with his seven-year-old son John.

In the event, Brinton found Alexandria 'very pleasant'[24] and decided to stay, during the early years spending his spare evening hours writing *The Mixed Courts of Egypt*, published in 1930 and still the definitive work. As a judge on the Court of Appeal of the Mixed Courts and from 1943 its president, one of the highest positions in the land, he was deeply immersed in Alexandrian affairs throughout the interwar heyday of the cosmopolitan city and the dramas of the Second World War, exactly the period corresponding to Lawrence Durrell's *Alexandria Quartet*.

Soon after his arrival in Alexandria, Brinton and his son John went to live in Ramleh, where a monkey rustling in the pepper tree in the garden made himself part of the family. Their neighbour and friend was Aida Borchgrevink, that 'marvellous woman'[25] as Brinton called her, with whom they would go riding across the sands, or they would go down to the sea at Stanley Bay, which lay almost at the bottom of her garden. A crescent of rocks embraced the bay where Forster had taught himself to swim, though it had become more frequented since the war. Its shallow pools were the playground of wading children searching for crabs, sea urchins and brightly coloured fish, you changed in flamboyantly painted little shacks that were kept at home and erected at the start of the season, and a White Russian general and his wife sold ices by a Chinese pagoda planted incongruously on the Egyptian shore. That is how John remembered it before the rocks and pools disappeared, the painted shacks were replaced by terraces of concrete cabins, and even the shape of the beach was altered when the Corniche road was built in the 1930s, 'the sea blue and sparkling and the white breakers galloping in slowly till they exploded on the sandy beach, a mass of silver bubbles'.[26]

Winter was the wildfowling season on Lake Mariut, the ancient Mareotis, and Brinton, chancing his motor car, would work his way round the sodden fringe of the lake or skim across it aboard a hydroplane, sometimes staying at the ezbah of his Coptic friend and fellow judge Sobhi Ghali Bey. As was typical of these rustic country estates, 'there was a rather primitive sort of owner's house, a plain one-storey building, simply furnished but comfortable, where we lived richly on the products of the farm', while from the fields came 'the curious plaintive sound of the waterwheel – the sakiya – turned by a blinded buffalo, its music floating in the air'.[27] Shooting snipe meant rising early to wade through water and mud; if duck, 'we would install ourselves for the night in a small wooden cabin among the reeds and a couple of hours before dawn would distribute ourselves into ancient kayaks together with our native helper, a raggedy dweller in the marshland, and proceed to our appointed barrels. With the decoys set out around us, we would wait the signal of our host, listening meanwhile to the sweep of invisible wings just above our heads; then come our host's signal, the first shot, and thereafter, for a couple of hours, the cannonade would be continuous. Whether one hit or missed, it was an exhilarating sport, and no one could be indifferent to the appeal of the natural scenery seen in the twilight or at dawn out in the Egyptian marshland.'[28]

Each weekday morning John rode the tram eastwards to Victoria College, a private boys' school run on English lines, while his father caught the tram in the opposite direction for the half-hour journey into town, sitting 'up on the roof so as to survey the scenery afar and the humanity down below, for there is always something interesting as you rattle in through the outskirts'.[29] As well as surface colour, there were 'the excavations incident to clearing away the land between here and the city. It is interesting, the many Roman cisterns they have discovered in digging for foundations in Alexandria.'[30]

An early case that came before Brinton concerned the tomb of Tutankhamun, which he had visited soon after its discovery in November 1922. Until that time Egyptology was a loosely regulated archaeological Klondike, in which foreign excavators were granted concessions that gave them rights over access and to a share of what they found – with some justice, as the expertise and cost were theirs and also the historical interest. The Egyptians themselves had been largely incurious about the past, but with Britain's abolition of its Protectorate in 1922 and the granting of limited independence, Egypt's sensitivity towards matters touching on its sovereignty became more acute, and the discovery of Tutankhamun's uniquely unviolated treasure-stuffed tomb soon excited nationalist passions. In the question of finders' versus Egyptian rights, Howard Carter found himself cast in the role of an imperialist villain determined to deny Egypt its heritage. His counsel warned that of the Mixed Courts judges sitting in Cairo to hear the case, one English, one French, one Italian and two Egyptians, 'the Egyptians would be instructed as to the verdict they should return and, to make quite certain of the outcome, the Italian would be bought'.[31]

In fact the court ruled in Carter's favour, but in 1924 the government took the case to the Court of Appeal at Alexandria, where Brinton was one of the five judges sitting in chamber. 'We held that the order of the government was an administrative act with whose execution the Mixed Courts were without jurisdiction to interfere. This decision put an end to the litigation and the controversy was quickly adjusted.' Once the government had established that it had the upper hand, both sides made concessions, 'which happily permitted Mr Carter to continue the work he had so brilliantly begun'.[32]

The case had become a cause célèbre and Brinton, who throughout his career was partial towards the establishment of Egyptian rights, was gratified by its outcome, which seemed to set a pattern for future relations between Egypt and foreigners. About the worst he had to say about the Egyptians concerned their handling of the water supply – the Nile, the canals, the irrigation system, the vast and complex hydrology of the country: 'This is probably the weakest spot in the Egyptian administration. It's here, and perhaps here alone, that the English have made their services welcome to the people at large.'[33]

His position on the court also occasionally involved Brinton in ceremonial duties, as when each year during the long summer months the king would transfer his court from the burning heat of Cairo to Alexandria for its Mediterranean breezes. The Egyptian government followed as well as the entire diplomatic corps, including the British, their new consular residence atop the hill of Abou el Nawatir becoming home to the high commissioner for the season. The judges of the Mixed Courts were among those who welcomed the king on his arrival at the train station at Sidi Gaber and who each autumn bade him farewell, as Brinton described in his diary: 'Down to Sidi Gaber to see the King [Fuad] off for Cairo. The same old ceremony, but, as always, elegant and snappy, with plenty of military display. The Cabinet was there and the usual long double line of pretty much everybody. The King's train backs in from the palace and he gets off at one end of the platform and walks down the Royal Alley Way shaking hands. I stood behind, but he spotted me and we said "How do you do" as usual. I felt a little apologetic, as I did not call on him at either end of this year's holiday. However, if I had thought of it, I would have gone just to see his new rooms at Ras el Tin Palace. He is a well-dressed dapper fellow, with an agreeable manner, and quite accomplished in the superficial arts, at least, of being a king. He can afford to do things up in style and people seem to like it, although he is about as far as a king could be from any contact with his people. It offered an occasion to sell my piano to our Consul for thirty-five Egyptian pounds. Delighted to do this, as I need the pounds and don't need the piano.'[34]

When Brinton dined with an Egyptian colleague on the court a few days later, they spoke of the king's extravagance. 'The English apparently are satisfied, as it's a question of "I tickle you, you tickle me". They don't oppose the King and he doesn't oppose many of their demands which are equally without justification.'[35] The chief fault of the British in Egypt, thought Brinton, was their 'natural aloofness'.[36] The opinion of the American Minister to Egypt was more forceful, when on a visit from Cairo he invited Brinton to dine with him at the home in Moharrem Bey of the American consul in Alexandria, who had rented the studio 'in the garden of Mr Ambron, a well to do and cultured Italian with artistic tastes'.[37] 'The Minister insisted that England doesn't want to settle anything out here at present but is constantly on the lookout for trouble and intends to stay', and went on to describe the English 'as the most diabolical propagandists in the world, and was bitter in his denunciation'.[38]

The remarks were prompted by a recent chain of events in which two of the most prominent players were Forster's wartime friends Robin Furness and George Antonius.

Returning from a summer's visit to America in 1926, Brinton observed that 'the harbour is the same as always, lively, interesting and cosmopolitan. Two British battleships to remind one who owns Egypt. The dock the same swarm of noisy humanity, again reminding us that vociferation is one of the Egyptian's favourite pastimes.'[39] A while later Aida Borchgrevink came to tea, as 'full of her experiences and as keen as ever':[40] she had just returned from a summer in England, where Forster had been her guest at the cottage she rented in the Lake District. But Brinton was more interested in the news she brought from England of his friend Sir Maurice Amos, who as Lord Allenby's Judicial Advisor had confirmed Brinton's appointment to the Mixed Courts and who, along with Furness, Oriental Secretary at the High Commission, had been largely responsible for the 1922 Declaration that had granted Egypt a large measure of independence. Since then a fresh outbreak of nationalist violence had cost both men their posts and had brought to Egypt the battleships Brinton had seen on his return to Alexandria.

In the autumn of 1924 Saad Zaghloul, the newly elected Wafdist prime minister, was invited to London for talks with Ramsay MacDonald, head of Britain's first Labour government, who had often voiced his sympathy for the Egyptian nationalist case. This followed Zaghloul's declaration that he was ready to negotiate with Britain 'with a view to arriving at an agreement which will guarantee the independence that we demand, while respecting such British interests as are reasonable and acceptable'.[41] The interest that mattered above all to the British was their defence of the Suez Canal, but on his arrival in London Zaghloul announced that he would accept nothing less than the total withdrawal of British troops as a precondition to negotiations, effectively leaving nothing to discuss. The problem was that even as Zaghloul had been making overtures to the British, he had become a prisoner of the unconditional promises he had been making to the Egyptian people, typified by his slogan 'Complete independence or death'. His rhetoric, as MacDonald reminded him, was also exposing to danger those British officers serving in Egypt under the terms of the 1922 Declaration, in particular Sir Lee Stack, whose position as Sirdar – that is, governor-general of the Sudan and commander-in-chief of the Egyptian army – Zaghloul had bitterly described as an affront to national dignity. Returning from London empty-handed and fearful of losing his popular support, in mid-November Zaghloul organised a massive demonstration against the king outside Abdin Palace in Cairo, demanding with cries of 'Saad or revolution' that he back the unilateral rejection of the four reserved points. Three days later Stack was murdered in Cairo by Wafdist extremists.

Lord Allenby, the high commissioner, who against much opposition from the local British and other foreign communities and despite the apprehensions of his own government had helped put Egypt on the road towards full independence and counted Stack as a friend, felt betrayed. Angrily he set Amos and Furness to drafting an ultimatum demanding strong measures and compensation, which together with Allenby's order that British troops occupy the Customs in Alexandria, its receipts the major source of revenue for the Egyptian government, caused Zaghloul to drop all resistance and resign.

Allenby himself departed the following year and was replaced by Lord Lloyd, who blamed events on the authors of what the new Conservative government in London saw as the too liberal 1922 Declaration. Amos was put out to grass in England, while Furness resigned to become professor of English at Cairo's Fuad University after discovering that Lloyd preferred the 'devious courses'[42] advanced by his special advisor George Antonius. And so, not without the help of the future author of *The Arab Awakening*, the gunboats arrived in Alexandria harbour, their purpose to discourage Zaghloul from resuming the premiership after the Wafd had once again won the elections in 1926 with a large majority. Though Zaghloul died in 1927, for nearly a decade to come the Wafd would continue to block all attempts at a settlement with Britain.

Between the wars Alexandria's British community, owing to its political dominance in Egypt but also to the considerable commercial success of many of its members, enjoyed a position of social prominence out of proportion to its numbers. Families like the Barkers, Peels and Carvers, while usually careful to ensure their sons' British birth and education (Eton, Winchester, Sandhurst), had lived and worked in Alexandria for two and three generations and were names to conjure with on the Cotton Exchange, just as in other spheres Whittal was in Istanbul and Jardine or Swire in Shanghai.

But generally the British, though of Alexandria's cosmopolitan society, were too doggedly insular to be in it, especially those in the administration and the military. The city's Sporting Club, where Brinton played tennis, was 'on the high road to Australia, and all players of any note found their way to our international tournaments', while 'in a world of Arab ponies and British military posts, polo was a matter of course', as well as twice-weekly race meetings in summer, golf, bowls, croquet and cricket, which was 'played with religious zeal'.[43] The British had founded the club in 1890 and their social horizons were reflected in the composition of its general committee of eighteen members. In the years following the First World War, ten were British, two were Greek, one was an Alexandrian Jew with British citizenship, one an Armenian, another a Syro-Lebanese Christian, while native Egyptians were represented by a Muslim and two

34   Anthony de Cosson (with shovel) and friends on a desert expedition in 1934. They have just been found by Judge Brinton and his wife Geneva (the tall woman, second from left), who helped dig them out of the sand at Qasr el Qatagi, 28 miles south of Burg el Arab. De Cosson, who was Bramly's son in law, played an important part in revising Forster's guidebook, and his own *Mareotis*, published in 1935, was one of Durrell's major sources when writing *The Alexandria Quartet*. The friends used Bramly's old carpet factory as their weekend Desert Club, then, in 1937, they brought Burg el Arab to life when they obtained permission to build houses within its walls.

Copts. The Muslim was Prince Omar Toussoun, popularly known as 'the king of Alexandria', who was president of the club and a cousin of King Fuad. There were also three ex-officio members, one always a regimental officer from the British barracks at Mustafa Pasha, another an officer of the Royal Navy chosen from a visiting cruiser and the third a delegate from the Eastern Telegraph Company, whose purpose, like the British presence in Egypt itself, was to ensure communications between Britain and India.

By and large, as his after-dinner diary entries for the 1920s show, Brinton found the British rather dull and short on style:

His wife was perhaps the gayest and simplest and most attractive of the English women here. But that's not saying much.

Solid little English circle where, needless to say, they play charades. One might almost say that this is a favourite British indoor pastime. But it's not a bad one at that. It's astonishing how some of the stiffish mothers one sees walking around Ramleh with their eyes straight before them can unbend when it comes to a national institution like this. The ladies entered into the business with great zest, and certainly everyone seems to be satisfied with it as a form of amusement.

Afterwards to Kenneth Birley's Ball at San Stefano. A big affair, birthday party for his daughter, but left an impression of the commonplace. He didn't spare expense, but there was no style or chic. Largely because the English here admit of no such qualification – a very conglomerate and ordinary lot, with one or two exceptions. Glad to get away at half past twelve. The affair made a poor contrast beside the entertainments of the Greeks and other Levantines in town.[44]

Brinton was always ready to defend the 'style and fashion of Alexandria', by which he meant Levantine society, against the 'shabby genteel' English colony.[45] Tall and slender, with a craggy profile as though cut from the rock of Mount Rushmore, Brinton enjoyed the society of 'well-dressed women, Greeks and Syrians'.[46] There were frequent invitations for tea, dinner and games of cards at the home of Michael Salvagos, a leading cotton exporter and president of the Greek community, whose classical-style villa (now the Russian cultural centre) and gardens on the corner of the Rue des Ptolémées and the Rue des Pharaons occupied an entire block in the heart of the Quartier Grec.

Salvagos' wife, Argine, was 'the leader of society' and with her striking violet eyes had been 'one of Europe's most beautiful women, the toast of Paris in her youth'.[47] She was the daughter of Emmanuel Benachi, whose marriage to Virginia Choremi sealed the business alliance that made Choremi Benachi and Company the largest cotton exporters in Egypt and one of the three or four largest in the world.

Argine Salvagos shared 'the family charm'[48] with her sister Penelope Delta and her brother Antony Benachi: elegantly dressed (he had a mannerism of turning up his cuffs over his coat sleeves), and with his pointed moustache and affable manner, Benachi was 'the most stylish figure in Alexandria'.[49] The extended Benachi family had several homes in the Quartier Grec, one on the corner of the Rue des Abbassides and the Rue des Fatimites where Brinton would visit Antony Benachi: 'Work until five. Go to Antony Benachi's for tea. A very stylish and beautiful affair – the last word in tea parties. The house is unique as a museum – jewellery, arms, medals, porcelain, embroideries, textiles, almost every sort of art in its finest examples. Dancing – which no doubt continues late. But I have to hurry back to work [on my book].'[50]

For a time Benachi was the moving spirit in the Amis de l'Art, with which Brinton became involved through his interest in its stepchild, the Groupe Littéraire, a lecture and discussion society: 'We – or rather he – gave two remarkable exhibitions but there was no suggestion of organisation', Brinton remarked of Benachi in his diary towards the end of 1926. 'He spent money as he felt like, regardless of the budget, but then made up the deficit himself. No particular objection to this, but it does not get very far. That's the trouble here, most everyone has some personal vanity they want to exploit. He is fond of art, but his conception of a club doesn't go much beyond showing off his own things and those of his friends.'[51]

Then came the news that Benachi was leaving Egypt: 'It was an amusing enterprise while it lasted, and a pleasure to smoke big cigars in beautiful homes, while we of the committee pretended we were running the club. Of course we were doing nothing of the kind. Benachi, what a charming figure: handsome, well-groomed and with a style to him that would make him a personage in any society. He expects to leave Alexandria for a new home in Athens. I shall be sorry for this.'[52] All agreed that the Amis de l'Art had no choice but to wind up, as Benachi was 'entirely responsible for the princely scale on which our expenses have been ordered – that is to say, he has ordered them and has paid them. We discussed the advisability of a final exhibition of seventeenth-century art and concluded to try it out. The Baron [Alfred de] Menasce is interested and it will be a lively little enterprise. The wealthy Levantines will of course lend their best pieces and bring their friends to admire them. In the meantime let's hope that our Groupe Littéraire gets going independently.'[53]

To see the contents of 11 Rue des Fatimites today you must go to the famous Benaki Museum in Athens ('Benaki' being the more acceptably Greek version of 'Benachi'). The Hellenistic jewellery, the Graeco-Roman and Coptic cloths and embroidery, the ninth-century carved wooden door from Baghdad, the Fatimid and Abbasid glassware, the reconstructed seventeenth-century reception room from a Muslim house in Cairo, almost everything down to the pendant once worn by Queen Christina of Sweden, all this and more was shipped out of Alexandria in the spring of 1927 and four years later endowed and presented by Antony Benachi to the Greek state.

Smyrna had been a warning for the Greek dream in Egypt. That catastrophe and also rising Egyptian nationalism, together with the prospect that the British might negotiate an end to the Capitulations or bargain away their reserved point that protected foreigners and minorities, unsettled the Greeks of Alexandria. At the same time, economic development in Greece had been spurred by the arrival of the one and a half million refugees from Asia Minor, who created a vast pool of cheap labour and a new market for locally produced goods. Gradually, Greek Alexandria was marginalised economically, politically and culturally, as Athens consolidated its position as the sole centre of Hellenism.

In the same year that Benachi left Alexandria, a historian of the Greek community was writing that 'day by day Hellenism in Egypt is losing ground in the land of its ancestors'.[54] But as one who celebrated the fleeting moment, had filled the city's streets 'with exquisite music, with voices', and who perhaps was not displeased that he would be its last and greatest exemplar, Cavafy affected not to mind when a friend remarked that there was no more literary movement in Alexandria. 'And if there is no literary movement here, Alexandria does not lose anything', he said. 'Perhaps it is all for the best. Those young men could have devoted themselves to commerce.'[55]

Benachi tried to take his friend Cavafy to Athens too, but the poet steadfastly refused to leave Alexandria and died there in 1933. 'Mohammed Ali Square is my aunt', he liked to say, 'Rue Chérif Pasha is my first cousin and the Rue de Ramleh is my second. How can I leave them?'[56]

The builders of the city Cavafy would not leave were Italians, who more than any other community were the architects and engineers of modern Alexandria. But while almost as numerous as the Greeks, the Italians were less well organised, had a much smaller elite and were generally of a more humble social level. The Greeks were often independently minded entrepreneurs who made their way in businesses large and small, whether in the cotton trade, in tobacco imports and cigarette exports, as manufacturers or as grocers and café owners, and a large number also had white-collar office jobs. Little of this was true of the Italians, who for the most part were manual workers and clerks.

Yet in the first half of the nineteenth century, Italians had played a considerable role in the development of Egypt's administration and services, which accounts for Italian being the early lingua franca not only of Alexandria but of the country as a whole. They ran the medical and sanitary services and much of the postal service, but then lost ground to British and Egyptian administrators. Increasingly, large numbers of Italians eked out a hand-to-mouth existence as knife-grinders, waiters or stonemasons and accepted wages lower than those of other foreigners. When Mohammed Ali allocated quarters of Alexandria to the various foreign communities in around 1830, he gave land to the north of the square that later bore his name to the British, who built their Church of St Mark there, land to the south to the French and Greeks, and the areas to the east, abutting the old Turkish town on the Anfushi headland and Karmouz on the site of ancient Rhakotis, he assigned to the Italians, which by the late nineteenth century had degenerated into slums all but indistinguishable from those of the native quarter, and where many of the inhabitants all but forgot their Italian origins.

Nor did Italy's overseas ambitions solve their problems. Rhodes and the rest of the Dodecanese were happy to be freed from the Turks in 1912 but angry that their Italian liberators came and stayed, which earned for the Italians of Alexandria the antagonism of the city's Dodecanese and other Greeks. Italy's conquest of Libya in 1911–12 did not win them any friends in Muslim Egypt, and their reputation suffered further when the Senussi Bedouins, armed by the Turks and Germans, drove them out of Libya during the First World War.

This was the condition of Alexandria's Italians when Mussolini came to power in 1922, in Italy maintaining the monarchy but instituting his own fascist dictatorship and in Libya beginning a ten-year reconquest. For many, what fascism seemed to mean then was not what it clearly came to mean later, and the Italian community in Alexandria, too poor to provide sufficiently well for itself, was grateful when money poured in from

Mussolini's Italy to build better hospitals and bigger schools and provide them with well-paid staff, to open clubs and mount excursions, and to send students free to Italy for their summer holidays.

Also part of Mussolini's appeal was the notion that the Mediterranean was once a scene of Roman greatness, its monuments standing witness all round Mare Nostrum. If Alexandria's very name gave Greeks a claim to domicile, then Mussolini's revived memory of Antony's conqueror reminded the city's Italians that Alexandria had once been theirs.

Along with communal regeneration and a place in the world came an awakened sense of national pride, felt not only by the city's lower classes. The Italians of Alexandria were taught to fly the flag; pictures of the king went up in their schools; and on their blackboards they wrote, 'O sole tu non possa veder mai nulla più grande e più bello d'Italia e di Roma' – 'O sun may you never see anything greater and more beautiful than Italy and Rome.'[57] Soon these were joined by pictures of Il Duce himself, and the children of the community were put into black shirts and blue neckerchiefs and enrolled in the fascist youth.

Returning home to Ramleh one afternoon in late 1926, Brinton was joined for tea by Della Rovere, an Alexandrian Italian on the staff of the court. 'We had an interesting talk about the new Italy. He is active in the Fascist movement here, which is directed by a Triumvirate which has a membership of 500. To talk with a fellow like that impresses you with the fundamental strength of the movement in its being able to secure the enthusiastic conviction of middle class thoughtful fellows like himself. He promised to send me literature.'[58]

'Thursday, January 20th, 1927: Took tea at Mrs X, a white-haired lady immersed in Theosophy, who talked for an hour on Krishnamurti, evidently regarding me as a possible convert. Was impressed by her charm of character, but everything she said seemed to be the most purely gratuitous assumptions. But if they work for her – and others – well and good for them.'[59]

As successor to Furness the Foreign Office appointed Walter Smart, its Oriental Secretary in Tehran, who after landing at Alexandria during that gunboat summer of 1926 and before catching the train to Cairo made it his first point of business to call round at the Rue Lepsius. Negotiating the ground-floor bordello he mounted the stairs to Cavafy's apartment, where the old poet's conversation so wove its enchantment that he almost forgot his purpose in coming to Egypt and thought the reprimand worth it when finally he arrived at his post several days late. Though Grafftey-Smith, who served under Smart in Cairo, described him as one of the 'giants' of the Foreign Service, a man of 'the finest ambassadorial timber',[60] he was to become an ambassador only in the fiction of Lawrence Durrell. During the Second World War Smart befriended Durrell, who later admitted he was 'my model for Mountolive',[61] the British ambassador to Egypt whose name serves as the title of the third volume of *The Alexandria Quartet*.

Smart was effectively barred from advance to ambassadorial rank when he allowed his wife to pursue an uncontested divorce some time after his arrival in Cairo. Eventually, in 1932, he married Amy Nimr, who had returned home to Egypt after the war from the bohemian life of Bloomsbury, a new-look woman with an Eton crop, a taste for *Ulysses* and the French avant-garde, and a talent as a brilliant painter that she had developed at the Slade School of Fine Art.

Amy's background was Syrian of a progressive kind. Greater Syria (today's Syria, Lebanon, Jordan and Israel) had been conquered by the Turks in 1516, as was Egypt the following year, and became part of the Ottoman Empire. The first awakening of Arab resistance to Turkish rule came in the 1880s and was led for the most part by Christian Arabs in Beirut who were influenced by Western culture and political ideas. But their movement failed to attract much support from the more traditionally minded Muslim Arabs, who were also less inclined to oppose the Turks with whom they felt a religious if not an ethnic affinity. Under the khedives and from 1882 the British, Egypt became the only country in the Middle East to achieve anything like European standards, material or political, and it attracted among others many Christian Syro-Lebanese. One of these was Fares Nimr, who had attended the Syrian Protestant College (now the American University in Beirut) and was an Anglican convert from Greek Orthodoxy. When the Ottoman sultan ordered the arrest and execution of Arab nationalists, Nimr swam out to a ship anchored in Beirut harbour and sailed for Alexandria, going on to Cairo where he founded the influential newspaper *Al Moqattam*, which took a warmly admiring though not uncritical view of the British. His wife bore him three remarkable daughters of whom Amy was one; another was Katie, a passionate Arab nationalist, who married George Antonius.

By the First World War Arab discontent against the Turks had broadened to include large numbers of Muslims as well as Christians, and what they were led to believe, both those of Arabia and those of Greater Syria, was that by joining the British against the Turks they would achieve self-rule. This applied also to Palestine, whose Arab population at that time, both Muslim and Christian, stood at around six hundred thousand. In addition there were about eighty thousand Jews, mostly from Poland and Russia, who in the face of pogroms and persecution had settled in Palestine during the nineteenth century. Of these about twelve thousand were followers of the Zionist movement, which had begun in the 1880s at the same time as Fares Nimr and his colleagues were founding their movement for Arab independence. The evident weakening of the Ottoman Empire and hence the chance to carve out a new world was a common factor, with both Jews and Arabs looking to England to satisfy their conflicting aims.

When Judge Brinton described Alexandria as 'brilliant and sophisticated, far beyond any city in the Mediterranean',[62] he was thinking not only of the Nuovo Teatro Alhambra on the Rue Missalla and the Mohammed Ali Theatre on the Rue Fuad, where Pavlova danced and Toscanini conducted, where the opera season was brightened by the stars of La Scala and where a succession of plays from Paris and London were performed by visiting companies. Despite his reservations about the Amis de l'Art, he located the true brilliance of the city in its great houses, where exhibitions, lectures, concerts and theatrical entertainments were presented by those 'representing the old business firms which had built the city's prosperity and whose families brought to the city the culture and traditions of foreign lands. Among these the Jews were strongly represented and enjoyed a high position in the social world. They were conspicuous too in the city's intellectual life. In fact it was in the Jewish homes that one was most apt to meet the prominent figures in the European literary world.'[63]

Brinton was thinking in particular of Baron Felix de Menasce's great rambling house on the corner of the Rue Menasce and the Rue Rassafa in Moharrem Bey. Baron George de Menasce, Felix's son by his first wife, lived there too and was a more than competent classical pianist whose Tuesday afternoon concerts, in which he was often accompanied by like-minded friends, became an Alexandrian institution. His half-brother Jean, Felix's son by his second wife Rosette, was that friend of Cavafy's and promoter of his poetry whom Forster had met at Lady Ottoline Morrell's. Whenever he returned from Europe to stay with his family in Alexandria Jean would speak of his friendships with a wide variety of literary figures, among them T. S. Eliot, who called him 'my best translator':[64] he translated *The Waste Land* and later *Ash-Wednesday*, 'East Coker' and other of Eliot's works into French. Felix and Rosette's two daughters lived in the house as well, Denise until she married Alfred Mawas, who practised at the Mixed Courts, and Claire for several years after her marriage to Jacques Vincendon, who was secretary-general of the Land Bank of Egypt, of which her father was director. Claire Vincendon's passion was the theatre, which was how Brinton and most other people got to know her; she acted in and designed costumes for the entertainments she staged for guests at the great house in the Rue Rassafa, where her daughter Claude was born in 1925.

Whenever Chaim Weizmann, leader of the World Zionist Organisation and the eventual first president of Israel, visited Alexandria, he would 'invariably'[65] stay at the home of Baron Felix de Menasce and his wife Rosette, the maternal grandparents of Claude Vincendon, who became Lawrence Durrell's third wife. But it was not while Durrell was in Alexandria that he and Claude met; she walked into his life on Cyprus a decade later, in 1955, while he was still writing *Justine* and just after his second wife, Eve Cohen, had left him. There his encounter with Claude inspired him not only to finish the book but to expand what till then he had intended as only a single novel into a quartet, its span the interwar years and the Second World War in Alexandria, bringing something to it of her own memories of the city as well as characters and stories from her family history.

The Menasces, like the overwhelming majority of the Jews in Egypt, were Sephardim, those who at the division of the medieval world between Islam and Christendom found themselves living in Muslim lands. They adhered to the same theology and basic Jewish practices as the Ashkenazi Jews of Christian Europe but differed in their cultural and

35 Baron Felix de Menasce, with (from left to right) his daughters Claire and Denise, and his son Jean. The Menasces were among the most prominent families in Alexandrian society and made important contributions to the brilliance and sophistication of its cultural life.

historical experience. In contrast to the Ashkenazim, the Sephardim (the name means Spanish) enjoyed the more tolerant society of Muslim Iberia, where the Arab princes accepted them as virtual equals, and where Jews rose to high positions in government, prospered in commerce and were eminent in the learned professions until they were driven from Spain in 1492 and from Portugal in 1497 by the Christian Reconquista. Many Sephardi exiles went to Italy, while most found refuge in the Mediterranean provinces of the Ottoman Empire. (Iberian Jewish culture was highly developed and the Sephardi refugees tended to dominate the oriental Jewish communities in the areas where they settled, explaining why Jews indigenous to Islamic countries have come to be known as Sephardim, although many of them are not in fact of Spanish or Portuguese descent.) In pre-nineteenth-century Egypt, despite a measure of popular prejudice and abuse directed against all non-Muslim minorities at the time, they enjoyed freedom of religion and a less oppressive government than anywhere else in the Ottoman Empire, where in turn conditions were preferable to those endured by the Ashkenazim in Eastern

Europe. In these relatively relaxed conditions they became prominent as merchants, moneylenders and farmers of taxes and customs duties.

With the advent of Mohammed Ali, Jewish immigration was actively encouraged, principally from Italy and Greece during the 1820s to 1840s, as part of his programme to develop and modernise Egypt with the help of foreign investment and expertise, and indeed the Jews were increasingly seen as merely one more constituent in the generality of foreign minorities. A fresh wave of Sephardim came to Egypt in the late nineteenth and early twentieth centuries from North Africa, Italy, Greece, Turkey, Syria and Iraq to enjoy the stability and liberalism of British rule. The Sephardim were the despair of visiting Zionists, among them a Viennese journalist who reported in 1904 that 'Egypt today is still the freest country in the world', but who complained that in consequence its Jews were 'without comprehension' in the 'face of all questions of Jewish culture or nationhood'.[66]

This was the world to which the Menasces belonged. According to Felix de Menasce, the family came to Egypt via Aleppo, the great entrepôt city of northern Syria, where spices, fabrics, precious metals and gems brought on the backs of camels from the East were traded for European manufactures. Both there and in Cairo, where the Menasces settled in the eighteenth century, Jews played a major role as merchants and moneylenders, virtually controlling the markets and concentrating the entire caravan trade in their hands.[67]

Felix de Menasce's grandfather was born in 1807 in the Haret el Yahud, Cairo's Jewish quarter, immediately west of Khan el Khalili, the famous bazaar in the heart of the city, from where he rose to become the private banker of the Khedive Ismail. This was Yaqub (Jacob) Levi Menasce (the original surname was Levi, but sometime early in the nineteenth century if not before the sobriquet Menasce was added, the French form of the Hebrew 'Menashe' or the Arabic 'Menasha', meaning fly whisk), who was one of the earliest businessmen in Egypt to recognise the opportunities offered by European trade and founder of the international banking house of J. L. Menasce and Sons. The 'de' was added in 1876 when he obtained Hungarian citizenship together with the title of Baron of the Austro-Hungarian Empire for puffing the sails of Habsburg trade between the Adriatic and the Levant. His move from Cairo to Alexandria in 1871 seems to have split Alexandria's Jewish community, presumably with the baron opposing the traditionalists, though the details are not clear. Later the rift was healed, but meanwhile he built the Ecoles Fondation de Ménasce on the Rue Sultan Hussein, which provided less well off members of the Jewish community with a secular education taught mostly by Roman Catholics. (Here, as the foundations were being dug, the huge Ptolemaic column was unearthed that was later erected in the Municipal Gardens to commemorate the retaking of Khartoum – that same column where Forster and Mohammed met at their first rendezvous.) He also built, perhaps likewise in opposition to the Rabbinate and its Grand Synagogue on the Rue Nebi Daniel, the Menasce synagogue just off the French Gardens, and he established the Menasce cemetery adjacent to the Protestant, Coptic,

Greek and Syrian Orthodox, Armenian and Catholic cemeteries at Chatby, where he was buried in 1882 and still lies among a plethora of barons and baronnes de Menasce (the title could pass to all his descendants, both male and female) and other members of Alexandria's *haute juiverie*.

The banking firm of J. L. Menasce passed to Yaqub's grandsons Jacques, Elie, Felix and Alfred de Menasce, who were sent to Europe for their education and to manage the bank's various branches there before returning to Alexandria. Felix, born in 1865, studied at the University of Vienna and at the age of twenty proceeded to England, where he was placed in charge of the bank's London branch. Meanwhile Jacques, as head of both the family and the firm, was extending the Menasces' range of business interests in Egypt, venturing into the construction of railways and waterworks and acquiring extensive landholdings in Upper and Lower Egypt, primarily for the cultivation of sugar and cotton.[68] In 1890, in association with his brothers, Jacques built the Menasce Hospital, which enjoyed a high reputation among Jewish and non-Jewish patients alike, and in the same year became president of Alexandria's Jewish community, an office he held for twenty-four years until the outbreak of the First World War, transforming the community into a 'model of order and organisation', with even Zionists, who preferred to scoff at prospects for intercommunal harmony, commenting favourably on the low level of social and religious tension in Alexandria.[69]

In comparison with his older brother Jacques, Felix de Menasce was a bon viveur who by 1914, though not yet fifty, had been retired from business for nearly twenty years, and though he continued to hold directorships in numerous companies and financial institutions and was associated with local philanthropic activities, these were hardly more than the notional involvements of a man who otherwise gave every impression of devoting himself to the enjoyment of his considerable wealth. He had the family ability, his grandson Jacques Mawas remembers, 'to be always cheerful, to live in the present, to never regret the past, to never wonder what will happen tomorrow'. He was certainly not a religious man: 'I never remember one Jewish feast in his house, and my mother says as far as she remembers there never was.' And so he remained to the end of his life, yet by 1918 the unforeseen consequences of the war and his marriage to a remarkable, mysterious and beautiful woman found Felix de Menasce, like his counterparts the Benachis, pursuing a great idea.

When war broke out in 1914, the Menasces, as Austro-Hungarian citizens, found themselves classified by the British as enemy aliens. Jacques de Menasce was obliged to resign as president of Alexandria's Jewish community, which like his family had enjoyed the protection of the Austro-Hungarian Empire. His successor the financier Edgar Suares was a distant relative by marriage, but as his family had come from Spain via Livorno he was an Italian citizen, and in the First World War Italy was Britain's ally. In March 1916 Suares approached the high commissioner, saying that there were Jews who favoured a German protectorate over Palestine, but that Britain could bind world Jewry to its cause by itself establishing a protectorate and opening up Palestine to Jewish settlers who would manage its internal affairs.

A similar proposal had already been put to the British government the previous year by the banker and Liberal politician Sir Herbert Samuel, the first unbaptised Jew to hold cabinet office, after he had met Chaim Weizmann. A naturalised British citizen born in Russia, Weizmann had been introduced to Samuel by C. P. Scott, a former Liberal MP and the owner-editor of the *Manchester Guardian*, who found Weizmann 'extraordinarily interesting – a rare combination of the idealism and the severely practical which are the two essentials of statesmanship. What struck me in his view was first the perfectly clear conception of Jewish nationalism – an intense and burning sense of the Jew as Jew . . . and, secondly, arising out of that, necessary for its satisfaction and development, his demand for a country, a homeland, which for him, and for anyone sharing his view of Jewish nationality, could only be the ancient home of his race.'[70] Already in *Tancred*, his 1847 lyrical romance, Benjamin Disraeli,[71] a Sephardi convert to Anglicanism and future Tory imperialist prime minister, had a Jew of Jerusalem prophesy that 'the English will take this city; they will keep it'. But if Weizmann ignited Scott's Bible-reading romanticism, he did nothing to disturb Scott's Liberal opposition to the extension of Britain's imperial commitments, for Palestine, Weizmann told him in November 1914, would not be a dependency but an ally, 'an Asiatic Belgium in the hands of the Jews', who 'would create a strong buffer guarding the Suez Canal'.[72] Weizmann and Samuel first met that December, and in early March 1915 Samuel proposed to the cabinet a British protectorate over Palestine and its settlement in the course of time by three or four million Jews, who once having formed an overwhelming majority of the population would be granted self-government. Later that month, comparing the intended role of the Jews in Palestine to that of the British in Egypt, Weizmann told Scott that the Jews would 'take over the country; the whole burden in organisation falls on them, but for the next ten or fifteen years they work under [a] temporary British protectorate'.[73]

On 11 December 1917, after being reminded that a donkey had sufficed for One greater than he, General Allenby entered Jerusalem on foot, the first Christian conqueror of the city in eight hundred years. But meanwhile Weizmann had won a still greater victory when the British government, with the Liberal Lloyd George as prime minister and Arthur Balfour as foreign secretary, issued a statement of its policy regarding Jewish aspirations in Palestine. This was the famous Balfour Declaration of 2 November: 'His Majesty's Government view with favour the establishment in Palestine of a National Home for the Jewish people and will use their best endeavours to facilitate the achievement of this object, it being clearly understood that nothing shall be done which may prejudice the civil and religious rights of existing non-Jewish communities in Palestine, or the rights and political status enjoyed by Jews in any other country.'

The announcement of the declaration was postponed to 9 November, the next publication date of the *Jewish Chronicle* in London, though the British press in general and the government let it pass as a minor event. In Alexandria, however, on 11 November, in scenes reminiscent if not on the scale of the Greeks' reception of Venizelos two and a half years earlier, eight thousand Jews massed at Weizmann's urging to welcome the news. Four months later, in March 1918, Weizmann himself sailed into Alexandria harbour and was cheered through the streets by a large and enthusiastic crowd of Jewish refugees from Palestine waving Zionist banners (now the flag of Israel) and singing the Hatikvah (the Zionist and now the Israeli anthem) and was greeted by numbers of notables led by Edgar Suares and Baron Felix de Menasce.

'Rosette de Menasce was an amazing woman', recalled one Alexandrian, Bernard de Zogheb. 'She was French, very French, a flamboyant woman with red hair, a terrific personality and a shady life before marrying the baron.' She was born in Paris in – but there the difficulties already begin. There is a story that at a dinner party during the Second World War a young English officer was asked, 'How old do you think that woman over there is?' Glancing down the length of the table and catching her face in the candlelight, he replied, 'Oh, about twenty-three'. In fact she was approaching seventy, but nobody knew for sure. Felix died at the age of seventy-eight in 1943 after paralysis had confined him for a decade to the great house in Moharrem Bey, but when Rosette died in 1949 even her family could only guess at her age: she had prevailed upon the French consul to alter her passport to conceal her true date of birth, and her brilliant blue eyes and fine complexion meant she always looked much younger than she was.

Rosette was not yet twenty when she arrived in Alexandria in the early 1890s as the mistress (some say posing as the wife) of Georges Philippard, director-general of the Messageries Maritimes. But how did she come to marry Felix de Menasce, and what sort of life had she led before? 'Little girls shouldn't ask questions', she would say to her daughters when they asked. She would nevertheless speak of her mother as having been born a Danton, giving rise to speculation that Rosette was the great-grandniece of the revolutionary. She made no mention of her father at all, but claimed to bear the surname Lariba de Bustros and spoke of a Carlist connection, a link with the Bourbon pretender to the Spanish throne: Danton and Bourbon, a fabulous symmetry. Rosette was rumoured to have been a dancer in Paris, where according to an Alexandrian friend she had a sister, the actress Charlotte Lyses, who was first mistress to the actor-manager Lucien Guitry and then wife to his son, the actor and dramatist Sacha Guitry. Certainly when Charlotte and Sacha came to Alexandria they would stay with Felix and Rosette in Moharrem Bey.

Rosette had not been long in Alexandria when Philippard was jailed for fraudulent business dealings and his real wife showed up with their children. With one thing and another Rosette was left stranded, and this seems to have been the moment that she met Felix de Menasce, who followed her back to Paris. But if it was a sudden and passionate affair, it was not an easy one: Felix was married to his cousin Celine who had recently given birth to their son George; Rosette also had a son, born illegitimately and left

36   Baronne Rosette de Menasce at the Municipal Stadium. 'Rosette de Menasce was an amazing woman', recalled one Alexandrian: 'She was French, very French, a flamboyant woman with red hair, a terrific personality and a shady life before marrying the baron.'

behind in France, with whom she must have remained in covert communication, for when she died he came to Alexandria – 'I remember him very well', says her grandson Jacques Mawas, 'he looked very much like her' – to claim his inheritance.

Through the turn of the century Felix and Rosette lived in Paris, where Celine, who ran off with her violin teacher, died in 1900 and was buried in Père-Lachaise. Claire (Claude's mother) was born in Paris in 1901 and a son Jean in Alexandria the following year, but only Denise, born in 1909, was legitimate, as Felix and Rosette were not married until 1903. At some point Jean learnt the truth, either after his mother's death or perhaps because she confided to him in her lifetime, for her birth and marriage certificates were found among his effects. These show that Rosette was born illegitimately in 1875, though her parents, who named her Rose Claudia, married immediately after. Rosette's father was Cyprien Larriba (not Lariba), a chauffeur born in Spain; Rosette's mother was Claudine de Bustos (not de Bustros), a maker of ladies' boots, her father in turn a shoemaker who indeed was married to a Claudine Danton, though they lived in south-central France, far from the great Danton's birthplace east of Paris. Felix and Rosette were married in Geneva, first in a civil ceremony before the Austrian consul, then at the

Grand Rabbinate the following day, and this explains why Felix delayed so long in marrying, even at the cost of two illegitimate children: for all that he was not a practising Jew, he would not marry Rosette, a Roman Catholic, until she had undergone the long process of conversion to Judaism, for only then would his children be properly Jewish.

Now as the Baronne de Menasce, Rosette imposed her personality on Alexandrian society. It was a society in which conversation was conducted by slipping in and out of several languages in the course of a single sentence, but while Felix was fluent in French, Italian, English, German and Arabic, Rosette's ventures beyond French were often descents into alarming malapropisms, as when during the First World War she told a high-ranking British dinner guest, 'I caught cold in your bed', at which Felix's monocle fell into his soup. She had meant to say that she had caught cold in his house, 'bed' being her mispronunciation of the Arabic 'beit', meaning home. 'Se non è vero, è ben trovato', Felix would sigh, 'If it's not true, it's a good story', which became something of a family motto.

Then with the death of Jacques in 1916, Felix, as the oldest surviving brother, was thrust into assuming responsibility for the family business and the family's role in community affairs, and it was now, with her taste for drama and adventure attaching itself to her newfound identity, Jewish and aristocratic, that the Baroness Rosette de Menasce gave her encouragement to Felix in the Zionist cause.

Weizmann's disembarkation at Alexandria on 20 March 1918 marked the beginning of his close friendship with Felix and Rosette de Menasce. Going beyond the role of gracious hostess, Rosette became Weizmann's lifelong correspondent, informing him of events and moods in the city, complaining, for example, about the Christian Syrians, who practised, she said, 'disguised but certain antisemitism'.[74] Weizmann had arrived as head of the Zionist Commission, whose purpose was to safeguard Jewish interests in Palestine, a task that involved overcoming Arab fears about Zionism's ultimate intentions. To that end, the commission went on to Cairo, where Weizmann met with Fares Nimr together with members of the Palestine Committee of Muslims and Christians and gave them assurances regarding the Jews' limited ambitions in Palestine.

Taking the overnight train from Cairo, Weizmann arrived in Palestine on 3 April, the commission arriving the following day, one of its members wasting no time in confiding to his diary on 7 April that 'The Arabs in Palestine are a blot on the landscape', adding that perhaps their leaders 'can be bought off'.[75] For Weizmann the contrast between theory and reality came as an intellectual and emotional shock. In London both he and the government had shared comfortable assumptions about the implementation of Zionist plans, but in Palestine the British military authorities faced the practical problem of handling the sensibilities of the Palestinians, who had not been consulted on the Balfour Declaration and while responding politely to Weizmann's assurances remained disconcertingly suspicious. Within two months of his arrival he had decided that the Palestinian Arabs had a 'treacherous nature'[76] and were 'a demoralised race with whom it was impossible to treat'.[77] Ronald Storrs, who was governor of Jerusalem from 1917 to 1926, was sympathetic towards Zionism but regretted the arrogance of some Russian Jews on the commission and thought it a pity that the Zionists did not make more use of Sephardim, who, having the same oriental background as the Arabs, would have been ideal agents for negotiations. 'The Zionists', Storrs wrote, 'are completely informed upon every aspect of the problem, save that of Palestine and the Palestinians. They do not know the languages, nor will they employ the Egyptian Jews who do know them: the consequence is that their frank intentions of policy alarm the present aborigines only less than their reassurances.'[78]

But in Egypt Felix de Menasce found things to do. In the summer of 1918, after returning from Jerusalem where he was present as Weizmann laid the foundation stone for the Hebrew University, he helped found the Alexandria Pro-Palestina Committee and became its first chairman. The purpose of the committee was to encourage and finance settlement in Palestine, though, as Israeli and Egyptian statistics show, underlining the wellbeing and security enjoyed by Jews in Egypt, fewer than four thousand Jews emigrated from Egypt to Palestine in the three decades from 1918 (many of these not Egyptian Jews but from elsewhere in the Middle East, or Ashkenazim from Eastern Europe who had paused in Egypt en route to Palestine), while the number of Jews in Egypt steadily increased right up to the creation of the State of Israel in 1948, the mass exodus only following the Suez war of 1956. The committee's accomplishment, and it was a critical one, was rather to help finance the emigration of twelve thousand European Jews to Palestine between 1920 and 1927, one in seven of all Jews emigrating there worldwide, at a time moreover when the entire Zionist venture was at risk because even as Jews were coming into Palestine, many were leaving, 1927 showing a net emigration of Jews from the country. Felix also became president of Alexandria's Palestine Restoration Fund and represented Egypt at the London Zionist Conference in 1920 and at the Twelfth Zionist Congress at Carlsbad in 1921.

Meanwhile, Felix de Menasce played an important role in discussions that could well have changed the course of history. From the Jewish point of view, Zionism, involving many sacrifices, was an idealistic movement; but to the Palestinians it was the enforced colonisation of their country by an alien people, and in 1920 and again in 1921 Christian and Muslim Palestinians exploded in bloody protests against the British and the Zionists. Weizmann's response was twofold. At Carlsbad he secretly authorised the purchase of weapons to be smuggled into Palestine for use by the Haganah, the Zionist underground militia, while in March 1922, with Weizmann's encouragement, Felix de Menasce, together with David Eder, a British member of the Zionist Commission, and Asher Saphir, a Palestinian-Jewish journalist with excellent ties to the Arabs, entered into secret negotiations with members of the All-Arab Congress in Cairo. The parties concluded that the problems between Arabs and Jews in Palestine were largely a consequence of conflicting British promises and that both sides should set aside the Balfour Declaration and arrive at a bilateral agreement sealed by a formal contract. Further meetings early in April brought the parties to a point where they were ready to implement these ideas. But the talks, which immediately followed the granting of limited Egyptian independence, were a step too far for the Colonial Office, whose policy was for Britain to retain its controlling hand in Palestine. Once the League of Nations ratified the Mandate for Palestine that summer, which enjoined Britain to enact the terms of the Balfour Declaration, there was little incentive for the Zionists to continue talks with the Arabs, with consequences for stability and peace in the Middle East and for cosmopolitanism in Alexandria.

What interest there had been in Zionism among the Jews of Egypt after the First World War waned steadily throughout the 1920s, and in 1929, when scores of Jews were killed or injured in a week-long riot in Jerusalem that arose from a dispute over religious practices at the Wailing Wall and from reports of the alleged intention of Jews to desecrate the Muslim holy places, open Zionist activity in Egypt virtually ceased altogether on the advice of Jewish community leaders, who were anxious not to import Palestine's troubles. Felix de Menasce for one, who had become president of Alexandria's Jewish community in 1927, confined his activities to within Palestine, making large donations to the Jerusalem hospital, buying land (as did his son George) atop Mount Carmel, and becoming a member of the council of the Jewish Agency, which succeeded the Zionist Commission and acted as a kind of autonomous Jewish government for Palestine. But already it was too late. The Wailing Wall riots of 1929 marked the complete breakdown of understanding between the two sides and the beginning of a bitter and irrepressible conflict that during the 1930s began to seep into Egyptian politics too. Fares Nimr, whose *Al Moqattam* newspaper had till then endorsed certain Zionist policies, now looked back on his meetings with Weizmann and said, 'He lied to me. He was not a truthful man.'[79]

A famous scandal rocked the Jewish community during Felix's term as president, a scandal that arose from within the Menasce family itself. After leaving Oxford, Jean had gone to the Sorbonne to study oriental languages and under the influence of the philosopher Jacques Maritain had converted to Roman Catholicism, becoming a Dominican and assuming the name Pierre. In addition to publishing work on Persian inscriptions, in 1931 he wrote *Quand Israël aime Dieu*, a book on Hassidism, whose teachings were originally a popularised form of the Jewish mystical tradition known as the cabala. But his continuing interest in Judaism, indeed his active Zionism both before and after his conversion,[80] did nothing to ameliorate his father's feelings, and it was with the greatest difficulty that the two were brought together and attempts made to heal the relationship when Jean visited Alexandria in 1932. Then amid the awkwardness came the scandal, for instead of lying low Jean went to celebrate mass at St Catherine's Cathedral. The Jewish bankers and brokers at the Mohammed Ali Club turned their backs as he passed, but nothing could stand in the way of Rosette's pride in her son, and she followed him to St Catherine's to hear him preach. In that same year Felix de

37   Felix and Rosette de Menasce raised their family in this great rambling house on the Rue Rassafa in Moharrem Bey. It was also home to George de Menasce, whose Tuesday afternoon piano concerts here became an Alexandrian institution. Whenever Chaim Weizman, leader of the World Zionist Organisation, would visit Alexandria, he would stay as a guest of Felix and Rosette, the maternal grandparents of Claude Vincendon, who was born in the house and became Lawrence Durrell's third wife.

Menasce resigned the presidency of the Jewish community, but when he suffered a stroke a year or two later, it was because he had discovered that Rosette was having an affair with Elie Ades, who belonged to one of the richest Jewish families in Egypt and wanted to marry her, though as Rosette put it to her daughter Claire, 'Do I want to exchange being la Baronne de Menasce for plain Mrs Ades?'[81] And so the affair continued while Rosette stayed with Felix, who remained paralysed at the house in Moharrem Bey for the rest of his life.

This was about the time that Jacques and Claire Vincendon moved with Claude and her younger brothers out of the Rue Rassafa and into an apartment at 63 Rue Fuad, opposite the Municipality. Their marriage had been another cause of distress to Felix de Menasce, as Jacques was a Christian, and though Chaim Weizmann found them 'very much in love' when he met them in Alexandria just after they were wed, he was probably echoing Felix when he dismissed Jacques as 'an utterly colourless Frenchman'.[82] The building was owned by Claire's half-brother Baron George de Menasce, who let them live there at a peppercorn rent. George and his father Felix lived on their considerable investment incomes which were administered from offices on the mezzanine – investments that extended beyond Egypt. En route to Palestine in 1935, Weizmann made another of his frequent visits to Alexandria, where as usual he stayed at the Rue Rassafa, but on this occasion he missed George de Menasce and so wrote to him afterwards from London:

> To my great satisfaction, I hear you have recently made a great deal of money in Palestine, and to my still greater satisfaction, I hear you have invested this money in some property in Palestine; I need not say that I wish you the very best of luck. But I feel that I am entitled to a small commission on this transaction, as to some small extent I was instrumental in introducing you to Palestine, and consequently in your land purchases there. I think neither of us is sorry for what we have done in this direction! I spoke to your father about it, and I think he agreed with me that my case is a good one. I would like to have my commission in the form of a contribution to the Institute in Rehovot. I leave it to you to fix the amount – anything between £500 and £5,000 will be welcome – but I do seriously hope that you will not refuse me; I am quite sure that this transaction will bear fruit as much as your first one on Palestinian soil!

> With kind regards and much love, I am,

> Yours ever,

> Ch. W.[83]

The Vincendons' apartment was enormous ('we used to cycle down the corridor'),[84] with rooms to spare for Carmen, an Italian-speaking Yugoslav who was Claire's *femme de chambre*, and the children's nanny Polly O'Meara. Claude and her brothers were taught French at school, spoke Italian with Carmen, and from George the chauffeur they picked up some Greek. But their first language was English, and this they learnt with a slight Irish lilt from Polly, forcing their French-born father to learn English too. Polly O'Meara had been hired by Felix and Rosette after Claire's birth in 1901, and she continued in the family until well after the Second World War, providing Claude with a stock of reminiscences reaching back over fifty years. In the mid-1950s when Claude began living with Lawrence Durrell and as he was writing *The Alexandria Quartet*, Claude was herself writing a series of novels, one dedicated to Polly O'Meara and another to her uncle George de Menasce, to which she appended the motto 'Se non è vero, è ben trovato', adding, 'In common with other story-tellers, I have used true and fictitious ingredients. None of the characters is a portrait of any one person . . . but some reflect facets of several personalities.'[85]

This last remark was a nod towards the *Quartet*, in which Durrell was now drawing on Claude's knowledge of the city as he wrote about the Coptic Hosnani family – the

38   The marriage in 1931 of Denise de Menasce (second from left) to Alfred Mawas, who stands between Rosette and Claire. At the far left is Polly O'Meara, the repository of the family's history. Polly had been governess to Rosette's children, was now governess to Claire's children, and would become governess to the children of Claire's daughter Claude, who would pass on Polly's stories about the Menasces to Lawrence Durrell when he wrote *The Alexandria Quartet.*

crippled father, the beautiful mother, and the two Hosnani sons, one a financier, the other a religious mystic – and the cause in which they became involved, a Jewish Palestine that would stand as an ally with the Copts against growing Muslim power in Egypt. Except that inside Durrell's mind the models for the Hosnanis were not Copts: they were the brilliant flowering of cosmopolitan Alexandria; they were Jewish and their name was Menasce.

The apartment building was divided in two, each half with its own entrance and lift, the roof serving as a common playground for Marta Loria, who lived on the first floor at 65 Rue Fuad, and Claude and her brothers on the top floor at 63. 'I used to see Claude a lot up there, she was very pretty. But she belonged to a different group of people; my father was very Italian, this is probably one reason, and she was younger than me.'

    There were nevertheless links between the two families. Marta's father, Alessandro Loria, was an architect who most famously left his mark on the city with the Hotel Cecil, a crenellated Moorish palace overlooking the Eastern Harbour near the Italian Consulate. He was commissioned to build the hotel by Albert Metzger, a German who during the First World War had discovered the inconvenience of being an enemy alien and had since become a British citizen; when he opened his hotel in 1929, Metzger at first called it the Regina Palace but within a year renamed it the Cecil after the grandest of London hotels.[86] It was immediately recognised as the finest hotel in Alexandria, and for Durrell 'it was always preferable to Cairo's Shepheard's Hotel because of its proximity to the sea'.[87] The Cecil became a recurrent landmark in the *Quartet*, where Justine 'would perhaps be waiting, gloved hands folded on her handbag, staring out through the windows upon which the sea crawled and sprawled, climbing and subsiding, across the screen of palms in the little municipal square which flapped and creaked like loose sails'.[88]

Giuseppe Alessandro Loria was born in Mansourah in 1880 and after spending time in Tuscany and Cairo, he finally settled in Alexandria in 1914. There he married into the wealthy Campos family of lawyers and *commerçants* and built their home at 6 Rue Neroutsos, the continuation of the Rue des Ptolémées, on the south side of the Rue Fuad. Loria lived and worked at 65 Rue Fuad, his rear-facing apartment on the first floor and his offices on the mezzanine below. 'My father's life was his work', remembered his daughter Marta. 'He worked hard, seven days a week; he had no hobbies. Only during the last ten years of his life' – he died in 1937 – 'would he take a day off, wandering out by Mareotis and into the surrounding desert.' There during the First World War Felix de Menasce had bought from the Bedouins a vast tract of land with the intention of settling it with immigrant Jews if Balfour failed to declare Palestine a Jewish homeland; in the event, Menasce had Loria develop part of the site as the winter desert resort of Ikingi Mariut – the spot that had been Forster's Solitary Place.

In a city whose architecture was playfully eclectic, no one played over such a variety of styles as Alessandro Loria, who also built the Italian Hospital at 3 Rue du Palais to the east of the Rond Point (now Sharia Dalal Dessouki off Midan Wabour el Maya); the new Jewish Hospital at 40 Rue Moharrem Bey; the National Bank of Egypt with its mosaic medallions and ascending arabesques on the Rue Talaat Harb in the centre of town; and several of the most delightful buildings along the sweep of the Eastern Harbour, including, to the east of the Cecil, the Venetian-style Lido House Hotel, now crumbling like the Majestic and long given over to offices and rented rooms, but its delicate tracery of arches and its intricately patterned coloured brickwork still lending the Corniche a carnival air.

Looking at childhood photographs of herself dressed in the black shirt and blue neckerchief of the new Italy, Marta also recalled that 'my father was a real fascist'. Nor was that all, for along with the Cecil, the hospitals, the bank and the rest, there is another monument to Loria in the city: in the garden of the Grand Synagogue on the Rue Nebi Daniel is a building which houses the Rabbinate and what remains of the Jewish community association. Inside, inscribed on its walls, is a list of the community's principal

39   Jean de Menasce, who converted to Catholicism and became a Dominican in France, scandalised Jewish society in Alexandria when he returned to the city in 1932 and gave a sermon at St Catherine's Catholic Cathedral. Jean had known Cavafy and promoted his poetry at Oxford; T. S. Eliot called him 'my best translator' after he did *The Waste Land* into French.

benefactors, among them the Menasces, the Suareses, the Cattaouis, the Riches, the Banouns – and Alessandro Loria, who as well as being a good Italian fascist was a good Alexandrian Jew.

Along with the Cecil, the Atelier is one of the most frequently mentioned landmarks in *The Alexandria Quartet*. Durrell himself lectured there on T. S. Eliot and Cavafy, his friend Clea Badaro painted there, and it is at the Atelier that Durrell has his alter ego, Darley, first meet Justine:

> I had been persuaded to lecture on the native poet of the city at the Atelier des Beaux Arts – a sort of club where gifted amateurs of the arts could meet, rent studios and so on. . . . What an impertinence to lecture upon an ironist who so naturally, and with such fineness of instinct took his subject-matter from the streets and brothels of Alexandria! And to be talking, moreover, not to an audience of haberdashers' assistants and small clerks – his immortals – but to a dignified semi-circle of society ladies for whom the culture he represented was a sort of blood-bank: they had come along for a transfusion. Many had actually foregone a bridge-party to do so, though they knew that instead of being uplifted they would be stupefied.

When it was over,

> I noticed that they had left behind them one solitary student of the passions and the arts. . . . She looked to me a trifle unbalanced, as she watched me with a candour I found embarrassing – it was as if she were trying to decide to what use I could be put. 'I liked' she said 'the way you quoted his lines about the city. Your Greek is good. Doubtless you are a writer.' I said: 'Doubtless'. Not to be known always wounds.[89]

The Atelier was founded in 1935 by the painter Mohammed Nagui (brother of Effat Nagui, whom Durrell met when he returned to the Ambron villa in 1977) and by Cavafy's friend Gaston Zananiri, though it might not have been founded at all had not Brinton introduced Zananiri to Thomas Whittemore of the Byzantine Institute of America. In 1932 Whittemore had just pulled off a remarkable coup. At the Turkish conquest of Constantinople in 1453, the great sixth-century Byzantine Church of the Haghia Sophia had been converted to a mosque and its offending mosaics plastered over. There was no chance that so potent a monument could ever be returned to Christian use, but Whittemore had persuaded Kemal Atatürk to allow him to restore the mosaics and expose them again to public view by converting the church-cum-mosque into a museum.

Whenever Whittemore visited Alexandria, he stayed with the Brintons at Bulkeley, from where he would call on Zananiri at his home near the Sporting Club. There, as Zananiri put it, 'He gave me details of the nights he spent with Kemal Atatürk to obtain the authorisation to uncover the mosaics.' The least of the mosaics could rouse Whittemore to ecstasies, as when he uncovered a number of small black crosses on the lunettes of the narthex and on the soffits of the vault, saying, 'They constitute no trivial repetition of a single shape; but each meets the vision as if charioted on a billow of light, each with an appeal as thrilling, and compelling, and personal as it seems possible to experience.' Zananiri was no less thrilled by Whittemore. 'One day I was driving with Whittemore and he said bring me to the desert. I took my car and we went outside Alexandria in the desert of Mariut. There we climbed up a cliff and there was a remarkable silence, and Whittemore told me, "Listen to the tumultuous silence of the desert – Ecoute le silence tumultueux du desert". And so I wrote a poem.

> The silence is profound
> Listen to the advent of evening
> We are alone here with our desire,
> our hopes.'[90]

Soon, however, their relationship exploded in a scene of homosexual jealousy involving a lithe young American called Kirk Prince ('of an old Southern family'), whom Zananiri had installed at La Maison sur la Dune at Mandara, his isolated retreat standing among

40 The architect Alessandro Loria, who delighted in Venetian and Moorish styles, most famously built the Hotel Cecil on the Eastern Harbour Corniche.

palms along what were still then the coastal dunes towards Montazah. When Zananiri and Kirk Prince were not together, 'we exchanged letters, letters which were remarkable!' – letters that disappeared one day when Kirk Prince found out about Thomas Whittemore. 'I said what did you do with our letters? He said our love letters? They are for the sewage! I've destroyed everything!' and with that Kirk Prince sailed away from Alexandria.

Zananiri followed him to Athens, accepting a convenient invitation from the Greek government to give a series of lectures. Cavafy had only recently died, and Zananiri, who had spoken at his graveside, proposed a talk on the poet. But the Greek government would not hear of it 'because of Cavafy's reputation', so Zananiri lectured on the Byzantine Church instead. In Athens Zananiri found that Kirk Prince had become a *danseur mondain* at the Hotel Grande Bretagne: 'the drinking was working into his head, and the American diplomatic attaché was obliged to embark Kirk on a boat back to the States. That was it' – the end of an affair that, as Zananiri spoke of it at the Couvent des

Dominicains on the Rue du Faubourg St Honoré in Paris more than sixty years later, made him tremble with emotion.

Zananiri's lectures on the ecclesiastical history of Byzantium were given in Athens in 1934 at a place called the Atelier, where the Greek government had also invited Mohammed Nagui to exhibit. Both men placed Egypt, with its mixture of religious and cultural traditions, within the context of the wider Mediterranean, as expressed by a major work of Nagui's, *The School of Alexandria*, a nod to Raphael's fresco *The School of Athens*.[91] In Nagui's painting, its background a panorama of ancient Alexandria's Eastern Harbour, the centre is dominated by Alexander the Great, with St Catherine, Archimedes and the Arab philosopher Averroes standing in the foreground, flanked by a host of notable modern native Egyptians on one side, among them the writer Taha Hussein, and Egyptian residents of foreign descent on the other, among them Cavafy.[92]

Nagui was typical of those artists, writers and intellectuals who were prominent in Egypt between 1919 and Nasser's coup d'état in 1952. A Turko-Egyptian who had studied law in Lyon and the fine arts in Florence, he was an ardent supporter of Zaghloul's nationalist movement while being fully integrated into Alexandria's Levantine society. As for Zananiri, 'my idea has always been the world, ecumenism'. On his father's side his family were Syrian Greek Catholics who had settled in Alexandria in 1610, while 'my mother was a Jewess, a Hungarian, a beautiful woman. I'm a mixture, as Alexandria was a Jewish, Greek and Syrian city.' In 1931 he had gone to Palestine, in Jerusalem meeting Madame Ben Yahuda, the widow of the man who, by compiling his great dictionary, almost single-handedly renovated the Hebrew language, transforming the word of the Prophets into the tongue of everyday life. Zananiri was inspired to write an account of Ben Yahuda's life and work, but in doing so would hardly have seen himself as promoting a devisive cause; instead Zananiri looked back to the past, to the empire of the Ptolemies. 'For me Alexandria was a universe. Alexandria hadn't changed. When I would drive my car along the Corniche and saw all the people parading along, I said to myself these are the same people who lived here two thousand years ago.'

The idea of a cultural centre like the Athens Atelier appealed to both Zananiri and Nagui, and together they decided to transplant the idea to Alexandria, the former responsible for its literary activities, the latter for fine arts, while for music they drew in Forster's old friend Enrico Terni, an anti-fascist Italian Jew.[93] But their intention was greater than to found a centre where a diversity of arts would be brought together under one roof; their hope for Egypt's future, their political as much as their cultural hope, was that it should follow the diverse yet inclusive Mediterranean model of cosmopolitan Alexandria.

Brinton unwittingly followed in Forster's footsteps along the shores of Mareotis even before the publication of the first edition of *Alexandria* towards the end of 1922. That was the year, as his son John recalled, that they first met Wilfred Jennings Bramly: 'Being adventurous spirits we began to explore the surrounding country. We drove east to

Rosetta and south to Cairo. Then we turned our brand new Model T Ford westwards and headed one Sunday towards the desert of Mariut. We had heard of Bramly Bey, this remarkable man who was Governor of the Western Desert Province of Egypt and who lived in his own capital town of Burg el Arab, and we were curious.'

In those days motor cars venturing into the desert passed through a stone gateway on the outskirts of Alexandria, where travellers' names and reasons for their journey were 'recorded in a large red book by a coal black Sudanese, a member of the Frontier Administration's Camel Corps. If we did not return at the appointed time a search party would be sent out. I remember a large sign over the gate stating that only Fords and Rolls Royces were recommended for desert use and felt comforted.'

In a while they were bumping along a wretched track, following the stone cairns that led the way. 'After driving for an hour over low ridges with an occasional glimpse of the sea on our right, we saw, from the crest of a rise, towers and battlements looming in the distance. We drove up to a fine stone tower pierced by an arched entrance. On each side were Roman lion-headed gargoyles. A Bedouin gate-keeper approached and took the card my father held out to him. He salaamed and disappeared into the recesses of garden and buildings. Soon we heard steps approaching and a slightly nasal voice called out a greeting. "Come in, come in. Where have you been anyway? Told you were coming. My man telephoned ahead. Watch your step. I'm Bramly. Glad to see you. Lunch will be ready in a few minutes. Family upstairs. Delighted you've come, Judge Brinton, and brought your boy."' As they passed through the high encircling walls – 'Windsor Castle', as Bramly called it – 'a new life began for us. From that day Burg el Arab became our second home.'[94]

Bramly's original intention for Burg el Arab was that the Western Desert, instead of being held by force, should become a place of security and prosperity by engaging the interests of the Senussi Bedouins who roamed both sides of the Egyptian-Libyan border. They had been stirred up by Turkish and German agents during the war, and it had taken thirty-five thousand British troops to contain them. But for centuries there had been a carrying trade across the desert between Egypt and the interior of Africa, and Bramly's idea was to facilitate that trade and also to draw the Senussi into some measure of social and political intercourse with Egypt by creating his 'town', not as a place of residence – the Bedouin preferred to live wherever they pitched their tents – but as a terminus for their caravans, with a storehouse and market place, a court of justice and a mosque, and a library in which they could keep their genealogies and other tribal records. The Senussi were enthusiastic and soon looked upon him as their protector and friend, calling him, in a play on 'Bramly', Abu Ramleh, Father of the Sands.

But work on the town was overtaken by the urgent need to do something for the widows of Senussi tribesmen killed during the war. Early in 1919 the British military authorities gave Bramly LE200 to distribute among them in compensation, but when he pointed out that this would barely amount to a pound a woman, he was told to use the money as he thought best. Bramly speculated in wool, which when it came onto the

41   Burg el Arab in the late 1930s. Bramly designed each of the towered houses for the new residents who made the desert settlement their home. Later, in *The Alexandria Quartet*, Durrell would make Burg el Arab the site of the Summer Palace built by Nessim for the mysterious Justine.

market a few months later increased his capital to LE300, and with it he built just to the east of the town a tower with adjoining cloisters – the carpet 'factory' where eventually 450 women and girls wove small rugs of camels' and goats' hair in a traditional pattern of indigo on white, which when sold in Alexandria earned them LE12,000 a year.

Egyptian independence in 1922, however, was a disaster for Burg el Arab, nationalists condemning it as unpatriotic, an intolerable gesture towards the Bedouins, who were traditionally Egypt's enemies. Official difficulties were thrown in its way, funds were cut off, and in 1924 Bramly resigned, leaving 'this austere beautiful town',[95] in Forster's words, standing silent and empty.

Bramly retired a mile to the north, where on the crest of a ridge overlooking the arm of Mariut, with views towards Taposiris and the sea beyond, he again set to work, this time on a home of his own. He was 'a born builder', Judge Brinton remarked, 'an artist in stone', and from his long association with Italy – his maternal grandmother was the daughter of a marchese of Ferrara – showed 'a leaning to the Italian'.[96] His house, which he planted about with olive groves and built over an ancient cistern fed by rainwater that filtered through the rock, suggested a world almost as self-contained as the medieval monastery it resembled, with round-arched windows set high in the walls and a great dining room giving on to a vegetable garden enclosed on one side by a vaulted arcade. The furnishings were few but well chosen – some lovely pieces of Italian and Jacobean furniture, beautiful Persian carpets that had been received as gifts from pilgrims on their way to Mecca, and the blue and white rugs of the Bedouins.

But off in the distance the Bedouin's carpet factory stood abandoned to the blowing sands. The nationalists were not to be blamed, was Forster's reaction: 'Old countries can't learn their lesson, so how should young ones? Egypt for the Egyptians, Britain for the British, France for the French! No country has seen that nationalism leads to dis-comfort within and disaster without.' The whole business was 'sad', but also 'inevitable' and 'quite comprehensible', he wrote in 1924.[97] Thirty-four years later and two years after Nasser's seizure of the Suez Canal and the combined British, French and Israeli attack on Egypt in 1956, Bramly, then in his eighty-eighth year, was thrown out of the country by Egypt's new rulers, his home on the ridge handed over to Field Marshal Abdel Hakim Amer, who was 'suicided' after the debacle of the 1967 Six Day War for which he had shown himself lamentably prepared. Nasser himself later occupied Bramly's home, which became and remains a presidential rest house: there Anwar Sadat secretly planned the 1973 October War.

But before that, in the 1930s, Burg el Arab was to have other inhabitants. In the pages of *The Alexandria Quartet* it is the 'summer palace' built by Nessim Hosnani for his wife Justine; in reality it became the desert retreat of Judge Brinton, his second wife Geneva, a fellow Philadelphian whom he had married in 1927, and several of their friends. At first they were content to motor out from Alexandria on weekend excursions into the Western Desert, picnicking on the shores of Mariut, bathing in the amethyst sea within sight of the temple of Osiris at Abusir, or sometimes venturing as far as the escarpment behind Alamein, where cautiously they would work their way down into the vast and lifeless Qattara Depression several hundred feet below. Carrying tents, spare tyres and supplies of food and water, and spades for digging themselves out of the sand, they were a self-sufficient camping community for whom the desert was a playground. But in time they sought something more permanent and turned to Bramly for a solution. With his help the government allowed them to rent and refurbish the living quarters of the old carpet factory for use as a weekend Desert Club, then in 1937 it permitted the con-struction of houses to Bramly's design within the walls of Burg el Arab itself.

The rebirth of Burg el Arab coincided with work on the second edition of Forster's *Alexandria* and involved many of the same people. Frank Cramer-Roberts, a civil engineer and member of the Desert Club, helped Forster with the military history of the Napoleonic period and with some of the maps. Anthony de Cosson was not surpris-ingly the most adventurous member of the Desert Club, for as well as being director of the Desert Railways, he had learnt much about desert lore from Bramly, who was his brother-in-law. In 1935 de Cosson published *Mareotis*, the classic account of the topography, history and ancient monuments of the northwestern desert of Egypt and of Lake Mariut, which Durrell, when he came to write *The Alexandria Quartet*, was to read and heavily underline. His authority was felt in many parts of the revision of Forster's guidebook, though usually through the contributions of his niece, Bramly's bright and vivacious daughter Vivien, who was then just into her thirties. 'Miss Vivien Jennings-Bramly', Forster would write in his new preface, 'has been both editor and contributor', revising the text and rewriting entire sections, 'notably the sections on the Graeco-Roman Museum, and on the Western Desert, which she knows so well. Without her, nothing could have been achieved.'[98]

Soon the new residents of Burg el Arab had the pleasure of seeing the camels arriving with their loads of stone and watching their houses rise before their eyes. 'And beautiful stone it was, much of it from the ruins of ancient structures in the surrounding neighbourhood', wrote Judge Brinton. 'The presence of ancient wall handles carved into some of the blocks was evidence enough of their earlier usefulness, say a couple of thousand years ago.'[99] The benefits of ownership had been pressed on the Brintons by Vivien: 'You would still have it as a possession should some of the many "ifs" the future frowns with make your stay, or our stay, in this country impossible – But "Gather ye rose buds (desert houses – pleasures – and for us dear neighbours) while ye may." '[100]

The ominous course of international events very soon altered relations between Egypt and Britain. The Italians, through their conquest of Libya in the 1920s and now through their invasion of Ethiopia in 1935, threatened to close on Egypt like a vice, convincing Egyptian leaders of every party that after all they should concede Britain's case for its strategic interests as expressed in the reserved points of the 1922 Declaration. Elections in May 1936 were won by the Wafd under Mustafa Nahas, who as prime minister led an all-party delegation in negotiations with Britain that within a few months broke through the deadlock of fourteen years.

The Anglo-Egyptian Treaty, signed in August 1936, replaced the Declaration with an alliance that allowed for a British military presence of ten thousand troops along the Suez Canal, the freedom of the skies for the Royal Air Force and the use by the Royal Navy of Alexandria's Western Harbour. Britain had got its way on the first two of its four reserved points, the right to protect its imperial communications and to defend Egypt against foreign aggression.

On their side the Egyptians celebrated the treaty, as it provided for the alliance to be renegotiated after twenty years, meaning that Egypt could be shot of the British within a generation. Though Egypt had also to concede Britain's indefinite control over the Sudan, the treaty pledged British help in getting the Capitulations abolished, and the following year agreement was reached at the Convention of Montreux to end the Capitulations forthwith while allowing the Mixed Courts to continue for a further twelve years.

In *Mountolive*, the third volume of *The Alexandria Quartet*, Durrell described what must have been the anxieties of some as this period of grace slipped away: 'Europeans had still the right, by treaty, to submit their judicial problems or answer charges against them at Les Tribunaux Mixtes, European courts with European lawyers to prosecute or defend. But the Egyptian judicial system (if one could dare to call it that) was run directly by men of Memlik's stamp, the anachronistic survivals of a feudalism as terrible as it was meaningless.'[101] Come 1949 and Europeans too would be subject to the Egyptian judicial system.

But most non-Muslim families of foreign origin had lived in Egypt for generations and very few thought there would be no future for them in the country they called home. They trusted that equal treatment before the law would mean they would suffer no discrimination in employment or in the running of their businesses, and they also put their hopes in the creation of a middle class that would include Egyptians and foreigners alike, and in which the place of foreigners would be assured by their expertise and by the proverbial tolerance of their hosts. It was also comfortable to believe that nothing had changed since 1919 when Saad Zaghloul had declared, 'The present movement in Egypt is not a religious movement, for Muslims and Copts demonstrate together, and neither is it a xenophobic movement or a movement calling for Arab unity.'[102] Zaghloul's conception of nationhood, which he derived from European liberal thought, was territorial and inclusive, and indeed Copts especially but also Jews were prominent members of the Wafd. With the signing of the treaty, however, and the lessening of British influence, there was a rise in pan-Arabism and Islamism and signs of a deterioration in the relationship between the vast Muslim majority and the Coptic, Jewish and foreign minorities, leaving some with a certain sense of anxiety, what one called 'this little fear'.[103]

Meanwhile, on 28 April 1936, while negotiations for the treaty were still underway, Sir Miles Lampson, the British high commissioner, was urgently summoned from an official lunch by Walter Smart, who told him that King Fuad had died that morning. A week later Fuad's sixteen-year-old son, who had rushed back from his studies in England at the news and had come up by train from Alexandria, was greeted by Lampson at the Cairo railway station. 'Farouk looked pale and decidedly spotty! Poor boy. . . . I quite realised that in the next little time things were going to be extremely difficult for the young King and that he was going to feel the want of someone to lean upon.'[104] Lampson, who was a giant of a man and towered over the Egyptian leaders with whom he was conducting the negotiations for the British, had thought Egypt should become part of the British Empire and agreed with Anthony Eden, the foreign secretary, that despite a treaty the option should not be ruled out for the future. But as it was, the Anglo-Egyptian Treaty meant that Lampson would be high commissioner no longer, the post replaced by that of ambassador to a sovereign state. But the man remained and was no less patronising than before, especially towards Farouk whom he continued to call 'the boy'. 'I personally regret', said Grafftey-Smith, 'that Sir Miles Lampson remained in

Cairo as Britain's first Ambassador. . . . He was physically and temperamentally inca-pable of giving any convincing impression of change, and this had unhappy conse-quences.'[105]

'I can still see him', Judge Brinton recalled of Farouk, 'as he entered the great hall of the Mixed Courts on the occasion of the signing of the Treaty of Montreux, a slim fair-haired young man acclaimed by the press – and indeed by his people – as Egypt's "Prince Charming". A curious remark which he once made to my wife often comes back to me: "You know I was brought up the hard way". Curious, yes, outwardly – but perhaps to those familiar with the whole story, holding much of the secret of a grim disaster.'[106]

Early in 1937 out at Burg el Arab Vivien Jennings Bramly was lamenting the with-drawal of their local detachment of British troops. 'We are expecting a batch of Tommies to tea. It may be our last, I am sorry to say, as I hear they are leaving. We will miss our post – and so I expect will the bedouins.'[107] She was busy just then dashing back and forth in her motor car between Burg el Arab and Alexandria, where she would stay with the Brintons when following in Forster's footsteps through the Graeco-Roman Museum. 'The visitor who "goes through" it', Forster had written in the first edition of his guidebook, 'will find afterwards that it has gone through him. . . . He should not visit the collection until he has learned or imagined something about the ancient city, and he should visit certain definite objects, and then come away – a golden rule indeed in all museums. He may then find that a scrap of the past has come alive.'[108] Vivien would pass her revisions on to Judge Brinton along with numer-ous asides, which Brinton in turn sent to Forster, much to Vivien's abashment. 'It made me rather uncomfortable to see how much I had been quoted to Mr F!' she wrote to Brinton's wife Geneva in Ramleh. 'Should any further mention ever be made, though, I think a word should be said of the quite exceptional pleasure I got from visiting the Museum in his (ghostly) company.'[109]

In all her dashing about, Vivien did in fact find that the museum and indeed the city would often go through her rather than she through them, and for remedy she would turn to the Brintons. What was the future of the casino at San Stefano, did the Ramleh tram stops still have the same names, and what about the Hellenistic necropolis found in 1933 beneath the British barracks at Mustafa Pasha, went one appeal to Judge Brinton: 'I have seen the tomb', she told him, 'but could not describe it accurately from memory. Could you get someone to go down and take notes in situ? Mr Marshall has an excel-lent clear way of putting things and is most familiar with Forster's own method.'[110] And from Burg el Arab in a flap to Geneva: 'Do you remember those last notes in our canter round the Museum? I may have stuffed them into that "working copy" of Forster's guide left in my room (at your house) – that is their best chance. Or they may have flown somewhere – under a bed – or even in the library – I'm afraid they will then be quite lost. If so I shall have to beg you – or anyone you find at a loose end – to trot over to the Museum and verify or correct one or two things.'[111]

Eventually by July 1937 the research, rewriting and editing of the second edition was all but done and Vivien set sail from Alexandria to go over the revised text with Forster in London. 'I told you', she wrote to John Brinton, 'you might sometime get an SOS re the Guide: Brace yourself, for the time has come. Mr Forster and I have been through it all together – our last session ending close on midnight! – and the result, though very satisfactory, left a few loose threads which we will be most grateful to you to tie up if and when you can. Poor John! You will I fear have to run about a good deal.'[112]

This call to run about the city seemed a welcome reintroduction to the Alexandria that John had left ten years before. Ask Adriani the date of the black bowl signed by Monomachus, began the list from Vivien and Forster. Has the inscription by the entrance to the Coptic cathedral ('shortly to be removed') been removed? Does the gun still lie in the sand atop the hill of Abou el Nawatir? Does a chain of reefs still close the entrance of the Western Harbour? Is the pretty mosaic under a broken tin shelter at Canopus still there? Are the Chaldeans still looking for a plot of ground on which to build a church? But John's heart sank when he returned to his childhood playground at Stanley Bay and found that the little dusty path he had followed down to the sea was a broad highway, that the circle of rocks was built over with rows of identical cabins and with a concrete terrace where an orchestra played jazz tunes and people sat at tables drinking beer. Since being civilised, Stanley Bay had gained something of a reputation for being a haunt for paedophiles. The Russian general with his white goatee and his wife who made the delicious ices were gone, replaced by a café brimming with waiters. But at least the Chinese pagoda had survived. 'Bravo! I thought. A Chinese pagoda in Egypt looking out over the Mediterranean. It shouted defiance.' And as though in a vision the scenes of his childhood returned, the gaiety, the colour, the shouts of wild delight, but then 'the dream faded slowly away and I felt I had seen my shadow in the sand'.[113]

Back in 1926, the year before his father married Geneva, John had been summoned to America by his mother to continue his schooling, though only until the age of sixteen, when he was put into her family's business. The McFaddens of Philadelphia were one of the biggest cotton brokers in the United States, and John was apprenticed first at their branch at Waco, Texas, then at Memphis, Tennessee, where he met and fell in love with Josephine Ingram, a spirited and beautiful blonde debutante. But at news of their engagement, the McFaddens tried to keep the couple apart, arguing that John was too young to earn his way in the world. So they eloped, and at the end of February 1937, a month after their marriage, John, twenty-one, and Josie, twenty, sailed into the harbour at Alexandria.

'John's father met us and he couldn't be nicer. He's really a darling and he told John I was terribly pretty and very charming. I think he likes me', Josie wrote to her mother. Brinton also helpfully queried her on the essentials: 'He asked me about my French and said I'd have to start practicing it and asked me about my tennis game.' Arriving home at Ramleh, Geneva 'came out and took me in her arms and welcomed me', and gave her and John 'a wonderful big room with a tremendous window through which the sun is

42　The Brinton family in a beach cabin at Sidi Bishr in Ramleh. From the left: Judge and Geneva Brinton, Josie and John Brinton, and on the far right a friend of the family, Charmian.

now pouring', while 'at night we sleep under huge mosquito netting which stretches over the entire bed and tucks in tightly under the covers. I love it. I feel exactly as if I were living way out in the tropics.' The following day, 'we went on a picnic about noon with some friends of Tante's' (as John called his stepmother, Josie calling Judge Brinton 'Mr Tante') '– Lady Barker and her daughter, about thirty-five. It was down on the beach. There's a wonderful beach here with a long string of bath houses. . . . Imagine being able to swim in February. It's as warm as late May in Memphis here now.'

'Alexandria', Josie wrote to her mother, 'is about six or seven hundred thousand, twice as big as Memphis n'est pas? Great tall palm trees and arabs – thousands of arabs in great long robes that look like night shirts and red fezzes. There are the most wonderful street noises, birds chirping and cries – they sound like the negroes selling fruit at home and yet they are long drawn out and of course in Arabic – It's so hard to remember the servants are Arabic and not negro. When we came the house man who's been with John's father for years shook my hand and then kissed it – I was amazed naturally. It's all so much nicer than John painted it even and I'm just as happy as a lark. We're going to a dinner party and to the opera tomorrow night – really it's as gay as Memphis I believe. Everyone is so nice to you. It's a lot like Memphis, it really is.'[114]

A week later Josie went with John and Geneva for 'tea with some delightful English people who live in the desert. The father of the family is a sort of king of the Bedouins – the Arabs who live in ramshackle tents in the desert. He has built this lovely home out there for little or nothing. He is now building a mosque for the Bedouins who live near his place.' That evening they went to 'this club house' where 'we had dinner and sat around the fire and read. Then John and I took a walk in the desert. There was a full moon and it was so lovely. Not a soul anywhere around except every now and then a Bedouin tent. The club is part of an old Arab village. It looks like the headquarters of the Foreign Legion you see in the movies. The name of it is Burg el Arab.'[115]

A few days later Josie was telling her mother how 'It's really necessary to know how to speak French here. We went to a luncheon the other day that an Egyptian gave and everyone spoke French. Course I could understand a little but I was afraid to speak anything but things like bonjour and good bye.'[116] But though the language of the city was French, the French themselves were generally too immersed in patriotic nostalgia to get into the swim of Alexandrian society. The Tortillias, however, who were descended from an engineer who had come to Egypt with Ferdinand de Lesseps, were an exception.

'Really, Mummy, this was like the movies!' Josie wrote home a fortnight after her arrival, having begun her day with a visit to Gharbaniat, three miles west of Burg el Arab. 'A man named Tortillia who lives in Alexandria and has a beautiful Persian house in the city has built a veritable castle way out in the desert. It is enormous with a swimming pool and a deck tennis court. There must be ten bedrooms, a beautiful entrance hall with tapestries and armour, a game room downstairs with a ping pong table and five or six bathrooms with modern plumbing – And he only uses it for weekends in the desert! It's beautifully furnished. There were eighteen people for lunch – ten nationalities! French, English, German, Hungarian, Romanian, American, Egyptian, Italian and I forget the other two. We had shrimp, chicken, wines, the most delicious dessert you've ever tasted – Really you can't imagine how amazing it all was way out in the desert, miles from civilisation.'

'We got home about five o'clock and then Johnny and I had to dash off to a cocktail party on a British warship. Doesn't that sound exciting? It was HMS (His Majesty's Ship in case you're puzzled) Furious. The ship was anchored about a mile out in the harbour so we had to take a motor launch from the dock out to the ship. Course it was streaming with lights and flags and the most beautiful sight. The Furious is an airplane carrier so they converted the place where the airplanes are carried into a sort of long room. All the planes were taken out and the flags of all nations hung along the sides. The American flag was right opposite the English flag. There was an orchestra and a place for dancing. Really it was wonderful fun.' After dinner and dancing back in town, Josie summed up her day: 'There's almost nothing one can't get in Alexandria. It's a very modern, up-to-date city. My Max Factor lipstick was all used up so I had to get another one which I did right away.'[117]

And if everything about Alexandria seemed 'amazing' to Josie and 'like the movies', she discovered that even 'the movie house is amazing' when she went to see *Romeo and Juliet*: 'The picture of course is in English but down at the bottom the conversation is shown in French and then they have a small screen on the side of the main one on which the conversation is shown in Greek and Arabic. Doesn't that sound cosmopolitan?'[118]

Oswald Finney and his wife Josa were Jasper and Geneva Brinton's closest friends in Alexandria, and by virtue of being the richest foreigner in Egypt Finney was the unofficial head of Alexandria's British community. Being childless, the Finneys all but adopted John and Josie, who lived rent-free in one of their properties overlooking the sea at Glymenopoulo; they were also benefactors of the Archaeological Society, and inside the Rabbinate Oswald Finney's name appears on its walls, his donation to the Jewish community exceeded by not even the wealthiest Jews themselves. It may all have been good business, for Oswald had, as Josie said, 'his finger in every pie in Alexandria'.[119] Together with Greek and Jewish partners, Finney had become a major player in the cotton export market (the Alexandria Commercial Company) and in local textile manufacturing (Filature Nationale d'Egypte); he also produced oxyacetylene, controlled the making of yeast and the distribution of milk, had wide investments in property, and from 1925 was the proprietor of the Société Orientale de Publicité, the group that published the leading English- and French-language newspapers in the country, the *Egyptian Gazette*, the *Egyptian Mail*, *Le Progrès égyptien* and *La Bourse égyptienne*.

By force of their fabulous parties and legendary wealth the Finneys epitomised the gilded age of Alexandria between the wars. 'All the German, French and English tennis stars have been here playing in an international championship', Josie wrote to her mother. Also Micheal MacLiammoir's Dublin's Gate Theatre troupe was in town. 'We've been going to the tennis matches every day and the theatre every night and cocktail parties and teas in between. Monday night we all went to Mrs Finney's dance for the tennis players. She's the one who has four Rolls Royces and lives in an entire building and calls me her namesake. The dance was loads of fun, champagne and caviar being served as if it were water and jam.'[120]

In making his fortune Oswald accounted his luck to Josa, who was an unsophisticated girl of sixteen when he, in his forties, met her in Trieste in the 1920s. Most probably her background was respectably middle class, the Brintons thought, and certainly both were Roman Catholics, she ardently so. However, Josa's past remained a mystery, giving rise to extravagant rumours in Alexandria, among them that Finney had met her in a house of child prostitution. Three years passed before he married her, and meanwhile, as he was grooming her to become a society hostess, what Judge Brinton called Finney's 'apparently infallible business judgement'[121] made him fantastically rich, so that from owning a single apartment at 3 Rue Rolo (now 3 Rue Docteur Ahmed Abdel Salam, just north of the Rue Sultan Hussein), from which he was too superstitious to move, he

43　Josa and Oswald Finney on the roof terrace of their house in Alexandria. Finney, who dealt in property, newspapers, cotton and onions, was the richest foreigner in Egypt and the unofficial head of the British community.

was able to take over one floor after another until he was master of the entire building, ripping out its insides and rebuilding it as an Italianate palazzo.

'I've never seen anyone with as much pep and vivacity', was how Josie described Mrs Finney at their first meeting. 'She rushes around absolutely hysterically, really runs all over this enormous house.' Two lifts and a marble staircase rose through five floors in all, from the gymnasium and swimming pool on the ground floor to the fourth floor ballroom and rooftop terrace with its erotic statuary in Graeco-Roman style and a spectacular panorama of Mareotis, the city and the sea. 'Throughout everything there is a great profusion of marble and ah yes – Mr Finney collects tapestries and he has enormous ones that cover an entire wall. The ballroom is lined with them. Really I was so amazed I was wide-eyed. They gave a lovely costume ball just before we arrived. They're constantly giving parties.'[122]

The Finneys' annual costume balls usually coincided with Alexandria's carnival season. 'Carnival time could not pass unnoticed in our cosmopolitan town', recalled

44   The Finneys' ballroom. By force of their fabulous parties and legendary wealth, the Finneys epitomised the gilded age of Alexandria between the wars. Durrell wrote their famous annual costume balls into *The Alexandria Quartet*, where they are the settings for intrigue and murder.

Count Patrice de Zogheb. The last days before Lent were enlivened by rejoicing and masquerading in the streets, houses and places of public entertainment. 'There was a procession of carnival cars full of gay beauties with masks and dominoes romping through the streets. In the evening, there would be a veglione or masked ball, usually in favour of some charity or other, at the opera house and revelling would go on till dawn all over the town.'[123]

Everyone who was anyone looked forward to the Finneys' costume balls – the Benachis, the Choremis, the Zervudachis, the Peels, the Barkers, the Carters, the Tortillias, the Ambrons, the Rolos, the Menasces, the Vincendons. Patrice's cousin, the Countess Mary de Zogheb, noted in her diaries her attendance at nearly every Finney ball from 1927 – dressed variously as a pierrot, a car mechanic, a sailor, a harlequin, a gypsy, a Tyrolean, a Cuban peasant and in 1939 a Palestinian. Being a countess, she could afford to dress down rather than up, and her costumes paled against most, as when one rotund Armenian went as Henry VIII with six wives in tow, though no one dressed down quite so much as a rather smaller Greek who equipped himself with a mahogany toilet seat around his middle and a cistern with chain-pull above his head. 'My mother', as Mary de Zogheb's son Bernard said, 'couldn't be bothered to do very much. Once she went as a beggar woman and sat on the doorstep begging, and everybody passed by without giving her anything, except one opulent large Jewish lady who said to her chauffeur, "Give the lady a shilling", and afterwards at the ball my mother said to her startled fellow guest, "You were the only generous woman."'

'We see Daphne du Maurier around everywhere we go', Josie wrote home to Memphis, 'and the other night we went over to have a drink.'[124] But Alexandria bored Daphne du Maurier stiff and, apart from her abhorrence of cocktail parties, not a hint of it appears in *Rebecca*, the novel she began writing while her husband was stationed in the city with the Grenadier Guards in 1936–7. '[We] were living in a rented house, not far from the beach, Ramleh I believe it was called, and while he was occupied with military matters

45   Some of the guests at the Finneys' 1938 costume ball. Jacques Vincendon stands on the left, with his wife Claire looking up at him. Rosette de Menasce is the woman standing farthest to the right, and her daughter Denise stands next to her.

I was homesick for Cornwall. I think I put a brave face on the situation and went to the various cocktail parties which we were obliged to attend. . . . I wondered if . . . I would have been jealous if my Tommy had been married before he married me. He had been engaged once, that I knew, and the engagement had been broken off – perhaps she would have been better at dinners and cocktail parties than I could ever be. . . . Seeds began to drop. A beautiful home, a first wife, jealousy. . . . I paced up and down the living room in Alexandria, notebook in hand.'[125]

'John's father is trying to get him a job in the printing business', Josie reported home. 'John has always loved that sort of thing and his father thinks that is what he should do'.[126] By April he had been taken on by Whitehead Morris – 'He's so glad to be out of the cotton business'[127] – but working for its manager, William Walker, 'was no sinecure', as John later told Forster, explaining the mean appearance of the second edition. 'Walker for some reason was terribly stubborn about using small type', and more than once John had come close to being fired for attempting to set the guidebook to a more generous and readable design. 'But I did get some sort of revenge. I was able to salvage a few of the notes and maps you made for Mr Mann for the 1922 edition. Walker threw them one day, in a temper, into his waste paper basket. They are now bound up in my copy of the guidebook. They are in safe and appreciative hands and I hope you don't mind my having them.'[128]

Behind Walker's outbursts was a case of *amour-propre*. When Judge Brinton had first approached Whitehead Morris, he had failed to realise that the price he was quoted was for a reprint rather than a revision of the first edition. Now over a year into the project, as Whitehead Morris discovered the scale of the alterations, they demanded more money. Brinton went to the Municipality, getting them to take a thousand copies at LE200, which together with the five hundred agreed by the Tourism Bureau and the five hundred required by the society itself brought the final print-run up to two thousand copies. But it was not just a question of finding extra money, Walker wrote to Brinton towards the end of 1936, for as 'the owners absolutely of the copyright in Mr E. M. Forster's Alexandria Guide', Whitehead Morris retained 'all control on any emendations, projected alterations, revisions, or additions and no expense should be incurred or will be admitted by them which has not their definite approval'.[129] In short, Walker was asserting himself as the final arbiter of both what went into the guidebook and what did not, as well as the manner of its production.

Brinton sent a warning to Forster, who replied, 'I am rather concerned at what you say about Mr Walker. . . . I will gladly send him a line soon, if you think it desirable – and if you will give me a hint of the sort of thing I should write.'[130] Thinking it best to let Walker first have sight of the work, Brinton submitted the guidebook with its provisional alterations on 8 April 1937, just days after John had started with Whitehead Morris, applying the gentlest pressure by explaining that 'Most of these have already been approved by Mr Forster . . . but you will of course wish to submit the text as you approve of it for his final approval.'[131] A fortnight later Forster was writing to Brinton: 'I have also heard from Mr

Walker, and enclose a copy of my reply, which I hope you will think is sufficiently tactful towards him. I am very gratified to you for your hints, and I feel sure that you are right in arranging that he should communicate with me direct. I will keep you informed of everything this end, and you will be in complete contact your end through your son.'[132] And so the conspiracy advanced, Forster's letter to Walker reading, 'I am very glad that a new edition of the Guide has your approval. It certainly has mine, and I feel under great obligation to the initiative and to the constant helpfulness of Judge Brinton in the matter. I believe that you are already in touch with him, and I hope that you may think well to consult with him from time to time, since I myself am not on the spot.' But then came the words at which Walker, one imagines, lost his temper, throwing the old maps from the 1922 edition into his wastepaper basket: 'As to the plans, I fear I do not agree with you that the original ones will be adequate. Many changes have taken place since the book was written, these will duly be mentioned in the revised text, and if the plans remain out of date they will mislead the tourist and cause the book to be criticised adversely.'[133] It was the story with Mr Mann all over again.

Judge Brinton, who followed Vivien to London in the summer of 1937 and met Forster there, kept him abreast of 'the pleasant little human comedy which the guide is playing in Alexandria', saying it 'has really become an institution (and I feel like the chief inmate). It crops up daily. I have almost come to lean on it for mild stimulation – and agreeable little thrusts and panics.'[134]

After further delays and strikes at Whitehead Morris, the second edition of the History and Guide was finally published in December 1938, delivering up Forster's city in time for a new generation brought to Alexandria by war. 'Mrs Stich gazed over the balcony into the gardens', wrote Evelyn Waugh in *Officers and Gentlemen* in a scene set in the city in the spring of 1941:

'Forster says they ought to be "thoroughly explored"', she said. 'Something for another day.' To Guy. 'You've got his Guide?'

'I've always wanted a copy. It's very scarce.'

'Just been reprinted. Here, take mine. I can always get another.'

She produced from her basket a copy of E. M. Forster's *Alexandria*.

'I didn't know. In that case I can get one for myself. Thanks awfully, though.'

'Take it, fool', she said.

'Well, thanks awfully. I know his *Pharos and Pharillon*, of course.'

'Of course; the Guide is topping too.'[135]

CHAPTER 5

Mixed Doubles as Usual

> Today – Mixed doubles as usual. Is there a war – anywhere – one feels like
> asking – in such a scene as that?
>
> Jasper Yeates Brinton, diary, 20 June 1940

In December 1938 a review in the *Egyptian Gazette* welcomed the republication of *Alexandria,* but then went on to add a historical coda: that with the ascendancy of Egyptian nationalism the modern city 'has [had] its heyday . . . and now the latest of the Alexandrias is also, unless we misread the signs, in its decline. And so with infinite gratitude to Mr Forster and all those who have made his work again available, we – borrowing from Cavafy, the poet of modern Alexandria –

> like a man prepared, like a brave man,
> bid farewell to her, to Alexandria who is departing.'[1]

But in less than a year everything had changed; the withdrawal of the British from Egypt seemed hardly more than a hiccup, and for the old Alexandria it was a reprieve of a kind.

On 3 September 1939, two days after Hitler's invasion of Poland, Britain declared war on Germany. The Egyptian government, acting on its obligations under the 1936 treaty, placed all ports, airfields and means of communication at the disposal of the British and imposed martial law. The Egyptians also introduced censorship of the press and mails, and to help run it brought in Robin Furness. Diplomatic and commercial relations with Germany were broken off, and all German men in the country, about twelve hundred, were interned and their property sequestrated.

Most of these were members of the Nazi Party thanks to Alfred Hess, founder of the party in Egypt, who like his older brother Rudolf was born in Alexandria, where at the turn of the century their father had been an eminent figure in the affairs of the foreign communities. Fritz Hess ran a prosperous wholesaling business in the Rue de France, where apart from importing Rhine, Moselle and Bordeaux wines he was sole agent for several English, Austrian and German firms, among them Krupp. In 1908 he sent his eldest son to school in Germany, from where he was meant to return to Alexandria and enter the family business. But Rudolf, who found his father overbearing, stayed on in

Germany and fought in the war; not that he had much to return to, as the British had expropriated much of the family property in Egypt. Instead he went to university in Munich, where he was among the first to join the Nazi Party, and in 1923 he took part in Hitler's abortive beer-hall putsch. Afterwards, while the two were in prison, it was to Hess that Hitler dictated *Mein Kampf*.

Yet even in the 1930s, when Hess was deputy Führer, he always found time to write to his mother and father at the family home in the Alexandria suburb of Ibrahimiya, where his letters were routinely intercepted by British intelligence. Of Alexandria he wrote to his mother – though this was after he had been sentenced at Nuremberg to life imprisonment – 'What a paradise it was in our garden at the edge of the desert. Do you remember how we would gather violets together, and how glorious they smelled?'[2]

Egypt, however, was not a belligerent, and beyond observing the letter of the treaty, the government's cooperation was grudging and minimal, reflecting the attitude of most Egyptians that the war meant little or nothing to them. As one woman, a relative of the nationalist politician Sidki Pasha, said to Gaston Zananiri, 'You see, we have always been here in Egypt the slaves of the foreigners. If these people who are the enemies, if they come and save us from what we've known for generations, better to be under the thumb of an enemy than to accept foreign domination.' And, for all the convolutions of her reasoning, she was not alone in her conclusion. Returning in October 1939 with his wife from a summer holiday in Europe, Judge Brinton found their ship filled with 'chers collègues' of the Mixed Courts: 'While most of them, like the British and ourselves, were violently anti-Hitler, others asked a little timidly, "Would it be such a bad thing if Hitler won?" Alexandria has always been a city of divided sentiments.'[3]

In the early stages of the war, however, the imminent threat to Egypt was not from Germany but from Italy, whose fleet was in the Mediterranean and whose troops were in Libya and Ethiopia, half a million strong. Against them stood the ten thousand British soldiers that had been allowed to remain in Egypt during peacetime under the treaty. But as yet Mussolini had not committed himself, and between Britain and Italy there was an uneasy peace. In Alexandria they watched and waited.

On 10 May 1940 Josie Brinton, just turned twenty-four, wrote to her mother in America: 'Of course today's events have us all trembling in our boots here for now that Germany has gone into Holland and Belgium, Italy is bound to do something in our direction! Egypt is having a trial blackout for a whole week and as soon as an air raid warning goes we all have to get off the streets and under shelter and we've had to pin blue paper over our shutters. All the street lights are out except for a few which are painted blue and all the headlights on the cars are painted blue.' At the end of May the Egyptian government declared Cairo an open city, meaning it would not be defended against enemy occupation and was therefore entitled under international law to immunity against bombardment and attack. Cairo blazed with lights for the rest of the war and its open-air restaurants and hotel-roof cabarets glittered. But things were different in Alexandria.

From Belgium the German army wheeled south into France and on 10 June, as the Germans stood almost at the gates of Paris, Italy finally declared war. 'There's a permanent blackout now so no one goes out at night – it's too difficult driving – besides being afraid to be caught in a raid', Josie wrote home to Memphis, and there were air-raid alerts throughout the day: 'I went into town this morning to do some shopping and I parked the car and went into a shop to buy some material for a dress when – "woob-woob-woob" – the alarm sounded. The shop quickly shut its doors and everyone rushed off the streets and to the nearest shelters while a police car patrolled the streets with an amplifier saying "Prenez alerte – dépêchez-vous, dépêchez-vous" – terribly eerie. That alarm lasted 45 minutes and we won't know until tomorrow's paper what it was about. Anyway no bombs were dropped. One old lady in the shop had hysterics and another woman asked the shopkeeper if he played cards – saying we might as well play something.'[4]

America would hang back from entering the war for a further year and a half, but Josie had faith in British grit: 'Well, the Germans declared they'd be in Paris by the 15th of June and they marched in today', she wrote in her diary on 14 June. 'God knows when and where this war will end now – the English will never give up till they've licked Hitler or until they're all dead.'[5]

Now the air raids began in earnest, the target the Western Harbour, though within the first days bombs had fallen on Cleopatra, and over the coming weeks and months they would drop with sporadic aimlessness throughout Alexandria, in the Rue Chérif Pasha, at the Ramleh tram terminus, at Gabbari and Mex to the west of the city and in Karmouz near Pompey's Pillar. At Stanley Bay a floating mine exploded off the Corniche.

Meanwhile, Whitehead Morris had printed a guide of another sort, a double-length sheet of paper headed 'Air Raid Precautions, Protection in the Home', advising on measures against incendiary bombs ('tackle bomb at first possible moment after entry'); treatment of windows, doors and fireplaces against air explosions, gas attacks and flying splinters ('do not sit below or in front of openings'); the best form of shelter ('preferably on basement or ground floor'); equipping of shelter ('bucket behind hanging curtain'); and what to do while in occupation of shelter ('do not use up oxygen unnecessarily'). Judge Brinton was tempted to ignore the raids altogether but felt it was 'bad form and pretentious', and so built a shelter in his garden using a piano crate set into a hole and covered with a mound of earth. Furnishing it with a chaise longue and a couple of chairs, it proved 'far from unsocial. Sometimes the company would include distinguished visitors. And for long sojourns, modest refreshments were available.'[6] Some of those living in the centre of the city, as fearful of boredom as of the enemy, dug deeper and wider and installed bridge tables. Others made use of Roman cisterns; one at Mustafa Pasha could hold a thousand people.

But on 20 June Judge Brinton wrote in his diary, 'Mixed doubles as usual. Is there a war – anywhere – one feels like asking – in such a scene as that?'[7] And indeed in between

46 Indian troops stationed at Burg el Arab in the summer of 1940. In the autumn they were replaced by the RAF.

the fall of bombs, the Alexandrians still flocked to the beaches, and members of the Royal Yacht Club by Ras el Tin Palace on the Western Harbour still sailed their dinghies in its waters. Among them one June morning were John and Josie, who were with Cyril Barker, of one of the oldest cotton-broking families in Alexandria, and his wife Gabriella. The two men went sailing, while 'Gabriella and I [together in a launch] had a long discussion about love and sex, etc. She tells me English women have the least morals of all!'[8] – Josie had recently been reading several books by D. H. Lawrence, including *Lady Chatterley's Lover*. 'The characters seem so unreal and unlifelike; still, maybe they represent the people in the enlightened world to come.'[9] Then an air-raid warning sounded; Gabriella said that if they were afraid, they could go back to the club, but instead they stayed out in the harbour: 'All the flags on the ships were strung up and the Ras el Tin station was signalling away like mad. The Sunderland bombers grouped around the Boat House were all moved out and dispersed and about eight destroyers weighed anchor and single file went out to sea. All most exciting!'[10]

By the mid-summer of 1940, when Josie walked past the Scuole Littorie to 'such cat-calls and shouts I never heard',[11] the Italian school had been pressed into service as a detention centre for Italian men of military age. The moment Mussolini had declared war, Italian nationals became enemy aliens and were made to register, their businesses and property were sequestrated, and thousands were interned in camps about the country, their families abandoned to their fate.

But there was considerable confusion over applying the measures. Many Italians were of Egyptian birth but had claimed Italian nationality simply to enjoy the protection of the Mixed Courts, while the Italian occupation of the Dodecanese meant that numbers of Greeks also held Italian papers. In fact the Greeks of Egypt were fiercely anti-fascist, and since 1938, when Mussolini introduced anti-semitic legislation, so had been most (though even then not all) Italian Jews. 'Our own staff', reported Barclays Bank in Egypt, 'were for the most part of Egyptian birth, but a number of these were of Italian stock and some had actually become Italian nationals prior to the war. At the outbreak of the war with Italy the whole of the Italian members of our staff in Egypt, numbering 75 in all, were suspended. Of these, however, only five were immediately interned, although this number was slightly increased at a later stage. Some of those suspended were of Jewish or Greek origin; ultimately, after a few months' suspension, about 20 of these were reinstated.'[12]

Though her fascist father had died in 1937, Marta Loria was not allowed to work until after she had married a Royal Navy officer in 1942 and became a British citizen. A friend of hers from early in the 1930s, when their families would erect their bathing cabins adjacently at Stanley Bay, was Herta Pappo, an Italian Jew. The war 'was a difficult time for us', Herta remembered. Her father, a cousin of Enrico Terni, had recently retired as manager of the Banco di Roma and the Land Bank of Egypt, both on the Rue Chérif Pasha, but all the same 'we were under surveillance, him especially, and they gave us identity cards and we had to report'. Nevertheless, being Jewish was an advantage and 'otherwise we had no problems'.

Others affected by the new security measures were numbers of foreign artistes working in the nightclubs at Alexandria. Going to the Excelsior cabaret one night early in June 1940, Josie discovered that 'they're sending lots of the girls away for they are Hungarians, etc, and might be fifth columnists'.[13] Some were deported, others went to Cairo where precautions were not taken until later; in Alexandria there were plenty of Greek, Cypriot, Maltese and other girls to take their places.

A couple of weeks later there was another departure of a more unsettling kind. 'At breakfast the phone rang', Judge Brinton wrote in his diary on 18 June. 'It was Josa Finney – to say goodbye. At first I thought it was just to Cairo. It took some time for the extraordinary news to sink in that they were leaving Egypt. In an ordinary year this would have been just a summer exodus – and made earlier; but now – with Egypt threatened – it came as a great shock: as if a pillar was shaken and tumbling. Oswald spoke too:

"Cape Town – America" – He would be the first they would look for.'[14] The previous day a radio broadcast from Rome had mentioned Finney by name, saying it was due to him and to his newspaper empire that Egypt was pro-British and anti-Italian, and that they would deal with him when they conquered Egypt. News of the French cabinet's resignation had also just come through, and that a new government headed by Marshal Pétain, the aged hero of the Battle of Verdun in 1916, had asked Hitler for an armistice; with the surrender of Britain's one European ally, Finney decided that the situation was lost.

After some havering over whether to sail or go by air, the Finneys flew to Cape Town early in July, 'showering gold pieces literally', gold louis and English sovereigns, among their friends before they went. Judge Brinton saw them off with a colleague, who told them their departure was 'the most demoralising thing that has happened in Egypt yet', while in his diary Brinton confined himself to reporting his terse farewell, 'Whatever you do will be all right for us but my feelings same as yesterday only stronger', adding to himself, 'It is only fair for at least one friend to tell them his views. They hear so little of what they don't agree with.'[15] At the embassy there were those who would have stopped Finney from leaving, and among the British community there were many who viewed his departure with contempt.

Though the Finney balls ceased with the outbreak of the war they long remained famous and were probably the occasions Durrell had in mind when writing the climax of *Balthazar*, when at the Cervonis' carnival ball Narouz drives a hatpin through Toto de Brunel's skull, thinking that he is killing Justine. Oswald made occasional brief visits to Alexandria, the last time in June 1942 when Rommel's advance towards Alamein sent him packing again to South Africa, where he died in September. Josa returned to Egypt and continued to run the Finney enterprises with Oswald's younger brother Harold until everything was sequestrated by Nasser. The house, however, was returned to her by Sadat, and just before her own death in 1983 Josa sold it to the Bank of Commerce and Development, which accepted her condition that nothing should be altered. And so on the ground floor the manager's office is in the huge cloakroom by the front door and the staff work at desks set upon a marble floor laid over the still intact sunken swimming pool and hot baths of the gymnasium. Upstairs, the living rooms, bedrooms, library, billiards room, card room and ballroom stand vacant, except for a portrait of Finney hung on a wall, this too one of Josa's conditions. For many years, even after its sale to the bank, it remained home only to Hajj Ahmed, the housekeeper who had been with the Finneys from the beginning, who had seen the house through its birth and life and who now swept it of dust in its final embalming.

'A very black day this', Judge Brinton wrote in his diary. The day before, 22 June, Pétain had accepted Hitler's terms, which subjected northern France and the Atlantic coast to German occupation while condemning central and southern France, under Pétain's government at Vichy, to collaboration cloaked in nominal neutrality. And now, on the twenty-third, Pétain was discussing an armistice with Italy as well. 'What next? Every-one talks of the French fleet. A few ships are here – including two battleships. Can they be saved to the Allies?'[16] Going round to see a French friend, Brinton found him 'crushed' and tried to console him: 'I asked him – can one people really crush another people today? And then we talked of what is France: so much more than any govern-ment. Can France really be crushed? Is not France immortal?' (In a similar scene in *The Alexandria Quartet* Darley meets his old friend Georges-Gaston Pombal: 'We gazed at each other for a long moment of silence, with emotion. Both knew that the silence we observed was one of pain for the fall of France, an event which symbolised all too clearly the psychic collapse of Europe itself . . . an irremediable failure of the human will.')[17] But if some flame still burned among the French, then what would they do with their fleet? The question nagged at Brinton's mind: 'I only hope the underlying antipathy between the two countries [France and Britain] won't boil up too much now. France couldn't fight any longer. Could she have transferred her fleet? Why didn't England take it – a week ago?'[18]

The British were anxious not to offend French pride and rather than seize their ships hoped that they would rally to the Free French under Charles de Gaulle and fight side by side with the Royal Navy. In broadcasts from London General de Gaulle declared that France had lost one battle but not the war, that this was a universal war in which immense forces were yet to come into play, and that every Frenchman who still bore arms had the right to continue the resistance, so ensuring that France would be present at the final victory. But in the early days following de Gaulle's appeal, there were few who answered his call. Of the thirty-eight thousand men of the French Army of the Levant, all but a thousand remained loyal to Vichy, and it took an expedition of British, Australian and Free French troops from Egypt in July the following year to bring Syria and Lebanon under Allied control. The story was no better among the French forces in North Africa, and even in Egypt, where by and large the French community pledged itself to the Free French, the French minister in Cairo and the consul in Alexandria were stubbornly pro-Vichy – so that de Gaulle, when he came to the city, found a welcome not among French officials but at the homes of sympathetic compatriots such as Rosette de Menasce and her daughter Claire.

Such was the sense of German omnipotence and the conviction that Britain faced imminent defeat that even outside France, where Frenchmen still could choose between resistance and submission, the majority holding positions of administrative and mili-tary authority wallowed in a mood of resignation and took refuge in a narrow legality to justify their loyalty to a France that was in the hands of Pétain's puppet government. Among these were the French naval commanders in the Mediterranean.

Pétain had ordered his fleets to return home, while the British were equally deter-mined to prevent them from going. As part of the armistice terms accepted by Vichy, the Germans had insisted on the surrender of the French fleet, but the British feared that Hitler would use it in his likely invasion of Britain. At Alexandria, the home base for the Royal Navy's Mediterranean Fleet, the commander-in-chief, Admiral Sir Andrew Cunningham, dissuaded Admiral René Godfroy from attempting to sail his ships out of the harbour. Meanwhile, the main French fleet was at Mers el Kébir, the military port for Oran in Algeria, where a British force sailing from Gibraltar went with proposals: that the fleet should either sail to a British port and put itself at the disposal of the Royal Navy or sail to a port in the French West Indies and accept demilitarisation. When these alternatives were declined, the commander of the Gibraltar Fleet Admiral Somerville offered the French the option of scuttling their fleet at Mers el Kébir. On 3 July when that too was refused the British opened fire, within five minutes sinking or disabling the principal French ships.

The Royal Navy was hardly proud to have undertaken so lamentable a task, but though Mers el Kébir cost the lives of twelve hundred Frenchmen who until a fortnight earlier had been allies, even General de Gaulle, while calling it detestable, agreed that there had been no alternative. Quite apart from the military necessity, there was a widespread defeatist mood to combat. 'All the former neutrals', Brinton observed, 'hope England will blow up and make peace – so that they will not be troubled. I hope England will fight only harder. But she hasn't many friends around here.'[19] In such circumstances, as Churchill understood, Britain's one sure ally was its own resolve, and he called Mers el Kébir 'the turning point in our fortunes, it made the world realise that we were in earnest in our intentions to carry on'.[20]

Godfroy, however, was outraged when he heard the news and, getting up steam, prepared to fight his way out to the open sea. Appalled at the prospect of an all-out naval battle in Alexandria's Western Harbour, Cunningham pleaded with him to change his mind. But when Godfroy remained adamant, Cunningham went over his head, appealing directly to his officers and men by means of messages written on large boards mounted on a flotilla of boats encircling the French ships. Godfroy relented and accepted Cunningham's generous terms, which permitted him to use Vichy codes to transmit information back to France, and provided for the repatriation of most of his crews, while the remainder, after discharging the ships' fuel oil and removing the breechblocks from their guns (but retaining, as Durrell wrote in the *Quartet*, 'both their small-arms and a sense of shame'),[21] stayed on as maintenance parties, victualled and paid by the British.

For the daily life of Alexandria the presence of Force X, as the French fleet became known, meant recurrent street fights between the Vichy sailors when they came ashore on leave and the Free French who would taunt them with 'Have you any mussels and oysters to sell?'[22] And it could also make pleasure-sailing in the harbour dangerous, where it was a recognised rule that a wide berth should be given to the grim unbattled fleet whose pampered but pariah crews could display fits of paranoia, taking potshots at members of the nearby Royal Yacht Club when a sudden shift of breeze might bring their craft in too close. In one of these was Claude Vincendon, fifteen in 1940, who could often be seen with her father sailing their dinghy in the harbour. Eighteen years later when she was living with Durrell in France, she described such an incident in her novel *The Rum Go*, which Durrell then borrowed and embroidered for the final volume of the *Quartet*, having the sailors of the captive fleet open fire on Pombal's dinghy, killing his mistress Fosca. Godfroy himself would come ashore, but was socially ostracised and could find it difficult to scratch up a game of tennis. Two years later in 1942, during the nervous months between the first and second battles of Alamein, when the British considered blowing Force X out of the water, Godfroy would owe his survival and that of his fleet to the judicious mediation of Jasper Brinton.

In a few sudden months the whole of the Atlantic coast of Europe from the North Cape of Norway to the Spanish frontier had fallen into German hands, while across the English Channel Britain was girding itself against a Nazi invasion from the French ports. At the same time, the Germans and the Italians controlled two thousand miles of coastline around the Mediterranean, which only the Royal Navy's bases at Gibraltar, Malta and Alexandria prevented from becoming an Axis lake. On the Libyan border stood the Italians, and though the British had by now raised their troop levels in Egypt to fifty thousand the enemy still outnumbered them by ten to one. If the British should be overwhelmed, if Alexandria should fall, then the Royal Navy would be driven from the Mediterranean, neutral Turkey would be surrounded, Greece, Cyprus and Palestine, together with Egypt and the entire Middle East, would be lost, and the Axis, soon to be joined by Japan, would hold much of Europe, Africa and Asia in thrall.

But as the fighting drew nearer, the rounds of cocktails and dinner parties took on a note of defiant insouciance. In summer the blackout precautions made people's houses unbearably hot, and at Ramleh they sat out in their gardens in the starlight and moonlight as the enemy passed overhead. 'At first the bombings', Judge Brinton said, 'were a bit disconcerting, they made such an awful racket, but soon we got used to them, and after a while came to look on the aerial illuminations which accompanied them as a sort of gigantic display of fireworks',[23] while John, who would rush up onto the roof with his binoculars, then clamber back into bed with Josie, pronounced that all he really cared about now was 'sex and air raids'.[24]

Early in September, when enemy aircraft trespassed upon a social evening in the Quartier Grec, Josie wrote home, 'Last night we went to have cocktails at Lady Barker's and about 8.00 just as we were leaving the air raid alarm went and we had a really proper raid lasting until quarter to ten. The noise was like a thunderstorm and you could hear bits of shrapnel falling in the streets – from the anti-aircraft guns. No damage was done at all and only one or two bombs dropped. They aren't so good, the Italians. We're all getting so hardened and used to these raids.'[25]

In the skies over London and the southeast of England the Battle of Britain was raging at the time, and in Alexandria, just then the only other city in the world to share London's distinction of being the victim of Axis attacks, Josie was filling her diary with accounts of air raids in each. 'A very bad air raid over London last night, 500 people

47   An air raid over the Western Harbour in 1941, seen from the Eastern Harbour Corniche.

killed and 1400 seriously wounded. Severe damage, according to the BBC.'[26] And so with satisfaction and a sense of common cause she listened to Churchill's broadcast on 11 September, 'a really good speech – probably be in future history books – he called Hitler "that wicked man" '.[27]

> These cruel, wanton, indiscriminate bombings of London are, of course, a part of Hitler's invasion plans. . . . This wicked man, the repository and embodiment of many forms of soul-destroying hatreds, this monstrous product of former wrongs and shame, has now resolved to break our famous Island race by a process of indiscriminate slaughter and destruction. What he has done is to kindle a fire in British hearts, here and all over the world, which will glow long after all traces of the conflagration he has caused in London have been removed.[28]

Two days later, on 13 September, Italian troops crossed the border from Libya and advanced sixty miles into Egypt.

On the day the Italians crossed into Egypt, advancing through Sollum and Buq Buq to Sidi Barrani, Judge Brinton set off to the British front line at Mersa Matruh, which for months had been suffering aerial bombardment. 'Decided to make a contribution'[29] was how he put it, so he bought a second-hand Ford and fixed it up as a mobile canteen which he called the 'Van Brinton' and drove it out to the front, where he donated it to the YMCA. Before leaving Alexandria he bought two tin helmets, one for himself and one for Geneva while he was away. Coming back he got a ride with Bramly, who had also driven to the front to help the Senussi who were pouring over the border to escape the Italians.

In fact, despite his superior numbers, Marshal Graziani ordered his invasion force to dig in at Sidi Barrani, where the Italians and their supply lines back into Libya were remorselessly attacked by British gunboats and carrier aircraft, giving time for three armoured regiments to risk running the length of the Mediterranean on five fast ships from beleaguered England. The danger was less the Italian surface fleet, which though larger than the Royal Navy's Mediterranean Fleet showed a singular reluctance to leave the security of its harbours, than Italian submarines: to avoid them men and supplies bound for Egypt had to make the twelve-thousand-mile voyage round the Cape – as did the mail, so that letters between Egypt and Britain or America took up to three months to arrive. The more writing home became like setting messages adrift in bottles, the more reassuring Josie's letters became. 'I know how worried you must be and it's useless to tell you not to be but what else can I say. If you saw the carefree life everyone leads here you'd wonder what all the excitement was about', and she continued with a story going about town, 'that in the Mediterranean now all the English sailors had to do was lean over the side of their ships and shout "waiter" to have an Italian submarine come to the surface! Tomorrow we're having a cocktail party and then several of us are going to town to dinner and dancing. Sunday we're going to see Garbo in *Ninotchka* which has just gotten here.'[30]

On 23 October Judge Brinton went to a 'reception for Polish soldiers at the Union Club (hot and smoky) where I met Mr Eden – breezy pleasant good looking fellow. I said "We're in the war now". He said "That's for you to decide." '[31]

Anthony Eden had arrived in Cairo on 14 October,[32] and though the Battle of Britain still hung in the balance he had flown to Khartoum, where the British were preparing to liberate Ethiopia, and had visited the Western Desert, where General Sir Archibald Wavell was planning a counterstroke against Graziani's sedentary forces at Sidi Barrani. But Britain's effort to fight the war in Africa while supplying itself from North America against the Nazi onslaught at home was taking a terrible toll at sea: five hundred British merchant ships had been sunk by the time Eden arrived at Alexandria.

When Brinton said, 'We're in the war now', he was referring to America's recent agreement to lease Britain fifty mothballed destroyers dating from the First World War. It was the prelude to the Lend-Lease Bill, which was approved by Congress the following March

48 On the day the Italians invaded Egypt, Judge Brinton, seen off by his wife Geneva, went to the British front line in a second-hand Ford he fixed up as a mobile canteen, which he called the 'Van Brinton'.

and which on the face of it seemed a generous measure: the United States would provide Britain with ships, aircraft, tanks and munitions, leasing them on a rental basis with payment delayed until after the war. But before the arrangement could come into effect, Britain was obliged to pay all the debts it could from its gold reserves and by the sale of its commercial assets in the United States, and subsequently was forbidden to sell any goods abroad that contained Lend-Lease material or indeed any goods at all, even if entirely British-made, that were similar to goods received under Lend-Lease.

Though by the late nineteenth century both America and Germany had overtaken Britain as industrial powers, Britain, by drawing on its accumulated wealth, had managed to remain a force in the world. But now with its assets gone and its exports curtailed, Britain at war was reduced to dependency on a still non-combatant United States. 'We are not only to be skinned', Churchill remarked privately, 'but flayed to the bone.'[33]

It might have been otherwise had Britain decided to fight a limited defensive war. But right at the beginning of his premiership Churchill had declared an all-out global fight to the finish. 'You ask what is our policy?' he broadcast in May 1940. 'I will say: It is to wage war, by sea, land and air, with all our might and with all the strength that God can give us; to wage war against a monstrous tyranny, never surpassed in the dark, lamentable catalogue of human crime. . . . You ask what is our aim? I can answer in one word: victory, victory at all costs.'[34]

In that call for 'victory at all costs' could be heard the voice of a proud history, but though Britain emerged triumphant from the war, its large debts and decimated trade brought it to the verge of economic collapse. 'Never forget about the Greeks that we are bankrupt', Cavafy had warned. 'That is the difference between us and ancient Greeks, and, my dear Forster, between us and yourselves. Pray, my dear Forster, that you – you English with your capacity for adventure – never lose your capital.'[35]

At three o'clock in the morning on 28 October Mussolini, without reference to Hitler, delivered an ultimatum to Greece, saying it was necessary for Italian forces to occupy certain mainland ports as well as Corfu and Crete, to which General Metaxas, who had opposed the Asia Minor venture in 1922 and since 1936 had been dictator, famously answered, 'No'. Sailing at once from Alexandria, the Royal Navy established a base at Chania in Crete; then on the night of 11 November a squadron including the aircraft carrier *Illustrious* approached the Italian coast and launched a daring aerial torpedo attack on the enemy fleet at anchor in Taranto harbour, sinking three of the Italian navy's six battleships and badly damaging a fourth.

On the same day Josie recorded that 'the Greeks have absolutely annihilated one of the crack Italian Alpine divisions',[36] and over the coming weeks as the Greek army continued to drive the Italians back into Albania, she wrote how all the Greeks of Alexandria were 'rushing about like mad',[37] 'celebrating in Pastroudis' and 'marching about in a snake dance at the Excelsior, including the band, which played all the national anthems. We sat singing at the tops of our voices.'[38]

In the wave of enthusiasm that swept through the Greek community, fifteen thousand men volunteered for service in Greece, and an entire division was quickly raised. Early in November the *Moqattam* expressed the general feeling towards Greece by publishing a leading article that said, 'The sympathy of the whole world goes to this brave people which has refused to belie its past', and when later that month *La Bourse égyptienne* printed an appeal from Greece to all Hellenes living abroad, within a single night the Greeks of Egypt subscribed double the amount that Egypt was spending for the entire year on its own national defence. The Arabic-language *Mussawar* drew particular attention to the generosity of the old familiar families of the Alexandria community – the Choremis, the Benachis, the Casullis, the Salvagos and others – mentioning that Greeks held nearly thirty-five per cent of all the shares of the banks and limited companies in Egypt.[39] Their literary movement had died with Cavafy, but the Alexandrian Greeks were still an economic force to be reckoned with.

Since spring, Geneva, with Josie's help, had thrown open her home in Bulkeley to convalescent soldiers, sailors and airmen each Monday, and to enlarge their welcome the Brintons moved in December to a bigger house with an extensive garden in Glymenopoulo. The place enjoyed a reputation for informality, and convalescents, once they had been restored to active service, would often return there to spend their leave.

One, a pilot, would announce his visits, recalled Judge Brinton, 'by a preliminary flight over our house and a familiar buzz which was like the ringing of a doorbell. On hearing it someone would proceed to the airport to pick him up.'[40] Indeed throughout Alexandria it became the fashion for society ladies who formerly would not have been caught dead receiving anyone less than an admiral, general, ambassador or banker to open their doors once or twice a week and provide meals and entertainments for servicemen.

Women also volunteered to help out at the services clubs that were springing up about the city. Among the first of these was the Britannia Club at 26 Rue Fuad, 'proof of the British ability', as Judge Brinton put it, 'to accomplish the largest results possible on the smallest resources'.[41] The atmosphere was distinctly English, with comfortable armchairs and shaded lights, and 'a dainty little sitting and tea room for the use of women members of the Forces', reported the *Egyptian Gazette*.[42] The various rooms were decorated and furnished by residents of Alexandria, among them Baron Charles de Menasce, son of Felix's brother Alfred, Jasper Brinton and, during one of his fairweather visits, Oswald Finney, the last two also contributing thousands of books, creating the best reference library in Alexandria. Also, towards the end of 1940, the Karam 'palace', an imposing private mansion standing in tree-shaded grounds in the Rue de Corinthe behind the Graeco-Roman Museum, became the United Forces Club, its oak-panelled walls, marble pillars and richly decorated ceiling making it the most luxurious service club in Egypt.[43] 'It's really very grand, almost too grand I'm afraid',[44] thought Josie who worked there alongside Durrell's future friend the painter Clea Badaro. Teas and drinks were served in the garden, and there were daily entertainments, with dancing every Sunday and Monday at five o'clock either on the special dance floor outdoors or in the magnificent hall within.

There were also Gabriella Barker's concert parties, musical reviews that were taken round the camps and hospitals, her troupe including, in Judge Brinton's estimation, a score of the most glamorous women of Alexandria whose 'social éclat was quite prodigious'.[45] During the summer Burg el Arab had served as a base for Indian troops, then in the autumn for the RAF, while the Brintons, who had military passes, continued to come and go. At the judge's invitation the concert party came to perform for the RAF at Burg el Arab over the weekend of 9 and 10 November. After lunch at Dar el Qadi, the House of the Judge, the Brintons' desert home, 'drinks at the officers' mess – and the show on at 7 o'clock. Air raid in the middle. The squadron leader rose and said, "Quiet – sit down – we'll go on with the show". Buffet afterwards. Breakfast for 16 in our loggia.'[46] Among those who signed the guest book at the Dar el Qadi that weekend was Claire Vincendon. Her daughter Claude was also part of the troupe, and later recalled their effect on servicemen, how 'the long-threatened concert party had descended on them in force and battered them into unresisting acceptance'. To Brinton, though, the concert parties were a great success: 'The same old songs – oft repeated – became identified with well-known and charming young performers – and the lilt and melody of some of the favorite numbers must have touched many military hearts.'[47]

There was an innocence about Alexandria then, in those early days of the war, an innocence that some would say the city never really lost. 'It was unthought of for an unmarried girl, or even an unmarried boy', recalled Bernard de Zogheb, 'to leave the family house and have a flat of their own. OK, some of the boys had bachelor apartments, *garçonnières*, where they went for a quickie now and again, but no girl lived by herself, away from her parents. If they had fun, they did it discreetly. Certainly most girls in Alexandria went to their weddings as virgins – girls of all the communities. We were brought up to think that sex was a mortal sin.'

To Claude Vincendon the dancers at the Excelsior cabaret 'typified Wicked Women'[48] who inhabited a world beyond her contemplation. She recalled how later in the war, when she was nineteen, her girlfriends, mindful of their mothers, would have their escorts take them home before the clock struck eleven – though she herself enjoyed an unusual freedom and sometimes stayed out later. Even ten or eleven for an unmarried young woman meant that she was leading a pretty fast life: Marta Loria had to be home by seven and counted that generous; six o'clock was more usual for the girls she knew. Maria Leoncavallo, whose grandfather had been a judge on the Mixed Courts, was born and until recently remained in Alexandria, preferring it to Milan and Venice where she also lived – it was the home, she said, of her memories, of where she 'bit life hard and life bit me; but never mind, I like this bite'. The bites, however, were not those of her girlhood: her father would not allow his daughters even to go to the cinema, and instead entertainments were confined to receptions at home: 'I would dance, my mother would sing, my sister would play the piano – in our house *le plaisir* was always *très limité*.' For the Syro-Lebanese Jacqueline Klat it was hardly different: 'Nice girls in Alexandria were very strictly chaperoned and were not allowed to take so much as a step on their own. If they did, it was assumed they were up to no good and obviously "not nice". It was only halfway through the Second World War, when – according to the good ladies of Alexandria society – every girl's morals had gone to the dogs, that [we] were even allowed to go to a movie without the governess.'[49] Josie met a war correspondent who was having a difficult time: 'Poor thing, he's very lonely cause he hasn't met many people here – and mostly Greeks and he says when he wants to take them out they always say they can't go without "papa" and "mama".'[50]

Meanwhile, the Archaeological Society continued to promote the city's past. The Graeco-Roman Museum was closed but its portico became the meeting place for the 'free conducted tours for members of His Britannic Majesty's Forces to points of historical interest', with 'special tours for officers and nursing sisters'. Using offprints supplied by Whitehead Morris of the relevant sections of Forster's guide, they would be taken round Pompey's Pillar and the catacombs of Kom el Shogafa, to the Anfushi tombs and Fort Kait Bey, to the necropolis at Mustafa Pasha, and sometimes farther afield to Rosetta, by 'attractive female guides'.[51]

Under cover of darkness on the night of 7 December British and Indian forces moved forward from Mersa Matruh and on the following night slipped through a gap in the

49   Josie (left) and John Brinton (centre) at a nightspot with friends.

enemy's lines to fall on the Italians from the rear. By 11 December Sidi Barrani was taken and the Italians at Buq Buq, farther to the west, found a British armoured brigade standing across their line of retreat, while all along the coast Royal Navy ships sailing out from Alexandria kept up a devastating bombardment. Wavell had intended to stun the enemy temporarily; in the event, so complete was the Italians' demoralisation that Libya was unexpectedly left open to a British advance.

Within days the first prisoners were arriving in Alexandria, where they were put into a stockade at Sidi Gaber, 'all looking very miserable and awful',[52] Josie said; 'like beasts, like lambs, and everybody went to look', remembered Anahide Merametdjian, an Armenian woman of the city. In all, thirty-seven thousand prisoners were taken in this opening engagement, and when Bardia, just over the border, fell on 6 January another forty-five thousand Italians surrendered, followed by thirty thousand more when a newly arrived Australian division captured Tobruk on the twenty-second. Quick to capitalise on reports of the desert victories, the gulli-gulli man who performed with snakes in the bar of the Hotel Cecil took to naming his spellbound mice 'Buq Buq' and 'Sidi Barrani'. But there were many servicemen who were not amused by Egypt's attitude to the war, one convalescent writing in Geneva's guest book cum diary:

> Shame on the false Egyptian
> that lingers in his home
> while Sir Archibald Wavell
> is marching on to Rome.[53]

If not Rome, then at least all Libya lay within Wavell's grasp. Following the surrender of twenty-five thousand Italians after the battle of Beda Fromm on 5 February, the whole of Cyrenaica with its supply ports at Tobruk and Benghazi was in the hands of the British who were poised to advance on Tripoli. The results so far had been fantastic. With never more than two divisions, one of them armoured, the British had advanced more than five hundred miles, annihilating Graziani's army of ten divisions, capturing a total of 130,000 Italians and 400 tanks at very light cost to themselves. But already some of Wavell's forces had been diverted for the liberation of Ethiopia, and now on the twelfth the order came from Churchill to halt the advance into Tripolitania and prepare to send as many as possible of his tanks and men to Greece.

The British had intelligence information suggesting that the Germans intended to invade Russia, but that first, to make good Mussolini's Balkan blunder, Hitler would turn south and go into Greece himself. Privately, Churchill thought Greece was probably lost; but as his generals told him there was a chance of making a fight of it, he was prepared to weaken his North African defences to go to Greece's aid. It was a matter of honour, Churchill told the House of Commons, 'to give them all the aid in our power. If they were resolved to face the might and fury of the Huns, we had no doubt but that we should share their ordeal.'[54]

By the end of January 1941 Lieutenant Robert Crisp, a South African serving as a tank commander with the British army's 3rd Battalion, Royal Tank Regiment, had got as far as Tobruk on a reconnaissance mission. Now he was back in camp at Amriya, halfway to Ikingi Mariut, awaiting orders, as he thought, to rejoin the headlong advance across Libya. But while he was envisioning his future in terms of the minarets and palms of a score of towns stretching clear along the North African littoral, away in London plans were already being laid that would see him at the end of March shivering in the snow and sleet along the mountainous frontier of northern Greece.

Oblivious meanwhile to his fate, Crisp launched himself upon the cabarets of Alexandria. His favourites were the Phaleron, just west of the Grand Trianon on the same square as the Hotel Cecil, and the Excelsior on the Corniche not far east from the Ramleh tram terminus. The Phaleron had been the leading cabaret open to commissioned officers during the First World War; now it had been refurbished with numerous large mirrors and an abundance of lights and thrown open to NCOs and sergeants too, who came less for a meal ('the restaurant aspect plays a minor role', as a wartime guidebook delicately put it)[55] than to dance with the Greek hostesses who doubled as call girls. At the Excelsior, open to civilians and commissioned officers only, you came for the weekend tea dances or like Josie and her friends for the jazz band in the evenings when you were expected to dine. But whether Crisp went to one or the other, the artistes seemed always the same, 'completely international in the way in which only a stateless person can be. There was a community of such girls who rotated around the Middle East and North Africa performing their uninspired cabaret turns, drinking weak tea at the price of double whiskies, earning their living by entertaining men in a variety of ways.'[56] Melissa of *The Alexandria Quartet*, Darley's Greek girlfriend and the mistress of the old furrier Cohen, was a dancer at the Etoile, which from Durrell's description was at the Corniche end of the Rue de l'Ancienne Bourse, where according to the same wartime guidebook the cabarets were 'not of the highest class'.[57] Her performance was 'banal', Darley thought, and 'bad beyond measure; yet watching her make those gentle and ineffectual movements of her slim hands and feet (the air of a gazelle harnessed to a water-wheel) I was filled with tenderness at her mediocrity'.[58]

Crisp's lieutenant's pay threatened to limit his operations until one night at the Excelsior he did a Zulu war dance in an interval between cabaret turns. Persuaded by the audience's applause, the management waived his bill, and from then on he became a regular. 'Thereafter, whenever I came in for supper the band would break into a tribal rhythm, inviting me to perform my primitive gyrations and stompings which might have intrigued a Zulu but which he would certainly have found unrecognisable.'

That was how he met Vera. She was a cabaret girl at the Excelsior, where she danced in a Spanish costume, 'not the clickety-clack, castanetted, whirling sort, but slow-moving and sensuous, in keeping with the full curves of her body and thighs and an immobile quality in features of considerable beauty'. Following one of his performances, she joined Crisp at his table and spent the evening with him for free, afterwards joining him whenever he returned to the Excelsior. Crisp was a handsome, tall and powerfully built man, an exceptionally able sportsman and courageous soldier;[59] he was also a sensitive man with 'a squeamish reluctance to indulge myself in the ultimate expenditure with the attractive but extravagant cabaret girls and hostesses who peopled the Alex night' – 'an absolute horror of that sort of relationship'. He knew that among these girls there was also another kind of payment that might be expected, but somehow he felt sure he meant something to Vera other than a calculated marriage and a passport out of Alexandria. When Vera was not dancing her Spanish dance and he was not doing his Zulu routine, they delighted in each other's company like any other couple at the Excelsior – 'I was something a little different, perhaps, from what she was used to', while he 'enjoyed the potent femininity of her, her trust in me, and the anticipation of the moment when this girl who had sold herself to so many men would give herself to me freely, completely and happily'.

Then the night came when Crisp accompanied Vera back to her apartment, but this time instead of leaving her in the large entrance hall went up with her in the lift. She said nothing, but he noticed how she looked at him with a strange and uncertain expression in her eyes. Putting her finger to her lips, she turned the key in the lock and opened the door, standing aside to let him see in but putting her hand gently on his chest when he made to walk through. 'The first thing I saw was a man's elegant over-coat hanging on a stand in the hallway. I was conscious of the atmosphere of luxury that surrounded everything – Persian carpets, furniture, pictures on the wall – everything had the mark of wealth and good taste. Then I saw the bright red fez. A man's voice called from an unseen room. Vera answered quickly, in French, and looked at me with such a pleading for understanding that I nodded and smiled. And went away. She watched me until the lift had sunk out of sight. The red fez gleamed at me past her thigh.'

One evening along the Corniche they had lain on the sand and she had stared up at Berenice's Hair hanging in the night sky. 'I leaned across and kissed her very softly, not touching her with my hands. The smile stayed there while I kissed her.'[60] The war, he thought then, stretched ahead of them with all its arrivals and departures, with all its uncertainties. Now before he sailed in March with the British Expeditionary Force to Greece he returned once more to the Excelsior, and in the calèche going to Vera's apart-ment he kissed her. If she sensed it was for the last time, he did not tell her, nor that it was she who was paying him with this last innocent touch of her lips, paying him with a memory that he would take into the battles to come.

At the beginning of March the hastily assembled expeditionary force of British, Australian and New Zealand troops drawn from Wavell's desert army sailed from Alexandria to bolster Greece against the expected German attack from Bulgaria. The plan was to defend the northern port of Thessaloniki and then if necessary to pull back to a line running along the Aliakmon River to Mount Olympus. To the west the Greeks were to hold the mountainous border with Albania where they had beaten back the Italian invasion the previous winter.

On 6 April the Germans invaded, but while rapidly advancing on Thessaloniki, they simultaneously drove on Belgrade, leading to the swift collapse of the ill-prepared Yugoslav army. Within days the Wehrmacht was pouring through the Monastir Gap into central Greece, isolating the Greeks on the Albanian front while wheeling round the exposed left flank of the British Expeditionary Force holding the Aliakmon line. Outmanoeuvred by the enemy's highly mechanised forces and at the mercy of the Luftwaffe's superiority in the air, all resistance was quickly broken, and long before the twenty-fourth, when the British command gave the order to evacuate, the roads south to the ports and beaches of Attica and the Peloponnese were choked with vehicles and men. 'Last night with you', broadcast Athens radio on the twenty-sixth, 'happy days with victory and liberty – God with you and for you, good luck.' To which Alexandria replied, 'We shall not forget you and look forward to the day of freedom.'[61] When Athens radio came on the air again the following lunchtime it spoke with a different voice: 'Achtung!

50 An Italian air force reconnaissance photograph taken from an altitude of 1000 metres shows ships of the Royal Navy's Mediterranean Fleet and Vichy's Force X in the Western Harbour. A breakwater runs along the right of the photograph; the harbour entrance, at the top right, was closed at night by a floating boom.

Achtung! This morning at eleven o'clock the National Socialist flag of Germany was hoisted above the Acropolis in Athens. Heil Hitler!'[62]

For the British, Greece was another Dunkirk; though ten thousand troops had been left behind, including seven thousand men left ashore at Kalamata in the southern Peloponnese after a fierce battle around the harbour, fifty thousand men had managed to escape to Egypt by 1 May. Now with the Luftwaffe operating from Greek airfields, Crete also came under attack. Despite reinforcements from Alexandria the Germans succeeded in an audacious parachute invasion, and by the end of May the island too was evacuated. Out of a defending force numbering twenty-six thousand, more than four thousand had been killed and five thousand taken prisoner, while the Royal Navy lost well over two thousand men with nine ships sunk and another thirteen badly damaged, including two battleships and the navy's sole aircraft carrier in the Mediterranean.

Meanwhile, with similar airborne drops expected imminently on Cyprus and the Suez Canal, Egypt faced a renewed threat in the desert to the west, where a young German general, Erwin Rommel, who had arrived in Libya to stiffen the Italians at Tripoli, had broken through the weakened British defences, had encircled Tobruk, and now stood on the Egyptian border at Sollum. When the War Office suggested that Britain might also have to evacuate Egypt, Churchill flew into a rage, though behind his directive to his commanders that he expected the troops there to fight to the last man was the realisation that even he believed that Egypt might well be lost. The German grand admiral was determined to make it a certainty: in support of Rommel he proposed to Hitler a decisive naval offensive against Alexandria and the Canal, a step which he considered would be 'more deadly to the British Empire than the capture of London'.[63]

'Is an erratic but most likeable individual with literary tastes', read a confidential British Embassy report on Judge Jasper Brinton; 'Is pro-British and essentially broad-minded, although sometimes unexpectedly stubborn.'[64] Titled 'List of Personalities in Egypt', the report was probably prepared by Walter Smart, the Oriental Counsellor, and was sent by Sir Miles Lampson, the ambassador, to Anthony Eden in 1941; covering 194 influential Egyptian and other non-British figures in the country, it was meant to help the foreign secretary assess whom Britain could rely on. They could certainly rely on Judge Brinton to be eccentric; when not sitting on the Mixed Courts or running the Archaeological Society, he had taken, at the age of sixty-two, to floating about in the Western Harbour by night to help protect the British fleet from air-raid attacks.

The harbour was encircled by batteries of anti-aircraft guns, while scores of barrage balloons, raised every evening and lowered in the morning by means of wires attached to windlasses, formed an effective screen against low-flying planes. Also to ward off enemy submarines the harbour was closed each night by a floating boom. But there was still a danger from aimless bombs and parachute mines, and it was principally to mark where these fell that at the request of Admiral Cunningham a few of Alexandria's yachting enthusiasts had formed the Volunteer Inshore Patrol.

'The whole enterprise', Judge Brinton observed, 'was conducted with a high standard of efficiency.' Owners of private craft were invited to contribute their use, and a roster of crews was drawn up with each volunteer serving once a week. Four sailing craft would go out each night from the patrol's headquarters at the British Boat Club in the customs area by Minet el Bassal, two taking up positions inside the harbour, the other two riding outside the boom, 'a distinctly choppy business' at times. Their orders were 'to be at the station throughout the night from dusk to dawn. . . . Close observation must be kept seawards, and accurate bearings and times of falling mines and bombs, etc, taken and recorded in the log book.'[65] Though some of the boats had cooking facilities and sleeping accommodation, nobody used them; even when off watch 'no one wanted to miss the interesting sights and sounds accompanying a night in the harbour': the wail of sirens heralding the approach of enemy aircraft, a dozen searchlights prowling the sky, then at the first glint of silver the anti-aircraft guns opening fire with a terrible roar, louder it was said than anything heard during the London Blitz, the flaming arcs of their shells snatching like claws at their targets, while down below beneath a hail of shrapnel the spotters bobbed about in their boats, enjoying what Brinton called 'one of the most exciting civilian war jobs', which was also, he thought, 'very much of a lark'.[66]

In the darkness before dawn on 1 May 1941 an Australian transport making the perilous crossing from Crete arrived at the boom of the Western Harbour, the ancient Eunostos of 'safe return'. The boatload of refugees had been expected for some time, and John Cromer Braun along with two other field security sergeants assigned to meet it had spent several days in idleness, eating ice cream and drinking coffee at Pastroudis on the Rue Fuad and regaling themselves on beccafico, the little birds that are a Levantine special-ity, washing them down with quantities of Mareotic wine. Now suddenly at four in the morning they were awakened in their barracks at Mustafa Pasha and told to bustle down to the docks where the near moonless night screamed with a barrage of tracer fire.

As the dawn call to prayer unwound from the dissolving darkness and the last enemy planes fled west with the night, the boom was opened and the waiting transport entered the harbour, passing along rows of camouflaged warships to its berth. Disembarkation began at mid-morning, Braun checking identity papers as the passengers filed off, 'for the most part a pathetic line of retired schoolteachers, professors, widows and other expatriates from Athens and the Peloponnese'. Amid the collapse and confusion of resistance in Greece, refugees fled southwards across the Mediterranean to Egypt, where as a precaution against infiltration by Axis agents they were carefully screened. Braun was standing at the head of the gangway when 'a stocky, round-faced figure' came forward, his wife just behind and his infant daughter on his shoulders. He took his pass-port and read 'Lawrence Durrell':

> 'Writer?'
>
> 'Yes.'
>
> 'Once of the Villa Seurat?'
>
> 'Yes.'
>
> 'Friend of Henry Miller?'
>
> 'Yes, anything wrong with that?'[67]

This did not seem the best moment for Durrell's notoriety to proceed him: until the outbreak of war he had been living on Corfu, where in 1937 on his twenty-fifth birth-day he completed *The Black Book*, his savage portrayal of a swaddled spiritual and sexual culture that he called the 'English Death'. T. S. Eliot, a director of Faber and Faber, greeted the novel as 'the first piece of work by a new English writer to give me any hope for the future of prose fiction'[68] but for fear of an obscenity prosecution would not publish it without cuts. Durrell refused, and instead an unexpurgated edition was published in Paris with the help of Henry Miller, whose own *Tropic of Cancer*, banned in Britain and America, was enjoying a *succès de scandale*.

'No, not at all', replied Braun, whose poetry had been published in London before the war and who was also a keen admirer of Miller, 'I would just like to talk to you about it.' After passing through Egyptian immigration, Durrell, Nancy and their ten-month-old daughter Penelope were placed in separate transit camps for men and women, Durrell at Agami, west of the city, where Braun went to join him that evening. 'We spent the whole night in a slit trench watching the air barrage while we talked about Paris and Henry Miller and literature till the next day when they were reunited – my recollection is that they were put on a lorry, the three of them, and sent to the Luna Park Hotel in Cairo.'[69]

Refugees had been pouring in for over a week, most having gone without food for days, many without papers, money or anywhere to go, over a thousand settling on Alexandria's seafront beaches, while the city's hospitals filled with soldiers from the Balkans and Tobruk. Durrell had seen nothing of Alexandria, but in that brief stay of barely twenty-four hours he had been received better than he would ever admit, always recalling his arrival in the most aggrieved and exaggerated terms. 'The first thing the British authorities did was to take our passports and lock us up in a concentration camp', he told an Egyptian journalist when he revisited the city in 1977. 'The heat was overwhelming and we were guarded by Czech soldiers armed to the teeth. We stayed there for three or four days until a consular visit established that I was a British press attaché.'[70]

Durrell's account, so at variance with Braun's, invites being taken with a large dose of salts: spinning tales to journalists, academics and anyone else who attempted to interview him became a habit with Durrell later in life. Yet even back in 1941 he had told something of the same story to his old friend from Corfu, Theodore Stephanides, lovingly described by Durrell's younger brother Gerald in *My Family and Other Animals* ('Gerry, this is Doctor Theodore Stephanides. He is an expert on practically everything you care to mention. And what you don't mention, he does. He, like you, is an eccentric nature-lover').[71] Stephanides, born in India to an English mother and a Greek father, had joined the British army in Greece and as a medical doctor with the rank of lieutenant in the Royal Army Medical Corps had stayed with the British forces throughout the battle of Crete until the island's fall at the end of May, when he was among the last to be evacuated to Egypt. Posted to a military hospital in Cairo, Stephanides soon tracked his friend down at the 'Lunatic Park',[72] as Durrell called the Luna Park Hotel, 'a rather ramshackle place that the authorities had requisitioned to house British refugees . . . a terrible place and terrifically overcrowded', though at least Durrell and his family had a room to themselves.

51 This photograph of Lawrence Durrell, with his daughter Penelope on his shoulders, was taken just before his family escaped from Greece, a scene repeated when he disembarked at Alexandria.

Stephanides and Durrell had last seen one another on a November day in Athens in 1939. There was much to talk about: remembered friends and recent adventures, not least the hair-raising escapes each had made from the Greek mainland to Crete, Stephanides in an antiquated Greek merchantman that was dive-bombed three times en route, Durrell and his family dodging the Luftwaffe in an overloaded and listing caique, the traditional fishing boat of Greece. 'But their luck held', Stephanides recalled, 'and they arrived safely in Alexandria, where they thought their troubles were at last over. But things did not turn out quite so pleasantly. The moment they set foot ashore [they] were pounced on by the military authorities and interned in a concentration camp where they were even more overcrowded than at the Luna Park Hotel', and where there was some delay before the Durrells 'were able to prove their bona fides'.[73]

'That just wasn't true', says Braun. 'Our job was to move them off as quickly as poss-ible. I said, "Look, you don't have to waste your time on him. He's what he says he is, there's no doubt about that."' Arrivals were put into holding camps, 'but not under prison conditions – but so they didn't go wandering off while we were getting the trans-port together. He certainly did not suffer any constraint. He could not have been in Alexandria more than twenty-four hours. Nobody wanted to crush up the port because there were other boats to come in, and nobody knew what the military follow-up would be.'

Nor, contrary to what Durrell told his Egyptian interviewer in 1977, was he a British press attaché when he arrived at Alexandria from Greece; neither was he 'with the Foreign Office at that time' and therefore 'entitled to passage on a battleship',[74] which was the line he spun to a French interviewer in 1972. But then as Stephanides once said of Durrell, 'Sometimes he would get so carried away by pulling other people's legs that he would end up by tweaking his own also.'[75]

Had Durrell really experienced any difficulties when landing at Alexandria, they would have been sorted out there and then by Braun's superior, Alan Wace, who was in overall charge of the operation. Wace was a professor of classical archaeology at Cambridge and had been excavating at Mycenae until the outbreak of the war, when he was taken on by British intelligence in Athens. As soon as it became clear that Greece would have to be evacuated, he was sent on ahead to Alexandria, arriving there on 21 April, where his task was to be at the docks to oversee the vetting of refugees as they arrived. Wace was eminently suited for the job: he had already performed a similar service when he controlled the movement of civilians from Greece to Egypt while working for intelligence in Athens during the First World War; if Durrell's passport and Braun's recognition were not enough, a few questions from Wace would have quickly established Durrell's identity.

Fantasy aside, the truth was that the Italian threat and the exhaustion of their small private incomes had driven Durrell and Nancy from their Corfu idyll which they had inhabited since early 1935, and they had come to Athens in search of work. In September 1939, as Britain declared war on Germany, the British Embassy in Athens was caught short-staffed, and people like Stephanides and Durrell, who were able to speak both Greek and English, were taken on to provide translated abstracts of the Greek press. The whole thing lasted about a month, remembered Stephanides, until permanent staff arrived from England 'and all the temporary wallahs were thrown out on their ears'.[76] Meanwhile, Nancy had become pregnant, and Durrell followed his embassy stint with teaching for the British Council, first in the capital and then at Kalamata in the southern Peloponnese.

In the opening months of 1941 it looked increasingly likely that the Greek success in repelling Italy's winter invasion from Albania would sooner or later bring the Germans into the Balkans. 'Sitting on the crater',[77] was how Durrell described the suspense to Henry Miller from Kalamata. 'I am not writing needless to say: too much noise in the world to hear one's own voice', but then in a postscript: 'Ironically enough yesterday afternoon the cloud lifted and I saw the whole Book of the Dead lying below me like a forbidden superb city. I am ready to begin it now: it's a marvellous conception and complete.'[78] 'The Book of the Dead' was Durrell's working title for what eventually became *The Alexandria Quartet*.

CHAPTER 6

Personal Landscape

Do you think we will get back? Not to the past of Greece, I mean, but to
our own past in Greece? . . . The past and future join hands here; whatever
happens we will get back.

Lawrence Durrell to George Seferis, October 1941[1]

Whatever the truth about Lawrence Durrell's arrival at Alexandria's Western
Harbour, the ferocity of his reaction betrayed a deeper disturbance. Unlike
Forster, who came to Egypt voluntarily and was determined to have experiences there,
the 29-year-old Durrell arrived badly shaken by his ejection from Greece. 'The loss of
Greece has been an amputation,'[2] he would later write in Alexandria, but the separation
from wholeness came long before that. Greece had been an attempt to restore it; Egypt
the place to which he was driven by inexorable forces, and where he felt cut off, helpless and trapped.

In the early hours of 1 July 1942, exactly fourteen months after disembarking at the
Western Harbour, Durrell was revisiting Alexandria. He and Nancy were still living in
Cairo, where during the previous summer Walter Smart, Oriental Counsellor at the
British Embassy, had given him a job in the embassy's Publicity Section. Now Durrell
had been issued with a revolver and despatched on the night train to the coast, his
instructions to destroy the files of the British Information Office. The atmosphere was
sinister as the blacked-out train moved north through the Delta darkness, from time to
time making unexplained halts amid an unnerving silence. The Afrika Korps had broken
through the Egyptian frontier, taking Sollum, Sidi Barrani and Mersa Matruh in rapid
succession, and as the Eighth Army was falling back on Alamein Rommel was writing
exultantly to his wife, 'Less than one hundred miles to Alexandria!'[3]

On that Wednesday morning of 1 July when Durrell reached Alexandria, the railway
station was jammed with evacuees. German bombers had been striking with ever
increasing force in their nightly raids over the Western Harbour, and panic had broken
out in the city on Monday when the Alexandrians saw the Royal Navy's Mediterranean
Fleet set sail for the safety of Haifa and through the Suez Canal to the Red Sea.

When Durrell reached the Information Office he found that it had been wrecked by a bomb, so instead he walked about the streets of what seemed a city of the dead. A funeral pall of smoke rose from the chimneys of the British Consulate on the Avenue Alexandre le Grand just east of the Ramleh tram terminus, where documents were being furiously burned. The same was happening at military offices and installations throughout the town and at Cairo, Ismailia and Port Said. Everywhere the word went round that the British had lost Egypt. Shops and bars and cafés were closed, their iron shutters rolled down, and from empty rooms the unanswered ring of telephones carried through Alexandria's empty streets.

But not everyone recoiled from Rommel's advance. Bearing gifts of fruit and cigarettes, some Italian residents of the city were stopped at a British guard post as they tried to drive out towards the front line to welcome the confidently expected Axis army; there were stories of cafés along the Corniche placing orders with local butchers for wurst; and Durrell noticed that several enterprising establishments had already posted signs reading 'Willkommen Rommel'. With nothing else for him to do, Durrell made a list of these, reporting them to the military authorities when he returned that evening to Cairo.

Since 1940 the war had swung back and forth across the desert, the Italians and Germans advancing eastwards from Tripoli, the British advancing in their turn westwards from Alexandria, each army stretching its lines of supply like a piece of elastic, until after the halt and attrition of battle the elastic hauled the advancing army back towards its base. Following a failed offensive in June 1941, Wavell had been replaced as commander-in-chief by General Sir Claude Auchinleck, who in November launched Operation Crusader, its purpose to relieve Tobruk and, in Churchill's words, 'to beat the life out of Rommel & Co'.[4] But in beating Rommel back towards Tripoli, the advance told against Auchinleck's own supplies, while towards the end of May 1942 a replenished Rommel made another lunge eastwards, overwhelming Tobruk on 21 June and capturing thirty-five thousand British, South African and Indian troops.

The fall of Tobruk was completely unexpected and shattered any feelings of complacency about what the British ambassador Sir Miles Lampson was wont to call 'the ups and downs of the Western campaign'.[5]

A run on the banks began on 24 June, the banking halls 'a seething mass of men and women'. At Barclays Bank in the Rue Chérif Pasha a system of queuing was introduced, not something that the public was used to, which had to be enforced by resort to corrals of chains and wooden benches and by bank employees who 'stood on the benches and occasionally hauled out by the coat collar people who were trying to push ahead of their turn'.[6]

The storm burst in all its fury on 29 June, when Mersa Matruh was overrun and Rommel's army seemed to race like a flood towards Alexandria. Radio broadcasts and newspaper headlines grew increasingly ominous: 'Egypt will be defended to the last' – 'Reinforcements are known to be arriving' – 'There can be no disguising the fact that a very real threat to our whole position in Egypt exists' – 'Even if we lose Alexandria, there still remain good port and harbour installations at Haifa for our Fleet'.[7]

On the day that Mersa Matruh fell, Countess Mary de Zogheb wrote in her diary, 'Panique en ville. Flotte et amirauté, Wrens, etc, évacuent, clubs et hostels militaires fermés';[8] otherwise out at Ramleh life went on in its usual routine: tea at the Beau Rivage Hotel, the former summer residence of the Zoghebs at Glymenopoulo, with her Jewish friends Lady Harari, wife of Sir Victor Harari Pasha, a director of several companies belonging to the Cattaoui-Suares-Menasce-Rolo group, and Yvonne Rolo, wife of the cotton broker Max Rolo. But on 30 June the 'panique' had grown and there were 'beaucoup de départs', among them some Greeks, including the consul and members of the Salvagos family, but also many Jewish families: 'les Vincendon, les Max Rolo, les Menasce, les Roger Aghion, Marie Rose Goar – au Cap',[9] though it seems that none of them except the last yet intended to travel as far as Cape Town, Mary de Zogheb observing that most had no more immediate plans than to head for Cairo and Luxor. From there, along with other members of Egypt's minority and foreign communities – especially those known for their support for the British and their opposition to the Nazis – they could flee if necessary into the Sudan or to Ethiopia, Chad, the Belgian Congo, Syria, Palestine or farther afield. The important thing was to leave Alexandria, from which the Mediterranean offered no escape, contributing to the atmosphere of fevered anxiety and tension in the city.

On 1 July as Mary de Zogheb was helping to close down the United Forces Club, her son Bernard, back from his new job at the RAF base at Aboukir, recalled 'the streets being full of burnt paper blowing in the wind everywhere as everyone was burning compromising documents and even love letters from soldiers and sailors'. That night the bombing was especially heavy and the Zoghebs went down to the shelter where they were joined by only two other families; most of their friends and neighbours had fled, including all those who were Jewish.

But these were the better-off and of independent means, nor did all of these leave the city. 'My parents are too old to be chased about by Rommel',[10] said Lilia Ralli, the niece of Sir John Antoniades, who in 1918 had given his villa and gardens out by Nouzha to the Municipality. Lilia had been in Athens as the Greeks fought valiantly against the Italians, then with grim hopelessness against the Germans; the spirit of Greece had been mystical, she said, which she did not feel was the spirit in Egypt now, and this made her deeply unhappy. She had escaped as Greece was overwhelmed, and she longed to go back, to collect food, to cook communal meals, to help the starving – there were reports of the dead being carried in tumbrils through the streets of Athens daily. For others the despair had been crushing and immediate: on the day the swastika was raised above the Acropolis, Antony Benachi's sister Penelope Delta killed herself by taking poison. 'In Athens there had been no hope', said Lilia. 'No matter what happens here, it can't be worse than what happened there.'[11]

52   Winston Churchill lunching with the RAF at Burg el Arab between the first and second battles of Alamein.

Among those who did not flee Alexandria there were also many middle-class traders who had invested heavily in merchandise since the beginning of the year at the prospect of increasing import restrictions, and who were now prevented from leaving by the lack of ready money, while the limited incomes of small tradesmen and artisans of the lower middle class made even the thought of flight impossible.

Among the less well off was Moise Cohen, a moneylender in Mohammed Ali Square who lived with his wife and his two daughters in Mazarita. His eldest daughter, Eve Durrell, or Yvette Cohen as she was then, also remembers 'Ash Wednesday', as British soldiers were quick to make light of it, when the black snow of charred documents fell from the sky and the rumour went round that 'the British are deserting us'. She heard stories too, though never substantiated, of panicking evacuees dying in the desperate crush aboard the departing trains. But she did not believe that the British were running away and she gave no thought to doing so either. Eve had confidence in the British army and never doubted that Rommel would be defeated. But her father was not so sure. Eve was twenty-three, impetuous and beautiful, and her father was worried about what might happen to her if the Germans came. He scraped together some money and a day or two later told her to go to Cairo for a few weeks and stay with his sister there. 'No one else in the family went. He did not send his wife or my sister. I was the apple of my father's eye.'

On the night of Tuesday 30 June Judge Brinton brought his diary up to date by reviewing the events of the week that had passed. He and Geneva had just had 'one of our most delightful visits' out at Burg el Arab where the desert seemed very calm. 'Tobruk had fallen two days before, but Tobruk was a couple of hundred miles away and while the situation was serious no one anticipated any rapid advance. Parker came out Wednesday evening and told us of the rumour of a big advance east. Bramly was cross at the generals who let Rommel escape but didn't seem much alarmed. Talked to him of the Bedouin law problem.'

By the end of the week Judge Brinton was back in Alexandria, and on Friday 26 June 'Gaudin [the American consul] calls up to ask about our getting away. We tell him we're not getting away.' The consul then demanded 'a single good reason why you and Mrs Brinton should not leave Alexandria', and the Judge 'failed to amuse' when he told Gaudin, 'I'm building a chicken coop.' By Monday afternoon the consulate had shut and Gaudin had left the city; also 'the hen and the chicks were gone. Mystery. Two widely separated clumps of feathers on our rich lush lawn. Cat? Thief? Fox?' Brinton was philosophical: 'Such are the fortunes of war.'

Apart from building a chicken coop, for which he had 'with much pains collected the material',[12] Brinton had other reasons for not leaving Alexandria. 'Perhaps we had more confidence in the Eighth Army than others did or perhaps we felt that the lives of an elderly judge and his wife were not in any great danger from a German occupation. Perhaps also we were too much interested in the convalescent officers who were settled in our home. Then there was our house at Burg el Arab, half-way out to Alamein, which continued to make itself useful to the YMCA and to which we still had access.'[13]

It meant something too that an ancient Egyptian goddess stood as a talisman against Rommel at Burg el Arab. In the previous autumn of 1941, Brinton had received word as he was staying at his House of the Judge, Dar el Qadi, that South African troops at a then unremarked place called Alamein had unearthed some interesting granite blocks bearing hieroglyphic inscriptions. Driving out there with John and Josie and with Alan Rowe, who had replaced the interned Adriani as director of the Graeco-Roman Museum, Brinton learnt that the blocks were from an ancient way station erected in the thirteenth century BC in the time of Ramses II at the outset of his Libyan campaign. Similar blocks had been found at Gharbaniat, near the desert home of the Tortillias some twenty miles to the east, and at Karm Abu Girg, southeast of Amriya, suggesting a line of stations, probably for both defence and water, along Ramses' main northern highway into Libya.

The way station at Alamein, however, seemed to have been the most important of these, for it stood at the narrowest and most defensible point between Libya and Egypt, hemmed in by the sea on one side and by the plunging impassable Qattara Depression on the other, and had been singled out by Ramses to serve also as a monument recording his early triumphs. In addition to a conventional relief showing the pharaoh braining his Libyan foes, another depicted a female goddess, otherwise unknown in the records, called Imit-mit, meaning 'She-who-is-in-the-road', a 'good augur for the modern defenders of Egypt',[14] wrote Brinton when he published his find in the *Bulletin* of the Archaeological Society early in 1942. After obtaining the permission of the Antiquities Service he removed the blocks for safekeeping to his garden at Burg el Arab, where they remain to this day.

And so at Alexandria the Brintons stayed and waited. 'Bank crowded that night [Monday 29 June] Mersa falls. We go to movie – Cary Grant in superior rotten movie – but a change of thoughts.' And on Tuesday as Rommel drew up his forces at Alamein they went to the beach, which was 'rather deserted'.[15]

On Wednesday evening, 1 July, when Durrell returned to Cairo, he found the city in the grip of 'the Flap'. 'The trains were taking everybody away, sending off all the women and children. A delicious thing to experience actually. Pure vertigo of panic on the streets.' Durrell was taken round to Operations by his friend Group Captain Dudley Honor who was in charge of the air defences of Cairo, where in a big gloomy hall the positions in the Western Desert were marked out on a giant board by radio operators in touch with the front. In contrast to the civilian panic outside, at Operations the mood was growing quietly more confident by the hour; this had been the most dangerous day of the desert war, but the RAF, including squadrons of Hurricanes flown by Greeks and Free French, had been harrying the invaders from the air, and the Eighth Army had stood its ground at Alamein. After taking 'an enormous deep breath',[16] Durrell and Honor walked out into the night for a drink.

Though the July battle of First Alamein, as it became known, would continue until the seventeenth, already on the fourth Rommel was writing home to his wife, 'Unfortunately, things are not going as I should like them. Resistance is too great and our strength is exhausted', adding on the following day, 'It's not easy to have to hold on like this, only sixty miles from Alexandria'.[17]

On 5 July, with the sound of tank and artillery fire carrying on the desert wind, Mary de Zogheb was back working at the United Forces Club in the Rue de Corinthe in the Quartier Grec – 'beaucoup de travail et de soldats'[18] – with ten other women under the direction of Norah Peel, and on the sixth and seventh she was noting in her diary that her friends who had fled to Cairo at the beginning of the month had all returned to Alexandria.

53   Dar el Qadi at Burg el Arab. The Brintons had military passes and continued to visit Dar el Qadi, the House of the Judge, at Burg el Arab throughout the desert fighting.

By then, however, the British, American and other embassies and legations had sent many of their nationals out of the country, by air to Ethiopia, by sea to East and South Africa and by rail to Palestine. Durrell's daughter and wife were among those who left Egypt during the Flap aboard an evacuation train for Jerusalem.

'She is going for a week', Durrell wrote in *The Alexandria Quartet* of another departure for Jerusalem, 'but in the panic, half-asleep I can see that she may never come back. The soft resolute kiss and the bright eyes fill me with emptiness. . . . It is only as the train begins to move, and as the figure at the window, dark against the darkness, lets go of my hand, that I feel Melissa is really leaving.'[19]

Perhaps it was in a premonitory mood that after seeing Nancy off at Cairo station Durrell did something he had been avoiding for over a year: on 4 July he wrote a letter to Henry Miller. In lurid detail he told his friend how awful he found Egypt, adding that his wife and daughter had gone to Palestine.

Then some time in late summer Nancy wrote from Jerusalem. Mary Bentley was in the embassy's Publicity Section, where she worked with Durrell, as he opened the letter saying she never wanted to return to him. 'He was truly shattered, he could not believe she meant it, and I saw tears in his eyes.'[20] If only he could see her, he said to Mary; she turned to her fiancé, Dudley Honor, who found an excuse to fly a light bomber to Palestine and took Durrell with him. But Nancy was unmoved by her husband's pleadings. Again in September he went to see her, this time taking the train from Cairo, but there had been tensions in their marriage for several years, and now, she told Durrell, she had decided to make her own way.

What hurt Durrell as much as the separation from Nancy was the rupture he felt at the loss of his daughter Penelope. That January, with two friends he had known from Athens, Robin Fedden and Bernard Spencer, Durrell had launched *Personal Landscape* in Cairo, a magazine devoted to poetry. From its first number at the beginning of 1942 to its eighth and last in 1945, its three editors, who were also its chief contributors, 'were impelled', as Grafftey-Smith put it, 'to pronounce essentials in a world of flux and menace, and they did so, eloquently. The quality of their fantasy valuably restored the sense of proportion of others who lacked their special vision.'[21] In fact, throughout the three-year span of *Personal Landscape* Durrell's contributions rarely had anything to do with Egypt, and in Cairo he complained that he could 'write nothing but short and febrile like jets by this corrupt and slow Nile'.[22] But he had salvaged some poems from Greece, and in the first number of the magazine he published one addressed to Penelope, protective and enclosing:

> Sleep, my dear, we won't disturb
> You, lying in the zones of sleep.
> The four walls symbolise love put about
> To hold in silence which so soon brims
> Over into sadness: it's still dark.[23]

In the twelve months preceding those desperate desert battles of June and July 1942, the war had expanded far beyond Europe and the Mediterranean. On 22 June 1941 Germany had invaded Russia, its erstwhile ally, and was now driving into the Caucasus, threatening Britain's supplies of oil from Persia and Iraq, while on 7 December the Japanese had attacked the American Pacific Fleet at Pearl Harbor, followed in the same month by invasions of the Philippines, an American possession, and of the British possessions of Burma, Hong Kong, Malaya and Singapore. More immediately concerned about Japan, America had no plans to enter the European war, but its hand was forced four days after Pearl Harbor when Italy and Germany gratuitously declared war on the United States. A further eleven months would pass, however, before the first American soldiers crossed the Atlantic and went into battle, landing at Casablanca in November 1942, this to coincide with Anglo-American landings at Oran and Algiers under cover of a Royal Navy task force commanded by Admiral Cunningham, who had been transferred in April from Alexandria.

Meanwhile, the struggle in the Western Desert was yet to be decided. In Egypt things had stabilised since the Flap and as the summer months wore on Rommel was held at bay by the Eighth Army and the RAF, while the Royal Navy bombarded his forces from sea. Auchinleck had 'stemmed the adverse tide',[24] as Churchill said; indeed, it became clear in retrospect that he had turned it, making Rommel's ultimate defeat only a matter of time. But recriminations over the disaster in June and disappointment over the lack of an outright British victory had shaken confidence in the high command.

Early in August a restive Churchill came to Cairo, flying at fifteen thousand feet in the unpressurised cabin of an American Liberator bomber, his oxygen mask specially adapted so that he could wear it and still smoke his cigar. Auchinleck was given Kipling's *If* to read and posted off to India. General Sir Harold Alexander, the last man to leave Dunkirk in 1940, was appointed commander-in-chief Middle East, while General Sir Bernard Montgomery, who had a reputation for abrasiveness, was given command of the Eighth Army in the field, Churchill remarking that 'If he is disagreeable to those about him, he is also disagreeable to the enemy.'[25] After flying on to Moscow for a meeting with Stalin, Churchill was back in Egypt during the third week of August when he paid a morale-boosting visit to the troops in the Western Desert. Calling at Montgomery's headquarters on the coast at Burg el Arab, he went bathing in the Mediterranean, floating on his back and raising his legs in his famous V-sign salute.

By August the Mediterranean Fleet had returned to Alexandria under the command of Cunningham's successor Admiral Sir Henry Harwood, who resumed entertaining at his lovely villa at Laurens beyond San Stefano in Ramleh. On 28 August the *Egyptian Gazette* was reporting that Richard Casey, minister of state,[26] who recently 'had been indisposed, has now recovered and has been recuperating at Alexandria'. Indeed the evening before, Harwood had invited Casey and his wife to dinner, where so far as the other guests were concerned the conversation turned on some paintings, and on the twenty-eighth the relaxing pace seemingly continued as Harwood in his white uniform and Casey, dapper in slacks and a double-breasted blazer, were the luncheon guests of Judge and Geneva Brinton at their home in nearby Glymenopoulo.

But the luncheon had an urgent purpose. British intelligence had cracked Rommel's codes and had learnt that any day now he would attempt another lunge forward, leaving Casey and Harwood with only hours to decide whether to seize the French fleet in the Western Harbour. Being an eminent resident of the city and a Chevalier of the Legion of Honour, Judge Brinton had been asked by the British to undertake the secret and delicate mission of sounding out Admiral Godfroy. Brinton had therefore invited Godfroy to his home, and it was his report of this meeting that Harwood and Casey had come to hear.

Judge Brinton told them that he had found Godfroy to be a quiet, courteous and dignified gentleman with a British wife and underlying British sympathies, who was pained by the ostracism to which he was subjected by Alexandrian society but who nevertheless was perfectly clear in his duty as commander of his fleet. The ships belonged to France, and he was a servant of the Vichy government to which alone he was prepared to render account. He told Brinton that he would not consent to the removal of the fleet unless on the orders of the Vichy government, that he would not surrender even if he was so ordered, and that if any attack was made on the squadron from any source which he could not resist he would immediately scuttle his ships. Godfroy had also handed Brinton a long and carefully reasoned document, a 'Communication Générale de l'Amiral à la Force X', which stated that 'the French are unable to be a nation unless they obey a government, even if they do not like it'.

Shrewdly, Brinton expressed the Frenchman's dilemma to his guests in British constitutional terms, saying Godfroy's language recalled that of the Speaker of the House of Commons who in 1642, at the outbreak of the English Civil War, was asked the whereabouts of several MPs whose arrest had been ordered by the king, and who replied, 'I have neither eye to see, nor tongue to speak here, but as the House is pleased to direct me.'

All this having been reported to them over lunch, Richard Casey and Admiral Harwood decided to leave Force X alone.[27]

That summer was a breathing space. With the Reich's resources increasingly diverted towards its advance on Stalingrad, Rommel remained tethered to his niggardly line of supply which stretched a thousand miles westwards across the desert. Meanwhile, British convoys were rounding Africa and feverishly unloading stores, armour, ammunition and men at Suez for transport to the front. Rommel knew of the gathering danger and on 30 August wrote to his wife, 'Today has dawned at last. . . . We have some very grave shortages. But I've taken the risk, for it will be a long time before we get such favourable conditions of moonlight, relative strengths, etc, again. . . . If our blow succeeds, it might go some way towards deciding the whole course of the war.'[28]

Rommel struck that night, but Montgomery was prepared. In the four-day battle of Alam Halfa, named after a ridge to the east of Alamein, the Germans again were checked, allowing Montgomery's meticulous build-up of the Eighth Army to continue. In this he had the help of Jasper Maskelyne, the celebrated illusionist, whose grandfather's famous House of Magic had occupied the Egyptian Hall in Piccadilly during the last three decades of the nineteenth century – and after whom Durrell named one of the characters in his *Alexandria Quartet*.

Maskelyne was famous for his pre-war levitation act, in which he seemingly floated the body of a hypnotised woman above the audience and then made her disappear into thin air. Posted to Egypt with the Royal Engineers Camouflage Corps in 1941, one of his first tasks was to protect a vital shipment of tanks due to arrive at Alexandria's Western Harbour; for three nights running he succeeded in misdirecting German bombers to a dummy harbour in Lake Mariut, where fake explosions suggested that targets were being hit. Now in the run-up to Second Alamein, the British created the appearance of a vast army slowly assembling at the southern end of the Alamein line in order to deceive the Germans into thinking that an attack would come from that quarter sometime in November. Meanwhile, aided by Maskelyne's techniques for disguising tanks as trucks, the real and more rapid build-up came at the northern end of the line, where Montgomery was concentrating the bulk of the Eighth Army's 1,000 tanks, 2,000 guns and 220,000 men for an attack, which when it came in October took Rommel completely by surprise.

Not that Durrell's Maskelyne character bore any resemblance to the illusionist, but 'to do a Maskelyne' became proverbial among the Alexandrians, and the strange ring of the name carried associations that Durrell would develop in his vision of the city. As Jasper himself liked to tell the story, he inherited his name and skills of deception from a Norman knight who came to England before the Battle of Hastings as a spy for William the Conqueror, and was afterwards rewarded with the county of Wiltshire and took the name Maskelyne, meaning disguise or mask in Old French. After the war Jasper found new inspiration in the family name when he gave his revived stage career a lift by teaming up with a striptease artiste as Maskelyne and Femynyne. Illusion and shifting identities would be a feature of Durrell's *Alexandria Quartet*, and shifting genders too.

This was the situation in October 1942 when Durrell was transferred to Alexandria and put in charge of the city's British Information Office, though 'when I came here', he thought at the time, 'there was no reason to suppose that the war would ever end, that I should ever leave Egypt'.[29]

Durrell took a room at the Hotel Cecil with a view over the Eastern Harbour. Arriving in the city after coming from Cairo (the visitor feels it even today) there was the intoxicating vast blue of the Mediterranean and the promise of Europe on the seawind. 'Everything smelt good again',[30] as Durrell would write in the *Quartet*, and at night the sweep of the Corniche brilliant with lights made Alexandria seem like 'some great crystal liner . . . anchored to the horn of Africa'.[31] But the city that seemed to him so 'plangently Greek'[32] was also a reminder of all he had lost, and looking out over the harbour from his balcony at the Cecil, Durrell 'reflected on exile in general and my own in particular'.[33]

The pain of loss that the Greeks call nostalgia (from 'νοστος', return home, and αλγος, pain) was all too familiar to Durrell's experience and went to the core of his being. He met Nancy in Bloomsbury in 1932 where she was a painter at the Slade School of Fine Art, a slender blonde with a feline grace who at five foot eight towered over Durrell, who was five foot two. Her first memory of him was of 'a wistful, sweet person, very small and charming. Very gentle, very unhappy', and she remembered him saying of his upbringing, 'Even the best school is an orphanage if there is no home life to compare against it.'[34]

The previous year, at the age of nineteen, he had had his first collection of poems privately printed as *Quaint Fragment*, its title as much a wry description of himself as of his verses. In one poem, 'A Dedication' ('To My Mother'), he explained how he had fashioned his poems 'from the memories of hours forlorn / When I lived goodbyes, and crushed the stem / Of conscious sadness, pillaging the sap / Of tired youth', and concluded, 'I only plead / That I have lived them all these lonely few / . . . / Each one some little magic that belongs to you.'[35] Later, in a notebook dated 1938, he raised this to a metaphysical level, writing that at birth a part of consciousness is lost, and that 'the whole course of one's life is simply a search for this lost fragment' through 'a world of

54 In the autumn of 1942, when Durrell was posted to Alexandria, he took a room at the Hotel Cecil with a view over the Eastern Harbour.

mirrors'. In the same notebook he also drew a sketch map of Bloomsbury marked 'Plan for the Book of the Dead'.[36]

The 'hours forlorn' harked back to the break with his childhood in India, where Durrell was born at Jullundur in the Punjab on 27 February 1912. His father, Lawrence Samuel Durrell, who worked for the railways as a civil engineer, was the son of a Suffolk agricultural labourer of illegitimate birth who after enlisting in the army was posted to India in the 1870s. Durrell's mother, Louisa Dixie, whose people were also soldiers and engineers, could trace her family's presence in India back a generation further; they were Protestants who had come from County Cork some time before 1845.

In the eight years following Durrell's birth, the family migrated from one railway project to the next across the breadth of the Raj, from Jullundur to the isolation of Arakan Burma on the far side of the Bay of Bengal, from Mymensingh on the burning Ganges plain up to Kurseong in the forested hill country below Darjeeling. Isolation and the climate took its toll in disease and illness and anxiety; at Mymensingh, as Durrell turned four, his infant sister died of diphtheria. Then in 1920 Lawrence Samuel resigned his position as executive engineer with the Darjeeling-Himalayan Railway and took his family (now enlarged by another son, Leslie, and a daughter, Margo – Gerry was not born until 1925) down to the village of Sakchi, where a raw industrial site was being carved out of the steaming jungles of Bihar.

An ambitious and uncommonly able man, he established an engineering and construction firm, Durrell and Company, with the backing of wealthy Sikhs, and won a contract to build a tin plate mill, a brick-making plant, an office building, a hospital and over four hundred workers' houses, each with its own garden, for the Parsi industrialist Sir Dorabji Tata, transforming the Tata iron and steel works at Sakchi into the model town of Jamshedpur. Religious and caste prejudice were entirely unknown at Jamshedpur, and the workers, who ran their own newspaper, enjoyed a greater freedom of expression than in workplaces elsewhere in India. This, together with its 'fine housing . . . its hospital', continued to make Jamshedpur something special even after independence a quarter of a century later, when Margaret Bourke-White, the noted *Life* journalist and photographer, described it as being 'far in advance of any other industrial centre I visited in India'.[37]

Though Lawrence Samuel was known among friends and relations for his warmth and his fun-loving nature, he seemed a shy and distant figure to Durrell, who felt helpless and lonely within the awkwardness of their relationship. He rejected, at times with bitter contempt, what he saw as his father's faith in material and social advance, 'the awful ignorance of the Empire Builder, the would-be altruist, the dreary stupidity of the "team spirit"'.[38] He nevertheless acknowledged that he had inherited from his father his 'love of order and sense of responsibility', but he owed his 'laziness and bohemianism',[39] also his looks, 'small and dwarfish of aspect',[40] to his mother, whom he adored; she spoilt him terribly, or so he would say, adding that he could always get his way with her, though at the same time he saw and fiercely resented the far greater attention she lavished on her younger son, the less able and often sickly Leslie.

In 1921, when Durrell was nine, his father decided that it was time for him to get regular schooling – until then such education as he had received came from an Irish Catholic governess at home – and so he was sent on the day and a half's journey back up the railway line past Kurseong to St Joseph's College at Darjeeling, where, as he would often recall, 'the long austere dormitories looked out across the valleys towards Tibet. A huge ragged escarpment of famous mountains were our companions.' But there his curiosity ended. 'I knew nothing of Tibet, then, though I frequently met benign old lamas walking down the highroad to the plains twirling their prayer-wheels. Tibet was not "romantic" then or even interesting. Africa (darkest) was the country of romance – or Egypt – (Stanley, Rider Haggard, etc).'[41]

As for India, Durrell was largely insulated from that native life that teemed beyond the domestic pale of the Raj, and certainly he was no Kipling's Kim; rather the magic lay in what he called the 'perfect idleness'[42] of his childhood and most of all in the enclosing world that was his home: 'Our life in India was typically colonial, ie very much family-oriented'.[43] But after two years at St Joseph's, his father decided that he and his brother Leslie should be sent 'home' to England, for he knew that professional advancement went to those who got the 'hallmark',[44] as he put it, at a public school followed by university. Neither his father nor his mother had ever set foot in England, but to Anglo-Indians, as Durrell explained, it was 'home' in an inexpressibly poignant way; 'The Israelites could not have hung up a larger harp on the sound of it than the British did.'[45] Nevertheless, according to Durrell, 'My mother was against the idea. She said I was too young, that it was cruel to send me so far away. It was the first time I had witnessed a really heated argument at home; it was so calm as a rule. Seeing my mother cry was a real body-blow.'[46] Yet if anything he blamed his mother more for allowing him to go, and it was not only in verses of 'hours forlorn' that he never let her forget it.[47]

Durrell was sixteen and at St Edmund's School in Canterbury when in April 1928 his headmaster handed him a telegram from India: six days after being admitted to hospital for what his family called a tumour on the brain, his father, a young man still, only forty-three, had died of a cerebral haemorrhage. Durrell was numbed, but most of all he felt guilty at his inability to cry. Within two months a shattered Louisa Durrell abandoned India and came to England, where her son, who meanwhile had given up his studies for good, was once more united with his family – united in a land where they had been brought together by the coffin of his father's striving.

Both Durrell and Nancy had small private incomes, and after marrying in 1935 they left England for Corfu, though not before Durrell had assured the essential by persuading his mother to follow with the rest of the family. Drawn by the island's benign climate and its low cost of living, the idea was that Nancy would paint and Durrell would write, while the family would conserve what remained of the money left by Durrell's father. 'In Corfu, you see, we reconstituted the Indian period which we all missed. The island exploded into another open-air time of our lives, because one lived virtually naked in the sun.'[48]

Years later Durrell recalled the Eastern belief that everyone has two birthplaces, one where you were actually born and the other your place of predilection, 'the place where you really wake up to reality . . . and which nourishes you'.[49] For Durrell that place was the shrine of St Arsenius on the remote northeast coast of Corfu, where a fisherman had found the saint's icon washed up after a storm and had built a small shrine with a votive olive-oil lamp on a ledge above the sea. For Durrell, living with Nancy in the hamlet of Kalamai nearby, this was 'the place where I was reborn'.[50] There they plunged naked each morning into a clear blue Ionian sea pool, and there he finished *The Black Book* and felt that he had really become a writer. 'I shall really never, never ever forget a youth spent there, discovered by accident. . . . Youth does mean happiness, it does mean love, and that's something you can't get over.'[51]

But in September 1939 at the outbreak of war Durrell and Nancy stood on the balcony of their white house at Kalamai looking out across the straits to Italian-occupied Albania; having decided they ought to move for safety to Athens, they were clearing out books and papers, emptying cupboards and packing clothes. The war had come 'like a great severance', and Durrell felt 'cut to the heart and dumb. . . . Standing on our balcony over the sea it seemed like the end of the world.'[52]

To Forster, India was that newfound world that stimulated his imagination and his love; for Durrell, who yearned for his childhood but did not yearn for India, to which he never returned, it inspired no poem, no novel,[53] no travel book – instead that inspiration was found in Greece: 'I have been heavily stamped by Greece, ancient and modern. It comes across in my poems. . . . Before you can understand me, you must first appreciate Greece.'[54]

After a few days at the Cecil, Durrell moved in with a friend at Ramleh. Gwyn Williams' villa was in an area by then called Rushdi, in Rue Sirdar on 'Embassy Hill', the hill known to Forster as Abou el Nawatir, where he had gone to stay with Furness in 1916. Since then it had been crowned by the Residency, the home and headquarters of the high commissioners and since 1936 of Sir Miles Lampson, the ambassador, when during the summer months the king and his government, followed by the entire diplomatic corps, transferred to Alexandria. Instead of the gun that Forster saw lying in the sand, a relic of the fighting of 1882, there was now an anti-aircraft battery nearby. The villa might even have been the one where Forster had stayed nearly twenty-six years before, for Williams owed his move to Alexandria to Robin Furness, until recently professor at Cairo's Fuad University, where Williams had been a lecturer since 1930.

Gwyn Williams, then thirty-eight, had arrived in Alexandria a month before Durrell, where on the urging of Furness he had accepted the post as the first head of the English department at the newly established Farouk (now Alexandria) University. Williams' marriage had deteriorated in Cairo, and 'when my wife said she didn't intend to come with me, after the first shock I found that this suited me very well'.[55] There was good swimming nearby at Stanley Bay, while at the Sporting Club, within walking distance, Williams would play tennis with Felix Carver and Bobby Peel, and with the English department only a few tram stops west towards town at Chatby, the location, like his wife's absence, suited him perfectly.

For a while it suited Durrell too. From the Mustafa Pasha station he made the four-mile journey to work aboard 'the bucking, clicking tram'[56] (B for Bacos replacing the blue label, V for Victoria replacing the red) – Sidi Gaber, Cleopatra, Sporting, Ibrahimiya, Camp de César, Chatby-les-Bains, Chatby, Mazarita – arriving at the Ramleh terminus from where it was a short walk to the British Information Office at 1 (now 2) Rue Toussoum Pasha on the corner of the Rue Chérif Pasha in the heart of Alexandria. The office occupied three or four interconnecting rooms on the first floor, just above the mezzanine, its walls covered with anti-German posters in several languages, its windows looking out on the former Banco di Roma on the opposite corner. A few steps away where the Rue Chérif Pasha joined the Rue Fuad opposite the Mohammed Ali Club was the Maison Baudrot, its tea room, restaurant and American bar 'twinkling with lights and music',[57] as Durrell described it, and presided over by its

55 The beach at Sporting. In [...] [Alexandri]ans still flocked to the beaches all along the city's Mediterranean [...]

femme du monde risen fr[om] [...] [n]o-smoking Ariane Baudrot, whose talk was of the da[...] [woul]d cover her shoulders with nine white foxes from Sis[...] and sweep off to the Finney balls.

The many bars and ca[...] [info]rmation Office a 'refreshing port of call' for Gwyn Wi[...] [a]bility to choose and keep an efficient, pleasant staff' - [...], Miss Pattis for newspaper research, and Milto Axel[...] [super]visor. Durrell threw himself into his work, which wa[...] [p]apers, published in English, French, Greek, Armenia[...] [war]ds for appropriately upbeat stories, often writing the[...] [n]ow in his element', observed Theodore Stephanides, v[...] [mili]tary hospital at Amriya; in a city whose atmosphere c[...] [Gr]eek population, 'he was now his own boss and he was [...] [kno]wledge of Greek'.58 But Milto

Axelos' wife Céline, a poetess with a mane of golden hair, a small precious mouth and lively eyes, whom Durrell knew as a 'delightful woman',[59] remembered him as 'drunk three quarters of the time, a pretty boy, penniless'.[60]

At ten o'clock on 23 October 1942 the Alexandrian air shook with the hurricane roar of a thousand guns off in the Western Desert as Montgomery unleashed his artillery barrage and the Eighth Army went on to the offensive in the second battle of Alamein. In the early light of Saturday morning Sir Miles Lampson drove down the Desert Road from Cairo, passing masses of tanks heading off westwards, while 'the air round us was literally filled with planes. I have never seen so many planes before . . . bombers escorted by countless fighters . . . moving in every direction the whole time', while the sea off Mex was thick with small torpedo craft and tank landing craft returning from their night's business. Following lunch at the Residency Lampson went down to the beach at Stanley Bay, where he 'could hear the thunder of the guns quite clearly most of the time. After dinner this barrage became a solid unceasing roar and before I went to bed I went up on the roof and we could see the flashes clearly reflected on the low-lying clouds. Most exciting.'[61]

In town, as the moon went from full to new throughout the twelve-day battle, the Alexandrians went nightly onto their balconies, smoking and chattering, waving to one another across the narrow streets and exchanging grimaces of hope and resignation, while all the time straining their eyes towards the western horizon where their fates were being decided beneath a terrible halo of light. And each night, in a strange communion with the tens of thousands of soldiers out in the desert, both German and British, the Alexandrians twisted the knobs of their radio sets until a voice said something in German, and about Belgrade, and as soon as this magic word was uttered everyone fell to silence and waited. Since 1941, when the Germans captured the transmitter there, Belgrade radio had been broadcasting the usual type of family messages to the German troops scattered from the English Channel to the Russian front and to the deserts of northern Africa, and the programme always ended with that solemn sweet moment when Lale Anderson sang the original rather than some ersatz version of 'Lili Marlène'. 'We sat or lay there in a nostalgic trance', a British veteran recalled, 'listening to every word. And every night we did this, as long as we were there – Lili spoke to us and never became stale.'[62]

Anahide Merametdjian, who until recently ran a bookshop in the city, felt the sea shake as she was bathing at Sidi Bishr during Second Alamein: 'The war, well the poor boys would come, and so many died; when I go to the Alamein cemetery now I see it: they were twenty years old, they were so young. Some women had a wonderful time, they went to bed every night with a different officer or man. The Greek, Italian and Lebanese women gave themselves to the troops – they were very kind, the women, I realise that now.'

Since the summer of 1940 more than two million soldiers, sailors and airmen had passed through Egypt, and by Second Alamein Alexandria had changed. 'Is it fastidious to want to keep your head', Clea says in the *Quartet*, 'to avoid this curious sexual rush of blood to the head which comes with war, exciting the women beyond endurance? I would not have thought the smell of death could be so exciting to them! Darley, I don't want to be a part of this mental saturnalia, these overflowing brothels. And all these poor men crowded up here. Alexandria has become a huge orphanage, everyone grabbing at the last chance of life.'[63]

Anahide remembers the young men who came into the services clubs: 'Some were very shocked, others just wanted to change the clothes they wore. I once served two hundred cups of tea in two hours, and we used to make their eggs; one boy asked for twenty-five fried eggs. The ladies worked very hard in the canteens. And of course the boys liked to come and speak English; they all wanted to talk. Sometimes they asked me to go and dance with them. I would go and dance at parties – but I never went like the others. We had balls every week: British Benevolent Fund, Lebanese Fund, the Greek Fund, Armenian Fund, music, concerts, lectures. We women didn't pay for tickets to the balls; we would go to the bureau and sell the tickets to the men.'

For the officer uninterested in the preliminaries of a benevolent ball, the place to go was Mary's House east of the Rond Point beyond the Quartier Grec and Moharrem Bey; Marta Loria knew exactly where, as it stood by the railway line, opposite the Italian Hospital built by her father. 'Mary was a Greek who had only one eye – that's from looking through keyholes – and she set up this brothel with the help I suppose of the British army and navy, much to the disgust of the people living nearby, though it was very nice and very well organised. Then there was the time Mary's got a direct hit. They died in action. There was no other way it could be described: the officers had families, some had wives, and so they were posted as killed in action.'

Otherwise for the troops there was the road west out of town towards the military base at Agami where prostitutes presented themselves on the balconies, and where you eyed your choice from the street below before going upstairs. Or there were the well-worn bordellos along the Rue des Soeurs, Sisters' Street, named after those Brides of Christ associated with the Lazarist Church behind the Mixed Courts on Mohammed Ali Square. Before the Flap, Marta Loria married a naval officer, Ron Fuller, who added that for a time the navy itself operated a brothel just off the Rue des Soeurs with a medical officer permanently on duty. 'It created a big scandal, that the British should participate in such activity, and in the end under pressure it had to be closed, but by that time Alexandria had become much less important, when nearly all the activity had shifted along westwards. But originally, when the Mediterranean Fleet was there – we had a massive fleet there and every battleship must have had nearly a thousand men on board, and at times we had five battleships in port, apart from the cruisers and destroyers and all the rest of it.'

Gwyn Williams would watch 'for as long as one cared to look' at British servicemen and women in 'a motionless clinch' of 'Pompeian rigidity' pressed against walls. 'Egyptians were clearly puzzled', or so he thought, 'by this curious behaviour on the part of young people in uniform and used to stop and watch perhaps in the hope of detecting some movement that would indicate what was happening.[64] For Mario Colucci, though he was hardly more than a boy at the time, there was little mystery about it: he remembers seeing 'a Wren standing on the pavement outside the United Forces Club, her skirt hitched up, one foot on the wall, having sex with a soldier'.

'The city was always perverse' (this is Clea talking to Darley as the real Clea Badaro, who worked at the United Forces Club, may well have spoken to Durrell), 'but it took its pleasures with style, at an old-fashioned tempo, even in rented beds: never up against a wall or a tree or a truck! And now at times the town seems to be like some great public urinal. You step over the bodies of drunkards as you walk home at night. . . . Out of shame and sympathy I feel like turning my face away. . . . I force myself to serve them teas at their various canteens, roll bandages, arrange concerts. But inside myself I shrink smaller every day.'[65]

On 3 November 1942 Rommel wrote to his wife, 'Dearest Lu, The battle is going very heavily against us. We're simply being crushed by the enemy weight. . . . At night I lie open-eyed, racking my brains for a way out of this plight for my poor troops. We are facing very difficult days, perhaps the most difficult that a man can undergo. The dead are lucky, it's all over for them.'[66] Two days later the *Egyptian Gazette* carried a communiqué from General Montgomery: 'The enemy is in our power and is just about to crack. We have a chance of putting the whole Panzer Army in the bag and we will do so. Complete victory is almost in sight.'[67] Fifteen hundred miles to the north a grim battle was going on in the ruins of Stalingrad, and not many weeks later this too ended in complete disaster for the Germans.

Second Alamein, Rommel later wrote, 'turned the tide of war in Africa against us and, in fact, probably represented the turning point of the whole vast struggle'.[68] The decisive engagement was fought on 2 November, and the following day Rommel and the Afrika Korps started on their long retreat that within little more than six months would take them out of Africa. 'This is not the end. It is not even the beginning of the end. But it is perhaps the end of the beginning,'[69] announced Churchill at the Lord Mayor's Banquet on 10 November. For Alexandria, certainly, it was the end to danger as the war whirled away westwards.

On the fifteenth, church bells rang throughout the United Kingdom to give thanks for the victory in the Western Desert. The Alexandria Municipality joined the celebratory mood when it announced a proposal (never approved) for bestowing the name 'l'Avenue Montgomery' on the Rue des Soeurs.

Victory reopened the Mediterranean to the mails, so that letters no longer took months to pass round the Cape. Yet Durrell, who had hardly written to anyone for the past year and a half, saying he found the delays discouraging, continued to remain almost entirely silent. There is nothing comparable to Forster's stream of letters that provide almost a diary of his experiences. The war and Durrell's exile from Greece and now the break-

56 Admiral Harwood, commander-in-chief of the Mediterranean Fleet, and Richard Casey, minister of state, visit Judge Brinton at his home in Glymenopoulo to hear of his talks with Admiral Godfroy of Force X, before deciding whether or not to destroy the Vichy fleet in Alexandria's Western Harbour.

up of his marriage left him numb and dislocated in Egypt – 'I was in such a stupefied condition all the time I was living there.'[70]

The person Durrell most pointedly avoided writing to was Henry Miller. Their friendship began in 1935, when a few months after arriving on Corfu Durrell read *Tropic of Cancer* and wrote enthusiastically to its author in Paris, Miller replying, 'Your letter is so vivid, so keen, that I am curious to know if you are not a writer yourself.'[71] Miller's flattering enquiry and the correspondence that followed were immensely encouraging to Durrell, who looked up to him as something more than a writer. Miller was forty-three, twenty years older than Durrell, who came to adopt him as a father-figure, as one of his 'uncles' as Durrell put it: 'He was full of energy and enthusiasm which were wonderful guidelines for a young man.'[72] Durrell soon began work on *The Black Book*, 'my first real book',[73] in 1937 sending his only manuscript copy to Miller, who called it 'a colossal poem',[74] 'an event in my life'.[75] Since their first meeting in Paris later that year,

Durrell had tried to persuade Miller to visit Greece, and in the summer of 1939 he came, Miller giving an account of his adventures in *The Colossus of Maroussi*, his most joyous book and one of the best ever written on Greece.

Now hearing from their friend George Seferis that Durrell had escaped from Kalamata to Egypt, Miller had written several times care of the British Embassy in Cairo. Finally he received Durrell's letter of 4 July, and his answer reached Egypt sometime around Second Alamein. 'Well, so you are alive! That's marvellous', he wrote, and to the news that Nancy and Penelope had gone during the Flap to Palestine, 'That's incredible. How I envy you both! I wish I could be sent to Palestine or Syria or Timbuctoo – or Cairo. I swear I wouldn't mind the dirt, disease, or anything. It seems so rich to me, that world you are in. Even the crazy alphabet. Even the postage stamps look intriguing.'

Miller, who had returned to America at the outbreak of war, was for the moment in Hollywood, a 'Lotus Land', where he was looking for work in the movies, and where he was in touch with Aldous Huxley, was about to meet Jean Renoir, 'and I am great pals with Marlene Dietrich's daughter – who is just turning eighteen. That deserves another letter.' At Warner Brothers Studios 'I had a sunstroke one day walking thru the artificial movie streets of Casablanca', and he recommended that Durrell see *The Maltese Falcon*: 'There is a marvellous English actor named Greenstreet in it. A colossus!'[76]

The letter came as a painful reminder to Durrell, not only of the loss of his wife and daughter, but of his Greek world which Miller's reference to the 'colossus' evoked. He had received but had failed to acknowledge Miller's newly published *Colossus of Maroussi* in the spring, its eponymous figure their friend George Katsimbalis of Maroussi in Athens, a fabulous raconteur. Miller met Katsimbalis through Theodore Stephanides, whose great gift to Durrell was to introduce him to Greek intellectual and literary life. Corfu could hardly have been a better place to begin that journey, for after the fall of Constantinople the island passed not to the Turks but to the Venetians and so preserved a mingling of the old Mediterranean world, its families cosmopolitan and tracing their descent from Byzantine, Angevin, Norman, Greek and Roman imperial origins. Under the benign rule of the British from 1815 to 1864, Corfu became the birthplace of the Greek renaissance, especially after 1824 when the philhellene Lord Guilford established the Ionian Academy which attracted the founders of modern Greek poetry, men like Kalvos and Solomos who in turn inspired Kostes Palamas (1859–1943), he of Cavafy's inferior whisky, to whom Stephanides and his friends were devoted.

These friends included Katsimbalis and George Seferis.[77] Stephanides and Katsimbalis had declared for Venizelos' provisional government in Thessaloniki on the same day in 1916 and had fought together on the Balkan front after Greece entered the First World War. Later Stephanides had also fought the Turks during the disastrous Asia Minor campaign, while Seferis was himself a Greek of Asia Minor who had been born and raised in Smyrna. As Venizelists and intellectuals, all three were committed to the cultural rebirth of Greece.

With the decline of Greek letters in Alexandria, literary activity centred on Athens, where during the 1930s Katsimbalis edited a review called *Nea Grammata* (New Letters, recalling Stephen Pargas' *Grammata*) that published the works of such rising poets as Nikos Gatsos, Anghelos Sikelianos, Odysseus Elytis and Seferis himself. But Cavafy seemed remote from their experience: 'I was not interested in Cavafy at that time', said Seferis, 'or not particularly', and while he saw Cavafy as adding another stone to the edifice of *The Greek Anthology*, 'my reaction was coldly literary'.[78] Katsimbalis was dutifully working on a bibliography of works about Cavafy when he met the poet in 1932, suitably at Athens' Cosmopolite Hotel where Cavafy was recuperating from an operation on the throat cancer which was to kill him the following year. 'Take care, Katsimbalis', Cavafy managed to say. 'For God's sake don't write that it's the whole Cavafian bibliography for there will be a danger that you may be exposed and blamed for not knowing all the rest that has been written about Cavafy. And there's lots more, Katsimbalis.'[79]

Cavafy had good reason to be concerned for his reputation in Greece, where as yet he was hardly known and little esteemed. In 1925 Katsimbalis and Stephanides had edited and translated *Poems of Kostes Palamas* and in 1926 *Modern Greek Poems*, which included only one poem by Cavafy (a stilted rendering of 'Ithaka'), four by Stephanides and five by Palamas, and which carried the dedication 'To Kostes Palamas, greatest poet of modern Greece'. Durrell later recalled that he was introduced to Cavafy through the translation of Katsimbalis and Stephanides,[80] but at the time the poet that he too most admired was not Cavafy but Palamas.

An important reason why Durrell's Greek literary friends discounted Cavafy may be understood by comparing Cavafy's city, from whose black ruins there is no escape, to the city described by Palamas in his great poem 'The Dodecalogue of the Gipsy':

> And your Soul, accursed City,
> will not find rest;
> the ladder of evil it will
> step by step descend,
> and wherever it goes, wherever it stops,
> into a worse body will it enter.[81]

Palamas' city is Constantinople, which fell to the Turks in 1453, and for him it was also the city of the fall of man. But his is not a poetry that salvages memory and sensation from the wreckage of failure and loss; rather it heals the dislocations of history by presenting the interpenetration of the inner and the outer worlds in terms of a supernatural drama. The outer drama of cultural regeneration is achieved through the inner drama of spiritual redemption. After passing through a series of negatives, the city and the soul of man are touched by love, they shed all evil, and they are reborn as one with the universe, 'like the grass, like the bird, / like the breast of woman',[82] pantheistic, embracing and feminine.

57 Lawrence Durrell behind his desk at the British Information Office, Alexandria, 23 August 1943. On the reverse of the original print that he sent to his friend Mary Honor in Cairo, Durrell wrote: 'The Great L.D. surrounded by staff. Miss Philpott, Miss Pattis, Mr Axelos.'

A powerful chord was touched in Durrell, who felt himself a 'lost fragment', by Palamas' longing for rebirth and integration, for which the answer lay, said Palamas, in the poet's creative powers, his redemption of the world through his affirmation of life, a process requiring him 'to feel, to suffer and to accept'.[83] Only through the 'savage battle'[84] of writing *The Black Book* could Durrell rescue himself from the English Death and meet Palamas' prescription to feel.

No sooner had Durrell finished *The Black Book* than he was writing to Miller, in July 1937, about how he saw his life's work: 'I have planned an agon, a pathos, an anagnorisis'[85] (struggle, suffering, acceptance), explaining that his agon was *The Black Book*, while his anagnorisis lay far off as the Book of Miracles.[86] But next would be his pathos, which he referred to as the Book of the Dead – and which would ultimately develop into *The Alexandria Quartet*, Alexandria becoming for Durrell what Constantinople had been for Palamas.

On 21 November 1942 Miller again wrote to Durrell, sending Christmas wishes, adding 'Tell me something about you and Nancy. How do things go these days –

together, I mean? Are you still lambasting one another?'[87] Durrell had not replied to Miller's letter of 15 September, and he did not reply to this one either. Nor would he write to Miller again for over a year.

'For the majority of people', Durrell remembered, 'Alexandria was a dull hole with only good bathing and many French restaurants to recommend it. "There is nothing to see!" they repeated endlessly.'[88] But Gwyn Williams was already looking back on those twelve years he had spent in Cairo as 'a dark blank with only a few flecks of animation, a black hole from which I emerged a different person'.[89] The experience of an unhappy marriage was not the whole of it: he knew a little Arabic and liked the rural fellahin, but he cared little for the town Egyptian, or for Cairo, which he had explored 'less than any other town I have lived in',[90] while Egypt's pharaonic past struck him as 'cold and inhuman . . . revolting and absurd'.[91] Alexandria was not just an escape from all that: it returned him to the wellsprings of his own culture.

For much of the time Gwyn Williams had been a lecturer at Fuad University in Cairo, Robin Furness had been professor of English there. Williams always said he owed a great deal to Furness, who introduced him to *The Greek Anthology*, including his own translations of Callimachus, and then prepared the ground for Williams' move to Alexandria by ensuring his acquaintance with Cavafy's poetry and Forster's two books on the city, which as Williams was to discover 'eliminated the time between us and the Ptolemaic past'.[92]

Copies of the 1922 first edition of Forster's *Alexandria* were almost impossible to obtain and the 1938 edition was now also rare. But 'by a series of manoeuvres verging on sharp practice',[93] Durrell obtained a second edition, one of 250 copies specially inscribed by Forster for members of the Archaeological Society.

Durrell had been primed for Alexandria by his boss, the Oriental Counsellor Walter Smart. In the summer of 1941, a week into Durrell's job as foreign press officer at the British Embassy in Cairo, Smart came to his office, saying he and his wife Amy wanted to talk to him about his poetry, and invited him round to their house that evening. The Smarts lived in Zamalek, a smart residential quarter on the island of Gezira across from central Cairo, their house filled with Persian rugs and porcelain, with books and manuscripts in half a dozen European and Eastern languages, its walls hung with Picassos, Dalis and Daumiers interspersed with a few of Amy's own large and colourful canvases. To Smart's reserve and what Grafftey-Smith called 'the fine neo-Platonist texture of his mind',[94] Amy brought an exuberant curiosity in all things artistic and literary and the social energy to gather at their home many of the most interesting and original people in Cairo. She most likely had read Durrell's poems and had despatched Smart to his office with their invitation, and she also took Nancy under her wing when she discovered that she was a painter and like herself had studied at the Slade School of Fine Art.

The two men became lifelong friends from that very first evening, when Smart put Durrell at ease with the story of how he went to visit Cavafy in the 'Rue Clapsius' those fifteen summers ago, an occasion on which, according to Alexandrian gossip, he was 'very much surprised at what he saw when he tried the wrong door'.[95] Amy too was interested in Cavafy and would later contribute translations of his poems to *Personal Landscape*. Like other friends of Durrell's, they joined the cast of his private mythology and would reappear in altered guises in the pages of *The Alexandria Quartet*. Certainly Durrell would have Walter Smart serve as his fictional ambassador David Mountolive, and he would draw partly on Amy Nimr for Leila Hosnani, the great love of Mountolive's youthful days in Egypt – a character, however, who as the matriarch of the Hosnani family was also inspired by Rosette de Menasce.

In Alexandria, Durrell's knowledge of Cavafy was aided by another friend of the Smarts, Robert Liddell, who was already retracing the poet's footsteps through the city and would later write his biography. Though Farouk University opened officially only in September 1942, an advance guard of lecturers had been there since the previous year, among them Liddell, who had been teaching for the British Council in Athens. For Liddell, who had been raised in Cairo, his flight from Greece, where he had known both Seferis and Durrell, had at least the recompense of a homecoming, but he had never visited Alexandria until May 1941, when he went to say goodbye to Seferis, who had been director of the Foreign Press Bureau at the Ministry of Information in Athens and was now being posted to South Africa by the Greek government-in-exile in Cairo.

Together they walked round Cavafy's quarter in the bomb-inviting moonlight with Timos Malanos as their guide. 'Here he loved', said Malanos, outside the house in the Rue Lepsius. 'Here he died', and he indicated the former Greek Hospital, by then the navy's Fleet Club. 'Here they read the service over him', and they were by the door of St Saba.[96] The tour made a tremendous impression on Seferis. He had escaped from Greece not long before and then from Crete when it too fell, and as he walked about the blacked-out quarter, Cavafy's 'Those Who Fought for the Achaean League' came to his mind, perhaps because defeat had brought him to the city of the Ptolemies like the Achaean in the poem. He whispered the whole poem over to himself, but when he came to its puzzling epigram –

> Written by an Achaean in Alexandria
> during the seventh year of Ptolemy Lathyros' reign

– Seferis suddenly appreciated, and for the first time, that the poem had been written in 1922 on the eve of the Asia Minor catastrophe, and now he found himself rephrasing its coda:

> Written by an Achaean in Alexandria
> The year that our race was destroyed.[97]

Seferis no longer saw Cavafy as some distant poet coldly adding his stones to the edifice of *The Greek Anthology* but as a living presence tersely expressing his feelings on the unbearable tragedy of his people.

For Seferis the Asia Minor disaster had cut at the roots of his experience as both man and Greek. There against the backdrop of Homer's epics, of the voyage of the Argonauts and Alexander's marches, in a landscape filled with classical temples, vines and olives and Byzantine churches, refugees were marched down endless roads, were butchered or herded into detention camps or threw themselves into overweighted ships, their homes ablaze, their lives in ruin, a world destroyed. For Seferis it had been the worst conceivable calamity until the fall of Greece itself, and it was also the presage of the despair and tragedy that was now the common experience of all Europe. In Alexandria and through Cavafy he could still hear the voice of Hellenism, of a race that through all defeats and exiles had refused to perish: 'I am not a Greek', Cavafy had said, 'I am a Hellene',[98] and Seferis embraced him.

When Liddell returned to Alexandria a few months later to take up his lectureship at the nascent university, Cavafy seemed to him the city's genius loci. At a bookshop they still held memories of him, at a small Greek restaurant they remembered what he liked to eat, and at his favourite cafés along the Rue Missalla (by then renamed Rue Safiya Zaghloul for the wife of the nationalist leader) he met old friends of Cavafy who recounted stories about him and a little scandal, who drew caricatures of him on the backs of envelopes and cigarette boxes, who imitated his gestures and tried to reproduce his wonderful voice and the enchantment of his digressions through all times and places which he seemed to bring home to Alexandria. 'When we say "Time" we mean ourselves', they remembered Cavafy saying. 'Most abstractions are simply our pseudonyms. . . . We are time.'[99] Through the personage of Cavafy Alexandria haunted Liddell and became 'one of the cities of the soul'.[100]

Among the friends of Cavafy whom Liddell met were Gaston Zananiri, who gave lectures on the poet, and Rika Singopoulos and her husband the lawyer Alexander Singopoulos, Cavafy's literary executor, who showed him some of the poet's furniture and what remained of his library. 'Mr Singopoulos never impressed me', said Zananiri. 'I was impressed by Madame Singopoulos', who like Cavafy's earlier friend Penelope Delta was a sensitive woman of superior intelligence. Rika was Cavafy's closest confidante from 1926, when she married Alexander Singopoulos and they took the apartment immediately below the poet's at 10 Rue Lepsius. There she would meet Cavafy's friends, among them Forster when he returned to the city in 1929, and she would make notes, never published, on Cavafy's life and write down what he said. She kept him company, fending off his fear of loneliness in his last years, and when he was diagnosed with cancer of the throat it was Rika and her husband who took Cavafy to Athens. Almost his last words were those spoken to Katsimbalis about the bibliography, for after a tracheotomy he could not speak at all, so that back in Alexandria he communicated by writing notes on a paper pad. The day in 1933 when Cavafy went across the street into the Greek Hospital, Rika found a small suitcase in his apartment into which he could put his clothes and his folders of poems. 'When he saw the suitcase he was overcome with tears. We tried to calm him at this heart-rending moment when he was leaving his house for ever. He took the pad and wrote: "I bought this suitcase thirty years ago, in a hurry one evening, to go to Cairo for pleasure",[101] and now, as Rika retold the story, she spoke of how Cavafy left the Rue Lepsius 'Like a man for long prepared, like a brave man . . .'.

After Cavafy's death, Rika and Alexander Singopoulos brought out the first edition of his works, but there were also numerous pieces of paper of all sizes and quality, some of them pages torn from exercise books, others small irregular scraps, on which Cavafy had scribbled severely truncated, almost coded notes in English – some of them, as Zananiri recalled, after they had been out prowling at the tavernas. Rika and Alexander Singopoulos wanted them deciphered, and so they gave a sheaf of these papers to Michael Perides, another friend of Cavafy's, for Gwyn Williams to see. Many offered glimpses into his homosexual emotional life, while others, to Williams' surprise, bore first drafts of his poems written in English prose, which Cavafy would then rework into poetry in Greek.

Gwyn Williams was sworn to secrecy, but the experience must have informed his conversation and contributed to the sense he shared with Liddell and Durrell that Cavafy's presence was still palpable in the city. 'Before all the worthies of Alexandria, the wits of the Museion, the saints and martyrs, Pompey, Antony or Cleopatra, it is he of the truly great who is nearest to us, and most occupies our thoughts', so Liddell wrote of Cavafy in an issue of *Personal Landscape*, to be echoed by Durrell in the *Quartet* when he wrote of 'the city's exemplars – Cavafy, Alexander, Cleopatra',[102] giving pride of place to the poet.

With this interest around him and his copy of *Alexandria* as his guide, Durrell felt able to re-experience the city as Forster and Cavafy had known it, so that 'Magically' (seemingly overlooking the fact that his edition had been updated) 'nothing had changed that I could discern. . . . The only real change, as far I could judge, was the empty chair in the favourite café of the poet; but the circle of friends remained unbroken, men like Malanos and Petrides, who would later write books about their singular friend. They too had all glimpsed the phantom city which underlay the quotidian one.'[103]

Sometime in the autumn or winter following the battle of Alamein Durrell left Gwyn Williams' villa on the hill of Abou el Nawatir at Rushdi and, according to Robert Liddell, moved to the seafront at Anfushi, along the Corniche towards the Fort Kait Bey end of the Eastern Harbour.[104] Just behind runs the Rue Tatwig, several art nouveau buildings giving it a European face, but the street has always stood on the edge of two worlds. Behind the Rue Tatwig was the Arab quarter or the 'lower town' as Durrell called it, which in the *Quartet* is the entrance to a primordial world: 'We doubled back and entered the huddled slums which lie behind Tatwig Street, our blond headlights picking out ant-hill cafés and crowded squares with an unaccustomed radiance; from somewhere behind the immediate skyline of smashed and unlimbered houses came the piercing shrieks and ululations of a burial procession.' Here among its brothels Justine

58   A postcard showing the Terbana Mosque. Found in the Rue de France, the Terbana Mosque is just a few streets back from the European façades of the Eastern Harbour Corniche at Anfushi.

searched for her kidnapped daughter as Demeter searched for Persephone;[105] and here Mountolive, intoxicated and seeking revelation, immersed himself and, in a scene reminiscent of Dionysus being torn apart by the Maenads, was mauled by frenzied child prostitutes.[106]

But it is not all nightmare: replete with inversions and comical associations, it is a world made home by Scobie, septuagenarian ex-merchant-sailor, occasional transvestite and the local head of British intelligence, who is described as living in Tatwig Street, in 'the sordid purlieus of the town . . . in a couple of tumble-down rooms'.[107] He walks through the quarter in an aura of local respect and affection, kills his neighbours with bathtub whisky, and is celebrated after his death as a Coptic saint, venerated by Christians and Muslims alike.

Durrell's model for Scobie was Joseph McPherson, 'Bimbashi McPherson' as he was universally known on account of the rank of major he had held in the Egyptian Ministry of the Interior under the Protectorate, where for a time just after the First World War he had been acting head of the secret police. After his retirement he stayed on in Cairo, where early in 1942 Durrell and Nancy called on him, discovering a frail white-haired man, about seventy-six, with 'eyes of extraordinary luminosity and smiling kindness'.[108] Except for Scobie's 'Tendencies' ('Looking from east to west across this fertile Delta what do I see? Mile upon mile of angelic little black bottoms'),[109] Durrell's denizen of Tatwig Street was clearly inspired by his visit to the Bimbashi, who received Nancy and Durrell (as Scobie would receive Clea and Darley) in a simple room, among its few adornments a crucifix over his bed, a print of the Virgin Mary and a photograph of his mother whom he adored. ('The shabby little crucifix on the wall behind the bed. . . . Nearby hangs a small print of the Mona Lisa whose enigmatic smile has always reminded Scobie of his mother.')[110] An eccentric figure, McPherson would go about Cairo lost in thought as though leaving his purpose and direction to the white mule which carried him through the streets, a vision that helped endear him to his Egyptian neighbours who decided he was a seeker and a seer.

McPherson was a keen observer of moulids, those festivals surrounding the birthday of a holy man, Coptic or Muslim, which are often celebrated at the level of folk religion, a pharaonic deity transformed into a Christian saint who in turn resurfaces as a Muslim sheikh. Only the year before, McPherson had published his classic *Moulids of Egypt*, describing and colourfully commenting on the activities, sacred and burlesque, that in his lifetime still attended these holy fairs, the circumcision booths and the tattoo stalls, the dancing, the fireworks and the prayers, the puppet shows and the processions of prostitutes, and he inscribed a copy for Durrell and Nancy. As Durrell drew on the man, so too he would draw on the Bimbashi's book for his descriptions of the tumultuous moulids whose drums and chants and wild music beat against the backdrop of the European city in *The Alexandria Quartet*.

One person Durrell did write to throughout his time in Egypt was T. S. Eliot at Faber and Faber, but this after all was business. The previous summer Eliot had accepted a collection of Durrell's poetry, almost all of it written in Greece, which would be published as *A Private Country* towards the end of 1943. Now Durrell was writing poetry in Egypt too and had other plans afoot, declaring to Eliot in February 1943 that 'I am very happy', following this with the admission, as light-hearted as he could make it, that 'My wife is being rather a nuisance at this moment, but apart from the fashionable domestic malaise I am here, and revolving a book in the back of what is left of my mind.'[111]

Durrell was in fact admitting hardly anything more to Eliot than he was by his silence to Miller; not admitting the depth of his feelings nor that everything was over with

Nancy. But in a reflective poem called 'Alexandria', which has the ring of being written during the months he lived at Anfushi, he is standing on 'Promontories splashed by the salty sea, / Groaned on in darkness by the tram / . . . / Here at the last cold Pharos between Greece / And all I love . . .'. His thoughts are with 'the lucky now who have lovers or friends, / Who move to their sweet undiscovered ends', while 'As for me I now move / Through many negatives to what I am.'[112]

Opening the pages of the *Egyptian Gazette* on 8 April 1943, Durrell would have read its account of what must have been one of the strangest events to have taken place in Alexandria, a tea party held in the Kom el Shogafa catacombs near Pompey's Pillar to celebrate the fiftieth anniversary of the Archaeological Society:

> Recalling the Roman custom of honouring the dead by visits to the Catacombs on the two great occasions of the Feast of Roses and the Feast of Violets, the various rooms and passages of the Catacombs had been decorated with a great profusion of roses, of which an additional supply had been secured from Cairo. Floral garlands, which harmonised well with the carved garlands on the important tombs, had been gracefully flung on the walls and were twined about the columns, forming a scene which was beautiful as well as impressive.
>
> Tea was served in the Triclinium, or dining-hall, where in ancient times the friends and relatives ate ceremonially in memory of the dead. Carpets had been spread upon the great stone benches, where at one time the visitors reclined on cushions. While the effect on Wednesday was very far from the gloomy one that probably was presented in the Roman era, it enabled those present to sense the atmosphere of this unusually interesting historic spot.[113]

As president of the society, Judge Brinton gave a speech, in French, saying that these past years had been marked by fruitful excavations that amounted to a minor archaeological renaissance. He was referring to the appointment of Alan Rowe as director of the Graeco-Roman Museum after Adriani's removal in 1940 when Italy attacked Egypt. Rowe was very much a field man, and it was not long before he emerged from his office at the museum and began digging at Kom el Shogafa, where he opened up new tombs and found pieces of gold jewellery, and at Pompey's Pillar, where he was able to prove what till then could only be assumed, that the site was that of the Serapeum, where Serapis, combining the attributes of the Egyptian Osiris and the Greek Dionysus, was worshipped as the god of the underworld but also the god of the harvest.

Throughout these years of Rowe's activities fascinated members of the society would often visit him at Pompey's Pillar, calling in at the shed that served as his field headquarters. Here in *Justine*, Durrell describes crossing 'the wilderness of trenches and parapets thrown up by the archaeologist' to attend a meeting of the Cabal, those aspiring hermetics seeking revelation in the ancient Mysteries: 'The Cabal met at this time in

59   Baudrot, 1940. Alexandria's most fashionable restaurant, bar and patisserie, Baudrot stood on the corner of the Rue Chérif Pasha, just a block from the British Information Office and opposite the Mohammed Ali Club (right) on the Rue Fuad, where Forster first met Cavafy.

what resembled a disused curator's wooden hut, built against the red earth walls of an embankment, very near to Pompey's Pillar.'[114]

During Seferis' sojourn in South Africa, Durrell had been no more able to write to him than to Miller, instead publishing an open letter to him in *La Semaine égyptienne*, a Cairo review, on 28 October 1941: 'Do you think we will get back? Not to the past of Greece, I mean, but to our own past in Greece? I think of you, my friend, in the unfamiliar continent of Africa; a subtropical man out of his element, defeated by a world where the black compromise is king. . . . But what have you or I to do with history? We are dwellers in the Eye, dedicated to the service of this blue. The past and future join hands here; whatever happens we will get back.'[115]

Durrell talked of the Eye again the following spring when Seferis returned from Pretoria to Cairo, where he was now First Secretary of the Greek Legation. 'Here we miss Greece as a living body. But above all we miss the Eye, for Greece was not a country but a living eye', a watchful landscape harmonising itself to the dimensions of human existence – and an eye, thought Seferis, in which Durrell himself was mirrored as man and artist, 'he and his "private domain"'.[116]

'I love Larry, he's got wonderful moments',[117] said Seferis. In Durrell, he felt, there was 'a faith in happiness, a mystique of happiness perhaps'[118] – something childlike, which Durrell had expressed in a poem written in Kalamata in 1941, 'Letter to Seferis the Greek':

> Our happiness, here on a promontory,
> Marked by a star, is small but perfect.
>
> . . .
>
> Nothing remains but Joy, the infant Joy.

The essential ingredients of that small but perfect ambit were 'a woman, an island and a tree'.[119]

Seferis saw that he and Durrell shared a sensibility that was Mediterranean, but that loving a country as one loves a woman – 'for there is always a sensual element in our attachments' – was 'not always without its dangers'.[120] Seferis could never abandon Greece, for he himself was irreducibly Greek and Durrell was not – a matter of fundamental loyalty which eventually would lead to a painful breach between them.

In about April, if not before, Durrell took a room in a sprawling and gloomy apartment at 40 Rue Fuad on the north side of the street and a few steps east of the Rue Safiya Zaghloul (the former Rue Missalla).[121] The building was old and shabby even then, but just a ten-minute walk brought him to his office, passing Pastroudis and the Atelier, the Mohammed Ali Club and Baudrot. One April afternoon he was at Baudrot, at a party given by a small newspaper publisher, when a young woman came up to him and asked, 'And what do you do, Mr Durrell?' 'I'm a poet', he said. This was Yvette Cohen, or Eve as Durrell would call her, though more than a year passed before he wrote about her to Miller.

CHAPTER 7

Mirrors

> He is when all is said and done a sort of minor Antony, and she a Cleo.
> You can read all about it in Shakespeare. And then, as far as Alexandria is
> concerned, you can understand why this is really a city of incest . . . The
> lover mirrors himself like Narcissus in his own family: there is no exit from
> the predicament.
>
> *Justine*[1]

During the early months of 1943 Eve was working for *La Bourse d'Alexandrie*, a small newspaper run by a man called Raoul Kahil, which listed shares and commodities. Her job was poorly paid and amounted to little more than double checking the figures, selling advertising space and answering the telephone; she was unable to type and anyway there was usually little to do, so that most of the time she knitted. Kahil had sent out invitations to a tea party at Baudrot, and now on this day in spring the telephone rang with a call from the British Information Office, the voice announcing itself as Lawrence Durrell. As a courtesy, copies of the paper had been sent to him regularly, and Eve knew his name and liked it; she was a fan of the movies and had been repeating 'Lawrence Durrell' over to herself, attaching to it the figure of the actor Leslie Howard.

Durrell wanted to speak to Kahil to ask if he could bring a lady friend to Baudrot. Eve put him through to Kahil's home where his servant, who spoke no English, answered in Arabic to which Durrell replied in a mock-Arabic of his own, Eve listening in to their mutually incomprehensible conversation, which became more nonsensical and uproarious with every exchange, until she was bursting with muffled laughter. Interjecting, she told Durrell that the servant was saying that Kahil was out, but she was sure he would not mind if he brought his companion to tea. She was desperate for Durrell to turn up at Baudrot, girlfriend or not, so that finally she could meet him.

A few days later when Eve arrived at Baudrot,[2] she saw a crowd of people standing off to one side: 'Larry was attracting people like honey, like bees to a honeypot; that's the first experience of me meeting him.' But she was surprised and put off when she saw that the Lawrence Durrell whom she had pictured as the epitome of an English gentleman stood no higher than her eyebrows: 'He was small. Not my type of man', but he was being interesting and entertaining, 'and so I'll make an exception'.

'Hello, I'm the girl you spoke to on the phone'; it was all she could think of to say, but in her eagerness and without realising it, she had pinned him against the wall: 'He was frightened, terrified. I'd never frightened anybody in my life before. He was terrified. And he admitted it; it wasn't just my imagination; we discussed it afterwards. Probably he never had someone like me approaching him in that direct way.'

Then she asked him what he did. As always to that question he said, 'I'm a poet'. His answer made her feel uneasy; she thought of herself as inhabiting that same territory, a world of high imagination that was her own.

But Eve had not failed to notice that the girl Durrell had come with seemed to be someone he had to shepherd around; she was not a girlfriend at all. Meanwhile Eve had an errand to run: 'I left that party at six o'clock, I had to meet somebody to get rid of him. That was an affair I wasn't going to have, a top chap in his firm who wanted me as a status symbol.'

Durrell phoned Eve several times after that, but her life was in turmoil and she would put him off; 'I was keeping him a bit on the side.' Then one day when she felt she needed to talk to someone outside her usual circle she phoned him, and they arranged to meet at Pastroudis. Eve arrived early and went to the Atelier,[3] directly across the Rue Fuad, where she spent time chatting with a sculptor friend for whom she had recently modelled: he had done a near life-size nude statue of her as a nymph that now graced some Alexandrian garden. Meanwhile, from upstairs at the Atelier she could look through Pastroudis' large windows and see if Durrell had yet taken a table in the tea room.

Founded by Greeks after the fall of Smyrna, Pastroudis was 'patronised by the elite of Alexandria society' for whom it was 'the rendezvous of preference'.[4] The atmosphere was airy, animated and elegant, the mouldings and panelling in the art deco style. The patisserie on the Rue Fuad connected with the adjoining restaurant where afternoon tea was served, and in turn the patisserie and tea room opened onto a well-stocked bar at the rear with tables set out on the pavement. In layout Pastroudis is the same today, though it is run-down and somnolent now; but like an island set apart from the rush of time and the city, it preserves a special quality that invites the sharing of intimacies.

At about four o'clock Eve went down to Pastroudis where Durrell was waiting at a table looking onto the Rue Fuad. They talked in English as his spoken French was poor, and she remembered how he was diffident and shy. After a while he brought the subject round to Nancy, 'about his problems with his wife who was going to leave him and he didn't understand any of it'. He was miserable, but also 'he was very angry; he kept saying "She's gone up a tree; she just won't come down."' Eve had picked up most of her English from the movies, but this was not an expression that she had heard before, and at first she took it literally, wondering how this woman with her daughter made do while living in a tree in Palestine. 'She's gone up a tree and she won't come down!' Durrell said again in explanation.

It had long gone dark when Eve began talking about herself. 'We had found a willing ear in each other, and I told him about my problem with my boyfriend. He was Shock, he called himself Shock. S–H–O–C–K. I was going to be Madame Shock, which some people would say would fit me. To this day I don't know what his first name was, but I would have begun to wonder; eventually we would have come round to it. The whole thing was very leisurely, casual, you know. And really I accepted him as he was, and he was Shock, that's the way he liked to be known and that was fine by me. And that's why we went along together, because we were so tolerant of each other. He looked exactly like Danny Kaye, tall and blond, though without the humour. But he was very elegant. I liked that about him. At the time it meant a lot to me. We made a spectacular couple. It was my suggestion a few months before, let's get married, and his reaction was no, I don't marry. But now Shock had decided he wanted to marry me after all but said to me, "How do I know I can trust you?" I'd never thought about that; I had no answer to it. But I was worried about it. I was very worried.'

When she got her chance she said to Durrell, '"I have a question and I don't know how to answer it. What do I answer to a man who says to me how can I trust you?" I was so anxious to know something about myself, passionate about that, and this is what Larry liked about me. He paid me compliments which I so appreciated, because God knows I needed them like water to a desert. And so he thought a little bit and then he said, "You'd make the best wife for anyone who treats you well, but God help the man who doesn't." And the moment he said it I felt he was right, it got me absolutely right.'

They continued talking as they went out into the night, meandering through the maze of blacked-out streets towards the Eastern Harbour. For hours they walked along the Corniche, back and forth before Mazarita. 'I just didn't think I had any value to me at all, and he was able to say things to me like, "When I go out and visit these people, these Alexandrians, they don't hold your dignity and your way of knowing what is correct and what isn't, and how to conduct yourself in life." He didn't mean that I was a wise person or anything like that, but in the things that were important I seem to have had these qualities.' Eventually they turned into the Rue Champollion, unknowingly following in Forster's footsteps when he walked up from the Mazarita tram stop towards the Khartoum Column for his first rendezvous with Mohammed el Adl, and at the door of the block of flats where Eve lived with her parents on the first floor she and Durrell said goodnight. It was two o'clock in the morning. For ten hours they had been confiding vulnerabilities and discovering assurances in one another, and as Eve lay awake, unable to sleep, she struggled with the sensation that 'Larry was falling in love with me, but I was very much in love with somebody else.'

Eve was twenty-four at this time. She had been born in Cairo on 8 August 1918, but her first memories were of Alexandria, where her parents moved when she was two. She thought of herself as a child of the city and recalled her youthful delight in 'exploring all its twinklings'. But by the time she met the 31-year-old Durrell her life had reached a crisis.

60 Eve Cohen on the beach in Alexandria in 1941, two years before she met Durrell.

By then Eve and Shock had been lovers for two years. He was an Austrian Jew who had come to Alexandria in the late 1920s and was now about forty. His flat was just across the side street running between the Rue Champollion and the Jewish cemetery where she lived with her parents in Mazarita. Then came the night as they were leaving Shock's place that Eve's father surprised them at the corner. 'I was not a little girl anymore, and my father ought to have known by now but he didn't, and so I burst into tears.' Shock quickly said in her ear, 'We'll say I am your fiancé', to which her father, dumbstruck as he shook hands with Shock, was only able to say 'enchanté'. But later her father told her, 'You can't marry him', saying something about his reputation and adding, 'In any case, he is not like me.'

'I had a father who was very possessive and for very good reasons. He was also, I think, infatuated with me. It was the closest he had been to any human being. He didn't know how to be close anyway, poor devil, and nothing really helped him, certainly not my mother. And Larry understood this to mean, when I told him, that my father had interfered with me sexually, but he never did. We were Jewish religion; he was an honest-to-God man; he just didn't know what was happening to him, that's all. I think he was in love with me because I was the only person he understood in his life.'

Since Shock's impromptu announcement of their engagement, however, Eve's mother had been asking, 'Where is your boyfriend? Where is your fiancé? Where is he? Why don't I see him?' She was working herself up into one of her fainting scenes or a threat to throw herself from the balcony if she did not get her way. Shock had heard enough about Eve's family to know he wanted nothing to do with them; 'I don't think I can face your parents', he replied, when she said they were expecting him to call, and anyway, he added, 'How do I know that I could trust you?' The year before, after he had refused to marry her, she had felt free to see other men. 'But you didn't have to', said Shock, and Eve too began to wonder if she could trust herself, knowing that Shock was not the man she really loved at all.

Eve's paternal grandfather, Chalom Cohen-Arazi, a blue-eyed Sephardi patriarch as she remembered him, left Algeria in the 1870s with his wife Rahel, also born a Cohen, and settled in Egypt where all their nine children were born.[5] Speaking Arabic as his mother tongue and wearing the galabiyya and the tarboosh, Chalom established himself as a goldsmith and jeweller in the familiar oriental milieu of Cairo's Khan el Khalili bazaar.

Eve's grandfather on her mother's side, Mordahai Palacci-Miram, was likewise a Sephardi but from Constantinople, where he married Rosa Alterman, an Ashkenazi of German origin. Several of their children were born in Constantinople, including Eve's mother Stella, but to escape an outbreak of plague they came to Alexandria around the turn of the century, where Mordahai opened a picture-framing shop on the Rue de la Gare de Ramleh. The shop became fashionable and within a few years he was able to move his growing family, eight daughters and a son, into a substantial three-storey house (to which a fourth has since been added), with wrought-iron balconies to the front and rear and the heads of lions and satyrs projecting from the window mouldings, at 94 Rue Hassan Pasha el Iskanderini, which runs south off the Rue Moharrem Bey down to the Mahmoudiya Canal.

In 1917 Eve's parents Moise Cohen-Arazi and Stella Palacci-Miram were married in Alexandria and went to live in Cairo where they had met while Stella was training as a nurse. The families became even more closely linked when Nessim, Moise's older brother, married Stella's twin sister Ventura. 'Of all the brothers', according to Nessim's daughter, 'Uncle Moise was dark, and very different, very sensitive.'[6] But Moise was different too in being hopeless at business, which was why Stella returned to Alexandria in 1920 with her husband and infant daughter. 'My father wasn't bringing in the money, which was difficult for him as a man', Eve said, and unable to afford a place of their own, they moved in with Stella's parents. Stella was nevertheless anxious to keep up appearances. 'My husband is a banker', she would tell the neighbours, though after first going into business as a moneylender with his brother Nessim near the Terbana Mosque in the Rue de France he was now struggling to make ends meet at his own one-man exchange and lending bureau with a roll-down shutter at 9 Mohammed Ali Square between the Mixed Courts and the Bourse.

61 The Khartoum Column. After their long talk at Pastroudis and along the Corniche, Durrell walked Eve to her parents' home in the Rue Champollion just behind the Khartoum Column. The column was also where Forster and Mohammed el Adl had their first rendezvous.

Across the tram line from the Rue Hassan Pasha el Iskanderini, to the north of the Rue Moharrem Bey, were the luxurious villas and spacious gardens of Alexandria's successful bankers, brokers and property tycoons, families like the Menasces and the Ambrons, but when Eve was a child 'I didn't know that world existed.' Her grandparents' neighbourhood was a dense grid of streets and closely packed houses, where Arabic mingled with the sound of Ladino (medieval Spanish containing elements of Hebrew). In *The Alexandria Quartet* Durrell quotes from Justine's diary: 'These are the poor quarters of the white city; they bear no resemblance to those lovely streets built and decorated by foreigners where the brokers sit and sip their morning papers. Even the harbour does not exist for us here. In the winter, sometimes, rarely, you can hear the thunder of a siren – but it is another country. Ah! the misery of harbours and the names they conjure when you are going nowhere. It is like a death – a death of the self uttered in every repetition of the word Alexandria, Alexandria.'[7]

Eve's memories of her childhood neighbourhood were brighter. Then the inhabitants of the southern quarters of Moharrem Bey were a mixture of 'well-to-do Arabs and comfortable middle-class Jews', and she recalled it in a friendly way, remembering the sense of belonging and safety she felt when out playing on its streets. 'Owlet eye – barefoot childhood – in streets of Moharrem Bey, nightshirts, elfin blowing of horn of the ice-cream man during Ramadan when the faithful rise at two';[8] these were some of her memories that Durrell wrote down in his notes for the Book of the Dead. But he also recorded a darker side which escaped Eve's remembrance of her past: 'Not a street but I can say "There I was unhappy and there I traded part of my immutability for a chocolate ice." '[9]

Photographs of Eve in Moharrem Bey show a lively and beaming child, but what she remembered was a growing sense of loneliness, and she was told, though she did not remember, that she would faint when her mother left the room. 'My grandmother Rosa counted a lot for me; she completely replaced my mother at an early age, when I was three, as soon as I realised that my mother wasn't functioning' – that was the year Nessim's wife Ventura died. 'My mother was a twin. Disaster. My mother from the moment she lost her twin was half a human being. She was not complete. My father and I knew that. She wasn't normal. But we bore up with it at great cost.' More deaths followed: Stella lost a child in infancy and a son to diphtheria when he was three, and also there was a miscarriage. The baby's was the first dead body Eve had seen, this after the excitement of expecting his birth and looking under a cabbage where she was told that babies were found, though afterwards she recalled how its outer leaves had been rotten.

With a mother who seemed unable to cope, 'to even keep her children alive', Eve spent her days with her grandmother who looked after her and saw that she was fed. 'But she was a bit formal, Germanic, not an oriental. She never kissed me, never embraced me, never said come sit on my lap. She played pastra with me, she enjoyed winning at cards, she taught me determination. But I wanted warmth from her, to be cuddled, and nobody did.'

Then when Eve was six her grandmother Rosa died and she moved with her parents to Camp de César. The synagogue where 'my father read every time' was to the south of the tram station, their rented flat between the tram line and the sea. Ladino and 'bad French' were usually spoken at home, but her parents spoke Greek when they did not want Eve to understand, 'so I learnt quickly from a Greek neighbour'. Arabic she had from her father, 'the language of my roots', and Italian from attending the Italian Catholic School at Moharrem Bey, though now she was placed in the Lycée Français, a short walk towards Chatby from Camp de César.

At times they were very poor, and whether out of need or mania 'my mother changed homes at one time continuously', four different addresses at Camp de César all in a single street, and then out to Sidi Bishr where they rented a simple house in which her mother set a room aside to run a small dressmaking business. Eve admired what her mother had accomplished despite 'all her neurosis and all her weirdness', though now that Stella was making a major contribution to the family's income she became more wilful and domineering than ever, and she played on what she saw as her superior 'European' background to denigrate her inept 'oriental' husband. Eve grimly recalled how her mother would interminably play on the gramophone the one record they possessed, 'Lady Be Good' from the 1924 musical, evoking in Eve a sense of claustrophobia from which there was no escape – not from the tensions and rows between her parents or from the violence they inflicted on her, not from her mother's instability or from her father's frustrated need for love. In spring she went picnicking with her parents out in the desert around Mariut, where 'I would pick poppies which would come and go in a day.'

In better times her parents would employ a servant to do the cooking and cleaning. There was a succession of servants, all native Egyptians, and Eve would ask them to tell her stories. 'They were always about jinns, an underworld', as Eve describes it, 'one that lives in a symbiotic relationship with our own.' She remembered how a story might be about a woman, magnificently beautiful, but with the scaly legs and feet of a chicken: 'The moral was always that you had to accept whoever and whatever it was, no matter how off-putting it might seem; that this was the way to appease and avert evil, for you never knew who really was what, or whom you might offend or make angry or turn against you. This is the essential code of the Egyptian, to welcome the stranger, to make him a guest – all the stories reinforced this theme.'

At the age of ten Eve was still unable to read. 'I was battered. When I say battered, I don't mean that I was beaten, though I was, but that wasn't the real battering. The battering was of the spirit. And I was just lying low. In school I just couldn't absorb anything, so all I was doing was waiting.' For relief from her life at home she would go for long walks along the sea, sometimes walking the entire ten miles from the edge of the desert coastline at Sidi Bishr to Pastroudis, where she would spend the tram fare meant to take her to school on a favourite pastry.

For a while Eve was put into the American Mission School in the Attarine, then at twelve, the same year her sister Dolly was born, she was sent to the Scottish Girls' School.

The school is still there in the Rue Amin Fikri Pasha running down from the Rue Sultan Hussein towards the terminus for the Ramleh tram; and though it has been much extended and is called El Manar (meaning the Pharos or lighthouse, but also the minaret) English Girls' School, its original building still retains the plan of the Cross of St Andrew. The cross is emblazoned across the front of the school sweater that Eve is wearing in a photograph taken during her first year: above a wide full mouth and delicate nose, her eyes are levelled in a haunted stare, vulnerable, determined and touched with pain. She lived a great deal within herself and recalled how she sometimes heard voices; 'Yvette de la Lune' they called her at school because she was always dreaming.

In Miss Melanie Athanassian, Eve found a sympathetic and stimulating teacher who instructed her in biology, drawing and Bible studies. Melanie's family, Armenians from Constantinople, had fled in the late nineteenth century from the Turkish massacres, arriving penniless in Alexandria where as a refugee child she was admitted to a Roman Catholic school at the price of doing cleaning work after classes. Also she was forbidden to attend prayers because she was 'asthmatic'; only later did she understand that her illness lay in being a monophysite Armenian Christian: the sisters had banned her from prayers because she was a 'schismatic'.[10] Seeing something of her own childhood self in Eve's withdrawal, Melanie went out of her way to engage her, and it was at the Scottish Girls' School that Eve learnt to read. The Bible stories particularly appealed, especially the life of Jesus, and soon Eve's appetite for books was voracious, her taste omnivorous. At home there were copies of Stendhal's *Le Rouge et le noir* and *La Chartreuse de Parme*, though her parents had never read them; Eve read them both, *La Chartreuse de Parme* four times during her adolescence because she had fallen in love with its hero, the handsome, aristocratic and charmingly naive Fabrizio, and likewise in French she devoured Dickens, Molière and Racine, while at school Miss Melanie also taught her English – so that Eve could now speak English, French, Italian, Ladino, Arabic and Greek, though she never learnt to read or write in the last two languages.

All the same, though Eve liked to say she left school at sixteen, as though she had pursued her studies to their full measure, she left a year sooner, and again her photographs tell the story: she no longer is the withdrawn young girl but has awakened to her physical presence; and by seventeen she has become a beautiful gamine with sparkling eyes who explodes into smiles and swimsuits. 'That's when I got my parents off my back' and began moving about in 'separate groups, different sorts of lives'. In summer when 'the heavy perfume of jasmine hung in the Alexandrian air, when women wore necklaces of jasmine flowers round their necks', she would go to a beach house at Sidi Bishr rented by an older set of people, among them Raoul Kahil; 'the younger ones did not have to pay, it was understood that you just showed up on a certain day of the week to join in the fun. At quieter times the place was used for affairs.' Sometimes she was taken dancing at the Bellavista on the Corniche at Camp de César, at the Monseigneur, which had a Brazilian band and at the Excelsior cabaret overlooking the Eastern Harbour, or she would go to *thés dansants* at the Grand Trianon. With friends her own age she would sail in feluccas across the Western Harbour to where there were foundered ships, their decks just above the waterline, and they would dance in the moonlight to the music from a wind-up gramophone. Yet at the same time Eve was racked by self-questioning, so that her friends came to call her 'Miss Psychanalyse'.

Eve was still living with her parents, who had now moved to Mazarita, where her mother would call her 'pudique' because she could not bear to be touched, 'to have my being touched, because I had felt so mistreated as a child'. At times falling into depression and listlessness, and after being humiliated when her mother took her to a bordello because the examination for syphilis was cheaper there (and perhaps because it was more discreet), Eve decided that she had to leave home, and she became a trainee nurse at the Cozzika Hospital soon after it opened in 1937. Built on a rise along the south side of the Aboukir road about a mile east of the Municipal Gardens and the vanished Gate of the Sun, the 250-bed hospital was founded by the Alexandrian industrialist Theocaris Cozzika as a replacement for the old Greek Hospital in town with the intention that it should be 'as perfect as possible from an architectural and medical point of view'.[11] Here Eve had a room of her own, and here she had her 'first real affair' with the Greek doctor in charge of her course. The affair lasted a year (he had one each year with a new trainee nurse, Eve afterwards discovered), and soon everybody knew, including, eventually, her mother who took advantage of the situation by going to the doctor and demanding to be treated for free.

For all that, Eve felt that her affair with the doctor had steadied her and given her some confidence in herself, and it was now that she met the man with whom she truly fell in love.

Durrell assumed that Shock was the man whom he had displaced in Eve's affections. 'You are a hard woman', he later told her when once they saw Shock sitting alone at Pastroudis; 'Just as you dropped him, so some day you'll drop me too for another man.' But though Eve would tell Durrell a great deal about the men who had been in her life, and about her childhood and her family background, she never spoke to him about the depth of her love for Ruggero.

Eve recalled the night she met Ruggero, how a girlfriend invited her to a party that meant taking the tram to San Stefano and then walking some distance inland, and how 'my intuition told me the evening would be important for me, and that there would be someone there whom I would respond to'. Passing a church along the way, she went in and made a silent prayer and felt that God was telling her 'go'. The party had hardly got underway, and looking around she saw a man, 'he was a tall man, a head taller than me', standing across the room. There was an air of reserve yet confidence about him, and there and then she decided that 'this was a man I wanted to know very much'. She wasted no time, and walked straight up to him, and immediately they started dancing: 'We had to go on dancing all night because he had a terrible erection, because it was too shock-ing, too shame-making to stop.'

Afterwards, however, Eve phoned Ruggero and told him they could not go on. What she did not say was that she had been 'messed up sexually by a Jew' (Eve would hardly say more about it) who was 'perverse in that he watched me all the time and said I was wrong to enjoy sex'; that though she had gained 'experience in love' with the doctor, she nevertheless was frigid; and that she was terrified that Ruggero would not want her. But Ruggero insisted that they meet again, and soon they were going around together, often to the beach where they would swim and picnic, but never going out for a meal together: 'Having a meal at that time meant you committed yourself to that person', and Rugge, as she called him (pronounced 'Rugy', with a soft 'g'), an Italian Catholic who was the sole provider for his sister, mother and retired father, 'couldn't afford it anyway'.

It was a year before they went to bed together because they had nowhere to go where they could make love. 'When?' Eve would say to Rugge when they were out together, meaning when would they have sex together; 'Soon', he would tell her, and the months would pass. As for Rugge, he worked as a removals man, 'not with the usual Arab horse and cart' but for a smart Swiss-run firm, a job he gave Eve to understand opened up opportunities with women who wanted more than their furniture moved. 'When?' Eve would say again, and he would answer, 'Very soon'.

Already then, in that summer of 1939, though she did not talk about it with Rugge, she wanted to leave Alexandria, the only way, as she saw it, of escaping her parents, escaping 'the whole Jewish set-up' that she felt was suffocating her. Perhaps she would go to Italy, where at eighteen she had gone as a Balilla, a fascist youth ('That's something else I never told Larry about; he would not have laughed as you did'). A Jewish friend of hers with Italian citizenship had suggested that they take advantage of the free passage offered by the Italian government, saying no one would notice that she was not Italian, especially as she spoke the language. 'You simply presented yourself to the Italian authorities in Alexandria, were dressed in the uniform, made the salute and did exercises' – though at the last moment the friend dropped out, and Eve found herself sailing off to Italy alone. In all she spent a couple of weeks there, in Rome and Naples and along the coast in between, before returning to Alexandria, harbouring the idea of someday leaving the city.

That was two years before Mussolini introduced his anti-semitic measures of September 1938, by which 'mixed marriages' were strictly forbidden, and by which Jews were excluded from state education at all levels, were denied the 'high honour' of compulsory military service, and could no longer announce deaths in the newspapers, be listed in telephone directories, employ 'Aryans' or belong to leisure clubs or to the Fascist Party.

But now in 1939, the last Alexandrian summer before the war, the only thing that stood between Eve and Rugge was a place to make love. Finally he was able to satisfy her question of 'When?' by announcing a *garçonnière* at Stanley Bay that he had managed to rent with a group of friends and that she and he could have to themselves each Saturday. The place was one of a line of miniature apartments overlooking the sea, 'a perfect position', said Eve, 'as it looked as though we were going down to the beach', remembering how censorious Alexandria could be but how delicious it was to be young and in love. 'We were innocents, things were going on forever like that. It was a simpler world, we could trust it. Even the poor, poorer than us, they never went hungry. You could eat cheaply and well – falafel and foul, rich and poor ate it. And the patisseries, masses of them. Cinemas all over the place. We'd have to be millionaires now to live as we did then. We were happy, and the weather helped – always summer.'

Rugge lived nearby, but now that they were lovers they were anxious not to be seen together, and so he would call for her with a sharp short whistle, his fingers in his teeth. 'He never said anything that didn't ring me right. And his actions corresponded. His whole person was there along with what he said. And he said very few things. He wasn't a man of many words. But also he was very calm, completely different from Larry. He was obviously very emotional, but he contained it. He wasn't a man of histrionics.'

Only as June approached in 1940 did any difference arise between them. Ruggero was convinced that the Italians would win if they went to war, while she had been pro-British early on, so they had a bet on it, the loser to buy ten cakes for the winner. 'Anything might happen', he warned her, 'but you must live your life. If I say wait, you will wait, I know, but I do not ask', and he told her that the time would come when they would pass each other in the street and pretend not to see one another. 'Egypt seemed so solid. Life would go on as before, things would never change. It was impossible to conceive that within ten to twenty years it would become other, that it would become entirely another world. We thought it would go on for ever and ever.' And for a few more Saturdays they made love by the sea at Stanley Bay.

Then one Saturday Ruggero telephoned; Ruggero, who never phoned Eve at home, and she heard him say, 'they are taking me away now', and somehow he managed to hang on the line until she was calmer. He was interned far beyond Alexandria, where she wrote him letters and sent him cigarettes and felt badly towards the British.

'And that was the tragedy, at least that's how I saw it at the time, the tragedy of my life. The person I really loved had gone away out of my life, and I went completely mad about that. If I had my way in life, I would have wanted just one man. My man. And I found him – before Larry. But I made the mistake of thinking that one could have two such men in one's life. No, I never made the mistake of thinking – I mean my choice was always with Rugge – but the thing was that Larry, what happened with Larry was something very serious. It had nothing to do with him or me; it had to do with the combination of the two. We had what's called – they call it *le coup de foudre* – it's a lightning love affair. *Le coup de foudre* is something that all French people love to experience, and they consider it very lucky if they do, but I don't think so at all. Well, I mean, I was lucky in the sense that I met Larry, that's something different, but *le coup de foudre* was not lucky. What happened was that, between that meeting at Pastroudis and our big talk on the Corniche, I felt as if I was possessed. That's the way I can say it; that my self was not my own anymore; that I had no say in the matter; that whether I liked it or not I was stuck by that person, Larry. Cheek by jowl like that; we had to be together or else. It was physical, and Larry had it too; it was mutual. And that's *le coup de foudre.* If you haven't experienced it, then I can't say anything more, because that's all there is to it. There's nothing more to say. And we were absolutely miserable when we were separated. We felt like twins – no, not twins, worse than that. You know these people that are born attached to each other? Siamese twins.'

Meanwhile, Eve's parents were still waiting for news of Shock, of the man she was meant to marry. 'The horrendous situation with my family accelerated very rapidly, and within no time at all, two or three days, it reached a peak of complete hysteria.' Eve saw Shock again and they went for a walk in the Municipal Gardens, where he returned to the question of marriage; 'Maybe I change my mind', he said, and Eve exploded. 'I said no, you may change your mind, I don't. I've had enough of this. He didn't know what I was going through.' These days were 'charged with emotion and horror', and Eve 'got into a state where I was very confused'; everything seemed to be crowding in on her, her memories of Rugge, Shock's indecisiveness, her own doubts about herself, and her mother still shrieking, 'Where is your fiancé? Why don't I see him?' 'It's broken off, it's finished', Eve told her parents; 'You're mad', they screamed, 'You'll not be able to get married ever'; 'Who cares', I said, 'to hell with that. I was completely my father's ward and I had to do what he said, but I said I've had enough, I'm going out, and they said no you're not, and they locked me in. They were going to send me to an asylum; they thought I was going crazy.'

Early next morning her father came unannounced into her room. She was standing there naked, and she turned on him and shouted, 'How dare you!'; she was having her period and she threw her sanitary towel at his face, then went out on the balcony and screamed for help to Shock across the way. 'The whole neighbourhood came out and Shock too, as white as a sheet, onto his balcony in his bathrobe and slippers.' Get me out of here, she called to him, they have locked me in, and when he came over still wearing his slippers and her father opened the door, 'I thought sod you all. To hell with the lot of you. And I ran out like a rabbit.'

That same morning she telephoned Durrell at the British Information Office. 'There was no one else in Alexandria I could talk to. He was the only sane person I knew.' 'I'm coming', she said; they had arranged to meet at the beach later that day. 'What's up?' he asked. 'I'm leaving my family.' 'What are you bringing with you?' 'My swimsuit and my espadrilles.'

Eve arrived at his office in a terrible state. She remembered how he showed her a photograph that he had on his desk of himself with his daughter Penelope on his shoulders. It had been taken at Kalamata before he fled Greece, and it was exactly the way John Cromer Braun remembered Durrell disembarking at Alexandria. Cut adrift from his family as she now was from her own, Durrell embraced her and said, 'I love you.'

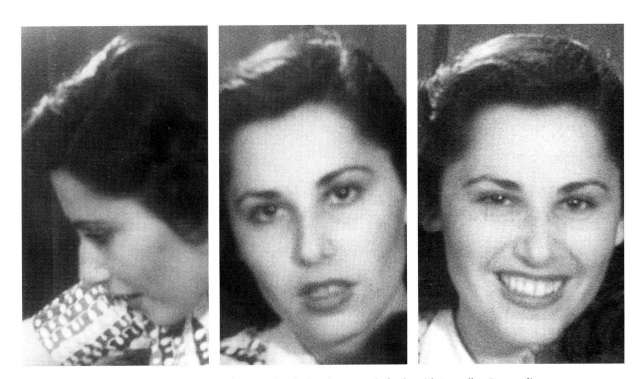

62 These photographs of Eve were taken just days before her *coup de foudre* with Durrell at Pastroudis. At the sight of a camera she tended to go into a vampish pose so someone put a child on her lap to make her relax. The vine-leaf pattern of Eve's dress was recalled by Durrell in *The Alexandria Quartet*.

Abandoning his office for the rest of the day, Durrell took Eve to the villa on Embassy Hill. Gwyn Williams was at the university, and they prepared a meal for themselves and began to talk. Eve told Durrell 'everything'; she found it 'cathartic' and wept; she 'vomited' it all out and was 'hysterical'. 'Larry slapped me across the face and was immediately sorry. I said no, I needed that. He was very good at listening; he was so gentle, so understanding and caring, and I felt completely safe and secure with him. There and then he asked me to marry him. It was all accomplished by noon. From that moment we were lovers.'

Eve stayed at the villa for three days, then deciding that she needed to get out of Alexandria for a while, Durrell sent her to Tanta in the western Delta to stay with Paul Gotch and his wife Billy whom he had first met in Athens in the summer of 1939. 'Billy and I both lost our jobs in London,' said Gotch, 'so we let our flat and on two pounds a week decided to see the world before the war started.' They bicycled to Rome and through Yugoslavia and Albania and were about to head north again into Bulgaria, 'and it was while we were in Athens at a cheap café that we met these two interesting people from Corfu. Larry was small, squat and lively; Nancy was tall, rather ethereal and very blonde.' The four fell into telling stories of their adventures, but in Durrell Gotch felt a warm sympathy, while his impression of Nancy was that she was 'rather cold'.

Gotch got a job with the British Council and was on his way to a training course in Cyprus when Italy entered the war; his ship was diverted to Egypt, where he was sent to Tanta as regional director. He met Durrell again on visits to Cairo, and at the time of the Flap, when they were evacuated to Jerusalem, the Gotches travelled on the same train as Nancy and all stayed at the same pension there.

By a series of chance snapshots enough of Durrell's private life had already been exposed to Gotch, whose easy-going nature must have seemed to Durrell the perfect balm for this latest complication. Eve spent ten days with the Gotches at Tanta, where she found the tranquillity she desperately needed. 'Billy and I got on with Eve very well, and she stayed quietly; we didn't do very much, just sat there.' Eve recalled the silence the Gotches seemed to inhabit, and how 'Paul carried England around with him – if you could not hear the sound of tennis balls behind you, it was your failure of apprehension.'

But though it was 'such a rest' to be at Tanta, 'I also felt terrible about the pain I was inflicting on my parents, who didn't know where I was.' The problem, when she returned to Alexandria, would be to allay the suspicions of her father, who 'behaved like he was my husband, he was so jealous', and those of her intrusive mother, who 'if something pleased me, she would wreck it', while not letting on that she was living with Durrell. 'That's one thing I wasn't going to make a mistake about: I wasn't going to tell my parents about him, because he's a divorced man, well he's ready to divorce; he's married. How can you marry somebody like that? And he's not a Jew.' At the same time Durrell was urging her to work, for though Eve thought his salary fabulous by local standards, he was complaining that he hardly had enough to live on. The all-round solution was the Cozzika Hospital, to which Eve returned as a 'stagière', or trainee nurse, and where she lived in the dormitory and was fed. 'So far as my parents were concerned, the hospital was my home, and Larry didn't exist.'

But Eve never slept at the hospital: 'I slept with Larry'; and every night she went to 40 Rue Fuad, to the dim flat on the second or third floor where Durrell inhabited a room. 'Things were very private between us', so though others lived in the flat too, among them 'a peculiar middle-aged couple', they kept to their rooms, and as she was hardly there in daylight hours she knew nothing about them. Instead she would rise early in the morning and go to the window to see if her calèche had come – she had made a standing arrangement with the driver to wait in the street below. It was the end of May or early in June and the morning sun was already hot, so that the horse and carriage would be waiting in the shade of the overhanging trees growing in the front garden of the classical villa diagonally opposite, on the corner of the Rue Fuad and the Rue Sidi el Kiachi. From there it was a ten-minute ride to the hospital.

The Cozzika Hospital is another of those places that figures frequently in the *Quartet*, as when in response to a phone call from Clea ('I am speaking from the Greek hospital. Melissa is here, very ill indeed. Perhaps even dying'),[12] Darley 'climbed the low bluff on which the hospital stood after threading the long bony spine of the Canopic Way. . . .

63   Durrell and Eve began living together in his flat at 40 Rue Fuad, where soon they were joined by Paul Gotch and his menagerie.

The sense of ghostly familiarity which was growing upon me now was due to the fact that we were approaching the little room in which I had visited Cohen when he was dying'[13] – Cohen being the man whose mistress Melissa had been before she became Darley's girl.

Now that Eve was Durrell's girl, one of their earliest outings was along the Rue Fuad where he took her into a photographer's studio. Only weeks before, Shock had done the same and the result was a charming sequence. 'Normally when a photograph is taken of me, I go into a pose and the pictures show me as vampish. The same thing was happening this time until someone, the photographer or Shock, suggested I sit with a child, a girl; you can just see her head in the corner of the photograph. This relaxed and brightened me and accounts for my beaming look.' Eve is wearing a light, summery outfit with a vine-leaf pattern: 'It was just at the time I took up with Larry.' Just at the time, it seems, that they met at Pastroudis: 'She for her part looked wonderfully, intimidatingly smart, with a new summer frock of a crisp vine-leaf pattern' is how Darley describes Melissa on the day when they exchanged 'that first kiss by the sea'. 'There and then I decided to love her. We idled arm and arm by the sea . . . our conversations full of the debris of lives lived without forethought, without architecture. We had not a taste in common. Our characters and predispositions were wholly different, and yet in the magical ease of this friendship we felt something promised us.'[14]

When Durrell took Eve into the photographer's studio, he took the camera from the photographer: Durrell posed Eve up against a mirror and took the photograph himself. Eve is smiling, she is smiling twice; in the foreground she is smiling full on, in the mirror she is smiling in profile. Durrell has given her a comb to hold; she did not know what to do with her hands. She looks poised and elegant, aristocratic; she is no longer the girl in the vine-leaf dress but looks like a woman of society, a woman who could be Justine. You do not notice when she smiles full on, but in the mirror her smile is touched with apprehension.

One night early that summer Judge Brinton was awakened by the sound of voices at his home in Glymenopoulo. Putting on his dressing gown he went down to investigate, and 'as I entered the drawing room I saw across from me, standing in front of the fireplace, a handsome figure, also in his dressing gown. Seeing me, he advanced and held out his hand with the remark "John's father, I presume."' The unexpected guest was King Farouk, who had met John and Josie at a party in town that evening. John was now the American military attaché in Cairo and during their visit to Alexandria he and Josie were staying with Judge Brinton. But rather than return to Montazah Palace Farouk had asked if he could spend the night, remarking, 'You know, I have no home.' As usual the house was filled with convalescing officers, and there was not a bed to spare, but the king had happily accepted their offer of a mattress on the drawing room floor.

'In truth he had neither home nor intimate friends', Judge Brinton reflected. 'How could he have when his position in the world was such that his closest associates, his ministers, left his presence walking backwards. And what kind of a home, for a man without a wife or family – his family life had broken up – was the immense establishment of Montazah, compared to our own friendly household, full of youth and liveliness and warm welcome.'

Farouk responded to the relaxed and inviting atmosphere offered by the Brintons. He was 'a naturally jolly person with a sense of humour', not least about his own position. On one occasion as he sat cross-legged on the floor to browse through some volumes on the lower bookshelves, he folded his arms across his chest and remarked with a smile, 'Oriental potentate, what!' 'He was always a good sport', Judge Brinton recalled, 'and I might add, since so many hard things have been said of him, that in all his contacts with members of our family, and there were many, a sense of dignity was never lacking.'[15]

Farouk became a frequent visitor at Glymenopoulo and also at Burg el Arab, once sharing the iron-frame bed in the tower room with John. 'Après-vous, Votre Majesté', John had said on that occasion, offering him the more comfortable side by the wall, but remembering he was king and 'en cas d'urgence',[16] Farouk insisted on the outside. And when John mischievously asked him if he intended to take the salute at a ceremonial procession of British tanks and troops, he replied, 'Why should I? They usually bring the tanks to me.'[17] But Lampson's notorious act of the previous year could not be shrugged off with a wry remark.

Farouk was referring to the night of 4 February 1942, when a battalion of British troops and a number of armoured cars and tanks surrounded Abdin Palace in Cairo. The locks were shot off the palace gate, the ambassador's Rolls Royce steamed in, and the six-foot-five Sir Miles Lampson strode through the halls to confront the king. He accused Farouk under the terms of the Anglo-Egyptian Treaty of 'recklessness and irresponsibility' which endangered 'the security of Egypt and of the Allied Forces', making 'it clear that Your Majesty is no longer fit to occupy the Throne'.[18] With a warship waiting off Alexandria to carry the king into exile, Lampson handed Farouk a letter of abdication and demanded that he sign it.

But it was not Farouk, rather Mustafa Nahas, the leader of the Wafd, who was endangering the British position in Egypt. While prime minister in 1936, he had signed the Anglo-Egyptian Treaty, ending the Wafd's years of implacable opposition to compromise with Britain. Meanwhile, the Wafd remained the dominant party in Egypt and the expression of its national aspirations, and the British saw its continued cooperation as essential to the smooth working of the military alliance.

Nahas, however, had lost office before the war, and now he put pressure on the British to restore him to power, threatening that the revolutionary outbreaks of 1919 might be repeated if the Second World War, like the First, brought economic problems to Egypt. When a bad harvest in April and May 1941 brought deepening shortages of flour, beans, oil and sugar and forced up the cost of staples to double their pre-war prices, the cry went round among the poor that the British army was eating all the food. Not that the Wafd when it had been in power showed much enthusiasm for improving the conditions of the working man or the fellahin; its interests were those of the landowners and of the wealthy middle class, but it drew its mass support by appealing to nationalism.

In August Nahas seized on the anniversary of the death of Saad Zaghloul to deliver inflammatory speeches in Alexandria and Cairo accusing the British of destroying the economy and so violating the Anglo-Egyptian Treaty. As the disturbances continued into the autumn, Eden drafted a telegram to Lampson complaining of the ability of the Wafd 'to influence public opinion according to the caprice of Nahas Pasha without incurring the slightest responsibility'. But Eden was less concerned with the immediate security of Egypt than with the perpetuation of British influence well beyond the end of the war, when in accordance with the Anglo-Egyptian Treaty Britain would be obliged to evacuate its forces and then, come 1956, to renegotiate the treaty itself.

64 Durrell took this photograph of Eve soon after they got together. Five years earlier he had written in a notebook that a part of oneself is lost at birth and 'the whole course of one's life is simply a search for this lost fragment' through 'a world of mirrors'.

Eden concluded that there was a bargain to be made with Nahas. 'I am prepared to believe', his telegram continued, 'that we shall not be faced with serious trouble in Egypt during the war unless things go very badly against us; but this will not necessarily be true in the period immediately following up the cessation of hostilities. It may in these circumstances be well to begin preparations at once for the return, before the end of the war, of a predominantly Wafd government, so that the Wafd shall not be indefinitely in a position to claim non-responsibility for what is happening in Egypt.'[19]

But if the solution was to install Nahas as the servant of Britain's long-term policy, the problem was King Farouk, who as Lampson had complained wanted to be the 'independent King of Independent Egypt'.[20] Even during the 1936 treaty negotiations, Eden's preference was for Egypt to become a colony, a view repeated by Lampson when he wrote in his diary in 1940 that 'I have for many years often thought that the best form of permanent relationship with Egypt lay in her incorporation, in some shape or form, within the British Empire.'[21]

Now in February 1942, on the eve of his Abdin Palace coup, Lampson demanded that the king invite Nahas to form a Wafdist government. But Farouk was disinclined to do what he was told by the patronising Lampson. Moreover, as in the days of King Fuad, the Wafd and the monarchy were rivals for the control of Egypt's destiny, and Farouk could claim that he was at least as popular with the people as Nahas, whom he saw as a political opportunist. Arguing, however, that the king's behaviour was inconsistent with the overriding requirements of the military alliance, Lampson ordered the tanks to Abdin Palace.

Yet Lampson's action achieved the opposite to its intended effect: it provoked nationalist outrage at foreign interference, destabilised constitutional government and introduced a bitterness between Britain and Egypt that would culminate in the Suez debacle.

Nahas was branded a traitor by the leaders of Egypt's other political parties, which while blaming the British, as he had done, for the continuing shortages and rising cost of living, heaped insults on the Wafd, which they accused of subservience to the embassy. But by the use and abuse of martial law and with the backing of the British, Nahas was able for the time being to fight off his political opponents.

Meanwhile, Egyptians' sense of shame over what had happened at Abdin bit deeply within the Egyptian army, whose supreme commander was the king. 'For the army, this event has been a deep shock', wrote one young Egyptian officer to a friend. 'Previously the officers only talked of enjoyment and pleasure. Now they talk of sacrifice and of defending dignity at the cost of their lives. . . . You see them repenting of not having intervened in spite of their obvious weakness to restore the country's dignity and cleanse its honour in blood. But', concluded the writer, once of Bacos and whose name was Gamal Abdel Nasser, 'the future is ours.'[22]

Sometime in June 1943 the shadowy tenants at 40 Rue Fuad vacated their rooms, leaving Durrell in sole possession of the large and gloomy flat. Hearing that Paul Gotch was being transferred to Alexandria, Durrell picked up the phone and asked if he would like to move in.

It puzzled Gotch why Durrell ever asked, and he was far from sure that it would be a workable arrangement: 'When Larry phoned up and asked how would you like to share a flat in Alexandria, I was a little apprehensive. I didn't know how domesticated he would be.' Gotch thought it must have been for the sake of respectability 'from the

Foreign Office point of view': that if Durrell and Eve were going to live together it was better that they lost themselves in a crowd. A crowd is what moved in on 28 June,[23] when Gotch arrived from Tanta with Billy his wife, Linnet his daughter, a nanny and a dog called Sappho, and also a friend of Billy's, Jean Hill, whom Eve remembered as having a squint in one eye. More probably Durrell wanted help in paying the rent while colonising the flat to his liking, for as much as he was a private and often secretive man, he also craved diversion in numbers, and for Durrell there might also have been echoes of India and Corfu in surrounding himself with a family.

Indeed the proximity between Durrell and Gotch extended almost twenty-four hours round the clock, for the British Council's Institute was on the floor immediately above the British Information Office at 1 Rue Toussoum. In the event Gotch found Durrell 'meticulous' in his social observances, so that from his office on the floor below he was 'always ringing up in that cultured accent of his, real pukka sahib stuff, to ask if he could bring somebody to lunch, that sort of thing', while back at the flat he was 'so tolerant' of the Gotches' menagerie. 'Eve and Larry couldn't have been nicer people to share the flat with. She adored Larry. It was a relief for her to find somebody who clearly loved her and with whom she was happy and prepared to live with, which was virtually what she was doing, in contrast to being forced to see people whom she didn't like and didn't want to marry.'

Durrell had a love for the absurd, the bizarre, the extraordinary and the grotesque, a taste he shared with Gotch and for which the howlers in the *Egyptian Gazette* and the *Egyptian Mail* provided them with a fair amount of material. Paul's prize was an advertisement showing a woman beaming by a brand new refrigerator, the tag line reading 'Every woman needs a frig.' Durrell's collection was pasted into a scrapbook titled 'Imbecility File – This Egypt':[24] there was Lord Louis Mountbattan 'with his louse-lipped smile'; 'Boobs of Heavy Calibre Dropped on Berlin'; and 'Britain has been going ahead with plans for the new prefabricated mouse for married couples.' Also an advertisement:

Beauty Parlour
Mme Margot Pop
Freckles
Radical electric
depilation, local
slimming treatment
by the peeling
method. Beauty
products. Special
prices for ladies
in uniform.
12 Rue Sesostris
3rd floor
Alexandria

65 Durrell's British Information Office was on the mezzanine floor of 1 Rue Toussoum Pasha, while above it was the British Council's Institute where Paul Gotch worked.

But apart from Pop, depilation and peeling, what must have made this advertisement for Durrell was the address and its association with Eliot's 'Madame Sosostris, famous clairvoyante, / . . . / With a wicked pack of cards', and the fact that Eliot had already identified Alexandria as one of the cities of the dead:

> What is the city over the mountains
> Cracks and reforms with bursts in the violet air
> Falling towers
> Jerusalem Athens Alexandria
> Vienna London
> Unreal[25]

Later Durrell would incorporate many of the themes and images of *The Waste Land* in his *Quartet*.

Eve remembered how Durrell and Gotch regaled each other with stories about 'those strange Egyptians', such as the one about the man walking along the street beside his donkey: the donkey was laden with a sack which attracted the attention of the police, who opened it, and out fell a load of human heads. Or another about the time that a taxi was found outside 40 Rue Fuad, the driver's head on the seat beside him, hacked off by three drunken RAF men serving at Aboukir who had been angry at being over-charged the fare. Both stories found their echo in *Justine*, when the French diplomat Georges Pombal tells Darley how the wife of the Swedish consul was found sitting in her car without her head: 'Some Bedouin women encamped nearby were among those interrogated. While they were busy denying any knowledge of the accident, out of the apron of one of the women rolled the missing head. They had been trying to extract the gold teeth which had been such an unpleasant feature of her party-smile.'[26]

Eve never really knew if these were just tales that Durrell and Gotch had picked up from gossip or from books and newspapers, though they always made them sound con-vincingly their own. 'On one occasion Larry came home from the office as white as a sheet. He had seen a smartly dressed effendi walking towards him along the street – black suit, polished shoes, a fez on his head. But as he drew close Larry saw that instead of a nose he had a cork stuck in the middle of his face. We all laughed, Paul and I and the rest of us, and refused to believe it, but Larry was serious and as white as a sheet to prove it.' He spoke too at this time of once encountering his doppelganger and the terror with which the experience filled him. Eve found Durrell's stories endlessly fascinating and amusing, 'even when he would tell the same stories again, because he would always give them some new twist', and she adds that 'he was an entertainer' who 'had a way of drawing people into his world'. But though 'he would make things up on the spur of the moment to suit the occasion, he believed what he said'.

The ambit of Durrell's world at this time lay close along the Rue Fuad, between the flat and his office, with ports of call in between. At number 30 were the offices of the Greek Orthodox Patriarchate, where Durrell made a friend of its librarian Theodore Moschonas, an Egyptian-born Venizelist who just then was writing a book on the patri-archate's role in the Greek War of Independence. In the same building was the Greek Club where Venizelos had come during his triumphant visit in 1915. 'Walking down the remembered grooves of streets which extended on every side, radiating out like the arms of a starfish from the axis of its founder's tomb' was how Durrell described this part of the city,[27] which housed most of the characters in the *Quartet*: Darley and Pombal shared a flat in the Rue Nebi Daniel; Clea's flat was in the Rue Fuad and her painter's studio in the Rue St Saba, at the Atelier; Justine and Nessim lived in a house set back from the Rue Fuad; and Balthazar lived in the Rue Lepsius, in 'the worm-eaten room with the cane chair which creaked all night, and where once the old poet of the city had recited "The Barbarians" '.[28] Durrell took Eve to the crossroads of the Rues Fuad and Nebi

Daniel and told her that Alexander was buried there, which was the first she had ever heard of it; and they walked round to the Rue Lepsius where Durrell stood outside 'in reverence' and recited 'Waiting for the Barbarians' in Greek – Eve said that the whole time Durrell was in Alexandria this was his favourite of Cavafy's poems.

Durrell and Eve would go to Baudrot and Pastroudis for a drink, especially to Pastroudis, which was Durrell's favourite rendezvous for meeting up with friends. But for a quiet meal together they would go round the corner from the flat into the Rue Safiya Zaghloul to the smart grill room or restaurant at the Santa Lucia, owned at that time by a Jew and a Greek, where Durrell kept a running account. 'Larry received his salary monthly and would immediately pay his rent and other bills, then spend whatever was left over. He had only one suit; he was always dressed the same, just changes of shirt, saying he could not afford clothes. But that was because he spent so much on drinking.' If he was feeling flush, however, he would take Eve to one of the expensive places in the little streets off the Rue Chérif Pasha, such as the Union Bar or the Petit Coin de France.

But Durrell never took Eve to the Cecil for a drink or a meal or for its entertainments, and in all her years in Alexandria she never once passed through its doors to be reflected in its mirrors like Justine: her earlier friends had thought it too staid and well beyond their class. Nor – and again unlike Justine – did she ever venture into the Turkish town apart from shallow forays to visit her father when he shared an office with his brother Nessim in the Rue de France. 'Yet Larry has written somewhere of me knowing all about the sex life of Arabs and the prostitution houses of Alexandria, and people have since come to me and asked about such things as though I was an expert. Nor did I ever tell him that I was half-Greek. Absolutely not. That was just Larry's usual fabricating imagination.'

Durrell got closer to the truth about Eve and their relationship when he spoke of them sharing 'a kind of refugee life'.[29] She was in full rejection of her parents and of what she felt to be their oppressive Jewishness, and her rejection extended to Alexandria as well as to everything Egyptian – to almost everything she knew and loved, in fact. On his side, as Eve recalled, 'Larry routinely made remarks against the Egyptians – it was like a tick. He had nothing but contempt for Egypt; he would come home in a rage, full of expletives about Egyptians.' Part of the reason, she thought, was that he hated not being in Greece. He might rail against the Egyptians, the English, the French and the Jews, but the Greeks were the one people he always liked, 'for the way they lived, for their outlook on life, though he might know them as rogues, liars, double-crossers and crooks', and she added, 'He was practically a Greek himself.' In mirroring his rejection in her own, she became 'the only person I have been able to talk to really'.[30]

But it was more than that. Durrell saw in Eve something broken, and part of her attraction was the healing he could bring her. 'I believed many foolish things at that time, and Larry reshaped me, he would question everything. It was a matter of principle for him that when he had won me round to his point of view, he would change

66   Pastroudis as it is today. Durrell and Eve began their affair here in 1943.

tack and take up the position I had just abandoned – always playing devil's advocate.' The effect was to tear down in order to rebuild, which Eve admitted she needed. 'The first time I was taken aback, I had a bit of a shock, but when it happened towards what seemed to be the whole lot, I would say you've taken everything away, I don't know what's me anymore. He knew what he'd done, and he helped me to start again, this time using my mind a bit more, which I'd never used before much. And because of that, well yes, he became more and more precious to me, because although it made me suffer a lot, I just shudder to think what would have happened had I not had this kind of treatment. It was the beginning, it was formative, and I started I suppose believing in myself, thanks to Larry, although he would build me up on one side and tumble me down on the other. He'd give me a kiss on one hand and a slap on the other.'

'But you never knew when he was going to be empathic and when he wasn't. When he was, he was marvellous. But Larry was the angel and the devil. No two ways about it.' Eve remembered an evening when they walked round the corner from the Rue Fuad to see *Casablanca* at the Rialto cinema in the Rue Safiya Zaghloul. But she could remember nothing of the film itself (and never wanted to see it afterwards) because she was crying the whole way through, and Durrell was saying, 'I'm sorry, I'm sorry' – 'He always said "I'm sorry" after beating me up and then he would beat me up again.' They had had a row before the film, something to do with Eve 'not knowing who Larry was. I never knew how interested in me he was: he seemed content to be within himself. I never understood him, not then, not now; he was a secret and he was changeable.'

Durrell had been working on *A Private Country*, a collection of verse that Faber and Faber would publish towards the end of the year, while on his occasional visits to Cairo for briefings at the embassy he lent a hand with *Personal Landscape*, whose sole issue for 1943 was due out in October. 'Mythology', one of Durrell's recent poems, would be included.

'Mythology' tells of a private world in which 'All my favourite characters have been / Out of all pattern and proportion', though it is also an example of how opaque and guarded Durrell could be with his feelings. The poem is full of imaginary names, like 'Tibble, Gondril, Purvis, the Duke of Puke, / Shatterblossom and Dude Bowdler / Who swelled up in Jaffa and became a tree'. Also there is 'Ramon de Something who gave lectures / From an elephant, founded a society / To protect the inanimate against cruelty'. And even Katsimbalis, though identified by name, is obscure for being 'heard but seldom seen'.[31]

But if 'Mythology' was not meant to reveal, its purpose for Durrell was to distil and record his sense of dislocation. And like the pocket scrapbooks he filled with wrappers, photographs and cinema tickets or an image captured in a line or two, those few words about Katsimbalis encapsulated for Durrell what seemed so distant from the groove of the Rue Fuad: the defiant spirit of wartime Greece.

Durrell had heard from Seferis, whose sister was there, of the thousands who gathered at Palamas' funeral in Athens in February 1943. Among them was Katsimbalis, who burst into a tirade of abuse against the German Embassy representative who was laying a wreath on Palamas' tomb, and then, though it was forbidden on pain of death, broke into the Greek national anthem. The immense crowd of mourners stood in terrified silence as a trembling Katsimbalis finished the first verse alone. Seferis' sister pulled on his arm as the German fixed him with a glowering stare; a terrible hush hung over the crowd but still Katsimbalis sang. Part way through the second verse Katsimbalis was joined by a friend and they finished the verse together. Then suddenly and with a mighty roar the anthem was taken up by the crowd, and with tears running down their thousands of faces they buried Palamas and sang for Greece. That was where Durrell wanted to be, and his thoughts were with his friend Katsimbalis, who for fear of being shot had gone into hiding, 'heard but seldom seen'.

On another leaf of Durrell's scrapbook, so to speak, was 'Ramon de Something', a memory from an evening when he and Nancy had gone to dine with Seferis, who was suddenly struck with a violent fever. Over and over in a state of delirium, he repeated the name of Ramon Gomez de la Serna, a Spanish surrealist writer. That was sometime after Seferis had returned to Cairo from Pretoria in the spring of 1942, and it was perhaps the last time Seferis, Durrell and Nancy had all been together. Nancy went to Palestine not long after, had 'gone up a tree and would not come down', since when she had been working for the official censorship in Jaffa, though probably not even Nancy would have recognised herself in Dude Bowdler nor seen in Shatterblossom the pain Durrell felt at losing his daughter. Meanwhile, during those months in Alexandria when Durrell had been living alone, he encrypted his feelings within a mythology and like Ramon de Something 'gave asylum to aged chairs in his home'.

With only his first name altered, Gaston Zananiri joined Durrell's mythology as a foot-note of sorts at the end of *Justine*; there among a list of tarot-like figures, or 'character squeezes', as Durrell called them, along with such as 'Melissa Artemis: patron of sorrow', 'Clea Montis: still waters of pain', 'Justine Hosnani: arrow in darkness', is 'Ahmed Zananiri: pole-star criminal'.[32] His presence in the *Quartet* amounted to more than that, however, if Robert Liddell was right in thinking that Durrell based his character Balthazar on Gaston Zananiri.

'They were brilliant people, writing, talking, drinking, smoking', said Zananiri of the people at the British Council, through whom he met Robert Liddell, seconded by the Council to Farouk University, and the British information officer Lawrence Durrell. 'Durrell had three lives. He had his group of those English young men teaching at the British Council. And then he was interested in the local people of Alexandria. And prob-ably there was his intelligence work, of which we never spoke.' Zananiri found Durrell 'an interesting man, a brilliant man who liked his drink, who liked jokes; I suppose he liked women. We were friendly, we had drinks together. He was Larry, Larry simply.'

Zananiri spoke to Durrell of those times when he first came to know Cavafy. 'I was a brilliant Alexandrian, of the posh society of Alexandria, the dancing, the balls, the evening parties. We had exhibitions and talkie-walkies, brilliant people; some of them quite superficial creatures. Society! Alexandria! Cavafy knew them all. He was conscious of his celebrity, very conscious and very proud; he always spoke like a poet', and here Zananiri clutched his hand at his throat, remembering Cavafy's last months with cancer – 'He was tortured', gasped Zananiri, his emotions caught by the memory. 'He used to come to my house, we sat in my garden, and he analysed with me his poems. What I did was to learn the psychology of Cavafy.'

The Alexandrians, thought Zananiri, could be 'very refined and others absolutely vulgar', but Cavafy understood that they all 'carried in their memories what the people of the past had tasted; they all lived this way unconsciously. Study Mahaffy. Although he's a bore, he'll enlighten you. His book gives you an idea of what Alexandria was in the past. But though Alexandria is two thousand years old, it's still Alexandria. There is something of the past which returns every moment.'[33]

67 Gaston Zananiri, who had been a friend of Cavafy's, also became a friend of Durrell's. Zananiri's dream was of a new Mediterranean culture waiting to be rescued from the war.

The identification of Balthazar with Zananiri is possible, for though Balthazar has much of Cavafy about him and lives in Cavafy's old flat in the Rue Lepsius, Durrell would have had descriptions of the flat and of Cavafy himself from Zananiri. Durrell wrote that Balthazar was a 'close friend of the old poet, and of him he spoke with such warmth and penetration that what he had to say always moved me',[34] a description fitting Zananiri, along with the observation that Balthazar 'spoke as if a different sort of time obtained here'.[35] And when Durrell wrote in *Justine* of the boys who stir and turn to watch every stranger 'in those little cafés where Balthazar went so often with the old poet of the city',[36] Durrell was clearly recollecting Zananiri's stories of his night-time adventures with Cavafy.

Zananiri would say to Durrell, 'You ask me what I am? I am an Alexandrian. Alexandria is not Egypt, Alexandria is not Africa. When you are in Alexandria you are on the Mediterranean.' But as Durrell knew, in the salons and cafés of Alexandria almost everyone, Greeks, Jews, Syro-Lebanese, had a story to tell of wanderings and survival, of Byzantiums fallen, of Smyrnas doomed. 'Durrell suggested that I write a book about the situation of the foreign communities who had brought new life to Alexandria. He suggested a history, *The Problems of Egypt*.'

Durrell had been reading Zananiri's *L'Egypte et l'équilibre du Levant au Moyen Age* published in 1936 and *L'Esprit méditerranéen dans le Proche Orient* which appeared in 1939. Both books were contributions to the discussion in intellectual and political circles about where Egypt's future lay at a time when it was still being asked who the Egyptians were and how their heritage should be defined. The answer would be critical, as those excluded from the definition could eventually lose their political rights and possibly their property, their homes and their country too.

Saad Zaghloul's vision of Egypt had been secular and inclusive, though he recognised the uniqueness of the Egyptian character that went back to pharaonic times, which appealed particularly to the Copts who prided themselves on being the pure descendants of the ancient Egyptians. The Muslim writer Taha Hussein, whom Mohammed Nagui featured in his painting *The School of Alexandria*, shared Zaghloul's views. But he emphasised that though Egypt had been invaded by the Arabs their numbers had been small, so that all Egyptians, whether Muslim or Copt, could claim equal heritage from the pharaonic past. He also spoke of Egypt's admiration for European civilisation, for its progress and its education, and said that Egypt was fundamentally like Europe. Many liberal-minded Egyptians of all backgrounds were attracted by Hussein's ideas, as they gave recognition to the role of Egypt's Jews and to its Greek, Italian, Syro-Lebanese and other settlers who had long acted as intermediaries between the Islamic and European worlds.

But Durrell would have been told by Zananiri of how he knew Ismail Sidki Pasha, a founding member of the Wafd, who later broke away from the party and became prime minister in the early 1930s. 'He cared for me like a son, like a nephew', yet even before the war he had told Zananiri, 'There is no future for you here', and advised him to leave Egypt. A new kind of nationalism was gaining ground, one which turned its back on history: Arabism stressed the shared language, culture and religion of the mass of the Egyptian people while rejecting the pharaonic, the Graeco-Roman and the Christian centuries preceding the Arab conquest and ignoring the subsequent multi-ethnic Ottoman period too.

In the late 1930s new militant nationalist groups combined Arabism with religion and xenophobia, among them the Muslim Brotherhood, which by the end of the decade had developed into a political force second only to the Wafd. In the liberal and secular pluralist state promoted by the Wafd, non-Muslim minorities had the chance to participate and to integrate; in the Islamic Egypt envisioned by groups such as the Muslim Brotherhood, minorities, if they were tolerated at all, would suffer discrimination and inequality. The rise of Islamic militancy, founded on a wholly fanciful belief in a bygone Muslim utopia, had its roots in rapid population growth and the ever more gaping divide between the rich and the poor. But the issue that gave focus to their sense of frustration and threat, that divided the universe into us and them, was Palestine.

Hitler's rise to power in Germany in 1933 saw a surge of immigration into Palestine which for the first time convinced the Palestinian Arabs that an eventual Jewish state was a real possibility. Then in 1936 when Palestinian leaders discovered that the Zionists were smuggling arms into the country they called for a general strike, which quickly developed into an uprising against the British primarily, but also against the Jews.

Suddenly Palestine became an issue that no Egyptian politician could ignore, and with it Arabism was crystallised as Egypt's defining identity. That Egyptian Jews were largely indifferent to Zionism, that Copts were the epitome of loyalty to Egypt, and that both Jews and Copts had played prominent roles in Zaghloul's nationalist movement meant nothing to those student demonstrators in Cairo, Tanta and Alexandria who in 1938 were heard shouting, 'Jews get out of Egypt and Palestine',[37] nor to those who confusingly demanded that the Copts should be expelled from Egypt and sent to Palestine to join the Jews.[38] Yet as long as Egypt was stable and prosperous, and the country was unaffected by war, the voices of extremism were still muted, so that in January 1939, when a representative of the Jewish Agency visited Egypt to discover why Zionism was unattractive to Egyptian Jews, he reported that 'in countries other than Egypt the Zionist movement expanded due to external factors – the spread of anti-Semitism and declining economic prospects', but in Egypt 'these factors do not exist at all'.[39]

Fuelled by a British proposal for the partition of Palestine into Arab and Jewish states, the Arab rebellion continued, persuading the British government to call a Round Table Conference in the spring of 1939 to which delegations from Egypt, Iraq, Saudi Arabia, Transjordan and Yemen were invited. That the British also now saw the Palestine issue in terms of a pan-Arab dimension was partly due to George Antonius, whose *Arab Awakening*, published the previous year, caused a sensation by revealing secret promises concerning territory and sovereignty made by the British to the Arabs during the First World War to win them as allies against the Turks.

But the book had also broken Antonius' heart, for in writing it he had come to see with terrifying clarity that the events he was describing were destroying his cosmopolitan world. Though a Christian, he had argued for an awakening that was to be understood, he said, in terms of the Arabisation and Islamisation of the entire Middle East, but as he was completing the final revisions he complained of the fanaticism, hostility and paranoia that he felt was growing out of control, and was disturbed by the 'general bankruptcy of moral standards and values' amid the rising chauvinist tide.[40]

With no compromise possible between the mutually exclusive claims of the Zionists and the Arabs over Palestine, the Round Table Conference ended in failure. But faced with the peril of a German war, the British imposed a settlement of their own. A White Paper issued in May 1939 envisaged the creation in ten years' time of an independent but bi-national Palestinian state, and it also limited Jewish immigration to seventy-five thousand over the next five years with no further immigration allowed without Palestinian Arab agreement. This was asking them to accept what the countries of Western Europe and the New World had refused when, in response to a conference called in 1938 by President Roosevelt, none except the Dominican Republic would accept more than a few thousand Jews suffering under Hitler's regime. Arab feeling throughout the Middle East was nevertheless conciliated by the British White Paper, and in Palestine, where a third of the population was already Jewish, the rebellion ceased.

All this was miles away from Durrell's longing for Greece. Yet in *Balthazar*, *Mountolive* and *Clea*, the last three volumes of *The Alexandria Quartet*, Durrell pursues the theme, absent from *Justine*, of the uncertain prospects of the minorities and foreigners in Egypt and of the Palestine conspiracy that drives the passions of the Coptic banker Nessim Hosnani and his Jewish wife Justine. ' "Yes, Justine, Palestine. If only the Jews can win their freedom, we can all be at ease. It is the only hope for us, the dispossessed *foreigners*." He uttered the word with a slight twist of bitterness.'[41] But that was only after Durrell met Claude Vincendon on Cyprus – Claude, the granddaughter of Felix and Rosette de Menasce and the niece of George.

Meanwhile, the White Paper outraged the Zionist movement, which turned emphatically against the British, though until a German defeat was in sight the Zionists could only bide their time.

By the early summer of 1943, Admiral Godfroy had bid farewell to Alexandria. Already in January on a visit to Egypt Churchill had spoken to Miles Lampson, who was now Lord Killearn,[42] about 'the intolerable position of having Admiral Godfroy and the French Fleet in Alexandria refusing to throw in their lot with us whilst receiving all their pay and food from British sources'.[43] Since then Godfroy had haggled and squirmed on the hook of his Vichy principles as the British gradually turned off the financial tap, until on 15 May, bowing to necessity, Force X sailed from Alexandria to join the Free French in Algeria.

Two days earlier, on 13 May 1943, the Axis commanders and their troops had surrendered to the converging British First and Eighth Armies and the American Second Corps in Tunisia, and nearly a quarter of a million prisoners had been taken. Six days later Churchill declared, 'The African war is over. Mussolini's African Empire and Corporal Hitler's strategy are alike exploded.'[44]

Now the liberation of Europe began. In June Alexandria's Western Harbour became 'stiff with ships',[45] part of a massive Allied armada assembling at British and Middle-Eastern ports under the command of Admiral Cunningham for Operation Husky, the invasion of Sicily that was set to commence on 10 July, its scale larger than that of the Normandy landings eleven months later. Of the half million troops that would land on Sicily, the slight majority would be British, the rest American, but all under the supreme command of General Dwight D. Eisenhower, an acceptance by Britain that the United States was now the senior partner in the alliance.

As the invasion fleet set sail from the Western Harbour, a sense of anticlimax settled on Alexandria, which already after the victory at Alamein, thought Gwyn Williams, had 'floated away from the world at war'. Though the military authorities decided that the blackout should continue as long as Crete and Greece were in enemy hands, for a while the old idyll seemed to return. 'The wealthy Jewish ladies and their salons, and the Wednesday afternoons of Baron George [de] Menasce could have been part of the Alexandria of Theocritus. For us, as for Theocritus, it was a city of consolable exile. . . . Love, good food, music, swimming, we had it all.'[46] As in Forster's time, 'sects and philosophies flourished', and 'there was Gaston Zananiri's dream of a new Mediterranean culture' waiting to be rescued from the war.

But there was no mistaking, Williams added, that 'Alexandria during the years 1942–45 was a city of causes that were being lost, even though militarily it was successfully defended.' It was a world symbolised by the names of people he and Durrell knew there – 'Zananiri, Sachs, Baddaro, Menasce, Zogueb, Suarez, Salinas, Kerekreti, Barber, Perides, Fumaroli, Papassunessiou, Oumoff, Barukh, Baladi' – but a world that instead of being linked to the Mediterranean was being 'rolled towards the sea'. 'It was out of this varied and dying ferment that Larry invented his *Alexandria Quartet*.'[47]

CHAPTER 8

Prospero's Tower

I sit in my tower and listen to ideas moving around inside, aqueous and dim like fishes.

Lawrence Durrell to Diana Gould, April 1944[1]

On 22 August Durrell went to the British Residency on the top of Abou el Nawatir hill in Rushdi to interview Noël Coward, who was staying there as the guest of his friend Lord Killearn. 'The day broke fair and excessively warm', Coward wrote in his diary, 'but I didn't notice it as I slept until twelve o'clock when, with my breakfast tray on my knees, I gave an interview to Larry Darrell [*sic*] who lived in Corfu and writes poems.'[2] He was so fed up, he told Durrell, with the wartime habit of stamping everything 'Confidential' and 'Top Secret' that he was stamping his own diary manuscript 'Highly Trivial'.[3]

Four nights before their interview Coward had been dining with Lord Killearn and Richard Casey in Cairo, where Casey spoke 'a good deal about the open arming of the Jews and the flouting of our authority' in Palestine.[4] Coward could safely be included in such discussions, as at the outbreak of the war he had joined MI6, the Secret Intelligence Service, first working in 'D' section, the dirty tricks department, then with the Political Warfare Executive, where he was engaged for a time in black propaganda, until it was decided that someone so much in the public eye could better serve his country's cause by entertaining the troops in the open employ of the Ministry of Information.[5]

Coward was on a three-month tour of the Mediterranean and the Middle East, and that same evening he gave a concert at a convalescent camp before flying off the next morning to Lebanon, Syria and Iraq. But in mid-September he was back in Alexandria, where he was invited by Harold Finney, Oswald's younger brother and business heir, to lunch at the Yacht Club, overlooking the Western Harbour by Ras el Tin Palace. 'Now the Yacht Club in Alexandria', Coward wrote in his diary, 'is select and exclusive to an alarming degree although I suspect that the bulk of the members have little or no connection with yachting. There were a number of elderly, mauve-looking ladies sitting on the terrace when we arrived. They were thickly coated with rice powder and hissing sibilantly.' Coward and Finney ordered cocktails and were congratulating themselves on being suitably attired for both the climate and the setting when the management noticed they were wearing shorts and shirts and asked them to leave. For all his influence in the city, Finney remonstrated in vain and they swept out with as much dignity as they could muster. Afterwards, dining in town, they comforted themselves with the reflection that 'as long as the Alexandria Yacht Club maintained its high moral standards, the war for freedom and civilisation really was worth winning'.[6]

During this return visit to Alexandria Coward also gave a concert at the Fleet Club. Italy had surrendered on 8 September, barely a week before, and the Italian fleet had just been brought into the Western Harbour in triumph, so that it was 'an exciting moment', as Coward said, when he entered the club's open-air beer garden where hundreds of British sailors, who had not been ashore for several weeks, were sitting at tables spread under the trees in an atmosphere of boisterous alcoholism. The Fleet Club was the old Greek Hospital where Cavafy had died, its garden the view of the poet when he stood out on his balcony and listened to the music of the city. This night the music was 'Don't Let's Be Beastly to the Germans' and raunchy variations on Cole Porter's 'Let's Do It', until 'sweating with relief' Coward leapt off the stage and was 'quickly submerged under a sea of sailors'.[7]

It was the stuff of one of Forster's, 'Alexandria Vignettes', but you look in vain through old copies of the Egyptian newspapers for Durrell's interview or an account of Coward's performance at the Fleet Club. On 29 August, however, the *Egyptian Gazette* did find two inches of space midway down its front page for a story taken straight off the UP wire. Headlined 'Hitler Has Deported 5 Million Jews', the bare figures were reported without comment: '5 million of Europe's 6.3 million Jews have been deported by Hitler, declares the Institute of Jewish Affairs. Over 3 million have been destroyed by starvation, murder or enduring forced labour.' Yet newspapers like *The Times* in London and the *New York Times* failed to report the story at all, as the British and American governments were suppressing details of the emerging catastrophe.[8]

The flat on the Rue Fuad in the centre of the city had been hot and stifling all that summer, and Eve remembered it as 'a very dark and gloomy place; nobody liked it'. All the same it came as a complete surprise when Durrell announced that he had found somewhere else for them all to live.

On Friday 1 October 1943, Durrell and Eve moved with Paul and Billy (who was five months pregnant), their two-year-old daughter Linnet, their nanny and their dog Sappho into the entire top floor of a neo-Baroque villa at 17 (now 19) Rue Maamoun in Moharrem Bey.[9] By then Jean Hill, Billy's friend, had gone her own way, but two new tenants were added to the menagerie – Harold Edwards, a British Council lecturer, and his Greek wife Epy, with whom he had fled from Athens at the time of the German invasion. The rooms with their ornately moulded ceilings were spacious and filled with light. There were bedrooms for the couples and one for the nanny together with the baby, and rooms to spare for guests; and there was a dining room and drawing room that everyone shared, and a large balcony overlooking the tree-shaded street where they frequently gathered and entertained.

An octagonal two-storey tower rose at the corner of the villa. From the roof a rickety stairway with wrought-iron railings climbed to the tower's upper room, which Durrell immediately claimed as his writing place. Only Eve was ever allowed in the tower: 'Often he would ask me up. I was in those days a very silent person, and my presence did not disturb his writing. I hardly ever spoke, because I was still coming out of my past.' She helped him with the furnishings, making curtains for the windows and cushions for the benches set against the walls, while he had a joiner make him a kidney-shaped desk which he placed at the centre of his room. It was all 'very smart alec and quaint',[10] he said, surveying his domain.

From his tower Durrell had a sweeping view over the southern quarters of the city and beyond. Romantics, he said, could see 'Pompey's Pillar, Hadra Prison, and the wet reedy wastes of Lake Mareotis stretching away into the distance and blotting the sky'.[11] Half a mile or so to the southeast, between the tram line and the Mahmoudiya Canal, were the narrow streets where Eve had spent her early childhood, a far cry from this leafy part of Moharrem Bey, which had been developed around the turn of the century as an upper-class neighbourhood comparable to the Quartier Grec. He could also look down into the villa's enormous garden enclosed within an eight-foot wall, where marble statues and granite columns stood amid an ever flowering forest of violets and ginger lilies, frangipani and banyan trees, with an overgrown tennis court and on the far side a painters' studio.

No sooner had they moved into the villa than Gotch and Eve realised that Durrell was familiar with its owners, the Ambrons. Zananiri, who described Aldo Ambron as 'a big shot, a Grand'Ufficiale' and his wife Amelia as 'a lady', said the door to their house 'was always open to society entertainments'. That must have been how Durrell met the Ambrons' daughter Gilda, thought Eve: 'She took a liking to him, and when she discovered he was looking for a flat, she said we've got this place upstairs.' With Eve still pretending to live at the hospital and not yet much in evidence, Durrell was welcomed by the Ambrons as though he was part of the family, and they invited him downstairs for meals prepared by Gilda. Eve supposed that 'the parents were feeling wouldn't it be nice if Larry, who was getting to be free – I think he talked a lot about his problems and so on to whomever would listen, and he was in the throes of being rejected by Nancy, and so there was intimation that he was a free man – therefore wouldn't it be nice if their daughter was married to somebody whom obviously she was so very fond of. And she was, poor darling. She was besotted with Larry, in a proper way: she was *une fille de bonne famille*, and she behaved beautifully.' 'Gilda adored Larry', Gotch recalled. 'She was in love with him.'

Gilda Ambron (pronounced with a soft 'g', as 'Jilda') was the only Alexandrian whose real name would appear in the *Quartet*. Twice in *Balthazar*,[12] the second volume, Durrell rolls out 'the majestic poetry of the names which had come to mean so much to me,

68 'Better times begin', Durrell wrote in his commonplace book when he moved into the Ambron villa in the Rue Maamoun, but his estranged wife Nancy and his daughter Penelope filled his thoughts.

the names of the Alexandrians',[13] and on each occasion, though the order of the names is changed, he ends with a falling toll on Gilda Ambron:

This was Alexandria, the unconsciously poetical mother-city exemplified in the names and faces which made up her history. Listen.

Tony Umbada, Baldassaro Trivizani, Claude Amaril, Paul Capodistria, Dmitri Randidi, Onouphrios Papas, Count Banubula, Jacques de Guery, Athena Trasha, Djamboulat Bey, Delphine de Francueil, General Cervoni, Ahmed Hassan Pacha, Pozzo di Borgo, Pierre Balbz, Gaston Phipps, Haddad Fahmy Amin, Mehmet Adm,

Wilmot Pierrefeu, Toto de Brunel, Colonel Neguib, Dante Borromeo, Benedict Dangeau, Pia dei Tolomei, Gilda Ambron. . . . The poetry and history of commerce, the rhyme-schemes of the Levant which had swallowed Venice and Genoa. (Names which the passer-by may one day read upon the tombs in the cemetery.)[14]

But Durrell's move to the Rue Maamoun may have had more to do with an introduction from the Smarts, who had long been friends of the Ambrons. Gilda's father Aldo was an art connoisseur and a founding member of the Amis de l'Art, whom Judge Brinton had described in his diary in the 1920s as 'a well to do and cultured Italian with artistic tastes'. Apart from shared cultural interests with the Ambrons, however, Sir Walter Smart's particular function as Oriental Counsellor (he had been knighted in June 1942) was to be informed on the entire recent political history of Egypt and on all its most influential figures. Since taking up his post in 1926, he had immersed himself in the affairs of the country and had cultivated all the appropriate people, developing them as contacts and sources of information. Smart included Aldo Ambron in the embassy's 'List of Personalities in Egypt' compiled for Anthony Eden in 1941, summarising him as a Jew from Rome and a resident of Alexandria, a civil engineer and an architect, a contractor and a property developer, a founder of the Banco Italo-Egiziano and a very wealthy landowner, who was president of the Italian Club and bore the title of Grand'Ufficiale of the Italian royal court.

Aldo Ambron Abramo Isaac, to give him his full name, had married Amelia, an Almagia by birth, and had a hand in her family's engineering and construction company, which in 1906 built that magnificent sweep of the Eastern Harbour's Corniche that Forster celebrated as being in the finest spirit of the Ptolemies. Ambron was also a director of the Société Egyptienne d'Entreprises Urbaines et Rurales, which was involved in the construction of apartment and commercial buildings, mostly in central Alexandria. His fellow directors were all captains of the thriving Alexandrian business community and for the most part members of the city's most prominent Jewish dynasties, among them Jacques Aghion, whose investments were in railways and sugar, the cotton and textile entrepreneur Raphael Toriel, the bankers Alfred and Jacques Suares, and also Baron Felix de Menasce. However it was that Durrell came to live at the Ambron villa, his move had brought him to the heart of Alexandria's *haute juiverie*.

Durrell liked Gilda, and they got on well; she was a lively, laughing, outgoing person, and moreover she was a painter, a good painter if a conventional one. All the Ambrons were artistic. Gilda's sister Nora was a musician, and her brother Emilio did etchings on Balinese themes, while her mother, mostly working in charcoal and chalk though sometimes in oils, drew and painted society portraits, her talent for capturing a likeness combining with a happy inclination always to stress the beauty and elegance in her sitters. This may have been because, as Marta Loria put it, 'the whole family was ugly', not least Gilda, who was 'ugly, small and round'. Bernard de Zogheb, while cautiously allowing that 'physically Gilda was not beautiful', went on to say that

69   Durrell's tower, 1994. An octagonal tower rising at one corner of the Ambron villa became Durrell's private writing place. He wrote *Prospero's Cell* here and also began his *Notes for Alex*, which evolved into *Justine*.

'she was short and rather stocky – or dumpy – with a sort of flat face and round eyes a bit like a bulldog or a pug'.

But the Ambron villa held another attraction for Durrell. Gilda and her mother worked in their studio at the far end of the garden, which had been built for Amelia in the early 1920s by the Ambrons' friend Alessandro Loria – what Judge Brinton called a 'toy house'[15] on his visit in 1926, when it was let for a time to the American consul. Though rising three storeys high, it was only a room deep and presented an all but windowless wall to the street behind; but several large windows which gazed north towards the Ambron villa filled the studio with voluminous light. With room to spare, the studio was shared with Gilda's friend and neighbour Clea Badaro when she was not at the Atelier, 'a very pretty blonde girl I was very keen on',[16] said Durrell, who had a clear view of the studio from his tower.

Clea spoke of the day that Durrell was first brought round to the studio, and though she hated it when people dropped in unexpectedly, she put aside her annoyance when he showed an interest in her work, her paintings of soldiers at the bars and cabarets around town, of harlequins, clowns and circus women on horseback, and she remembered also how he was fascinated by her name. 'Clea, the gentle, loveable, unknowable Clea', is how he introduces her in the *Quartet*, 'so disarmingly simple, graceful, self-contained . . . poured, while still warm, into the body of a young grace: that is to say, into a body born without instincts or desires.'[17]

'Larry described her very well', said Eve. 'He used her name, and he gave her physique absolutely.' 'She was tall', said Bernard de Zogheb, who became her friend, 'majestically attractive rather than beautiful, with blue eyes and her blonde hair piled up as they did in those days, forties fashion. She had a lot of charm, she had this warmth that came out at once, she radiated a sort of inner glow; though she could be very shy at times with people she didn't know.' When Eve had been modelling at the Atelier she would meet Clea in passing and regarded her with awe. A look of intelligence shone from her eyes, a knowing, an awareness, and a seriousness of purpose that made Eve feel 'like a lightweight'. She was 'stunningly beautiful' Eve said, 'but unlike many women in Alexandria who would have put on airs on that account, she was always modest and unaffected. Whatever Clea's private life, it did not spill out into public talk – this in a city where everyone knew and talked about everyone else's affairs. Everyone liked having her around, not a word was said against her; even women liked her.'

Clea sketched Durrell and they would talk. She was thirty at this time to his thirty-one. Since her childhood, she said, when she first began to draw, she had been recording her impressions on almost every piece of paper that came to hand, in school copybooks, on house accounts, in the margins of letters to her friends, stimulated not only by what she saw about her but also by her dreams. Her name, she said, Badaro, was Syro-Lebanese; her father, a Maronite Christian, had been a lawyer and involved in important financial affairs in Cairo where she was born. But her mother was a Greek from Smyrna, and to her friends, who thought of her as Greek, she was known as Kleaki, the Greek diminutive of Clea; that was what her parents had called her during her happy childhood in Egypt.

She was still a child when her mother died, and her father, who lost his fortune at almost the same time, took her and her older sister to Switzerland, where they all lived with her maternal grandmother in Montreux. There the days of happiness ended and were followed by years of sadness and stifled pain. Her father, who had been so loving to his daughters, cuddling them and spoiling them, suffered a breakdown and was paralysed by depression for the rest of his life. Instead of the noise and laughter of childhood that Clea and her sister had known, their grandmother, an austere disciplinarian, imposed a joyless reign of silence. In this cloistered existence, she told Durrell, she turned to drawing, mostly clowns and dancers suspended in the air and fairies riding on Pegasus-like horses; the circus had always been her passion. At seventeen she enrolled at the Académie des Beaux Arts in Lausanne and four years later returned to Egypt, where in Alexandria she found her spiritual home at the Atelier.[18]

Durrell makes allusions to Clea Badaro's life in the *Quartet*. There is the character-squeeze of 'Clea Montis: still waters of pain',[19] references to her mother, who has died,[20] and to 'her old father whom she worships'.[21] But though Durrell describes Nessim as a Copt, Justine and Balthazar as Jews, Melissa and Capodistria as Greeks, and so on through Scobie, Pursewarden, Pombal and the rest, uniquely Clea is portrayed without an inheritance, her nationality that of artist.

In fact, one of the things Durrell most liked about Clea was that she was not Jewish. 'We are surrounded, impregnated with Jews', he wrote in a notebook, who 'give a curious flavour to the Alexandrian backcloth: a curious pessimistic hysteria, and a ceaseless "conscience tourmentée" in the words of Clea. The Greeks give our city noise and flair; but the Jews flavour the whole financial and moral world with the weight of their urgence, a hunger for insecurity. Tranquillity is poison to them, and this lack of repose pushes forth mental constructions at such a rate that time is accelerated like certain cancerous growths.'[22]

This was something that Durrell had long thought about. While writing *The Black Book* he had written to Miller from Corfu, 'Now we have the timely recognition that each man is entitled to his own reality, interpret it as he wants. . . . There is only one canon: FAITH.' But there was a crowd of writers who out of fear gave experience the lie – 'Mostly Jews'. 'They will not admit the claim of the artist's experience to be as valid as any so called rational truth. They have no faith. THAT IS THE JEWISH NATIONAL DISEASE, LACK OF FAITH.'[23]

Clea Badaro, like himself, was making of her experiences an art of her own. This as well as her beauty is what he admired about her, that self-containment he wrote about; her faith in her originality and her confident authority in her art. She concentrates 'with single-mindedness upon her painting which she takes seriously, but not too seriously', he wrote of his fictional Clea in the *Quartet*. Her 'bold yet elegant canvases radiate clemency and humour. They are full of a sense of play.'[24]

70 Clea Badaro, who painted in the studio on the far side of the Ambron villa garden, served as a model for the character of Clea in Durrell's *Alexandria Quartet.*

At the end of *Justine* and also at the end of *Clea*, the final volume of the *Quartet*, Darley on his island is exchanging letters with Clea across the sea, he in his tower so to speak, she in her studio across the garden. They will come together, they know; sometime, somewhere.

Late in the summer of 1943, after Operation Husky had sailed for Sicily from Alexandria harbour, an elegant two-masted schooner sailed in from Mombasa. Its name was the *Samothrace* and its owner was George McFadden, a relation of Judge Brinton's by his first marriage, who in April the previous year had brought it over from Cyprus where he had been excavating the sanctuary of Apollo at Curium for the University of Pennsylvania. McFadden combined his pursuit of the antique with a love of the sea; in his spare time he had been translating *The Iliad*, and the walnut-panelled stateroom of his yacht, with its fireplace and furniture from the palace of James II at the Hague, was lined with shelves and cabinets of scholarly books. Before returning to America to join the navy, McFadden had had the *Samothrace* placed out of harm's way in Kenya; now it had been brought back to Alexandria where Judge Brinton was meant to find a buyer.

The man who sailed the *Samothrace* up from Mombasa was Charles Gibson Cowan, the author of *Loud Report*, published in 1938, which was an account of his impoverished Jewish background in London's East End and his years as a vagabond, a fairground barker and a confidence trickster. Since then he had enjoyed a modest success as a producer, playwright and actor, but his future, he felt, lay in writing.

With the idea of writing another kind of vagabonding book, this time cast across the Mediterranean, Cowan, aged thirty-six, had set sail from England in July 1939 in a rebuilt fisherman's yawl, the *Evelyn Hope*, with a 25-year-old actress called Elizabeth Gwynne, better known after the war as Elizabeth David, the author of the culinary classic *Mediterranean Food*.

Elizabeth had been born into an upper-class family with connections to the aristocracy, and at her coming of age in 1932 she was presented at court as a debutante. Shy but intense beneath her cool beauty, she found herself bored by the society of the callow young men of whom her mother approved. In reaction she announced that she would become an actress, and soon she met Cowan with his tousled, dark and piratical look: 'Never wear anything but a blue jersey and an old pair of flannel trousers', Elizabeth told him during their voyage through the Mediterranean, 'Never wash the salt out of your hair. Then perhaps I shall stay in love with you.'[25] Cowan would tie her to the mast and whip her, she confided to one of her closest friends, which if a joke was in any case suggestive of the way she saw their relationship.

As they travelled eastwards their journey was stalked by war. The Germans invaded France as they were at Antibes; they were interned for a while by the Italians when they sailed into the Straits of Messina; and when the Germans launched their attack on Greece, their island home of Syros was bombed. In the middle of May 1941 they escaped to Egypt, where worn with intimacy, hardship and danger Cowan and Elizabeth parted. 'We'll both think often of the things we have done together', she wrote to him that summer, 'of the canals and the wine and the red rocks of my beloved France, of the sea white with nautilus off the coast of Corsica, of dawn in the Bay of Naples, of a certain lobster mayonnaise we ate between one life and another, of mountains of golden oranges in Joseph's garden and those purple islands lying all around us from the top of the hill behind our hovel.' But it was an ambivalent farewell: 'Thank you for the lovely experiences you have given me and remember that you made the Isles of Greece more than just a beautiful name for both of us and that these things can be done again.'[26]

Durrell would later claim that he first met Elizabeth when she boarded the same caique in which he and Nancy escaped from Kalamata.[27] As well as being untrue, this was also

Alexandria

The "Samothrace"

Charles. Gibson. Cowan

71 These photographs in Paul Gotch's album record the arrival at Alexandria of Charles Gibson Cowan and the *Samothrace*.

an appropriation; he met her through Robin Fedden only after she arrived in Cairo. But then Durrell enjoyed a friendly rivalry with the older Fedden and sometimes imagined himself in his shoes.

One of the co-founders with Durrell of *Personal Landscape*, Fedden had grown up in Normandy and gone to Cambridge before travelling about the Middle East. In 1937 he wrote a monograph setting down his valuable observations on the Coptic monastery of St Anthony near the Red Sea, which he had visited the previous year,[28] and in 1938 he published *Suicide: A Social and Historical Study*, which made a special impression on Durrell.[29] Fedden was cultural attaché at the British Embassy in Athens when he met Durrell, who was temporarily working there just after the outbreak of the war, and he made a note after their first encounter of Durrell's 'elusive almost feminine grace, deep-set eyes, and . . . an impression of great sensitivity balanced by composure'.[30] He also wrote down some of Durrell's remarks, such as 'The poison of life is the desire for a permanent synthesis. . . . The problem of life is in the reconciliation of Time with Space.'[31]

Unable to reconcile his embassy position with his pacifism, Fedden resigned and returned to Egypt in 1940, where he lectured at Cairo's Fuad University. In Cairo his friendships were wide and various, and he moved easily between nightclubs and cock-tail parties and literary and diplomatic circles; he was a great friend of Amy Nimr's, and it was probably Fedden who recommended Durrell to her and to her husband Walter Smart. He was also a frequent visitor to Burg el Arab and counted John Brinton among his closest friends, which did not stop him trying to seduce Josie after a desert picnic: 'He tried to make love to me. He's really very attractive. He let me read a new poem he had just written',[32] perhaps the one called 'Personal Landscape': 'Smooth is the sand we trod last night / And very soft the contours of the hill.'[33]

Elizabeth was already familiar with Egypt long before her Mediterranean adventure with Cowan; in 1936 she had been the guest of English friends of her mother's in Cairo, who introduced her to Walter and Amy Smart through whom she met Fedden. His lively mind combined with his languid charm and easy humour left a deep impression on Elizabeth; years later she revealed that they had been briefly engaged, probably during a holiday they spent together in France in 1938, though she did not say.

Certainly this time round they were in very close touch, though Fedden was in Cairo while Elizabeth had found a job as a cypher clerk with naval intelligence in Alexandria. There she shared an enormous flat in the Rue des Pharaons in the Quartier Grec with Mike Cumberlege, an old friend she had first met in Malta, who worked with the SOE, the Special Operations Executive, and who was often away, running arms and agents in a caique to the resistance in Crete. Cumberlege was a romantic and engaging figure, and staying at his flat in Alexandria was a recipe for an affair. But after two years of vagabond-ing with Cowan, Elizabeth wanted the emotional repose to 'feel connected up again', and so she house-kept for Cumberlege and entertained without, as she said, 'sex rearing up its ugly head'.[34] Durrell, who had already met her in Cairo, may have been a visitor at this time,[35] the latter half of 1941, perhaps coming with Fedden, whose arrival in September was described by Elizabeth as 'the signal for a series of parties and picnics'.[36]

By this time Fedden was deeply in love with Renée Catzeflis, an Alexandrian whose father was a prominent Greek lawyer who always set his table with an empty place for her Italian mother, who had died young. Renée was brought up a Catholic, though her communion with the Church did not last beyond that day in confession when she was told by the priest not to repeat the sin she had just confessed to. In a city notorious for rumours, *toute Alexandrie* whispered that since her mother's early death she had fallen madly in love with her twin brother. Fedden had introduced Renée to Elizabeth, then blamed Elizabeth for not keeping an eye on her when during his visit in September he discovered that Renée and Cumberlege were having an affair. But the story goes that Renée was having an affair with Elizabeth too. It was 'a very intense relationship',[37] said a friend of Fedden's, George Lassalle, then working for British intelligence in Cairo, who met Elizabeth when she moved there in the autumn of 1942, and with whom she enjoyed an intimate friendship for years to come.

Elizabeth and Cowan had been exchanging lively letters since they last saw each other in the summer of 1941, and she wore the African jewellery he sent her as presents, but she refused to read Cowan's *Voyage of the Evelyn Hope*, which came chapter by chapter as it was written. And then when Cowan announced his arrival aboard the *Samothrace* at Alexandria harbour, she immediately sent him a telegram asking to be left alone, followed by a letter in which she wrote, 'I never want to feel a scrap of emotion for the rest of my life', and another saying, 'I do absolutely dread any emotion or the reminder of the unspeakable miseries of Italy and Athens and the first weeks in Cairo. . . . I will never never return to the kind of existence I led before the war. I am a thousand times happier doing a job I love, living among my friends, than I was bashing around the place never knowing where I should be next week. I have learnt to make up my mind for myself, and not be influenced by emotions.'[38]

The adventure with Cowan had broken the mould of Elizabeth's earlier narrow life; their affair had done its job and in that sense was over. For two years she had been experimenting and remaking herself, but now she found herself confused and disturbed by the rejected emotions that assailed her at the news of Cowan's return.

Durrell began hearing the story almost as soon as the *Samothrace* arrived at Alexandria when Cowan turned up at the British Information Office and soon became a regular visitor at the Rue Fuad flat and then at the Ambron villa, where Eve remembered him asking Durrell's opinion on the chapters he had written so far of *The Voyage of the Evelyn Hope*. Usually Durrell was generous and encouraging towards other writers and artists, but in this case he was pointedly less than enthusiastic, perhaps because both hero and adventure were precisely what he would have wished for himself. 'Charles was a flamboyant buccaneer, full of tall stories', said Eve. He had a way of always taking centre stage, she said, while in Durrell there was an envious part of himself that liked to play with Cowan, to torture him a bit.

Eve became very fond of Cowan, though just as his always scruffy appearance at first hid how good-looking he was, so she soon saw that beneath a guise of gaucherie he was a kind and gentle man. 'Charles was not a poser, not with me. He approached me simply and with courtesy and respect. He made a point of making a special gesture each time – he brought little things, it touched me so deeply.' And perhaps that also made Durrell jealous.

With the *Samothrace* still in his care, Cowan grandly entertained, inviting Durrell and Eve and the Gotches to parties in the Western Harbour, along with service girls and British and Egyptian friends, and sometimes John and Josie Brinton. But Eve best remembered the small dinner parties aboard the yacht, when six guests or so would play guinea pig to what she called Cowan's *grosso modo* cuisine, 'crude, like a man who enjoys cooking, everything thrown in with gusto', though Durrell later credited Cowan with teaching Elizabeth how to cook – 'Typical woman, she learnt everything from a man.'[39]

Durrell had the story of the *Evelyn Hope* from Elizabeth too, who would come down from Cairo and spend hours pouring out her heart to him at the Ambron villa. 'My first contact with her', Eve remembered, 'was on that balcony where we always congregated

72 Elizabeth Gwynne, *c.* 1943. Later better known as Elizabeth David, Elizabeth talked to Durrell with a burning intensity. Her power to conceal and reveal selectively gave force and mystery to her personality.

because it was such a lovely place. And there I was, and I was like an object, literally, I didn't count because she was so emotional. And she was talking all about Charles Gibson Cowan, what to do about him, and she wanted Larry's advice.' Cowan's irrepressible romanticism had a way of tugging at her heart, as when late in the summer of 1943 he had joined a secret mission to the Aegean islands organised by the naval section of the American Office of Strategic Services (OSS) and under cover of darkness had returned to their former island home of Syros, where he plucked a branch of dry thorn and sent it to her when he got back to Alexandria that autumn. Possibly Elizabeth was angry that Cowan had aroused her feelings and was forcing her to struggle against them, though Eve's definite impression was that Cowan had left her, and Elizabeth 'didn't know what to do about it'. Elizabeth juggled her visits to ensure that she and Cowan never met, but during those early visits to the Ambron villa, it seems, he was never out of her mind. 'He was the man of Elizabeth's life,'[40] said Eve, while she and Gotch also remembered that on several occasions Cowan had said of Elizabeth, 'She was the woman of my life and that is why I left her.'[41]

Eve, who found Elizabeth 'larger than life', yet not at all theatrical, observed a burning intensity about her, 'a single-mindedness which excluded everything and everyone during her conversations with Larry'. But though Eve kept to the background 'like a piece of furniture', when she was alone with Durrell she could tell him about Elizabeth's friend Renée Catzeflis, whom she knew 'not socially, as we lived in different worlds', but because they had both worked at the Cozzika – Renée for the Red Cross – and had lived for a time at the hospital, where Renée became 'the one woman who ever had an effect on me, an appeal'. Durrell, who had a gift for an interrogative way of listening, would soon have learnt from Elizabeth herself that there was a great deal more to her story than Cowan and the *Evelyn Hope*. What gave force and mystery to her personality was her power to conceal and reveal selectively, a game he would have enjoyed. But it is not clear if eventually she herself or Cowan or a mutual friend told Durrell that at the age of fourteen she had been raped by a member of her family. Certainly George Lassalle is said to have claimed that it was true, remarking what a nuisance it was, as it meant re-enacting the rape every time one made love to her.[42]

'She had (and there was no mistaking the force of this confession for it was accompanied by floods of tears, and I have never seen her weep like that before or since) – she had been raped by one of her relations. . . . From this time forward she could obtain no satisfaction in love unless she mentally recreated these incidents and re-enacted them.'[43] So Durrell wrote of Justine in *The Alexandria Quartet*.

As for Eve, 'It was like *Alice in Wonderland*. It was as if I had suddenly got myself into a book, the characters of the book coming alive. I wasn't sure what my part was to be.'[44]

Though Cowan sometimes spent the night at the Ambron villa, Elizabeth always stayed elsewhere with friends, often with George de Menasce at the family house on the corner of the Rue Menasce and the Rue Rassafa, just a five-minute walk away. Menasce had been married to an American heiress, Elinor Kaskel, and in 1924 they had a son, Pierre Levi de Menasce, but the marriage had very quickly broken down and Elinor returned to America with the child. For the rest of his life George de Menasce devoted himself to collecting beautiful things, his watchword 'circumspice',[45] which could as well have applied to his habit of collecting people. He delighted in leading Elizabeth about the house, introducing her to his remarkable collections of late Roman ware, Roman and Syrian glass, Mogul jewelled jade, Jaipur enamel, Persian jewels, coloured diamonds, jewelled watches and automata, eighteenth-century gold snuff boxes, Greek island and Turkish embroideries, fine paintings, rare carpets and Fabergé. His greatest passion, however, apart from music, was for Chinese works of art, especially porcelain, in which he built up a collection that was perhaps the finest and most extensive in private hands anywhere in the world.

Elizabeth had met Menasce, probably through the Smarts, during her visit to Egypt in 1936 and revived her acquaintance with him in 1941 when she came to work for naval intelligence in Alexandria. At the time of the Flap in July 1942 her section was moved to Port Tewfik near Suez at the southern end of the Canal, but she developed a serious foot infection and returned to Alexandria on leave, where Menasce, whom she soon came to regard as her kindest friend in Egypt, insisted that she be his guest. When her foot became even more inflamed, he took her to hospital for an operation and paid the bill himself, then brought her back to the Rue Rassafa where for ten weeks with the help of his own doctor he looked after her as though she was part of the family.

Once Elizabeth had sufficiently recovered, she went to Cairo, arriving just in time for Fedden's marriage to Renée Catzeflis in October 1942, an arrangement which, apart from gratifying their love for each other, gave Renée independence from the confining atmosphere of her family and allowed her, as she had always wanted, to live life on her own terms. It was Renée, now working at the British Embassy Publicity Section, who put Elizabeth onto a job at the British Ministry of Information, the clearing house for reports from agents, experts, diplomats and information officers on conditions anywhere from Tunisia to Persia, which were sifted, sorted and forwarded as required to the embassy, the intelligence services, the military and Whitehall, and were suitably filleted and dressed for circulation to the press. Elizabeth's task was to establish a reference library of books, journals, magazines and newspapers to be used freely by war correspondents and press attachés, and though it was not secret work, both through the publications she read and the sort of people she met she became in political and military matters one of the best-informed and well-connected people in Cairo. Fedden and Durrell would use her library, as would journalists like Alan Moorhead of the *Daily Express*, who later wrote famous books on the White and Blue Niles, and the traveller and writer Freya Stark, who had become a friend of Durrell's after he met her at the Smarts. Freya Stark also worked for the Ministry of Information and had set up the Brotherhood of Freedom to unite Arabs throughout the Middle East behind the Allied cause, and just now, in the autumn of 1943 as Elizabeth was visiting Alexandria, Freya was setting off on an eight-month lecture tour of America and Canada in an attempt to counter mounting Zionist propaganda there against British policy in Palestine. Elizabeth was proving an interesting friend for George de Menasce.

Indeed, by this time George de Menasce was already secretly raising money from a selected list of Alexandrian Jewish millionaires on behalf of Mossad Le'Aliya, the underground organisation responsible for illegal immigration into Palestine.[46] This was in contrast to the appeal to the Jewish community in Alexandria in December 1942 to donate funds care of Robert Rolo, the non-Zionist president of the community, to further the British war effort as the surest way of delivering the world from Hitler's tyranny. Associated with illegal immigration was the gathering of intelligence about the British and the Egyptians, along

73 Robin Fedden and his wife Renée Catzeflis after climbing the Great Pyramid.

with the theft from British warehouses of weapons and munitions confiscated from the retreating Germans which were then smuggled across Sinai to be used against the British and the Arabs in Palestine. But British intelligence reports to the embassy, it seems, had not yet made Walter Smart suspicious of Menasce's activities. Nor had Menasce been among the 'List of Personalities in Egypt', as it included only Egyptians and non-British residents: George de Menasce, who had been born in Liverpool, was British, and indeed for his generous services to the troops he was awarded an OBE.

A month before Durrell moved to Moharrem Bey, Felix de Menasce died, aged seventy-eight, after years of paralysis that had kept him confined to his villa in the Rue Rassafa. 'Keenly interested in Zionism' and 'a close friend of Dr Weizmann', read his obituary in London's *Jewish Chronicle* on 3 September 1943. 'Among those who attended the funeral were the Governor of Alexandria, who had been delegated by the King to convey the Royal condolences to the family, a representative of the Prime Minister, the Director-General of the Municipality, the Commandant of Police, the Consular Body, and the Chief Rabbi of Alexandria. Baron de Menasce is survived by his widow, two daughters, and two sons, Baron Georges de Menasce, a noted philanthropist and enthusiastic worker for the welfare of British and Allied Forces comforts institutions, and Father Jean de Menasce, of the Dominican Order and author of a book on Chassidism, *Quand Israël aime Dieu*.'

Durrell knew the Menasce house where Elizabeth went to stay, as sometimes he would go there with Gwyn Williams for one of its renowned musical afternoons. 'I remember', said Jacques Mawas, the grandson of Felix and the nephew of George de Menasce, 'during the war every Sunday afternoon there were concerts for the troops at the Rue Rassafa. There would be some hundred or two hundred people entertained and also fed. And on the Tuesday something else, when there were another two hundred guests. This was in addition to ten or fifteen friends and officers who were living there more or less permanently.' In fact at the Tuesday concerts George de Menasce himself played the piano,[47] often in duet with Gina Bachauer, who subsequently became internationally famous, and this was followed by a lavish tea with pastries from Baudrot or sometimes from Pastroudis.

'It is true', Durrell writes of Nessim in the *Quartet*, 'that at this period he had already begun to entertain with a prodigality hitherto unknown in the city, even among the richest families. The great house was never empty now. . . . Only the diplomatic corps smelt in this new prodigality a run of hidden motives.'[48]

The Palestine conspiracy which provides the political-thriller dimension of *The Alexandria Quartet* sees the Coptic banker Nessim Hosnani plotting to smuggle weapons into Palestine to foment a Jewish revolt against the British. Nessim's idea is that the Copts would suffer in an independent Egypt unless, to offset Muslim dominance, they helped create a steadfast ally in the form of a Jewish state in Palestine. But the Copts have always been resolutely Egyptian and anti-Zionist, and would never have lent themselves to any such conspiracy. Durrell himself, in a note prefacing *Mountolive*, the third volume of the *Quartet* – the one in which the ambassador David Mountolive discovers that his friend Nessim Hosnani is involved in an anti-British Zionist conspiracy – writes 'All the characters and situations described in this book . . . are purely imaginary. I have exercised a novelist's right in taking a few necessary liberties with modern Middle Eastern history.'[49] But though it is true that Durrell took some liberties, it is also true that they were necessary if he was to conceal the fact that the characters and situations he describes were far from purely imaginary.

74 Baron Felix de Menasce in a wheelchair, 1938; with him are several of his grandchildren. From left to right: Jacques Mawas, Eric Vincendon, Claude Vincendon (then thirteen years old) and Betty Mawas. Felix de Menasce was paralysed during the last years of his life and was confined to his home and gardens in the Rue Rassafa, where he died not long after Durrell moved into the nearby Ambron villa.

Forster's *Alexandria* introduced Gwyn Williams to the poets of the Ptolemaic city, and soon he was reading the Fifteenth Idyll of Theocritus, the poems of Callimachus in Robin Furness' translation and the epigrams of *The Greek Anthology*, and these gave him the notion of a flyting or verse war between the poets of Alexandria and those of Cairo. They were friends of his and they liked the idea: Robin Fedden, Bernard Spencer, Terence Tiller and Bryn Davies, all at Fuad University in Cairo, and in Alexandria Williams himself and Robert Liddell at Farouk University, and Harold Edwards and Durrell, who declared, 'Not since Troy has there been such a bash-up.'[50]

Gwyn Williams called on Robin Furness in Cairo to act as arbiter ('. . . resist, dear Robin, / the inevitable urge to lead your tribe in / this poetemachia. It better skills / your wisdom and your wit to hold the scales')[51] and in November fired the opening shot, roundly trashing the muses of the Cairo poets. The reply came from Bernard Spencer, who after insulting Williams, Edwards and Liddell, turned his fire on Durrell:

> But oh what startled Muse would not miscarry
> when in the swollen verse of Durrell (Larry)
> pornography and Greece and gaga marry.[52]

Durrell hit back against Cairo, where 'all you prostituted pens / Flow slimy as the unchristian Nile', its poets 'mere boabs of the Muses'. He defended himself against Spencer, 'a blubber hacker' or 'flenser', who 'when you've done / In place of skin and bone / Is gristle left alone'; while 'thou smart unbridled Fedden / Who doth with base iambic leaden / Stir the dark Khamseen with thy verse, / And in full flush / Glide with sassoon-like rush / From poetry to pose – or something worse.'[53]

Furness made just one intervention, and that a sly metaphysical observation on the Oneness of Tiller. This came after Gwyn Williams had written lines contemplating 'the mystery of the sex life of Mr Terence Rogers Tiller' – 'If Terence rogers Tiller / Then are we to presume / The latter's just ancillar?'[54] – to which Furness, arguing against the implied duality, insisted that 'If Terence rogers Tiller rogers too.'[55]

But it fell to Liddell, though he had been raised in Cairo and was often (as Durrell put it) 'tart',[56] to locate the Alexandrian muse in the allusiveness of the city:

> From Cleopatra, near the Camp of Caesar,
> This is my answer to the School of Giza.
> Never has any but some wretched tyro
> Yet thought of writing poetry in Cairo.
> What can your motive be, if not to mimic us,
> The fellow-citizens of the great Callimachus?
> You would do well then not to mock, but toady us,
> The heirs of Apollonius called Rhodius.
> . . .
> Nor ever will the Muses answer sulkily
> If wooed at Glymenopoulo or Bulkeley.
> (Our very tram-stops – could the names be sweeter
> Than Soter, Sidi Bishr or Mazarita?)[57]

It was the poetry that Forster had found in the city, and which Durrell incorporated in the *Quartet*: 'The very names of the tram stops echoed the poetry of these journeys: Chatby, Camp de César, Laurens, Mazarita, Glymenopoulos, Sidi Bishr.'[58]

For all that Eve was devoted to Durrell and had taken seriously his talk of marriage, she felt that things were not yet over between him and Nancy. During his early days with

Eve, he would talk of Nancy as being a 'nuisance', the same word he used to mask his feelings when he had written to Eliot earlier in the year, but he also spoke angrily about her, and it was Eve's impression that if Nancy were to return to Egypt and have him back, he would go to her like a shot.

Now in mid-November 1943 Durrell went to Beirut, telling Eve he was going to see Nancy who was staying there for a while. But it seems that she refused to meet with him face to face, and Eve recalled how upset he was when he returned to Alexandria ten days later: Nancy would give him no clear answer about what she intended, and he was worried that he might not see his daughter again.

The end of things with Nancy meant that it was time for a summing up, and while still in Beirut Durrell completed a long autobiographical poem he had been writing in Alexandria, 'Cities, Plains and People', which opens on his childhood:

> Once in idleness was my beginning,

> Night was to the mortal boy
> Innocent of surface like a new mind
> Upon whose edges once he walked
> In idleness, in perfect idleness.

Little was known then of better or worse:

> Sex was small,
> Death was small,
> Were qualities held in a deathless essence,
> Yet subjects of the wheel, burned clear
> and immortal to my seventh year.

> To all who turn and start descending
> The long sad river of their growth:
> The tidebound, tepid, causeless
> Continuum of terrors in the spirit,
> I give you here unending
> In idleness an innocent beginning

> Until your pain become a literature.

Corfu was a return to that magical world:

> So Time, the lovely and mysterious
> With promises and blessings moves
> Through her swift degrees,

> So gladly does he bear
> Towards the sad perfect wife,
> The rocky island and the cypress-trees.
>
> . . .
>
> Here worlds were confirmed to him.

But now the simile for Nancy and himself came to his mind:

> Of lovers, like swimmers lost at sea,
> Exhausted in each other's arms
> Urgent for land, but treading water.[59]

In December Durrell heard from Miller again, for the first time in a year: 'How are you all? I think of you often. Will the war soon be over, do you think? Will we see Corfu again?'[60]

And this time, at last, Durrell replied: 'I am in Alexandria now. . . . Nancy is in Jerusalem with the child. We have split up; just the war I guess. After Greece, Crete and the Alamein evacuation we got to understand what the word "refugee" means. Will you write some time – and disregard my bloody humours?'[61]

Finally he was admitting that he had lost Nancy, but he made no mention of Eve.

By now she had stopped working at the Cozzika Hospital (though her parents still thought she was there) and was living full time at the Ambron villa, where she was feeling listless and began to put on weight. This happened most years as winter approached, when her mood would swing from a manic high to a depressive low. In the summer she had weighed 110 pounds but now it had risen to 132, so that the talk at the villa was that Eve, not Billy, was the one who was pregnant.

Early in July 1943 Durrell had proposed a short book on the Greek War of Independence to the Department of Information of the Greek government-in-exile in Cairo. Hoping that Faber and Faber would publish it in England too, he described it to T. S. Eliot as an 'accurate and terse chronicle' of the revolt against the Turks during the 1820s, but one that he would embed 'like flint' in 'an imaginative portrait of a national character and landscape'.[62] But now in February 1944 Durrell was complaining to Eliot that his book 'still waits for cooperation from our gallant and maddening little allies', adding, 'Of all the uncooperating, talkative, thankless, political races they are the worst.'[63]

Durrell had intended that his book should argue a cause – by analogy the cause of the guerrilla resistance in German-occupied Greece. Several groups formed the Greek resistance, but the largest and most effective was the National Popular Liberation Army. As intended, its acronym, ELAS, was laden with patriotic symbolism in that it all but reproduced the Greek word for Greece (Ελλας), which helped it win widespread support within Greece itself and from anti-fascists and philhellenes abroad. ELAS was the military arm of the National Liberation Front (EAM), many of whose members were

Venizelists, among them Katsimbalis, who had remained in Greece, and it also had many sympathisers among Egyptian Greeks and among Greeks who had escaped to Egypt, including Stephanides.

Yet the Royalist Greek government-in-exile had now shunned Durrell's proposal. Behind their rejection was a British policy towards EAM/ELAS of such 'ignoble and stupid unimaginativeness' that it made his 'blood freeze'. In fact he had stumbled onto politically dangerous ground, for just at the time he was proposing his book, the British had awakened to the fact that while EAM/ELAS claimed to represent the future of liberal democracy, and though the majority of its members were on the democratic left, the movement was secretly controlled by the Greek Communist Party, for which resistance against the Germans was always secondary to the principal objective of advancing the interests of the Soviet Union and establishing by force a 'people's democracy' in Greece. Not that Durrell knew or cared very much what they were, but he realised that if he was not to 'accumulate a dossier of indiscretions',[64] he had better fall silent, though it made him feel, and not for the first time, that he was betraying the cause of the Greece he loved.

As Forster had done, Durrell saw the war that had overtaken his life in terms of an inner conflict. 'I see no end to the business', he had written to Miller from Kalamata in November 1940 after the Italian invasion of Greece. 'It will go on for years because we are no nearer to the individual solution – and the outer struggle is only a reflection of it.'[65]

All the same, he had been ready to fight, as Miller saw for himself on Corfu in the late summer of 1939. For Durrell the atmosphere was charged with memories of Byron, and he wanted to enlist, not in the British forces, but in the Greek army for service against the Italians on the Albanian frontier, 'because he thought more of the Greeks than he did of his own countrymen'.[66] Eventually he was dissuaded from going, but only after a terrible row with Nancy and some level-headed talk from the British consul. But again in February 1941, with Italian aircraft in the skies above Kalamata, Durrell went up to Athens and proposed to the British Council that he be released from his teaching duties, this time to join the RAF, to be told that their instructions were to keep their people at their posts to bolster local morale against the growing threat of a German invasion.

A month later, even while 'sitting on the crater' and thinking about his Book of the Dead, Durrell was writing to Miller in America, 'I am so happy that England and Greece are in this together; with all their faults they both stand for something great. . . . Over there you can have no idea how moving and awakening is the effort and the love expended by the ordinary people caught in this great rat-trap of war; in England the children putting posies of wild-flowers on the graves of the German airmen who have smashed their towns to powder. In Greece the shop-girls who have been hastily enlisted as nurses weeping over two poor Italians who had to have their legs amputated for frost-bite; the beggars running beside the columns of prisoners giving them bits of bread or an orange. . . . And on the other side the lying crawling meanness of the Italians who bombed Larissa during the earthquake: who bomb villages from 30,000 feet for fear of the single defending machine gun as at Pylos: and who run before the wretchedly clad, poorly fed Evzones in their scarlet shoes. One thing is certain, that these rats are not the masters of Europe, and never can be: and of course, as we prophesied at the beginning of the war the arch-rat is France. You will see her declare for Germany before long: all she wants is an excuse. All this, of course, has no connection with us in the ultimate sense: only as T. E. Lawrence said once, "There are times when right living is cried down, and then only the sword can preach." ’[67]

Instead Durrell was pushing a pen in Alexandria in the service of British propaganda, frustrated even in his attempt to write in the cause of Greece. ‘To console myself’, he wrote to Eliot, ‘I am writing a little book about Corfu.’[68]

Prospero's Cell would be the first and most charming of Durrell's island books, splashed with sunshine and wine, and for its mood and its folkways and its discursions in history it continues to be read as a bucolic travel book. By February 1944 he had written twenty thousand words, or so he told Eliot, which, if true, meant that he had already written half the book.

Yet as late as autumn 1943 Durrell was writing to Seferis, who had returned from South Africa and was Press Officer at the Greek Legation in Cairo, that ‘I have started working at night now and have begun a novel about Alexandria. It's a strange sensation. I've almost forgotten my grammar, a curious shortcoming when writing prose. I'm advancing slowly, like a blind man, feeling my way ahead, on ground which still feels ominously hollow.’[69] In fact he soon put his Alexandrian novel aside and turned to writing *Prospero's Cell*; it was as though before he could feel his way forward he first had to return to his past, to the magic he had shared with Nancy on Corfu.

While living on Corfu Durrell had entertained the fancy that Shakespeare had set *The Tempest* there, and had called his own white house at Kalamai ‘Prospero's Cell’. He saw in Prospero's farewell to his magical powers a mirror of the poet's own retirement to Stratford at the age of forty-six, for quite possibly *The Tempest* was the last of his plays, so that Shakespeare himself was laying down his ‘godly powers to the ebb and flow of his human and mutable life’,[70] a theme with which Durrell identified as war loomed over Corfu. But unlike Shakespeare's Prospero, Durrell had never really left his cell, and now in his tower at the Ambron villa he was stirring from his Alexandrian sleep: starting with a quotation from *The Tempest*, ‘No tongue: all eyes: be silent’, the words spoken by Prospero as he invokes the spirits,[71] Durrell began to write.

Prospero's Cell is presented in diary form, as though from April 1937 to September 1938, but a magical stillness hangs over it all. There is a timelessness about Durrell's youthful happiness on Corfu, a timelessness in which ‘Causality is this dividing floor which falls away each morning when I am back on the warm rocks, lying with my face less than a foot above the dark Ionian.’[72] Just as timelessness dissolves all sense of cause and effect, so it also dissolves ‘any strict dividing line between the waking world and the world of dreams. N[ancy] and I, for example, are confused by the sense of several contemporaneous lives being lived inside us.'[73]

Durrell would experience that sense of being inhabited as he listened to fishermen sitting about in a smoky taverna waiting for the wind to change. In their boasting, their cunning, their loquacity, he could hear the voices of Odysseus and his crew, though chronologically they were separated from *The Odyssey* by thousands of years. The Greeks were still very close to the earth and sea by which they lived, their character formed by a landscape of timeless mythology. They had not yet undergone that modern split between head and heart; they were part of the stream of life; and in the company of what Durrell called 'the immortal Greek'[74] he felt that he too was whole.

In *Prospero's Cell* Durrell's view of history is Olympian: 'Under the formal pageant of events which we have dignified by our interest, the land changes very little, and the structure of the basic self of man hardly at all.'[75] But there is the sense of events impending beyond his island cell: as vintage time approaches, Durrell interrupts the reverie of his diary with the entry 'Soon there is to be a war.'[76]

Prospero's Cell ends with an 'Epilogue in Alexandria', where Durrell cries out that 'the loss of Greece has been an amputation. All Epictetus could not console one against it.'[77] Against the laws and prescriptions governing the universe, whose purpose can never be subject to human influence, the stoic philosopher Epictetus had spoken of the necessity, 'αναγκη', to submit and endure. Does man, then, possess no freedom of action, no free will, no ability to reconnect what has been torn apart? Durrell answers, saying, 'History with her painful and unexpected changes cannot be made to pity or remember; that is *our* function.'[78]

Growing out of his experience of Greece was what Durrell called the Heraldic Universe, his mystic vision. A purely spatial dimension where time lies about in pools, a magical place where the artist creates in an atmosphere of playful freedom: this 'little world, the heraldic universe, is a cyclic, periodic thing in me: like a bout of drinking',[79] Durrell wrote to Miller in the summer of 1937 from Corfu.

'It is not a "state of mind"', he again explained in the first issue of *Personal Landscape*, 'but a continuous self-subsisting plane of reality towards which the spiritual self of man is trying to reach out through various media. . . . "Art" then is only the smoked glass through which we can look at the dangerous sun.' Because logic describes, so it also limits, 'its law is causality'; but poetry, transcending logic, 'invades a realm where unreason reigns, and where the relations between ideas are sympathetic and mysterious – affective – rather than causal, objective, substitutional. I call this the Heraldic Universe, because in Heraldry the object is used in an emotive and affective sense.'[80]

Durrell believed that pure rationalism was the ill of modern mankind. Logic, with its ruthless dualities of either/or, its conflict of opposites, was the work of the ego with its destructive belief in the power of the will. Durrell would make the same point when he later prefaced his *Justine* with a quotation from the Marquis de Sade's *Justine*: 'There are

Mareotis

75 Durrell's commonplace book. Sometime in 1943, Durrell joined a duck shoot on Lake Mareotis, an experience that would provide him with the climax to *Justine*.

two positions available to us – either crime which renders us happy, or the noose, which prevents us from being unhappy. I ask whether there can be any hesitation, lovely Thérèse, and where will your little mind find an argument able to combat that one?'[81] Durrell saw Sade as a child of the Enlightenment, the final flower of the Age of Reason, which had brought present-day Europe to destruction.

'Was he happy or unhappy, moral or amoral? He was outside the trap of the opposites', Durrell was writing in *Prospero's Cell*. 'Thought must be free. Let us dispense with the formalist whose only idea is to eliminate the dissonant, the discrepant. Let us marry our ideas and not have them married for us by smaller people.'[82]

For Durrell the battle was a spiritual one. In taking the rationalist road, society had lost its vision of wholeness – of inclusiveness, acceptance and love. But Durrell saw the realm of the artist as that boundless whole, and he believed that it was the task of art to heal what reason had torn asunder, or as he wrote in *The Black Book*, 'to invoke God'.[83]

Molly Tuby told the story of her grandfather (Jewish) walking along the Rue Fuad with his friend Count Patrice de Zogheb:

> Zogheb: 'It's a pity you're not a Christian, we have so many miracles.'
> Tuby: 'We have only a few miracles, but they are all true.'[84]

At the beginning of 1944 Durrell wrote himself an imaginary letter from Nancy. 'Dear fainéant, dearest lazybones. I have bought us a little twenty-foot cutter, with a Bermuda rig and a carvel hull; now we can set out for the Bay of Fauns: now you will be able to prove if you are the stern deep-sea character you pretend to be.'[85] He would include the letter in *Prospero's Cell* under his 'diary' entry for 25 June 1937, but in place of the line about proving himself, he would write, 'the whole world seems to be open before us'.

Then on the same blue paper and in the same red ink he wrote a new-year letter to Eve. Though giving it the guise of a literary production by stapling the pages together in the form of a booklet and writing 'A Little Letter to Eve – Alexandria 1944' on the front, in reality the letter was a private confessional in which he addressed his lack of confidence as a lover and as a writer.[86] 'Dear Yve, terrible fainéant and wicked black-eyed beast generally', it begins. 'It is nice to spend a few moments writing rubbish to you here.' The rest of the letter follows:

> Why are you so perversely exacting? You do not know. Why am I so unsatisfactory as a lover? I do not know.

> Firstly because you are an expert in selfishness and secondly because I am more selfish than you are.

> Secondly because in love il faut avoir de confiance a soi-même[87] and I haven't any – and you haven't though you pretend to have.

> Thirdly you are terribly secret and I am too profound for expression.

> I mean that my artistic difficulties as a writer are all reflected in my difficulties as a lover – expression, sincerity, style etc.

> But of course what stands in the way more than anything is the consciousness of treachery; we are all traitors by the faiblesse of smiles or moues or by intention and

we can't help it. So my pessimism guards me against your smiles to other people and your bloody gipsy familiarity with tout le monde. Then language! Yr English is not perfect – and you must feel as I would feel if I had to make love in Greek all the time: *nuance* is hard to understand.

But apart from all this I stand by your dark nut-brown gipsy face and flashy eyes and sombre sexy loveliness.

There at least we can meet and understand one another – and sometimes in bed I wonder whether everything else is not artificial – whether anything else matters really – the tendresse is the important thing.

What do you think?

And it is signed 'Your devoted', followed by a drawing of his head in profile, his nose improbably enlarged like an erect phallus.[88]

Eve had been frigid with Ruggero, while with Durrell 'I knew I was difficult with him sexually, but he must have known that I was more difficult with those who came earlier.' She had told him something of Ruggero and about her other former lovers, but 'his reaction was to think of me as a whore, lascivious, all "fucking this and that". He always assumed he was one of a series, and that I would leave him.'

But it may not have been only that. Perhaps beneath what he called her gypsy familiarity with everyone she met it was her silent withdrawals that most disturbed him. 'Excited curious about oneself – found no correspondence in another or world around me' – Durrell copied this remark of Eve's into a notebook for his Book of the Dead, a lost soul turned inwards upon herself. And immediately below it he copied something else she said: 'One good thing. I part easily. The bonds that matter I forge them in myself and take them with me. It is my innocence of spirit, my purity.'[89]

Durrell had been listening to Eve's story from the night of their long talk at Pastroudis and their walk along the Corniche, and he had embraced her when she fled from her parents' home and was having a breakdown. Her vulnerability appealed to him as much as her sensual beauty. 'I found Melissa', he was to write in *Justine*, 'washed up like a half-drowned bird, on the dreary littorals of Alexandria, with her sex broken.'[90] He knew that Eve's story went back to her childhood in Moharrem Bey, and he saw that inhabiting her woman's form there was the desperate urgency of a battered child, always searching for someone to love, for some nourishing thought or belief, and he wondered perhaps if he or anyone could ever really gratify her yearning.

But also he wondered how much of himself, withdrawn into his writer's cell, he could ever share with any woman. While reliving his life on Corfu and turning it into art, he sketched out on another sheet of blue paper an imaginary poem to himself from Nancy:

> dear fainéant, dear lazy bones
> now winter's at our heels

> I write you a New Year Letter
> From that great Court of Appeals.
>
> The empty heart whose silences prove
> So wretched a critic of last years.
>
> . . .
>
> You didn't say you love me
> You behave like William Blake.
> I begin to think that marrying you
> Was all a fine mistake.[91]

'Lately I had a short holiday in Beirut', Durrell wrote to Miller at the beginning of February. 'Here I am devilish gay and empty.' Now in the fifth year of 'this sickening war', he continued, 'our feelings are those of the periphery; everyone going quietly bad and mad inside. *Me too.*' Having struck the faint Byronic note, he launched into a crescendo: 'But the women are splendid – like neglected gardens – rich, silk-and-olive complexions, slanting black eyes and soft adze-cut lips, and heavenly figures like line-drawings by a sexual Matisse. I am up to my ears in them – if I must be a little *literal*' (and here Durrell took the trouble to write 'literal' in red). 'But one has never had anything lovelier and emptier than an Alexandrian girl. Their very emptiness is a caress. Imagine making love to a vacuum.' And in a postscript he added: 'Now I think of the correct simile for the Alexandrians. When they make love it's like two people in a dark room slashing at each other with razors – to make each other feel —?'[92]

But there was only one Alexandrian girl with whom Durrell was involved, the one he would not mention.

Towards the end of February 1944 a fresh north wind blew through Alexandria, exciting as a scattering breeze. 'The North Wind' was the sobriquet with which Durrell and his friends crowned a new arrival, Diana Gould, the future wife of Yehudi Menuhin. She was a dancer who had trained under Nijinsky and Anna Pavlova; as a soloist she had joined George Balanchine's company in Paris and the Markova-Dolin company in London, and when war broke out she had turned to acting on the West End stage. She had been raised in Chelsea, where writers, poets, actors, painters and musicians frequented her mother's home; her stepfather, Admiral Cecil Harcourt, had recently been scoring victories against the Italians in the Mediterranean; and also Diana was intelligent, sparkling, strikingly beautiful and very tall. In short, Durrell was reduced to gibbering infatuation: 'Dearest Diana, I am so miserable I don't really know what to write. You are so heavenly. . . . O merry widow! I love you.'[93]

Diana Gould was with an ENSA (Entertainments National Service Association) tour of Franz Lehár's operetta *The Merry Widow*, starring Cyril Ritchard and Madge Elliott, in which she played Frou Frou, a French dancer in Vienna. The production appeared first at the Cairo Opera House before coming on to Alexandria, where it opened on 25 February for a week's run at the Alhambra theatre on the corner of Rue Safiya Zaghloul (then still popularly called the Rue Missalla) opposite the Ramleh terminus. Her part amounted to one long talking scene and song, for which she had specially rewritten her lines in gutter French à la Toulouse-Lautrec, to the uproarious approval of the audience who understood every dirty phrase, and there was a high-kicking *pas de deux* in the last act. Fedden had told Durrell that Diana was coming to Alexandria, and he was dazzled when he saw her dance.

Diana was delighted in turn by Durrell's company, by his bewitching power with words, by the brightness of his ideas and humour, by his sometimes antic behaviour. He would call round at the Cecil, where she was staying, and accompany her to the theatre across the square, then wait for her at the stage door and take her off in a calèche to a favourite restaurant or accompany her to a glittering party given by someone of the Greek community. Once he brought her back to the Ambron villa, though Eve, as it happened, was not there or at any rate has no memory of the occasion. 'Oh God', said Gotch, who did remember. 'The vision is of Larry chasing her over the furniture. He said this is a fertility rite.' Billy's child was at this time nearly a month overdue. 'Bring her to the show, Larry darling', Diana commanded, 'and I'll kick it out of her'.[94] Indeed Billy barely got to the hospital in time after the curtain came down. Walking with Durrell through the streets of the city, Diana was aware of their physical dissimilarity, he short and fair, she so tall with long black hair, yet she felt entirely at ease with him. He 'wore Alexandria like a cape',[95] she thought, and while passing the late hours with him at a café, she was drawn by the 'depths and widths of his wonderful heart'.[96] All this while he showered her with a confetti of pained lover's notes, signing one of these 'Me', elaborating with 'The continuous I behind the discontinuous Me's'.[97]

Arriving from the alarms and deprivations of the London Blitz and with Rommel long since driven from the gates of Alexandria, the plenitude and gaiety of life in Egypt seemed to Diana a paradise. Among Durrell's circle of writers and poets she enjoyed the 'utter bliss . . . of "tiring the sun with talking and sending him down the sky"' – this from Callimachus' epigram to his friend Heracleitus – and for their benefit once performed an impromptu *entrechat* on the roof of the Cecil. 'Bliss it was at that hour to be young, and to be in Egypt was very heaven.' As Diana sailed away from Alexandria, she 'howled for the lovers I had left behind'.[98] But though Durrell showed up one day with his face covered in scratches from Eve, he was not one of those lovers.

All this happened very fast; Diana was in Alexandria hardly more than a week or two, yet the incidents of her passage shone out for all of them, most of all the day that Gwyn Williams drove Diana and Durrell out to Lake Mariut. 'One drop of rain this winter and in the spring the whole place will be covered with asphodel', said Durrell. There the cleanness of the wind and the pale cyclamen of the lake under an empty sky made Diana say, 'I've never seen so much room in a sky before', and Durrell replied, 'I'll write you a poem for that.'[99] Called 'Mareotis', it is dedicated to Diana Gould:

Now everywhere Spring opens
Like an eyelid still unfocused,
Unsharpened in expression yet or depth,
But smiling and entire, stirring from sleep.

. . .

But now the wind,
Not subtle, not confiding, touches once again
The melancholy elbow cheek and paper.[100]

The climax in *Justine* is a duck shoot on Mareotis – Durrell had joined a shooting party on the lake the previous autumn. And at the duck shoot, in an early plot outline of the novel, are 'all Justine's lovers'.[101] This is followed by Darley's discovery that Justine has vanished from the city: the woman he had loved so passionately has walked out of his life. Also in the final version of *Justine*, the allusion not only to Forster's History and Guide, Durrell wrote of the 'Rue de France, the Terbana Mosque', of the 'equestrian statue of Mohammed Ali in the square, General Earle's comical little bust', of 'Ikingi Mariut (gathering wild flowers together, convinced she cannot love me)', and of the sensation that 'the whole city had crashed about my ears'.[102] For out at Mareotis, Durrell asked Diana to marry him, and she told him that her lover was Robin Fedden.

Durrell wrote to Diana after she had departed, 'I have watched your name peel slowly off the hoarding in Sharia Missalla with a pleasantly ironic feeling of "If twere done twere better quickly done"; now Gary Cooper has replaced you, and I sit in my tower and listen to ideas moving around inside, aqueous and dim like fishes.'[103]

As the weather warmed in spring the Ambrons gave a garden luncheon. 'Déjeuner chez les Ambron au Jardin', goes the entry in Countess Mary de Zogheb's diary for 17 April, '– trente personnes – petites tables: moi, Alice Toriél, les Almagia, Larry Durrell, Lauren Macgrath (jeune actrice anglaise), Lieutenant Nasou, les Jean Lumbroso, les jeunes Engel, Marcel Gallo, les Shafik, les Cantoni, Madame Carlo Naggiar, Despina Salvago, Viri Delmar, les Terni, les Gotch.'[104]

One wonders if Durrell and Enrico Terni had a chance to talk, and if Terni told him about Forster and of singing Wagner underwater. Lauren Macgrath was with another ENSA theatre group and was shown round Alexandria by Durrell and Gwyn Williams, who took her down into the catacombs at Kom el Shogafa and told her of Orpheus and Eurydice, which in the surrounding eerie atmosphere caused her to pass out. 'Alexandria', remarked Williams, 'is a place where *l'éternel retour* is apt to catch you without warning.'[105]

Otherwise you wonder about Durrell's thoughts as he dined in the garden with these people, so many of whose names represented the builders of the city, of its 'poetry and history of commerce'.[106] These too were the city's exemplars – *négociants, commerçants, agents de change, exportateurs, banquiers, industriaux* – and especially those who would have reminded him of his father's world in India, the Almagias, who had built the Eastern Harbour Corniche; Aldo Ambron, civil engineer.

When Durrell came to build his Alexandria in the *Quartet*, this city 'inhabited by these memories of mine', it became a place imperial in its scope, where 'the communities still live and communicate – Turks with Jews, Arabs and Copts and Syrians with Armenians and Italians and Greeks. The shudders of monetary transactions ripple through and divide them. . . . Where else on earth will you find such a mixture?'[107] Amid the drum beat and wild music of a religious festival (a Coptic festival enjoyed not least by Muslims, for 'to a religious country all religions were one') rose reminders of the 'wants and powers of a great *entrepôt* . . . the whistle of steam-engines from the dark goods-yards or a sniff of sound from the siren of a liner, negotiating the tortuous fairways of the harbour as it set off for India'.[108]

As a British information officer, Durrell was in fact a propagandist, his job to manipulate what appeared in the press, a task he found particularly distasteful in April 1944. Not only were the British worried that the Greek government-in-exile in Cairo was losing its authority to communists within the resistance movement in Greece itself, but now it was faced with mutiny among the Royal Hellenic Forces in Egypt, consisting of volunteers from the local Greek community as well as Greek soldiers and refugees who had escaped from Greece.

The trouble broke out at the end of March, when the communist-dominated EAM established a provisional government in the liberated mountain areas of Greece, and the Royalist Greek government-in-exile refused its demand to help form a government of national unity representing all parties and all resistance groups. The mutiny began on 6 April with the First Greek Brigade, based at Bahig on the desert railway line near Burg el Arab. Within two days the insurrection had spread to the crews of three ships of the Royal Hellenic Navy out in the harbour at Alexandria.

The British surrounded the camp near Burg el Arab, with orders from Churchill that there should be no parley with the First Greek Brigade: 'Simply keep them rounded up by artillery and superior force, and let hunger play its part.'[109] Over three weeks later, on the afternoon of Saturday 22 April, a British cruiser, the *Ajax*, moored amid the *Apostolis*, the *Ierax* and the *Sachtouris*, the three rebel ships in the Western Harbour, and the British and Greek sailors exchanged greetings and jokes in the usual way. But at 2 a.m., through a screen of smoke, the pompoms on the *Ajax* opened fire, and about two hundred men, dressed in workmen's overalls and with blackened faces, leapt aboard the Greek ships and engaged in hand-to-hand combat. By eight in the morning it was all over; with about ten dead and forty wounded, the rebel sailors surrendered, and later that day the First Brigade surrendered too. Twenty thousand Greeks were disarmed in all, and after first being held in prison cages near Alexandria, they were sent to detainment camps in Libya and Eritrea.

Durrell learnt the outcome at breakfast at the Ambron villa on Sunday morning, when a Greek friend, Alexis Ladas, who had been staying over, staggered in exhausted, covered in soot and grease. The men with blackened faces had all been Greek officers loyal to the Royalist government-in-exile; Ladas had been one of them; it had been a battle of Greek against Greek. 'I hear you Greeks have been mixing it up', said Durrell, disguising any feelings in the matter. 'Fuck your mothers', Ladas shouted back.[110] And off to the British Information Office went Durrell on Monday, sick at what had happened among the Greeks, sick at the part British policy had played, and at 1 Rue Toussoum Pasha sat at his typewriter and steeled himself to write jubilantly of the victory.

Miller wrote to Durrell again on 5 May: 'When you write to me about the Alexandrian vacuum with razor blades flashing and all that I am in a paroxysm. Let's get there! Christ, it's dead here. . . . I'd give it all up to wander with you through those streets and see those sloe-gin fizz eyes, drown myself in that abattoir of love which you describe so eloquently.'[111]

'No, I don't think you would like it', Durrell answered. 'This smashed up broken down shabby Neapolitan town, with its Levantine mounds of houses peeling in the sun. A sea flat dirty brown and waveless rubbing the port. Arabic, Coptic, Greek, Levant French; no music, no art, no real gaiety. A saturated middle european boredom laced with drink and Packards and beach-cabins. NO SUBJECT OF CONVERSATION EXCEPT MONEY. Even love is thought of in money terms. . . . No, if one could write a single line of anything that had a human smell to it here, one would be a genius.'[112]

But a week or so later he was telling Miller how 'Alexandria is, after Hollywood, fuller of beautiful women than any place else. Incomparably more beautiful than Athens or Paris; the mixture Coptic, Jewish, Syrian, Egyptian, Moroccan, Spanish gives you slant dark eyes, olive freckled skin, hawk-lips and noses, and a temperament like a bomb. . . . It's funny the way you get woman after woman: and exactly what it adds up to I don't know: each more superficial than the last Gaby, Simone, Arlette, Dawn, Penelope.'[113]

But Durrell was not getting woman after woman. Possibly there was some brief affair, maybe more than one, after Nancy left him, but for over a year now there had been nobody but Eve. 'I don't think he was messing around with women in Alexandria, no, I don't', said Gotch. 'I think I would have known. We would have known because he would have not been in at meals or he would have brought the person – we'd have known.' Indeed, Gotch would almost certainly have known, for not only were he and his wife living at both the Rue Fuad and the Ambron villa, but Gotch was working at the British Institute on the floor above the British Information Office. Eve said there was never a night when Durrell failed to come home. He liked to charm and flatter women, she said, and he would flirt with women in her presence, but she did not mind that, and she did not know of it ever having led anywhere. The only commotion was over Diana Gould; Eve and Paul Gotch remember that plainly. It was the exception to the rule.

What Durrell was leading up to in his letters to Miller was the introduction of Eve, but he needed to make it seem that he had been very busy, meanwhile gorging himself on Alexandria's 'sexual provender'. Then almost *en passant*, as a single line placed a third of the way through the letter, he slipped in the remark that 'at the moment I am in mid-stream fighting my way through the rapids of a love affair with Gipsy Cohen, a tormented jewish-greek'. He knew that Eve was not half-Greek, but that was just the appetiser and two-thirds of the way through the letter he returned with ten more courses: 'Gipsy Cohen burns black and fierce under her Tunisian eyebrows; the flavour is straight Shakespeare's Cleopatra; an ass from Algiers, lashes from Malta, nails and toes from Smyrna, hips from Beirut, eyes from Athens, and nose from Andros, and a mouth that shrieks or purrs like the witching women of Homs or Samarkand. And breasts from Fiume. And what the hell?'[114]

In July Durrell gave Miller more: 'She sits for hours on the bed and serves me up experience raw – sex life of Arabs, perversions, circumcision, hashish, sweetmeats, removal of the clitoris, cruelty, murder. . . . Funny how one simplifies and pares away the inessentials. Sex now as a non-possessive form of friendship. . . . Simple needs this time. A girl who really fucks with the heart and soul and buttocks; an olive tree, a type-writer, and a few great friends like you. What do you think?'[115]

CHAPTER 9

The Unburied City

Once the first sense of estrangement is over, the mind finds its surcease in the discovery of the dream-city Alexandria which underpins, underlays the rather commonplace little Mediterranean seaport which it seems, to the uninitiated, to be.

Lawrence Durrell, introduction to the 1982 edition of E. M. Forster's
Alexandria: A History and a Guide

Alexandria, felt Durrell, was the only possible place in Egypt to live because it had a harbour and opened onto the sea – 'a way of escape'.[1] But in May 1944 he was able at least to travel west beyond the city and into the former military zone with Paul and Billy Gotch and Eve: 'Well, the last few days we've driven out through Bourg El Arab', he wrote to Miller, or rather he saw it in the distance, for Durrell mistakenly described it as a 'deserted crusader fort, nibbled battlements misty and like a mirage', from where they slipped down through 'thousands of empty rounds of ammunition, dirty bandages, twisted wreck of enemy tanks', to 'a long beach where the real Mediterranean comes up in great green coasters'.[2] In fact they had driven out by way of the Solitary Place, where Forster had foreseen a landscape buried under tins and barbed wire, and had come to Abousir, where Montgomery had had his headquarters during the battles of Alamein. Behind them on the limestone ridge was the Ptolemaic temple of Osiris, whom the Greeks identified with Dionysus, and the ancient lighthouse, a miniature Pharos, which to one side overlooked the western arm of Mareotis and to the other overlooked the sea.

'The sand was white', remembered Eve, 'and so fine it slipped through your hands like powder, the sea emerald as it washed over the beach, then turquoise and peacock blue going farther out, and the sky violet – and you sat amid this reverberation of colour.' After Durrell began to complain that she was no longer the svelte young woman he had taken up with, Eve had begun to lose weight and was becoming happy with her body again. All of them were naked, and Durrell was ecstatic as they gambolled in the waves. Eve noticed how he swam with a dolphin's grace, and how afterwards when they lay on the beach his skin seemed scented with honey. 'Strange transition to Cavafy's Alexandria', Durrell wrote to Miller of their return to the city that evening. 'For the first time in four years I felt I was in Greece.'[3]

Years later Durrell would commemorate those moments of joy near Burg el Arab by having Nessim build Justine's Summer Palace there, with its 'distant view of the old Arab fort, and the long drawn white scar of the empty beach where the waves pounded night and day'.[4] There too, as a thank-offering to old Panayotis, who served as guardian of their desert home, Nessim obtained 'a dispensation from the Patriarch of Alexandria permitting him to build and endow a small chapel to St Arsenius in his house'. Clea had found an old icon of him at a Muski stall in Cairo and had given it to Justine as a birthday present, Durrell saying in the *Quartet* that 'the choice of saint had been, as it always should be, fortuitous'.[5]

But there was nothing fortuitous about it for Durrell. Near Kalamai, and under the gaze of the icon of St Arsenius, which had been washed ashore in a storm, Durrell finished *The Black Book* and felt that he had been reborn. It was a rebirth too for Arsenius, who like Durrell had lost a world: in the early fifth century Arsenius became a solitary in the Wadi Natrun and was there when Berber tribesmen destroyed the first monasteries in 410, the year the barbarians sacked Rome. 'The world has lost Rome', Arsenius said, 'and the monks the Wadi Natrun.'[6]

Meanwhile, throughout the spring and summer Durrell was making trips up to Cairo, both to receive instructions from the embassy and to call on Robin Fedden, who was anthologising *Personal Landscape* for publication the following year in England. Fedden remarked on Durrell's 'exuberant vitality'[7] and said that his flying visits from Alexandria 'brought an immediate stimulus to the lax atmosphere, a sense of wider reference'; it was 'as though someone had uncorked a bottle of vintage champagne'[8] when he burst into a room.

Durrell in turn recognised that behind the slight stoop and stutter that were part of Fedden's disarming charm, there was a sharply critical mind interrogating the cultures of Europe and the East, and he looked up to him as he did to none of his other contemporaries in Egypt.[9] He became an extension of Durrell's own experience of the country, as when Fedden wrote in his introduction to the anthology of the resident foreigner's sense of 'cultural' and 'psychological isolation' in Egypt, where 'the current of thought sets towards Mecca and the European is inevitably swimming all the time against the stream',[10] which later found its way into the *Quartet* where Darley speaks of 'our isolation from the warm Gulf Stream of European feelings and ideas. All the currents slide away towards Mecca.'[11] Writing to Diana Gould in Naples a few weeks after she had sailed from Egypt, Durrell said, 'We are busy putting the anthology together; Robin has written a brilliant introduction – probably the best thing he has ever done.'[12]

Perhaps what Durrell also looked up to in Fedden was his easy success with women, and here too Fedden seems an extension of Durrell's experience to the point of masochism. 'Robin horribly missing you', Durrell wrote to Diana in April, 'almost as bad as me', describing himself as someone 'with no object in life beyond the search for mildness, fatness and poise'.[13] And in August he wrote of 'being only Sancho Panza

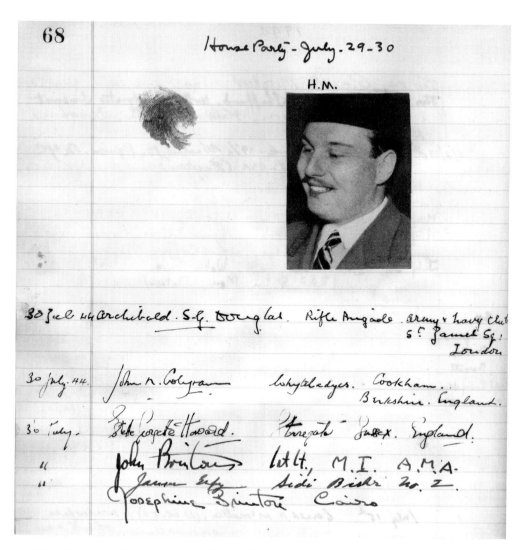

House Party - July. 29-30

H.M.

30 Jul 44 Archibald. S.G. Douglas. Rifle Brigade. Army & Navy Club
5. James Sg.
London

30 July. 44. John M. Colgrave. Whyteladyes. Cookham.
Berkshire. England.

30 July. Stete Crosbie Howard. Irregate Sussex. England.

" John Brinton. Let Lt., M.I. A.M.A.

" James Espy. Sidi Bishr No. 2.

Josephine Brinton. Cairo

76 King Farouk was often a guest at the Brintons' house in Alexandria. Rather than sign his name, he would leave his thumbprint in the guestbook. On this occassion in July 1944 the other guests included John and Josie Brinton, and also James Espy, who worked for the OSS, the forerunner of the CIA. Farouk was seeking American support against the British at this time.

to him and you in this, and conducting myself with tact before my master and mistress's windmills'. You are miserable, he told Diana, and 'I am miserable too, but far too deep down to sound in the upper registers. In a sort of gem-like way, solidly damped down but burning underneath – in the night-mind. Ugh bad dreams. But I am determined to be happy. It's a science like everything else, including making love. I am determined to be happy. So like Mr Coué I go through the motions and keep repeating to myself "Now you are going to be happy – really happy". Not puny sickly and bruised; not whining, self-commiserating, and hopeful. But happy by the fastidious exercise of love.'[14]

In January 1944 the British ambassador Lord Killearn had noted in his diary King Farouk's 'boorish and unpleasant'[15] behaviour, but a month later at a duck shoot where almost all the guests were Americans, Farouk 'was in his very best form and certainly is a most admirable host. It is pretty clear he has been having a considerable "get-together" with the Americans. But the whole atmosphere could not have been pleasanter or more intimate.'[16] After Pearl Harbor John Brinton had become the American military attaché; now one of the king's shooting guests was Lieutenant-Colonel John Dregge, John's boss at the American Mission, and another was James Espy, local head of the OSS (Office of Strategic Services), the forerunner of the CIA, who shared a flat in Cairo with John and Josie Brinton. Josie, who was now working as a secretary for the OSS, also noted this new emphasis, writing to her mother on 1 May, 'We went down to one of King Farouk's estates with him the other day and spent the night and the day. . . . We see a lot of him and find him so congenial and intelligent. He's very fond of the Americans.'[17]

Farouk was courting the Americans, and the Americans were courting Farouk. Meanwhile, in British circles Farouk's boorishness towards themselves was put down to an accident the previous November in which his speeding car collided with a British military vehicle. He was treated at a British military hospital for a fractured pubic bone of the pelvis. Many people would be disappointed at his survival, Farouk was reported to have said, upon whom he would be revenged, at which the king's uncle, Prince Mohammed Ali, a toady of the British whom they would have put on the throne had the Abdin Palace coup gone through, gleefully squealed to Killearn that Farouk was 'vindictive and cracked'.[18] Immediately after the accident, the prince had helped spawn the rumour that more than Farouk's pubic bone was damaged, and stories circulated that the king was impotent and that his behaviour and recent weight increase were due to a glandular and hormonal imbalance, though neither the Egyptian nor the British doctors who had treated him, and who had declared him fit within a week, reported any such thing.

Behind all this was the rumbling antagonism between Killearn and Farouk which broke out again in April 1944 when Farouk wanted to dismiss the prime minister, Mustafa Nahas. The Wafd in government was becoming increasingly unpopular and corrupt, while Nahas himself, as well as lining his family's pockets, was seen by many Egyptians as a foreign stooge who was attempting to undermine a still popular king. But the British, though becoming tarred with Nahas' brush, decided that he and the Wafd would be even more trouble in opposition and so continued to back him. If Farouk resisted there would be no question this time of calling off a coup: on 12 April Lord Killearn raised with Anthony Eden their old familiar project, suggesting in a very secret telegram that perhaps the time had finally come to 'take some more direct control of Egypt'.[19] On 24 April Farouk stepped back: it was the day after the suppression of the Greek mutiny, and having seen this display of British steel, the king decided to wait.

The Brintons saw Farouk in a different light from the British Embassy and Foreign Office, particularly John. Farouk, he believed, had intensely warm feelings towards the British but felt bitter at the way they dictated to him, and especially at the humiliations he had suffered at the hands of Eden and Killearn. He liked to play games to annoy the British, but he had no desire to betray them, thought John, who said that Farouk was certainly not pro-German, and that though he liked the Italians among whom he had been raised in his father's court, he was not pro-fascist either. Nor was John Brinton alone in his view: much of the British military high command in the Middle East was critical of Killearn's behaviour towards Farouk, among them Generals Wavell, Auchinleck and 'Jumbo' Wilson, Sir Alan Brooke, who was chief of the Imperial General Staff, and Air Marshal Sir William Sholto Douglas, who said the ambassador committed a major strategic error in 'treating King Farouk as if he were nothing but a naughty and rather silly boy. . . . Farouk was naughty, and he was still very young . . . but to my mind, and taking a hard-headed view, he was also the King of Egypt.'[20] Sir Thomas Russell Pasha, long the commandant of the Cairo police, was so outraged at the embassy when he learnt of the Abdin Palace coup (Lampson, as Killearn then was, had not troubled to tell him in advance) that he was reported to have 'set his face against these people whom he saw as destroying all the work of himself, his colleagues and his predecessors'[21] in developing a relationship of trust and goodwill with the Egyptians.

One afternoon not long after, Farouk called by the Rue Khalil Ibrahim in Glymenopoulo. Judge Brinton was sitting in his library after tea; Farouk sat down beside him, took a cigar, and enquired after the *Samothrace*. Farouk asked if it was for sale, Brinton said it was, and that concluded the negotiations: 'I'll send for her in the morning', said the king. No price had been mentioned, and in any case Judge Brinton felt it was bad form to discuss prices with royalty, but knowing that George McFadden was willing to sell for the insured amount, he talked a bit about the ship's papers and log and so on as they walked towards the garden gate, adding that it was insured with Lloyds and mentioning the amount, to which Farouk made no reply. But a few weeks later the Egyptian admiral in charge of the royal vessels invited Brinton to call at the palace and handed him a cheque for the intimated sum. Farouk painted the *Samothrace* blue and gave it sails of the same colour.[22] It can still be seen in the Western Harbour at Alexandria where it rots away.

On 22 August, when Durrell wrote to Miller again, he had just sent off *Prospero's Cell* to Faber and Faber in London, who accepted it at once. 'Now what? I have a wonderful idea for a novel in Alexandria, a nexus for all news of Greece, side by side with a sort of spiritual butcher's shop with girls on slabs.' He had put himself down for a job in Greece and was eagerly awaiting a visit that evening from Seferis, 'my best friend in Egypt',[23] who had just returned from London where the British, having intercepted top-secret messages about the Germans' imminent withdrawal from Greece, were urgently planning to send a military force to Athens to forestall a communist takeover. But as much on Durrell's mind were his wife and daughter: he could not get a word out of Nancy, 'who is behaving like a mad evangelist with a nice touch of anglo-saxon guilt. No news of the child either to which I was perhaps too much attached.'[24] Meanwhile, there was Eve, 'who says she is a burnt out soul from another planet, who is tired of everything except God; and he's tired of her!' – 'Gipsy Cohen provides a cyclone every day with a real generous and mad beauty which is touching and exciting.'[25]

Durrell edged closer to confiding to Miller that he had attempted a start on the Book of the Dead when he wrote again, later in August or early September, saying, 'My note-books are swollen like an amnion with notes for an Alexandrian novel.'[26] The reference to an amnion, the innermost sac enclosing an embryo, suggests the expectancy of cre-ative birth; also he had just learnt that a term had been put on his confinement in Alexandria: he was to be posted to Rhodes as public information officer as soon as the island was liberated from the Germans.

'I am coming alive slowly', he wrote later in September. 'The last three years has been a dull nightmare. I'm itching to write something', and again he spoke of the Book of the Dead: 'Got some marvellous dialogues for it – and an iron-frame plot. Shifted the action to Alexandria and made the two central characters twins.'[27] Enlarging somewhat on his theme in October, he once more mentioned to Miller an ambitious book about twins, saying that he had already written a bit of it, and adding that the greatest anxiety-art such as *Hamlet* centred on the Oedipus complex, and that to develop into a man one had to emerge from the Oedipal womb.[28] It was a book 'about incest and Alexandria', he wrote a few months later, which were 'inseparable ideas here'.[29]

For nearly two years now Durrell had been walking about Alexandria with Forster's guidebook in his hand, 'borrowing many of its gleams of wisdom to swell the notes for the book I myself hoped one day to write'.[30] In particular he was tracing 'the spiritual city underlying the temporal one'.[31] Indeed *Justine*, the first volume of *The Alexandria Quartet*, would become an excursion into the section in Forster's guidebook on 'The Spiritual City'. 'What is astonishing', Durrell has one of his characters say, 'is that he pre-sents a series of spiritual problems as if they were commonplaces and illustrates them with his characters.'[32]

Durrell's early attempt at an Alexandrian novel (from which *Justine*, the first volume of the *Quartet* would grow) survives in the form of a government-issue notebook; on its cover he wrote in pencil, 'The Book of the Dead, Manuscript I, Lawrence Durrell Under-world', adding in ink, 'Notes for Alex'.[33] Its earliest pages are written up entirely in pencil and correspond to the book about twins and incest that he mentioned to Miller.

Who were Durrell's original Alexandrians? In fact their names read like the cast of characters in a Noël Coward play: Charles, Damien, Claudia, John, Hogarth, Baroness Irma, Tessa, Melissa, Corège. Almost all his characters are British; they turn out to be like Durrell and his friends, not true denizens of the cosmopolitan city but exiled in Alexandria by the war.

Corège is a barber, Damien a flyer, while Charles at some point lived with Claudia, which is nearly all that Durrell writes about them before they change form or disappear. Melissa, whom Durrell identifies as 'Cohen', is a nurse working at the Greek Hospital, a 'black-eyed slave-girl tending everything, even the passions, without being asked',[34] but for the time being he has nothing more to say about her either. Instead Durrell's preoccupation is with John and Claudia.

John Faber has been 'split in the egg', for he and Claudia are brother and sister twins who live with 'the incontrovertible fact of being a half and a double at the same time'[35] – so that together they are Faber and Faber.[36] ('Double motif',[37] Durrell writes to one side; it is an idea he will pursue.) Claudia has been married to Hogarth, a psychoanalyst she first met in a mirror at the Café Royal in London. But she seems to suffer outside her twin sister-brother identity: 'Claudia held for observation until the arrival of a responsible relative: "insanity" but no pituitary disturbances.'[38] Faber's arrival in Alexandria reunites them and he and Claudia become lovers, perhaps not for the first time.

These early pages of 'Notes for Alex' can be traced back to Durrell's perception of himself as a quaint fragment and to the 1938 notebook in which he drew a map of Bloomsbury marked 'Plan for the Book of the Dead' and wrote that a part of oneself is lost at birth and that 'the whole course of one's life is simply a search for this lost fragment' through 'a world of mirrors'.[39] Durrell had also been reading Plotinus, heir to Plato, Aristotle and the Stoics and the founder of speculative mysticism in the West. Writing of Plotinus Forster said that 'Alexandria produced nothing greater.'[40]

Mirrors, fragments and prisms were central images for Durrell. In 'Notes for Alex' Durrell describes Claudia as 'hunting for something in Dostoyevsky which will give him a clue to her "prism-sightedness"',[41] as later in *Justine* he would portray Justine herself as sitting before multiple mirrors at a dressmaker's and saying, 'Look! five different pictures of the same subject. Now if I wrote I would try for a multi-dimensional effect in character, a sort of prism-sightedness.'[42] Likewise Plotinus used these same images of fragments, prisms and mirrors to explain man's experience of the universe.

Plotinus said that everything emanates from the One. The One overflows like a fountain, or pours forth streams of light like the sun, so that these emanations generate descending orders of reality. First there is the Intellectual Principle, which is a universe of pure forms. Next there is the All Soul, which emanates in turn; it uses those pure forms of the higher reality as models for giving shape to matter, which is the lowest of all things. This world of matter is the universe in which we live, but matter acts like a prism on the pure white ray of light emanating from the All Soul, causing it to fragment into numerous multi-coloured rays. These rays are our individual souls, each one a fragmented version of the light emanating from the All Soul – or to use another of Plotinus' images, the All Soul gives forth 'likenesses of itself like one face caught in many mirrors'.[43]

The world that Durrell is creating in his 'Notes for Alex' is Plotinus' lowest reality, in which Faber and Claudia, or anyone for that matter, can have only the most fragmen-

77   Durrell on the balcony of the Ambron villa in March 1944 with Billy Gotch and Jock Jardine of the British Council.

tary conception of totality. But barely aware of what they seek and confused amid this world of mirrors they nevertheless yearn for wholeness. Separation from the One has created that yearning to return, a yearning that Plotinus illustrated with sensual imagery, saying that lovers in their desire to unite are longing to lose their separateness in imitation of flowing back into the One. But for Faber and Claudia, as Durrell writes in 'Notes for Alex', 'Sex [is] a parody of the soul's pleasure in its conjunction, like the meeting of two images in a prism'[44] – a parody because instead of returning towards the One they are trapped within themselves. 'Twins have no history like other people.

Their world lacks a dimension', writes Durrell; 'born into a dependency it became con-tracted – its love, its triumphs, its fears – to the compass of that dependency. Love is turned inward, since the desire which springs from love is itself idolatrous.'[45]

One can recognise in this world turned in upon itself the sterile spiritual and sexual atmosphere of what Durrell had called the English Death. It also describes Durrell's view of Western culture, which in its pursuit of pure rationalism had become separated from a mystic vision of the boundless whole, what for Durrell was the Heraldic Universe. Using his twins as his exemplars, Durrell is describing a closed system, a world that has become shut in, where there can be no vision of wholeness, no inclusiveness or accep-tance, no true experience of love. He would describe Alexandria in this way in his final version of *Justine*: 'The symbolic lovers of the free Hellenic world are replaced here by something different, something subtly androgynous, inverted upon itself.'[46]

Through Forster Durrell had discovered 'the dream-city Alexandria which underpins, underlays the rather commonplace little Mediterranean seaport which it seems, to the uninitiated, to be'.[47] Here he could imagine the roots of Western culture lodged in Alexandria's slumbering mind: 'The city does nothing. You hear nothing but the noise of the sea and the echoes of an extraordinary history.'[48]

Not only was Plotinus the last great philosopher of antiquity, but his profound insights on the workings of the mind anticipated the observations of modern psy-chology. Plotinus was the first to write, for example, about the distorting mirror of wish fulfilment, how 'when our desires are aroused, imagination comes along and, as it were, presents us with the objects of those desires', a remark that impressed itself on Freud,[49] and he also wrote of the powerful influence of buried memories on our waking lives.[50]

A Freudian theme was probably already in Durrell's mind when he drew his 1938 sketch map of Bloomsbury marked 'Plan for the Book of the Dead'. Hogarth, his char-acter in 'Notes for Alex', bears a quintessentially Bloomsbury name, the Hogarth Press having been founded by Leonard and Virginia Woolf; moreover, he is described as an analyst, and this too ties him to the Hogarth Press, which first published Freud's works in English. Another Freudian association is found in Baroness Irma. Durrell describes her in 'Notes for Alex' 'as Ouida',[51] the pseudonym of the Victorian romantic novelist Marie Louise de la Ramée, who despite her name was English, as perhaps Irma is meant to be too. But the name Irma alludes to *The Interpretation of Dreams*, in which in order to demonstrate that dreams have a meaning and reveal the workings of the unconscious mind Freud analysed a dream he had had about one of his patients to whom he gave the pseudonym Irma. Freud regarded this book, published in 1900, and his interpret-ation of his Irma dream as the single greatest achievement of his life, as it became the foundation stone of psychoanalysis, the first scientific instrument for examining and healing the human mind.

For Freud dreams were messengers from the strange world of the unconscious, where each impulse seeks satisfaction independently of the rest, where ideas are linked not by logic but by association, where contradictions are ignored and opposites flourish, where negatives are treated as positives and similarities as identities, and where everything is changeable. Dreams provide clues to mental conflicts, which was their value to Freud, who wrote in his preface to *The Interpretation of Dreams* that 'anyone who has failed to explain the origin of dream-images can scarcely hope to understand phobias, obsessions or delusions or to bring a therapeutic influence to bear on them'.[52]

Durrell's characters are themselves like dreams dreamt by the dream-city, the meaning of their lives a mystery, for as he writes in 'Notes for Alex', 'Meanwhile in this year of exile only Alexandria itself is free to dream: while we are not free to record its dreams – or to look for meaning behind them.'[53] Durrell would portray this in *Justine* when, for example, the city invades Nessim's mind with dreams of its own history. He would wake to see 'the giant footprints of the historical memory which lies behind the recollections of individual personality',[54] so that 'while the gallery of historical dreams held the foreground of his mind the figures of his friends and acquaintances, palpable and real, walked backwards and forwards among them, among the ruins of classical Alexandria, inhabiting an amazing space-time as living personages'.[55] It was a madness, and 'in a real sense we all shared it',[56] says Darley, for 'man is only an extension of the spirit of place'.[57]

To this Durrell added another element, a sort of cosmic psychosomatic force propounded in a 'great undiscovered book – Groddeck's *The Book of the It*'.[58] 'What filled his talk at that time was Groddeck', remembered Eve, and Gotch remembered too: 'He introduced me to Groddeck, fascinating. I went out and bought a copy instantly.' Unlike Freud, whose career was grounded in the physical sciences, his fellow psychoanalyst Georg Groddeck was a Christian mystic who saw science as the maidservant of his anti-rationalist outlook. While accepting Freud's theory that behaviour is determined by conflicts between the conscious and the unconscious, Groddeck also believed that man suffered from the opposition of his ego to the world. In saying that 'I am', man imagines that he is free to act, and so to cure the ills of the world through the exercise of his will. But really man is inextricably part of the universe, and to heal himself he must trace 'a relationship between the *individuum* and the cosmos. . . . We understand man better when we see the whole in each of his parts, and we get nearer to a conception of the universe when we look upon him as part of the whole.'[59]

Though they do not see it, the lives of Durrell's characters are inseparable from the city they inhabit, 'the city which used us as its flora – precipitated in us conflicts which were hers and which we mistook for our own: beloved Alexandria!'[60]

This was the beginning of the book that would become Lawrence Durrell's *Justine*, and though it fills only about two dozen pages, he foresaw that it would absorb his energies entirely. 'I haven't enough force to work on it even if I had the leisure', he wrote to Miller in September. 'How painful it is to write from the nervous system. I shrink from it inside. I often feel that I sprained my soul on *The Black Book* and it will take some time to get strong again.'[61]

Before returning to the Book of the Dead he needed to settle his emotional turmoil and his practical affairs. It was time to look beyond the sense of dislocation that he felt in Egypt and beyond his broken relationship with Nancy and his child; soon he would be in Greece again, and he had made up his mind that he wanted to take Eve. 'To Miss Y. Cohen for invaluable aid in copying out manuscripts',[62] he added to the tail-end of his acknowledgements in *Prospero's Cell*. Eve had in fact copied out no manuscripts whatsoever; nor had she even been aware, despite her visits to the tower at the Ambron villa, that Durrell in his hours alone had been writing a book about Corfu, and Gotch too remained in the dark. The reason for Durrell's acknowledgement was to make her seem useful, for until he obtained his divorce from Nancy and was free to marry Eve, the only way he would be able to take her along to Rhodes was as his secretary.

Durrell was feeling how life might be without Eve, who since the late summer of 1944 had been working as a nurse at a United Nations Relief and Rehabilitation Administration (UNRRA) camp out by Aboukir to the east of Alexandria, looking after Yugoslav refugees, returning to the Ambron villa only at weekends. This was the time, if there was any, that Durrell stood a chance of having adventures among the female fauna of the city. 'I dealt with that in very subtle ways, not in scratchings', said Eve. 'We women from Alexandria, we have generations of ways of dealing with men.'

Then what Eve had been dreading finally happened; as she and Durrell were walking along the Rue Fuad one evening with a group of friends they bumped into her father. They were on their way to the British Council's Institute for a session of the Brains Trust, and Durrell invited Eve's father to join them in the audience, which put questions to a panel of knowledgeable people such as Alan Wace, who had been appointed professor of archaeology at Farouk University, while Gwyn Williams chaired the proceedings. Moise Cohen was fascinated by the novelty and stimulation of the evening, though he was also rather bewildered that his daughter should be there and uncertain of how Eve fit in with the company she was keeping.

Not long afterwards Durrell decided to show his hand by inviting Eve's parents out to dinner, bringing Gotch and Billy along as well. ' "I want you to say what a good chap I am, and that I hope to be able to marry Eve", and so we did, Billy and I. We had them out to a restaurant on the Corniche near the Hotel Cecil. And we talked, and they didn't seem to be remarkably peculiar in any way. They weren't outraged that here was this English fellow and another English fellow talking about their daughter. Her father was very straightforward, and her parents listened to what we said. But Eve has no recollection of this whatsoever; I don't even know if Larry ever told her.'

Egypt turned its back on the Mediterranean that September, when its government hosted a conference in Alexandria to advance the cause of Arab unity. As prime minister of the most populous and developed Arabic-speaking state, Mustafa Nahas was determined that Egypt should take the lead among Saudi Arabia, Yemen, Iraq, Transjordan, Syria and Lebanon, and in this he and the king for once saw eye to eye. For Farouk it was a

78   Theodore Stephanides, Durrell's friend from Corfu, visiting the Ambron villa in September 1944.

chance to play a commanding role in the new Middle East that would emerge from Western tutelage after the war. For their part, the British hoped to influence the direction of pan-Arabism so that it might serve as a bulwark against Russian-inspired communism in the region, and so Lord Moyne, successor to Richard Casey as minister of state, gave his encouragement to the gathering and facilitated the attendance of an Arab delegate from Palestine too. The conference was successfully concluded with the signing of the Alexandria Protocol on 7 October 1944, establishing the framework for the foundation of the Arab League, whose headquarters would be in Cairo.

On the following day King Farouk dismissed Nahas. Lord Killearn was temporarily out of the way on holiday in South Africa, and Farouk rightly judged that Nahas' stock had fallen so low that the British would not embarrass themselves by intervening on his behalf. When Killearn returned to Cairo in November, he had an audience with Farouk who was 'in good form and pleased with himself. The whole talk was of a very friendly nature but I took occasion just to rub in that he had now landed himself fair and square with the responsibility for the new arrangements.'[63]

But what brought Killearn rushing back to Cairo was not the dismissal of Nahas but the murder of Lord Moyne on 6 November. Walter Edward Guinness, 1st Baron Moyne, was a scion of the famous Irish brewing family and one of Churchill's closest friends. His death at once reminded Egyptians of the severity of Britain's reaction to the assassination of Sir Lee Stack in 1924, which had put back the cause of nationalism for over a decade, so there was considerable relief when the news came through that Moyne had been killed by two Jewish terrorists sent from Palestine, members of the Stern Gang, which saw the British presence in the Middle East as the chief obstacle to the realisation of a Jewish state.[64]

Moyne's murder shocked and angered Churchill, for whom it was a stain on Zionism and a betrayal of Britain. Only days before Moyne's assassination, Churchill had told Weizmann over lunch at Chequers that the least the Jews should settle for was partition into separate Arab and Jewish states, but that if they could 'get the whole of Palestine' it would be 'a good thing'.[65] Now he told the House of Commons, 'If our dreams for Zionism are to end in the smoke of assassins' pistols and our labours for its future produce only a new set of gangsters worthy of Nazi Germany, many like myself will have to reconsider the position we have maintained so consistently and so long in the past.'[66]

Moyne's murderers were hanged at the end of March 1945, a month after Ahmed Maher, Farouk's new prime minister, was shot dead by an Egyptian nationalist extremist. On the advice of Churchill and with the support of Farouk, Maher had declared his intention in parliament to bring Egypt into the war, for by joining the Allies even at this late stage Egypt would count as a founding member of the United Nations and would not be shut out from any post-war settlement as had happened in 1918, when it was denied a place at the Paris Peace Conference. But what the Wafd had wanted then, their opportunism rejected now. Once Nahas was out of office the Wafd reverted, as Killearn had feared, to being fiercely anti-British, and with the support of the Muslim Brotherhood and other militant nationalists they claimed that Maher was bending to Britain's will. Into this swirl of nationalist hysteria stepped a true believer, a young lawyer with a pistol. As Maher was leaving parliament, having just declared for the Allies, his assassin fired three shots at point-blank range, proudly proclaiming that there were many more like him who were willing to attack the enemies of the Egyptian nation.

Ahmed Maher's assassination was only the beginning. Over the next seven years governments fell, or were paralysed, by the bomb or the bullet or their threat, and murder stalked any politician who took a public stand against what extremists might construe as being pro-British or counter to Egyptian nationalism. The only issue that united all factions was Palestine, and now Farouk, as Lord Killearn had observed, had 'landed himself fair and square with the responsibility for the new arrangements'.

Early in March 1945 Robin and Renée Fedden were in Alexandria on their way to Burg el Arab to spend a few days with Jasper and Geneva Brinton. Fedden was talking of going to England as soon as the war was over, but for Durrell the way back to Greece was still closed. The Germans, who had garrisoned the Dodecanese after the Italian occupiers there surrendered, had yet to be dislodged from Rhodes, while in Athens an EAM uprising caught the British 'defending the Acropolis caryatid by caryatid', Durrell wrote to Miller, a consequence of what he saw as Britain's wrong-headed policy towards the Greek resistance earlier on. For Durrell Greece was a living body best left to heal itself of the passing aberration of ideology. 'What an extraordinary piece of history', he continued to Miller, 'what a final curtain on the smallest country in Europe; withstanding Fascism in the field, nazidom in the home, and now the reaction on the part of the people they love and admire most.'[67]

Durrell had been depressed throughout the winter, but 'Gipsy has been a life preserver',[68] and he managed to complete *The Dark Labyrinth*, a thriller set on Crete, though he had felt 'like a prisoner writing on the wall with a rusty nail in order to keep sane'.[69] 'I knocked it off in a month',[70] he told Miller after sending his manuscript to Eliot, for once only mildly exaggerating. 'Meanwhile I am waiting here to be posted to Rhodes. . . . They are liberating everyone everywhere. Soon it will be my turn.'[71] The prospect filled him with optimism, and a few weeks later he was happily telling Miller that his collection of poetry *Cities, Plains and People* was on the verge of publication by Faber and Faber, that *Prospero's Cell* would follow shortly and *The Dark Labyrinth* after that, while the Book of the Dead, of which 'I have drafted about twenty pages . . . will take me a year or so to do'.[72]

Meanwhile, he had 'unearthed some facts about a cabalistic group, direct descendants of the Orphics, who throughout European history have been quietly at work on a morphology of experience which is pure Pythagoras. There are about six or seven in the Mediterranean area. They teach nothing; they assert nothing; they do not even correspond; they are pre-Christian adepts. I am going along to see Mr Baltazian one of these days to find out all about the circle and the square. He is a small banker here.'[73]

This was Durrell deliberately making Miller salivate, as when he wrote to him of Alexandrian women, and likewise it was another instance of Durrell straying into fantasy. The elder members of Alexandria's Armenian community have no knowledge of a Mr Baltazian, but the name appears in Durrell's 'Notes for Alex' where it is immediately transformed into 'Balthazar'. The cabalist's identity was later claimed by Carlo Suares, who said that he was the model for Balthazar in the *Quartet*.[74]

This need not contradict Robert Liddell's belief that Balthazar was based on Gaston Zananiri. 'Larry did all sorts of things', said Eve; 'he took bits of several people to produce one character; he called people by one name and they had the character of another.' But sometimes as he did so, his creations took on for him a reality of their own: the Mr Baltazian Durrell mentioned to Miller may have been one such creation, almost as real to Durrell as a Zananiri or a Suares.

Born Carlo Giuseppe Suares in Alexandria in 1892, Joe, as he was known to his friends, was the son of Edgar Suares, who had been president of Alexandria's Jewish community during the First World War and had pressed the British to establish a Jewish homeland in Palestine. Carlo was an administrator of his family's Banque Suarès, though 'he did no serious work at the bank',[75] while after training for six years as an architect in Paris, he practised in Alexandria, Cairo and Jaffa for only four years, until 1924. By then he had married Nadine Tilche, whose family belonged to Alexandria's Jewish elite as much as the Menasces or the Rolos and could trace their presence in Egypt back to the six-teenth century. From then on Suares devoted himself to painting, writing and the eso-teric, and became a close friend of Krishnamurti, who at sixteen had been proclaimed by Annie Besant, the leader of the worldwide Theosophical Society, as the coming Messiah.

Durrell's interest in unusual characters and his fascination with the esoteric could have led him by any number of means to Suares' door in the Rue Borchgrevink at Saba Pasha. Oddly, a connection had already been made between Suares and Durrell: back in 1937, after receiving Durrell's manuscript of *The Black Book* from Corfu, Miller wrote to say, 'There is a strange French counterpart to your book in the way of a volume called *La Procession enchaînée*, by Carlo Suares, which I am now reading'[76] – 'French' because the book was published in 1934 in Paris, where in addition to his home in Ramleh (and until the war another in the Rue Nebi Daniel) Suares kept an apartment near the Eiffel Tower. Monsieur Coucou, a character in Suares' earlier works, reappears in *La Procession enchaînée*; he represents the cry of revolt and remorse of the conscience that is locked into the universe, and he says that if he had to give meaning to the word 'soul' it would be 'desire'. Monsieur Coucou seeks perfection, by which he means the liberation of desire: 'The only discipline that the soul demands is that of granting leeway to all desires, so that the most real always swallow others until the soul releases the solitary ultimate desire, which is that of being.'[77]

Coinciding with Durrell's tram journeys out to Saba Pasha and his conversations with Suares, this central idea of M. Coucou's appears in Durrell's 'Notes for Alex' and in his correspondence. At about the same time as Durrell was writing to Miller of Mr Baltazian, he also sent an airgraph dated 2 April to Diana Gould: 'Myself I have been drafting notes for the book of the dead which is to be about (a) incest (b) Alexandria (c) The Hermetics. I have been examining the doctrine of the modern cabbalists and have evolved from it a philosophy of self-indulgence very Alexandrian in its refinement. My Grand Inquisitor says: "What I have to offer the world is not a morality but an aesthetic. Where all religions tend to prohibit, exclude or sort out human behaviour, my aesthetic *in*cludes: Our object is the same: to remove envy, greed and other vices from the human nature. I say indulge them *but refine yourself* by them and thus refine them too. Take experience for a laboratory. No sin can remain sin if it is informed by this principle which I call the heraldic principle. Where you wish to conquer indulge and refine, never prohibit. Prohibition by the law of opposite increases demand." '[78] And in

'Notes for Alex', to which Durrell returned after sending Eliot his manuscript of *The Dark Labyrinth*, he repeated the last lines of his letter almost word for word. Below this Durrell has written, as one would an attribution, 'Mr Baltazian', who reappears on the following two pages as 'Balthazar'.[79] Ultimately this would appear in *Justine*, where Balthazar says, 'None of the great religions has done more than exclude, throw out a long range of prohibitions. But prohibitions create the desire they are intended to cure. We of this Cabal say: *indulge but refine*.'[80]

None of this has anything to do with the Orphics or the Pythagoreans, nor with pre-Christian adepts, whoever they were meant to be, but it does have a lot to do with Suares' friend Krishnamurti, who was a frequent and lengthy guest of Carlo and Nadine both at Saba Pasha and in the Seventh Arrondissement. Though Krishnamurti broke with the Theosophical Society in 1930, essentially because he found it bitchy, riven by snobbery and backbiting among factions claiming to be the more select, he remained a theosophist in the general sense of the word, holding the belief that man could obtain direct and immediate experience of the divine. But instead man perversely sought deliverance or salvation by and through an intermediary; he refused to work for his own liberation, pretending that first the world must be liberated. Krishnamurti replied that the problems of the world were bound up with the problems of the individual: cultivate your doubts, embrace every kind of experience, keep on desiring, while surrendering your narrow sense of identity, so that in assimilating and integrating all that you have experienced you will find that truth is ever present, that eternity is here and now. Suares, who had written *Krishnamurti*, published in Paris in 1932, gave a copy to Durrell who said that he found it excellent.

Durrell's notion of a cabalistic group of Mediterranean adepts also came from Suares, whose interests during the 1930s had expanded beyond Krishnamurti and into the world of Jewish mysticism, which just then was undergoing a revival. In particular Suares had been delving into the *Sepher Yetsirah*, a third-century account of the means by which God created the universe. The Psalmist wrote, 'By the word of the Lord were the heavens made; and all the host of them by the breath of his mouth',[81] and so the *Sepher Yetsirah* claims that the divine utterance included all the letters of the Hebrew alphabet which in their various combinations make up the holy language, the language of creation. To each letter is assigned a number, and these taken together were the instruments by which God created the cosmos in all its infinite variety. For the cabalist, this system of linguistical and numerical manipulation would reveal to him the real meaning, the true revelation, contained in cypher form within the book of Genesis and other holy texts, but it was also seen as a means of revealing the structure of universal energy. To Suares the release of this energy involved a transcending exaltation of the seven deadly sins, whose real significance, he believed, could be traced back to Gnostic origins; and to achieve full realisation of oneself, said Suares, it was necessary to become aware of the energies of these 'sins' and their true values so as to be able to integrate them into oneself.

It was a game of mystification that could seem godly, and indeed Durrell thought that Suares had gone off the rails since writing his Krishnamurti book and now believed that he was God. For that matter, to bring in matters of taste, Durrell found Suares' raucous canvases appalling – he painted one a day, based on a theosophical theory of colour. But Durrell enjoyed Suares' childlike enthusiasm and his innocence, his kindness and his warmth. Nadine could be a fierce and overbearing woman, but she worshipped her husband and condoned his many infidelities with partners of both sexes, and together they welcomed guests to their home at Saba Pasha with a wealth of hospitality.

Suares and his mystical Hebrew alphabet gave Durrell the idea in *Justine* for Balthazar's cabalistic group, with its exchanges of Hermetic philosophy written in Greek in boustrophedon form. But though there are rumours that Suares was working for French intelligence, and while at the heart of the medieval cabala was the belief that the spiritual dislocation of the Jews would be healed when they returned to Zion, there is otherwise no indication that his get-togethers at Saba Pasha were a screen for Zionist activities. That was left to Durrell's imagination when after completing *Justine* he decided to extend his Book of the Dead into a political thriller.

A change comes over 'Notes for Alex' as Durrell continued to work at it during the spring. Alexandria begins to emerge with a flavour of its own as he gives names to its streets and replaces his original cast of British exiles with a population of cosmopolitans, Balthazar among them. John Faber becomes John Masson and later the decidedly Anglo-French John Maçon, so that we see 'Claudia Maçon in her brother's arms'.[82] Also Durrell introduces a new character whom he identifies only as 'I', but from now on 'I', the precursor of Darley,[83] will tell the story: through his memory he will 're-enter, reinhabit the unburied city',[84] as he says in *Justine*, recording his experiences 'not in the order in which they took place – for that is history – but in the order in which they first became significant for me'.[85] With this new approach to writing his story, Durrell leaves off writing in pencil, more confidently writing in ink, as he would continue to do with only a few exceptions throughout the rest of 'Notes for Alex' and in all that followed.

The last significant change comes a couple of pages later when John Maçon and his twin sister Claudia disappear from 'Notes to Alex' – or rather they are subjected to yet another transmutation: reversing the names of Masson or Maçon, Durrell invents Nessim, who in the next few pages is introduced with his wife Justine. Yet Nessim and Justine are still twins so to speak, that 'magnificent two-headed animal a marriage could be',[86] as they will appear in the *Quartet*.

Churchill, Roosevelt and Stalin met at Yalta in February 1945. With the Western Allies still held at the Rhine, while the Red Army occupied the whole of Eastern Europe and stood within thirty miles of Berlin, the looming question was what Stalin would do when the war was over. 'The misery of the whole world appals me', Churchill wrote to his wife, 'and I fear increasingly that new struggles may arise out of those we are now

79 George de Menasce, 1940s. George devoted himself to collecting beautiful things. His watchword '*circumspice*' could as well have applied to his habit of collecting people and to his gift for intrigue.

successfully ending.'[87] After the conference the prime minister and the president came to Egypt, where Josie Brinton observed that 'Churchill looked fatter than ever, and Farouk looked almost as fat as he did', while 'Roosevelt looked very tired'.[88] Less than two months later, on 12 April, John and Josie were with Farouk when the king was handed a telegram: 'He read it and then in French said, "Ladies and gentlemen, I deeply regret to announce the death of the President of the United States". We could hardly believe our ears. He was very upset for he was a great admirer of Roosevelt.' Judge Brinton delivered an address at the memorial service in the crowded Church of St Mark in Alexandria. He had often been called upon to give an address on the deaths of colleagues, 'but this was the first time I had been able to speak in English on any such occasion. I was grateful that it was so. Such thoughts should be expressed in one's own tongue.'[89]

On the day that Roosevelt died, Durrell's writing plans were knocked into disarray. 'I'm going to a little white cell on a little blue island with a little dark girl',[90] he had written to Diana the previous week, intending to complete his Book of the Dead on

Rhodes. But on the twelfth an airgraph came from Eliot rejecting *The Dark Labyrinth*, saying in upper-case letters for clarity, 'THERE'S TOO MUCH MEAT IN IT FOR A POT-BOILING THRILLER, AND THE MEAT ISN'T WELL ENOUGH COOKED FOR SOMETHING BETTER', adding, 'ARE YOU PRIMARILY A POET OR A PROSE WRITER? DO YOU KNOW which you want to be?'[91]

Durrell did not answer Eliot's question, a sure sign that it had gone to the quick, but he readily accepted Eliot's criticism of *The Dark Labyrinth*, explaining that he had dashed off the book to pay for his divorce, and adding that he did not think that revising it was worth the effort or the time. But in fact Durrell was unable to leave it at that, and on Rhodes he would rewrite the book, reworking the plot and adding several new characters, among them the analyst Hogarth, discarded from 'Notes for Alex'.

When Rhodes was liberated on 1 May, Durrell's escape from the 'heat and bore of Islam'[92] and 'our long misery in the marshes of Mareotis'[93] loomed closer. A week later Germany capitulated. The war in Europe was over. The farewells to Alexandria began when Paul Gotch was posted by the British Council to Thessaloniki, and the rooms that he had filled with his wife and children at the Ambron villa fell suddenly empty and quiet.

Finally Durrell received instructions to visit Rhodes 'to inspect the premises', as he put it to Eve, where as public information officer for the Ministry of Information he would be serving under the island's British Military Administration, which was to oversee the transfer of the Dodecanese from Italian to Greek rule. On the afternoon of 30 May, in a mood of tremendous expectation mingled with uncertainty, Durrell set sail from the Western Harbour in a Heavy Duty Military Launch, feeling like Jonah travelling in the belly of the whale.

Back in Alexandria ten days later, and feeling that it was possible after all to get back to his past in Greece, Durrell wrote to Miller that he had found the island 'lovely in a rather Corfiot way'.[94] But more than a fortnight passed after his return to Alexandria before his posting to Rhodes was confirmed, and only now was he free to put forward his choices for the two office assistants he would need. Eve had to go for interviews at the Ministry of Information in Cairo, armed with an inflated curriculum vitae prepared by Durrell, which presented her as a journalist and linguist with excellent typing skills. 'I even brought a pair of spectacles to look efficient and was very well coached and said all the right things and had the right attitude and was actually received with great enthusiasm by the people who interviewed me', said Eve, who was appointed Durrell's administrative secretary on Rhodes.

Next Eve needed to obtain her travel papers, but now the Egyptian government told her that she was not a citizen and could not be granted a passport; she was a stateless person in her own country. Only in 1929 did the Egyptian government attempt to clarify who was Egyptian and who was not; this included any former subject of the Ottoman Empire resident in Egypt since 1914, and also the children of foreigners born in Egypt, provided they applied for Egyptian citizenship within a year of attaining their majority and gave up their foreign citizenship. Neither Eve nor her parents had applied for naturalisation, nor had a great many others for whom Egypt was home. Even if it occurred to them to apply, obtaining citizenship papers cost a good deal of money, which the less well off could ill afford, while by the 1940s the authorities were making naturalisation difficult for non-Muslims whatever their legal eligibility.

The Ottoman Empire had recognised its subject peoples not by their nationality but by their religion, and now the Egyptian authorities responded to Eve in the same way, telling her that she would have to obtain permission from the chief rabbi in Cairo before they would issue her with a *laisser passer*. The Rabbinate wanted Moise Cohen's permission, so 'I managed to wangle a letter from my father saying he was quite happy to let me go, which wasn't true at all, but it was because I wrote him a vicious letter saying listen, it doesn't matter what you're going to write, I'm *going*! So he wrote, poor guy, he must have sweated blood writing it, and so I thought I had things all right, and then nothing' – the Rabbinate wanted his signature verified.

Finally Durrell sent Eve to his friend Bernard Burrows, First Secretary at the embassy. 'So I went to Bernard and he said, "Well look I'm not supposed to be doing this", but he stamped the letter in testimony that the embassy recognised the signature as my father's. And I went back to the Rabbinate with it and these impressive stamps, and at long last the Rabbinate said, "We give you the OK"; that's how I was able to leave the country.'

Durrell passed the episode off lightly to Gwyn Williams, saying, 'We have panned out with the most extraordinary luck', though it had taken 'every wangle known to man', including 'the embassy, the army, the Quakers and the pashas'.[95] But beneath the foolery he was angry; it had nearly cost him Eve, and he blamed the Egyptians for it: 'I feel like a crusader when I think of Egypt', he later wrote to Miller from Rhodes. 'I'd gladly put an army corps into the country and slaughter the lot of those bigoted, filthy, leprous bastards!'[96]

One afternoon before they left Alexandria Eve called on Durrell at the British Information Office; she wanted to buy a pair of shoes, and so they went shopping along the Rue Toussoum. 'Wait here', she suddenly said to Durrell and rushed across the street. Eve had recognised Ruggero from the back: 'So you thought you would pass me without acknowledging that you had seen me?' Ruggero, now released from detainment, said that he had just been round to her mother's. He had never been before; going there was the convention for asking a girl's hand in marriage as they both understood but left unsaid. 'Is it serious?' he asked, looking towards Durrell. 'Very serious', she said. 'We intend getting married.' One last time she saw Ruggero before she went away. 'You never understood that I had to leave Egypt.' 'Why?' he asked, surprised that anyone should want to leave. 'Don't you see', said Eve, 'that everyone is going to leave?'

As Durrell and Eve sailed from the Western Harbour, he felt it was like 'a cloud lifting':[97] he was going back to Greece. Yet meanwhile the poetry of Cavafy was on his mind, but

80 Claude as Praxinoë, January 1946. The secret to how
Durrell came to write *The Alexandria Quartet* is contained in
this photograph of Claude Vincendon dressed for the role of
Praxinoë in the Fifteenth Idyll performed at Baudrot in January
1946. In his *Alexandria: A History and a Guide*, Forster had
written: 'Only through literature can the past be recovered and
here Theocritus, wielding the double spell of realism and poetry,
has evoked an entire city from the dead and filled its streets with
men.'

no longer 'Waiting for the Barbarians'. Instead in his 'Notes for Alex' Durrell translated
'The City',[98] which he called Cavafy's 'real monument to modern Alexandria':[99]

> There's no new land, my friend, no
> New sea; for the city will follow you,
> In the same streets you'll wander endlessly,
> The same mental suburbs slip from youth to age,

In the same house go white at last –
The city is a cage.
No other places, always this
Your earthly landfall, and no ship exists
To take you from yourself.[100]

'I am very happy',[101] Durrell wrote to Gwyn Williams from Rhodes. This time he was not going through the motions like Mr Coué: happiness bubbled up in his letters now, as again he had 'a woman, an island and a tree'.[102] Eve shared in his happiness: 'Rhodes in those days was pure enchantment. It was ours. It was our island. That was our honeymoon, the happiest time that Larry and I had together.' Nor was Durrell's recollection of his happiness with Eve on Rhodes diminished by all that followed; when he revisited the island thirty years later he said, 'They were the happiest two years of my life.'[103]

But for Gwyn Williams, returning to his post at Farouk University that autumn after a holiday in Britain, Alexandria had become 'empty and ugly and full of ghosts'.[104] Almost all his wartime friends had dispersed homewards or across the Mediterranean, and over the coming years he would watch as the city was Egyptianised, 'not from the working class Egyptian quarter but from official Cairo',[105] until it became 'a very different place, less intellectual, less decadent, more ordinary, more provincial'.[106]

The great rambling house on the Rue Rassafa was emptying. With her husband dead and her son Jean the Dominican now in France, Rosette de Menasce increasingly frequented her favourite suite at the Hotel Scribe in Paris. Her stepson George de Menasce was transferring his money abroad; also, he was gradually moving his Chinese jades and porcelains and all the rest of his collection out of Egypt, partly with the help of Professor Alan Wace, who arranged for a portion to go to the Fitzwilliam Museum at Cambridge. But then Wace, still working for British intelligence, embarrassedly had to distance himself from Menasce after learning from Sir Walter Smart at the embassy that their friend was spending much of his money on smuggling Jews into Palestine.[107]

Yet anyone attending the Royal Archaeological Society's dinner at Baudrot's on Saturday 26 January 1946 could have been forgiven for thinking that nothing was ever going to change. Following the Filet de Poisson Verdi and the Tournedos Henri V came a presentation of ancient life in Alexandria as conveyed by Theocritus in his Fifteenth Idyll. Claire Vincendon designed the costumes for the cast, which included her twenty-year-old daughter Claude in the role of Praxinoë. King Ptolemy Philadelphus and his sister-wife Queen Arsinoë have put on a magnificent service for the Feast of Adonis at the royal palace. As Gorgo and her friend Praxinoë press their way through ancient Alexandria's crowded streets complaining of the jostling throng of Greeks, Egyptians, Syrians and Jews, the audience could as easily imagine the scene in the modern city. Once inside all is delight; the palace is hung with gorgeous tapestries embroidered with lively scenes, and Praxinoë exclaims:

81 Prince Nicholas Romanov, heir to the imperial throne of Russia, Gilda Ambron (centre), and Countess Mary de Zogheb (right), in Alexandria. Later, when Durrell, by then on Rhodes, received the news that Gilda had died in an air crash, it seemed to spell the end of the Alexandria he had known.

What art even in the spinning is shown
The figures are living not woven or sewn.
True to life they stand and they move. How clever is man![108]

Many of those at Baudrot's that evening would have recalled how Forster in his *Alexandria* had written of the Fifteenth Idyll: 'Only through literature can the past be recovered and here Theocritus, wielding the double spell of realism and poetry, has evoked an entire city from the dead and filled its streets with men.'[109]

A few months after the production of the Fifteenth Idyll Claude suddenly left the city. She had been working as secretary to Tim Forde, a married Irishman serving as a victualler with the Royal Navy down at the Western Harbour, by whom she was now pregnant – 'He was much older, not good-looking, unappealing, rough', remembered Claude's cousin Jacques Mawas; 'a good sort, but not the man for such a refined and beautiful woman'. To ward off the censure of Alexandrian society, Claire Vincendon took matters in hand, sending Claude to London, where she worked as press attaché for the French Embassy before giving birth to a daughter, Diana, in November 1946. It took longer for Claire to fix Forde's divorce, so that the couple were married only after Diana was born; then leaving the navy Forde took Claude home to Cork, where they ran a pub at 4 Grand Parade.

Aldo and Amelia Ambron returned to Italy for the first time since Mussolini's 1938 anti-semitic laws, while Gilda flew back and forth between Rome and Alexandria to help King Victor Emmanuel III, exiled from Italy after the war, settle into their villa in Moharrem Bey. Then word came that Gilda Ambron was dead, killed in a plane crash in the desert near Mersa Matruh while flying between Italy and Egypt.[110] Durrell was shocked when he heard the news on Rhodes; it was as though it spelt the end of the Ambrons, said Eve: 'That world we had known at the Ambron villa had already become unreal.'

A Passage from Alexandria

And then the Guardian Spirit ['Aγαθός Δαίμον', Agathos Daimon] will desert the city which they founded and will go to god-bearing Memphis and their city will be deserted. That will be the end of our evils when Egypt shall see the foreigners fall like leaves from the branch. The city by the sea will be a drying-place for the fishermen's catch and passers-by will say, 'This was the all-nurturing city in which all the races of mankind lived.'

Oracle of the Potter, third century BC[1]

On 26 January 1953 Lawrence Durrell disembarked with Sappho, his infant daughter by Eve, at Kyrenia, a small harbour town on the northern coast of Cyprus. Soon he had bought a run-down house in the nearby village of Bellapaix, where he unpacked the materials for his Alexandria novel that had been long stored away, which included E. M. Forster's *Alexandria: A History and a Guide* and his own 'Notes for Alex'. On the front cover of a blank government-issue notebook he wrote in pen, 'Notes: The Caballi, Alexandria'. Then turning to the first page he wrote:

> *Alexandria*
> (a pathos)
>
> to Yvette, these documents of our beloved city

'I have escaped to this island with a few books and the child – Melissa's child', he began, writing what would become the opening page of his published *Justine*. 'I do not know why I use the word "escape". The villagers say jokingly that only a sick man would choose such a remote place to rebuild. Well, then, I have come here to heal myself, if you like to put it that way. At night when the wind roars and the child sleeps quietly in its wooden cot by the echoing chimney-piece I light a lamp and walk about, thinking of my friends – of Justine and Nessim, of Melissa and Balthazar. I return link by link along the iron chains of memory to the city which we inhabited so briefly together.'[2]

After leaving Rhodes in 1947, and a year teaching with the British Council in Argentina, Durrell worked four years for the Foreign Office as press and information officer at the British Embassy in Belgrade. Finally, in the closing months of 1952, and with savings enough to last his family for a year or so in Cyprus, he decided that at forty it was now or never if he was to write the Book of the Dead.

But then Eve began to fall into the kind of depression that had been so familiar before she met Durrell, and as she withdrew deeper into herself she became convinced that he did not care. In late November she suffered hallucinations and raged violently against him, saying she was leaving. 'Acute schizophrenic thought disorder with depressive features',[3] went the report of the psychiatric staff at a British military hospital in Germany, while Eve's psychiatrist wrote to Durrell, 'As you have already discovered, her delusions and ideation' are 'bound up with her early auto-erotic guilt feelings, her marked ambivalence towards her parents, and her craving for love objects'.[4] The story that had begun with Eve's disturbed childhood in Moharrem Bey had now overwhelmed their lives.

'Schizophrenia leaves a psychological overhang for nearly a year after the patient is well', Durrell wrote after arriving in Cyprus to his old friend Alan Thomas in England. 'I'm not saying that Eve's decisions etc will be altered necessarily – but one has to wait a bit to see whether they are just idées fixes or genuine thought-formations.' Meanwhile he suffered as he waited, wondering if Eve would ever come back to him, 'some days full of optimism' but 'some days gloomy and despondent'.[5]

Though Greek from the time of the Trojan war, Cyprus had known many masters; seized from the Venetians by the Ottomans in 1571 and planted with Turkish colonists, the island was handed over to Britain in 1877 in return for a defensive alliance against the Russians. For the British it was a watchtower looking out over the Middle East; for Durrell this was no return to the Arcadian landscapes of Corfu or Rhodes. 'Palm trees, camels, the smell of Syria', he wrote to Miller: 'a weird and rather malefic sort of island. . . . Cyprus is *oriental*. I'm trying to write a really good book now about Alexandria – at night when the chores are done.'[6]

After installing his mother at Bellapaix to help look after Sappho, in September Durrell began teaching English to sixth-formers at the Pancyprian Gymnasium in Nicosia, which in lieu of a university served as the island's most distinguished academic institution. It was also a hotbed of Hellenic nationalism. Archbishop Makarios, head of the Greek Orthodox Church on Cyprus and de facto leader of the majority Greek community, had once been among its students; so had George Grivas, a veteran of the Greek debacle in Anatolia in the early 1920s and commander of a Greek army division against the Italians during the 1940–1 Albanian campaign. A year and a half later, at a signal from Makarios, Grivas would launch an insurrection against the British in the cause of enosis, or union, with Greece.

With his teaching day beginning at seven in the morning, Durrell would rise at four-thirty and over a mug of black coffee add a few more lines to his novel, writing in long-hand in his 'Caballi' notebook so as not to disturb his sleeping household, before driving thirty miles round the shoulder of the coastal range and onto the plain of Nicosia. In those dawns and in the lengthening shadows of his return drive to Bellapaix he was composing his novel in his head; these were the passages he set down by candlelight the following morning in 'The Caballi'. At weekends he would type out the fifteen hundred words he had written there; it was a slow process of distillation.

'Never have I worked under such adverse conditions', Durrell wrote to Miller in October, but also 'I have never felt in better writing form.' Announcing the title of his novel as *Justine*, he said it would be '*4-dimensional. I'm struggling to keep it taut and very short*, like some strange animal suspended in a solution.'[7] Durrell was seeing Melissa and Justine as aspects of the same woman, Melissa the vulnerable Eve with whom he had fallen in love, Justine as the woman he feared that Eve had always been, a prisoner of her obsession with a traumatic memory. It was like looking at the same face from different angles in multiple mirrors. But also he was seeing himself as Darley and Nessim, the younger man who became entranced in Alexandria and the man of experience who suffers. It was a story, he found, that could be comprehended only four-dimensionally. From the incestuous twins of his 'Notes for Alex', whose world became contracted to the compass of their dependency, Durrell had now extended his central characters to four: 'The four of us were unrecognised complementaries of one another, inextricably bound together.'[8] Together they inhabit a womblike Alexandria, as he would describe it in *Justine*, where 'for the four of us the known world hardly existed; days became simply the spaces between dreams, spaces between the shifting floors of time'.[9]

Durrell was constantly referring to his 'Notes for Alex' and filled several pages towards the back with plans, elevations and three-dimensional projections of his house at Bellapaix, while amid calculations for various costs, including specially carpentered stained-glass windows, he drew cats and a rabbit for his daughter. In 'The Caballi', too, he drew elevations of his house and designs for a four-poster Turkish-style cot for Sappho. But also at the back of 'The Caballi', and entirely separate from the body of his evolving novel, he wrote a kind of daydream conversation about his daughter, Melissa's daughter, who was also called Melissa:

'It's a shanty. Dirty. Disreputable. But we're both healthy. I've built only one decent room so far. I am so happy. I have never been so happy before. Thank God for everything.'

'And little Melissa?'

'Asleep.'[10]

The conversation was with Clea.

In April 1954 Eve flew in to Nicosia. Durrell was delighted with Eve's return; she was 'very gay and pretty', he wrote to Stephanides, and 'Sapphy is tremendously pleased'.[11] Eager to reassure Eve that she was truly home, Durrell made over the house to her almost

I had a look at
the house. It was
quite dry inside

82 Durrell wrote encouragingly to Eve about the house he was fixing up at Bellapaix in Cyprus, but meanwhile he wondered if she would ever come back to him.

as soon as she arrived. But Eve's mood swings worried Durrell, who compared their situation at times to *Tender is the Night*, Scott Fitzgerald's autobiographical novel about his love for Zelda, his beautiful and exciting but unbalanced wife.

Eve recalled how things seemed to her: 'In less than a few days, in less than a week after I arrived, I was back to square one, when I said I had to go all the way back to hospital. This is a suicide situation not a life situation. I mean, nothing had changed with Larry. And I was determined that I wasn't going to die. Larry was behaving during that time abominably. I'm the sort of person who can't stand being abused. I'm not a victim. At the moment I realised I was being pushed into the role of one, then, you know, I began to say, "Who's the victim here, you or I? Maybe you." Listen, I would have killed him if it had come to the crunch. I can kill. Literally. Kill with a blow. I nearly killed someone like that, because he was trying to abuse me' – a man known to her father who had tried to seduce her on a beach in Alexandria. 'I have dreams about these things. I put it down to my Leo qualities. I mean, you try and frighten a lion; it'll go against you. It will rush against you. And this is what I did. I terrified the wits out of Larry.'

At about this time Durrell continued his story from 'The Caballi', but in a blue note-book on which he wrote, 'Justine Rough Draft',[12] and drew a view of Alexandria from the sea – a mosque, a church, the Pharos surmounted with its statue of Poseidon – combining all three epochs of the city's history. Then he filled a page of his notebook with another translation of 'The City', before resuming his novel with the reflections of Nessim, who had been driven to the brink of madness by the strange behaviour of Justine: '"My problem", he said to himself quietly, feeling his forehead to see if he had a fever, "is that the woman I loved brought me a faultless satisfaction never touched with her own happiness". . . . He could hear, like the distant reverberations of the city's memory the voice of Plotinus speaking, not of flight away from intolerable temporal conditions but towards a new light, a new City of Light. "Let us flee to the beloved fatherland. . . . Withdraw into yourself and look." But this was the one act of which he was now incapable.'[13]

In the summer of 1954 Durrell was recruited for the post of director of the Public Information Office of the Cyprus government, which he saw as a chance to promote the long-standing affection between England and the Greeks. British rule in Cyprus was the first in the island's history to be in any way benevolent, and its population enjoyed almost perfect civic freedom, as even the most convinced supporters of enosis agreed. He would run the government's Cyprus Broadcasting Service and revive the quasi-official *Cyprus Review*, commissioning friends and fellow philhellenes to write articles promoting Anglo-Hellenic harmony. Britain required a strategic presence in the Eastern Mediterranean close by the turbulent Middle East, and there was also the complication presented by the island's Turkish minority: neither they nor the Turkish government in Ankara wanted the island handed over to Greece. Surely the Cypriots could be won round to understanding Britain's needs and find in the continuance of British rule their own security and self-interest too.

But soon Durrell's Greek love affair began falling apart: in December British troops fired on student demonstrators in Limassol, wounding three, while Seferis, who had visited Durrell during his first winter at Bellapaix, now pointedly avoided meetings when coming to Cyprus. Remarking on Durrell's propaganda activities, Seferis accused him of using the island's cultural institutions and his old friendships from Greece 'to infiltrate and enslave consciences'.[14] In later volumes of the *Quartet* Durrell would portray the older novelist Pursewarden as a man whose friendships had been compromised by his work in the Foreign Service, as Durrell was beginning to feel his were too.

Just past midnight on 1 April 1955 the thunder of blasting bombs rolled through the streets of Nicosia, and like seismic aftershocks reports came in of more explosions in Limassol, Larnaca and Famagusta. Archbishop Makarios had given the order to General Grivas to begin the insurrection. Before the year's end 24 people would die, and in 1956 another 214, more than half of them Greek Cypriots, the majority of killings by Grivas' terrorist group EOKA, the National Organisation of Cypriot Fighters. 'We are having a bitter uphill struggle against this too-long neglected Enosis situation', Durrell wrote to Alan Thomas. 'I've scored a few goals but mostly it is saving shots. The pitch is greasy, ball muddy and Yours truly tired of it all.'[15] These thoughts were in Durrell's mind when he traced his outspread hand in 'Justine Rough Draft' opposite where he had written of Alexandria that 'Everywhere on these brown flapping walls I see the basic talisman of the country – imprint of a palm with outspread fingers, seeking to ward off the terrors which thronged the darkness outside the lighted town.'[16] And in a pocket poetry note-book he traced an outline of 'Sapphy's hand, April 1955, Dear Child be Happy. Larry.'[17]

Twice in July Durrell flew to London, where he was involved in consultations with the Colonial Office. When he arrived back in Nicosia the second time, Eve announced that she was leaving and taking Sappho with her. The worsening situation in Cyprus may have made his acquiescence easier, and he accompanied them as far as Athens, but the scene must have reminded him of Nancy's departure with Penelope to Jerusalem at the time of the Flap.

Durrell fell into 'a bad patch of distress and apathy'[18] after the departure of Eve and Sappho. Worn threadbare by the nightly bombings which pounded in the background of his loss, he stayed up late drinking at Nicosia's Cosmopolitan Bar, where towards the end of September he came close to being shot, only the barking of a dog warning him of gunmen lurking in the bushes outside. From then on he carried a pistol, telling Miller in November, 'We are in the middle of a very nasty little revolution here with bombs and murders on the Palestine pattern.' By now travel about the island had become dangerous and he had to lock up his house at Bellapaix, but 'in the midst of all this noise and slaughter I'm half way through a book called *Justine* which is about Eve and Alexandria before the war'.[19]

After New Year 1956 Durrell wrote to Miller again, saying he had 'just finished a book about Alexandria called *Justine*. . . . It's a sort of prose poem to one of the great capitals of the heart, the Capital of Memory.' After Eve had gone 'a lovely young Alexandrian tumbled into my arms and gave me enough spark to settle down and demolish the book'. Her name was 'Claude, a writer with something oddly her own'.[20]

Except for its frequent changes of scene, Claude Vincendon's life had been frustrating and pedestrian since her departure from Alexandria nine years before. After a period spent running their public house in Cork, Tim Forde decided that he and Claude should make a new start in Australia. They opened a greengrocery in the Sydney suburb of Vaucluse, where they were joined by Polly O'Meara, who had worked as a nanny for Rosette de Menasce and then for Rosette's daughter Claire Vincendon. Now Polly had come to work in turn for Claude, looking after Diana and also Barry, her newborn son, and she spoke of how life had been in the days of the great house on the Rue Rassafa, of Felix and Rosette, of uncles Jean and George, and of the days when Claude was still a girl, for Polly O'Meara was the living repository of three generations of Alexandrian history. The Fordes went next to Israel, where through Menasce connections Tim and Claude got jobs with the Federmann brothers' Dan Hotels group. Then again Tim was on the move; in Cyprus he was offered a job starting up a hotel in Bombay, but this time Claude said that she would not go, and it was now in the early summer of 1955 that she applied for a position in the French section of the Cyprus Broadcasting Service and was hired by the public information director.

Claude spoke perfect French and English, also Italian and some German and a smattering of Hebrew, Greek and Arabic, and she was businesslike and practical, good at figures and able to type. She was elegant too, blonde and slim, though agreeably she was taller than Durrell by only an inch or two. Also she was wonderfully humorous and could match him for loquacity and Irishness; from Polly she had her Irish lilt and from her days at the pub in Cork she had picked up a playful Irish tongue. Then again she could seem so entirely French, but with the adaptability of a Levantine. Telling Durrell that she was an Alexandrian, she added that she had 'always wanted to write'.[21]

After Eve left Cyprus, their affair began. Durrell afterwards described the scene: 'I used to make her come round to the villa at bomb time and set up a typewriter on the dining table. We drank red wine and worked like maniacs' – Claude was writing her first novel, *Mrs O*', based on her experiences as a publican in Cork. 'Every twenty minutes there was a boom and something in the town went up; the telephone rang. We disregarded everything. I answered the duty room, the staff room, Government House, Police Press – and back to *Justine*.'[22] Night after night they sat working on their books, their typewriters at opposite ends of the table on which they spread a map of Alexandria, 'tracing and re-tracing the streets with our fingers, recapturing much that I had lost, the brothels and the parks, the dawns over Lake Mareotis'. Against the noise of pistol shots and bombs going off at the rate of three or four a night, and calls coming in from the operations room of another ambush in the mountains, it was a 'very queer and thrilling period, sad, weighed down with futility and disgust, but marvellous to be able to live in one's book'.[23]

Later, in thinking of these nights and days with Claude, Durrell would write in the last volume of the *Quartet* how when Darley returned to the city 'A whole new geography of Alexandria was born through Clea, reviving old meanings, renewing ambiences half forgotten, laying down like a rich wash of colour a new history, a new biography to replace the old one.'[24]

In June 1956 Durrell was telling Alan Thomas that Faber were 'quite excited'[25] about his novel. His two-year contract with the Cyprus government was nearing its end and he had decided not to renew it. Most of his friends had left the island in April after EOKA began killing British civilians; in May Durrell was warned by the secretary to Makarios that his life was in danger; and early in June an incendiary bomb went off in Durrell's garage. 'It was time to leave Cyprus, I knew, for most of the swallows had gone.'[26] There was no further hope that the Cypriots could be held without uncompromising force; Britain was 'fighting the spirit of Greece',[27] and that was not his battle.

On a visit to Famagusta, 'the most haunting town in Cyprus, saturated with the memory of its past', he visited the ruined crusaders' cathedral of St Nicholas 'wearing

83   Claude Vincendon on Cyprus in 1955 or 1956, not long after she met Durrell. 'A lovely young Alexandrian tumbled into my arms and gave me enough spark to settle down and demolish the book', he wrote to Henry Miller.

its uncouth horns of minarets' – the church had been converted into a mosque by the Turks after they seized the island from the Venetians. Here he walked about the Gothic galleries overgrown with grass, reflecting that England, like Venice before it, was 'a sea-born power whose many bridgeheads were being slowly invested by the sea we had tamed and yoked . . . and conscious that one day our history must touch and marry [Venice's] own, to join the great confluence of tides which meet forever at the point where present meets the past in a death-embrace'.[28] In the graveyard he noted down inscriptions on the burial stones, Wilmot Montolif among them, whose last name he would later give to his fictional ambassador, while others he would sprinkle among the names of his Alexandrians, 'The poetry and history of commerce, the rhyme-schemes of the Levant'.[29] Though Durrell identified with the Mediterranean rather than with England, he regretted the passing of maritime empires, those foundations of cosmopolitanism. Then he returned to Nicosia and the preoccupations of his office, of 'the noisy contentions of demagogues and illiterates which had begun to fill the empty theatre of world affairs with the shrill waspish voice of the times – nationalism'.[30]

Claude was leaving with her children around the end of July, first staying with her brother Eric who now lived in Paris, then visiting her uncle George de Menasce in London and putting her children into boarding school in England. By the time Durrell joined her in London at the end of August, Claude would be ready to share their life together, and early in 1957 they would settle in France.

But before that, in mid-July, Durrell sent a letter to Faber and Faber: 'In the back of my mind I want to do a series, I don't know how many, of novels in the style of *Justine* about Alexandria, using the same people in different combinations.'[31] This was Durrell's first announcement that he would go beyond a single volume, and though later he would say that from the start 'I had planned four books',[32] this was untrue. Claude returned him to 'the capital of Memory', words he added by hand at the last moment to his typescript of *Justine*, and opened his eyes to an Alexandria that he had not seen before.

'A single chance factor has altered everything, has turned me back upon my tracks', he wrote at the beginning of the second volume, *Balthazar*. 'Justine, Melissa, Clea. There were so few of us really – you would have thought them easily disposed of in a single book, would you not? So would I, so *did* I. . . . Indeed, I saw my lovers and friends no longer as living people but as coloured transfers of the mind; inhabiting my papers now, no longer the city, like tapestry figures.'[33]

In reality that single chance factor was meeting Claude, who showed him that what he had known of Alexandria, its personalities and intrigues, was wrong or incomplete. Durrell's reference to the figures in the tapestries is his nod to Claude, who had told him of her role as Praxinoë in Theocritus' Fifteenth Idyll, where 'The figures are living not woven or sewn. / True to life they stand and they move.'

Durrell's undated letter mentioning possible sequels to *Justine* was date-stamped by Faber and Faber on receipt: 24 July 1956. Against the background of the events that followed, Durrell embarked on writing *Balthazar*, *Mountolive* and *Clea*, the further volumes that would make up his *Alexandria Quartet*.

On 26 July, the fourth anniversary of the overthrow of King Farouk, Nasser gave a speech from the balcony of the Bourse to a quarter of a million people pressed in and around Mohammed Ali Square. In 1917 Forster had been on that balcony too, watching the sparrows and thinking that whenever he was with Mohammed he caught 'glimpses of the happiness of thousands of others whose names I shall never hear, and know that there is a great unrecorded history'.[34]

The sparrows were gathering to chatter and roost in the trees around St Mark's as Nasser began his speech at 5 p.m. Ten times or more during the first two and a half hours he repeated the name 'Lesseps': it was the codeword for the Egyptian army to move towards the Suez Canal. Egypt had its political independence, he cried, but economic independence was necessary too, and to the wild cheers of the adoring crowd he roundly denounced imperialism and accused the Western powers of seeking to dominate Egypt and the Arab world through Israel, and by military pacts, the manipulation of arms sales and economic pressure. In particular he charged Britain, the United States and the World Bank of a conspiracy in refusing to finance the proposed construction of the hydroelectric High Dam at Aswan after he had purchased arms from the Soviet bloc. Asking rhetorically where Egypt was to find the money for the dam, he repeated the name Ferdinand de Lesseps, and to an ecstatic roar from the square he announced the military occupation of the Canal Zone and the nationalisation of the Suez Canal Company.

Britain had withdrawn its forces under treaty from the canal in June, leaving the zone in the hands of the largely British- and French-owned Suez Canal Company, which would hand over to the Egyptians when its lease expired in twelve years' time. But Nasser was impatient. He faced opposition from some quarters in Egypt and felt that his position was insecure, and he had already been considering nationalising the canal six months before the West's refusal to finance the dam: the old populist remedy of attacking the British in particular and the West in general came readily to hand.

But old reflexes were at work on the British side too. A quarter of Britain's trade passed through the canal and British ships accounted for a third of its users. Moreover, most of Britain's oil supply came through Suez. Anthony Eden, who was now prime minister, believed that if the nationalisation of the canal was left unanswered it would be a blow to British prestige and influence among its Arab allies in the region. Recalling Britain's pre-war appeasement of Germany following its occupation of the Rhineland, Eden began comparing Nasser to Hitler and called for his destruction. France had its own reasons for wanting to see Nasser go, believing he was supplying arms to the Algerians in an independence struggle that was tying down a quarter of a million French troops. Israel had already been planning to attack Egypt if the British buffer in the Canal Zone was withdrawn. Now in this combustible atmosphere Israel saw its chance to light the match by providing the excuse for an Anglo-French invasion of Egypt, its aim to internationalise the canal and to overthrow Nasser's regime – which would be replaced, so the thinking went in some quarters, by a coalition led by Mustafa Nahas.

On 29 October, with the prior agreement of their allies, the Israelis advanced through Sinai. On the pretence of preventing a clash between Israeli and Egyptian forces, British and French troops landed in the Canal Zone at dawn on 5 November – though not before British bombers flying from Cyprus and Malta pounded Egyptian airfields to protect Israel from counterattack, while French fighter planes painted with Israeli markings and flown by French pilots in Israeli uniforms cleared the Egyptian air force from the skies.

The original invasion plan was for Alexandria itself to be the target of attack. British and French airborne troops would drop on the limestone ridge running west from the city out towards Burg el Arab, from where they would seize the dock facilities in the Western Harbour. Meanwhile Alexandria would be bombarded from the sea by a fleet of a hundred British warships and thirty French, which would disgorge hundreds of landing craft for a marine assault on the city's beaches. Over the following days more troops would be disembarked in the Western Harbour, until a hundred thousand men in all would begin the march on Cairo and towards the Suez Canal.

Only a month before the invasion the plan was changed; fighting a major battle in a large city would not be acceptable to world opinion and the attack was switched instead to Port Said at the northern end of the canal, though airfields near Alexandria were bombed. As the air-raid alarms sounded in the sunset, Judge Brinton and his family boarded an American navy ship in the Western Harbour. During Arabi's rebellion in 1882, when the British had bombarded Alexandria, an American flagship had been there too, playing 'See the Conquering Hero' and 'Rule Britannia' on its decks as it steamed encouragingly round the British fleet, and later it landed marines to help restore order in the town. But now Anglo-American rivalry in the Middle East, where America believed that its own independence from a colonial past could get it on terms with Arab nationalists, meant that the US Sixth Fleet was engaged solely in evacuating Americans and other foreigners to Crete. 'It was a beautiful sight', said Judge Brinton as they left the harbour, 'with Farouk's palace, the Yacht Club, the light house and the long break- water to the north of us – and to the south and east the profile of the city with its docks and warehouses, its mosques and minarets.' He counted the years since he had sailed into Alexandria as a stranger facing an unknown future – 'Now roots have been torn up and life is not likely ever to flow in the same channels again.'[35]

British and French forces advancing southwards along the canal were within twenty-four hours of seizing Suez when Eden ordered a ceasefire at midnight on 6 November. 'I am not sure I should have dared to start', said the former prime minister Winston Churchill, 'but I am sure I should not have dared to stop.'[36] Instead a divided country at home and noises from the Soviet Union, but most of all strong pressure from the United States, had broken Britain's will.

The miscalculated Anglo-French invasion, followed by its ignominious withdrawal, invited contempt and became a triumph for Nasser, whose position was immeasurably strengthened at home and throughout the Arab world. In 1957 all remaining British and French citizens were expelled from Egypt; a third of Egypt's Jews, mostly those with foreign nationality, were driven into exile by police harassment and economic pressure; and the remainder of the foreign community dwindled as manufacturers and exporters were Egyptianised. In a climate of fear and anger the old cosmopolitan Alexandria was destroyed.

Alexander himself laid down the plan of the great city that was to bear his name. But as there was no chalk to mark the ground, he sprinkled grains of barley to indicate the

84 Cavafy's tombstone in Alexandria's Greek Orthodox Cemetery bears the simple epitaph, 'Poet'.

alignment of its streets and where its markets and temples should be and the circumference of its walls. Then suddenly huge flocks of birds appeared from Mareotis and the Nile and to Alexander's alarm devoured all the grain. Take heart, his diviners urged him, interpreting the occurrence as a sign that the city would not only have abundant resources of its own but would be the nurse of men of innumerable nations.

The modern cosmopolitan city saw itself as the revival of that dream. But wider forces were at work both within and without, and between the extremes to which they went, Alexandria was ground to a husk. A few foreigners, mostly Greeks, held on, running those small businesses – pensions, tavernas, bookshops and so on – which escaped the wholesale nationalisation measures of 1961 that were applied to Egyptians too. All talk of democracy and free speech was suppressed as Nasser, by now absolute dictator, used his vast secret police force to stamp out dissent. The disastrous 1967 war against Israel followed, and only after Nasser's death in 1970 did Egypt begin its return to political and economic liberalism, though this was matched by a growing Islamic conservatism.

Today the city is no longer *ad* but *in* Aegyptum and uniform in culture, though it is occasionally disturbed by reminders of its past. Recently a row broke out over the erection of a bronze equestrian statue of Alexander the Great, a gift to the Municipality from the government of Greece. Some objected to the statue being raised in such a prominent position near the ancient Gate of the Sun, while others objected to it being raised at all, saying that the founder of Iskandariya, as the city is called in Arabic, was a foreigner and did not belong.

An archaeologist examines the buried layers of a ruined city. But Alexandria, though deteriorating and poorer now, is not a buried city, and as you walk about its streets you see something of what would have been familiar to its inhabitants a lifetime ago. Yet despite the massive increase in population – around five million now against eight hundred thousand or so at the outbreak of the Second World War and five hundred thousand in Forster's time – the city is haunted by a sense of vacancy, for almost all the citizens of cosmopolitan Alexandria have long since gone away, leaving a new people without memories to inhabit the carcass of others' lives. For those wanting to see the city, the words of Plotinus apply: 'To any vision must be brought an eye adapted to what is to be seen.'

But not all the inhabitants of cosmopolitan Alexandria left the city; many have stayed behind in its Greek, Jewish, Protestant, Syrian Catholic and Latin cemeteries near the Gate of the Sun. Here lie the Salvagos, the Benachis, the Suareses and the Menasces; here Bacos, Loria, Badaro and Zogheb; and here lies Constantine Cavafy, on his tombstone the simple epitaph 'Poet'.

Amid the cemeteries is an ancient Ptolemaic tomb. The tomb perhaps of Alexander, some archaeologists now believe. And if not here then somewhere near, if he lies at rest at all, the founder of the city that bears his name, the first of the Alexandrians buried among the last.

NOTES

PROLOGUE
The Capital of Memory

1 Lawrence Durrell, *Justine* (1957), the first volume of *The Alexandria Quartet* (hereafter *AQ*), London 1962; all page numbers refer to the *AQ* paperback edition, London 1968, here 201.

2 *Justine*, *AQ*, 17.

3 Lawrence Durrell to Henry Miller, some time from late May to mid-July 1944, in *The Durrell-Miller Letters, 1935–80*, ed. Ian S. MacNiven, London 1988 (hereafter *DML*), 167.

4 *Justine*, *AQ*, 17.

5 LD to HM, *c.* January 1956, *DML*, 279.

6 Introduction to E. M. Forster, *Alexandria: A History and a Guide*, London 1982, xviii (hereafter *AHG*/1982). The first edition of Forster's *Alexandria* was published in Alexandria in 1922 and is extremely rare; the reader is more likely to obtain it in republished form. The 1922 edition was republished in New York in 1961 with a new introduction by Forster, and again in London in 1982 with Forster's 1961 introduction, a new introduction by Lawrence Durrell and an afterword and notes by Michael Haag. The afterword and notes of *AHG*/1982 were revised in a 1986 reprint published in London and New York. The second edition (hereafter *AHG*/1938) was published in Alexandria in 1938; it has never been republished.

7 Peter Adam, 'Alexandria Revisited', *Twentieth Century Literature* 33:3, fall 1987, 397. Cité du Livre at 2 Rue Fuad, next door to Baudrot, was owned by Nessim Mustacchi, a Greek Jew from Thessaloniki, whose son Georges

Moustaki later wrote 'Milord' for Edith Piaf.

8 *Clea* (1960), fourth volume of *AQ*, 700.

9 Adam, 'Alexandria Revisited', 400.

10 Ibid., 409.

11 Ibid., 407.

12 Ibid., 400.

13 *Justine*, *AQ*, 41f.

14 Jane Lagoudis Pinchin, *Alexandria Still*, Princeton 1977, 106. Pinchin quotes from Forster's papers at King's College, Cambridge, probably a draft for what became his essay 'The Complete Poems of C. P. Cavafy', in *Two Cheers for Democracy*, London 1951.

15 Pinchin, *Alexandria Still*, 109.

16 *AHG*/1982, xix.

17 Robert Liddell, *Cavafy: A Critical Biography*, London 1974, 181.

18 *Clea*, *AQ*, 702.

19 Ibid., 846.

20 Plutarch, 'Mark Antony', in *Makers of Rome*, trans. Ian Scott-Kilvert, London 1965, 340.

21 Edmund Keeley, *Cavafy's Alexandria*, London 1976, 6.

22 Letter from Claude's brother Eric Vincendon to the author, 10 July 1995: 'Claude and Larry NEVER met in Alexandria, only in Cyprus.'

23 LD to HM, *c.* January 1956, *DML*, 279.

24 Diana Menuhin (née Gould) to Alan Thomas, 10 February 1968. British Library.

25 *Clea*, *AQ*, 722.

26 *Mountolive* (1958), third volume of *AQ*, 393, where incidentally 'δαίμονοζ' is misspelt 'διάμονοζ'.

27 LD to HM, 17 January 1967, *DML*, 416.

28 Adam, 'Alexandria Revisited', 401.

29 *AHG*/1982, xix.

30 Adam, 'Alexandria Revisited', 397.

31 BBC transcript *Spirit of Place*.

32 Lawrence Durrell, 'Notes for Alex', 9. British Library. This is a notebook begun in 1944,

possibly incorporating notes from 1943. The page numbers are those assigned by the British Library.

33 Adam, 'Alexandria Revisited', 397.

34 Ibid., 398.

35 Ibid., 399.

36 Ibid., 398f.

37 Ibid., 400.

38 LD to HM, 8 February 1944, *DML*, 159.

39 *AHG*/1982, xix.

40 LD to HM, 25 November 1977, *DML*, 490.

41 LD to Alan Thomas, [October 1977], postmark Alexandria. British Library. Durrell lived in the Villa Cleobolus on Rhodes after the war, a time he describes in his book *Reflections on a Marine Venus*, London 1953; see chapter 5, 'In the Garden of Villa Cleobolus'.

42 *Balthazar* (1958), second volume of *AQ*, 209.

43 *AHG*/1982, 33, translation by Robin Furness.

44 In Arabic the pronunciation of his name is closer to 'Urabi' or 'Orabi', which are alternative transliterations.

45 *AHG*/1982, 103.

46 *Justine*, *AQ*, 152. See T. S. Eliot, *Four Quartets*, 'Little Gidding', II.

47 *Justine*, *AQ*, 27.

CHAPTER 1
A Tram with a View

1 E. M. Forster, 'Letter to Mohammed el Adl' (1922–9). E. M. Forster archive, library of Kings College, Cambridge (hereafter KCC).

2 *AHG*/1982, xxi.

3 E. M. Forster, 'The Complete Poems of C. P. Cavafy', in *Two Cheers for Democracy*, London 1972, 237.

4 *AHG*/1982, xxi.

5 EMF to Florence Barger, 28 April 1916. KCC.

6 E. M. Forster, 'Syed Ross Masood', in *Two Cheers*, 285.

7 E. M. Forster, *The Hill of Devi*, London 1983, 3.

8 E. M. Forster, locked journal, 1 November 1911, in Nicola Beauman, *Morgan: A Biography of E. M. Forster*, London 1993, 247.

9 EMF to Forrest Reid, 13 March 1915, in P. N. Furbank, *E. M. Forster: A Life*, London 1979, vol. 2, 14.

10 Furbank, *E. M. Forster*, vol. 1, 259.

11 J. F. C. Fuller, *The Decisive Battles of the Western World*, ed. John Terraine, London 1970, vol. 2, 290.

12 EMF to Malcolm Darling, 6 November 1914, in *Selected Letters of E. M. Forster*, ed. Mary Lago and P. N. Furbank, London 1985, vol. 1, 213.

13 E. M. Forster, *Howards End*, London 1973, 60.

14 E. M. Forster, unpublished diary, 4 August 1914, in Furbank, *E. M. Forster*, vol. 1, 259.

15 EMF to FB, 10 August 1915, *Letters*, vol. 1, 229.

16 EMF to Syed Ross Masood, 29 July 1915, *Letters*, vol. 1, 224.

17 *Guide to Egypt and the Sudan*, seventh edition, London 1916, xv.

18 EMF to his mother, 21 November 1915, in Furbank, *E. M. Forster*, vol. 2, 22.

19 *AHG*/1982, 110.

20 E. M. Forster, *A Room with a View*, Harmondsworth 1978, 36.

21 *Twentieth Century Impressions of Egypt*, ed. Arnold Wright, London 1909, 429.

22 Ibid., 423.

23 Ibid., 429.

24 Evaristo Breccia, *Alexandrea ad Aegyptum*, English-language edition, Bergamo 1922, 2.

25 Douglas Sladen, *Queer Things about Egypt*, London 1910, 153.

26 Ibid., 155.

27 Ibid., 154.

28 Breccia, *Alexandrea ad Aegyptum*, viiif.

29 Ibid., 59.

30 *AHG*/1982, 7.

31 Breccia, *Alexandrea ad Aegyptum*, viif.

32 Mabel Caillard, *A Lifetime in Egypt*, London 1935, 176.

33 Robert Furness to John Maynard Keynes, 25 April 1907, in Furbank, *E. M. Forster*, vol. 2, 24.

34 Laurence Grafftey-Smith, *Bright Levant*, London 1970, 70.

35 Ibid.

36 EMF to SRM, 29 December 1915, *Letters*, vol. 1, 232.

37 Edward W. Said, *The Question of Palestine*, London 1992, 20.

38 EMF to SRM, 29 December 1915, *Letters*, vol. 1, 232.

39 Foreigners were exempt from native law: civil cases were heard in the Mixed Courts, where foreign and Egyptian judges applied

the Napoleonic Code, while criminal cases were heard by the consuls.

40 Karl Baedeker, *Egypt and the Sudan*, London 1914, 15, 19.

41 *AHG*/1982, xxxi.

42 EMF to Malcolm Darling, 6 August 1916, *Letters*, vol. 1, 238. By 1911 'Anglo-Indian' had already officially replaced 'Eurasian' to describe people of mixed descent, but here Forster means a British citizen of long residence in India.

43 EMF to Edward Carpenter, 18 May 1916, in Furbank, *E. M. Forster*, vol. 2, 30.

44 EMF to Malcolm Darling, 6 August 1916, *Letters*, vol. 1, 238.

45 Robert Trevelyan, poet, was brother of the historian G. M. Trevelyan and of the Liberal MP C. M. Trevelyan, who advocated 'peace through negotiation' throughout the war. Goldsworthy Lowes Dickinson was a lecturer in political science at King's College, Cambridge, and a proponent of pacifism and of a 'league of nations' (a term he may have invented). His sisters at his London home in Langham Place were in part the inspiration for the Schlegel sisters and their home in *Howards End*.

46 EMF to SRM, 20 November 1913, in Beauman, *Morgan*, 284.

47 Benjamin Disraeli, speech at Crystal Palace, 24 June 1872, in *The Selected Speeches of the Earl of Beaconsfield*, ed. T. E. Kebbel, London 1882, 530–4.

48 Nicholas Mansergh, *Survey of British Commonwealth Affairs*, London 1952, vol. 3, 256.

49 *Howards End*, 320.

50 *The Hill of Devi*, 223.

51 *Howards End*, 320.

52 Ibid., 266.

53 Ibid., 179.

54 Ibid., 337.

55 Ibid., 258.

56 *A Room with a View*, 60.

57 E. M. Forster, 'Gippo English', *Egyptian Mail*, 16 December 1917.

58 EMF to Goldsworthy Lowes Dickinson, 28 July 1916, *Letters*, vol. 1, 236.

59 EMF to GLD, *c.* September–October 1916, in Beauman, *Morgan*, 295.

60 Working Men's College *Journal* 14, 14 March 1915, 61, 58.

61 EMF to Leonard Woolf, 12 February 1916, in Furbank, *E. M. Forster*, vol. 2, 25.

62 Forster, 'Gippo English'.

63 *AHG*/1982, 177.

64 Ibid., 178–80.

65 Grafftey-Smith, *Bright Levant*, 52.

66 EMF to Virginia Woolf, 15 April 1916, *Letters*, vol. 1, 234.

67 Ibid.

68 Ibid.

69 Liddell, *Cavafy*, 165.

70 EMF to Pericles Anastassiades, 1949, in *The Complete Poems of Cavafy*, trans. Rae Dalven, New York 1961, 288.

71 EMF to George Savidis, 25 July 1958, *Letters*, vol. 2, 271.

72 Now the Palace of Culture at 1 Sharia Horreya opposite the entrance to Sharia Salah-Salem, the former Rue Chérif Pasha.

73 EMF to his mother, 26 August 1916, in J. H. Stape, *An E. M. Forster Chronology*, London 1993.

74 EMF to GLD, 10 January 1917, in Stape, *Chronology*.

75 In Forster's time the trams bore coloured symbols to indicate their routes: stars, crescents, triangles, circles, trefoils, lozenges and labels.

76 Forster, 'Letter to Mohammed el Adl'.

77 EMF to Edward Carpenter, 12 April 1916, in Furbank, *E. M. Forster*, vol. 2, 35.

78 EMF to FB, 2 July 1916, *Letters*, vol. 1, 235.

79 EMF to his mother, 10 July 1916, in Furbank, *E. M. Forster*, vol. 2, 27.

80 EMF to FB, 2 July 1916, *Letters*, vol. 1, 235.

81 *AHG*/1938, iii.

82 *AHG*/1982, 33f., translation by Robin Furness.

83 Ibid., 173.

84 *AHG*/1938, iii.

85 *AHG*/1982, 182.

86 EMF to Laura Forster (aunt), 25 August 1916, *Letters*, vol. 1, 240.

87 EMF to GLD, 28 July 1916, *Letters*, vol. 1, 236.

88 EMF to FB, 16 October 1916, *Letters*, vol. 1, 243.

89 EMF to FB, 10 August 1915, *Letters*, vol. 1, 229.

90 EMF to Laura Forster, 1 January 1917, *Letters*, vol. 1, 248.

91 *AHG*/1982, 181.

92 E. M. Forster, 'The Lost Guide', lecture given at the Aldeburgh Festival of Music and Arts,

1956. KCC.

93 E. M. Forster, *The Longest Journey*, London 1989, lxvi.

94 Ibid., 3.

95 Diary, 18 August 1904, in Forster's introduction to *The Longest Journey*, lxvi.

96 *The Longest Journey*, 136.

97 Ibid., 136, 138.

98 Ibid., 137.

99 *Howards End*, 183.

100 EMF to FB, 8 November 1916, *Letters*, vol. 1, 244.

101 EMF to Malcolm Darling, 1 December 1916, *Letters*, vol. 1, 246.

102 EMF to Laura Forster, 21 December 1916, in Stape, *Chronology*, 61.

103 EMF to Laura Forster, 1 January 1917, *Letters*, vol. 1, 248.

104 EMF to FB, 6 January 1918, *Letters*, vol. 1, 280.

105 Ibid.

106 EMF to FB, 17 June 1917, *Letters*, vol. 1, 258.

107 EMF to FB, 6 January 1918, *Letters*, vol. 1, 280. For the unexpurgated text (as quoted here), see Furbank, *E. M. Forster*, vol. 2, 37.

108 EMF to FB, 6 January 1918, *Letters*, vol. 1, 280.

109 Ibid.

110 'Letter to Mohammed el Adl'.

111 These pressures were reinforced by the law. Homosexual relations between consenting adults were decriminalised in England only in 1967, when Forster was eighty-eight.

112 EMF to FB, 29 May and 1 June 1917, *Letters*, vol. 1, 256.

113 EMF to Forrest Reid, 2 February 1913, *Letters*, vol. 1, 187.

114 'Letter to Mohammed el Adl'.

115 KCC.

116 *AHG*/1982, 170.

117 Furbank, *E. M. Forster*, vol. 2, 38.

118 EMF to FB, 18 July 1917, *Letters*, vol. 1, 262.

119 EMF to FB, 4 July 1917, *Letters*, vol. 1, 260.

120 Furbank, *E. M. Forster*, vol. 2, 38.

121 'Letter to Mohammed el Adl'.

122 'Letter to Mohammed el Adl'. The word 'muddle' – derived from 'mud', which had a special resonance for Forster in Egypt and also in *A Passage to India* – occurs frequently in his writings, public and private. In his published work it first appears in *A Room with a View* (47): old Mr Emerson, finding Lucy without a Baedeker in the Church of Santa Croce at Florence, undertakes to show her the Giottos, then suddenly speaks to her of his son. 'He has known so few women, and you have the time. . . . You are inclined to get muddled. . . . Let yourself go. Pull out from the depths those thoughts that you do not understand, and spread them out in the sunlight and know the meaning of them.'

123 William Plomer, *At Home*, London 1958, 107.

124 EMF to GLD, 25 June 1917 (continuation of 5 May 1917), *Letters*, vol. 1, 253.

125 Constantine Cavafy, *C. P. Cavafy: Collected Poems*, trans. Edmund Keeley and Philip Sherrard, London 1978, 53.

126 Ibid., 41.

127 Liddell, *Cavafy*, 93f.

128 *Cavafy: Collected Poems*, 117.

129 The Italian reads, 'Our Consulate, our new, rich, magnificent Consulate, strong as our Cadorna [then in command of the Italian army on the Austrian front], deep as our sea, lofty as our heaven that moves the other stars, and quite convenient for the Ramleh Tramways terminus.'

130 EMF to Robert Trevelyan, 6 August 1917, *Letters*, vol. 1, 266.

131 E. M. Forster, 'The Poetry of C. P. Cavafy', in *Pharos and Pharillon*, London 1923, 91f.

132 Forster, 'The Complete Poems of C. P. Cavafy', 233.

133 Liddell, *Cavafy*, 179.

134 'The Complete Poems of C. P. Cavafy', 233.

135 Ibid.

136 Quoted in Diskin Clay, 'The Silence of Hermippos: Greece in the Poetry of Cavafy', in *The Mind and Art of C. P. Cavafy*, Athens 1983, 178.

137 'The Complete Poems of C. P. Cavafy', 233.

138 Ibid.

139 *AHG*/1982, 104, translation by George Valassopoulos.

140 *Cavafy: Collected Poems*, 28, 75, 146, 58.

141 Forster, 'The Poetry of C. P. Cavafy', 95f., translation by George Valassopoulos.

142 Plutarch, 'Mark Antony', 344.

143 EMF to FB, 31 July 1917, *Letters*, vol. 1, 264.

144 EMF to FB, 13 September 1917, *Letters*, vol. 1, 270.

145 EMF to FB, 18 February 1918, *Letters*, vol. 1, 286.

146 EMF to FB, 18 July 1918, *Letters*, vol. 1, 262.

147 Mohammed el Adl to EMF, 31 August 1917,

Letters, vol. 1, 262.

148　EMF to FB, 25 August 1917, Letters, vol. 1, 267.

149　Ibid.

150　EMF to FB, 13 September 1917, Letters, vol. 1, 270.

151　EMF to FB, 17 June 1917, Letters, vol. 1, 258.

152　Mohammed el Adl to EMF, 31 August 1917, Letters, vol. 1, 262.

153　Stape, Chronology, 174.

154　Lytton Strachey, to EMF, in Furbank, E. M. Forster, vol. 2, 40.

155　EMF to FB, 25 August 1917, Letters, vol. 1, 267.

156　EMF to FB, 9 August 1917. KCC.

157　EMF to SRM, 8 September 1917, Letters, vol. 1, 269.

158　Liddell, Cavafy, 208.

159　EMF to FB, 11 October 1917, Letters, vol. 1, 274.

160　EMF to FB, 13 September 1917, Letters, vol. 1, 270.

161　EMF to FB, 30 September 1917, Letters, vol. 1, 271.

162　EMF to FB, 31 July 1917, Letters, vol. 1, 264.

163　EMF to FB, 25 August 1917, Letters, vol. 1, 267.

164　EMF to FB, 13 September 1917, Letters, vol. 1, 270.

165　EMF to FB, 30 September 1917, Letters, vol. 1, 271.

166　EMF to FB, 25 August 1917, Letters, vol. 1, 267.

167　E. M. Forster, 'Our Diversions: Diana's Dilemma', Egyptian Mail, 26 August 1917.

168　EMF to FB, 8 October 1917, Letters, vol. 1, 273.

169　EMF to FB, 30 September 1917, Letters, vol. 1, 274.

170　Furbank, E. M. Forster, vol. 2, 41.

171　EMF to FB, 11 October 1917, Letters, vol. 1, 274.

172　Mohammed el Adl to EMF, 10 November 1917, Letters, vol. 1, 275.

173　KCC. It is a first-class ticket but at the concessionary half fare – one of the perks that so pleased Forster. Tickets were valid for stages, this one from the Ramleh terminus in town to the suburb of Cleopatra or vice versa. Most likely it dates from July 1917 or later, when Forster, following Irene, began living at Camp de César.

174　EMF to FB, 11 October 1917, Letters, vol. 1, 274.

CHAPTER 2
Alexandria from the Inside

1　EMF to GLD, 5 December 1917, in Stape, Chronology, 63.

2　EMF to FB, 18 February 1918, Letters, vol. 1, 286.

3　E. M. Forster, 'A View without a Room', an appendix in A Room with a View, 232.

4　EMF to FB, 18 February 1918, Letters, vol. 1, 286.

5　Of the twenty-six newspaper articles Forster wrote while in Alexandria, twenty-two were written after he had clinched his affair with Mohammed.

6　E. M. Forster, 'Alexandria Vignettes: Cotton from the Inside', Egyptian Mail, 3 February 1918; republished as 'Cotton from the Inside', in Pharos and Pharillon, 74.

7　Breccia, Alexandrea ad Aegyptum, 15.

8　E. M. Forster, 'XX Century Alexandria: The New Quay', Egyptian Mail, 2 December 1917. The Cosmograph was a cinema.

9　E. M. Forster, 'Alexandria Vignettes: Between the Sun and the Moon', Egyptian Mail, 31 March 1918; republished as 'Between the Sun and the Moon', in Pharos and Pharillon, 87. Forster was following the opinion of his day in placing the Gate of the Sun somewhere in the vicinity of the Municipal (today's Shallalat) Gardens. Indeed, the remains of both Arab and Ptolemaic fortification walls can be seen in the gardens, and the Arabs built their Rosetta Gate there, most likely on the site of an older Hellenistic gate. But traces of an outer line of ancient fortification walls have been found a mile or so farther to the east, and there is an argument that it was this outer gate that was called the Gate of the Sun.

10　E. M. Forster, 'Alexandria Vignettes: Handel in Egypt', Egyptian Mail, 6 January 1918.

11　'Between the Sun and the Moon'.

12　E. M. Forster, 'A Musician in Egypt', Egyptian Mail, 21 October 1917.

13　EMF to Norman Douglas, 10 November, 1917, Letters, vol. 1, 275.

14 'The Poetry of C. P. Cavafy', 97.

15 'The Complete Poems of C. P. Cavafy', 234.

16 EMF to Robert Trevelyan, 23 August 1918, *Letters*, vol. 1, 294.

17 Liddell, *Cavafy*, 180.

18 Gaston Zananiri in conversation with the author. See also Liddell, *Cavafy*, 180.

19 Liddell, *Cavafy*, 163.

20 'The Poetry of C. P. Cavafy', 94.

21 In 1883–90 Sir Colin Scott-Moncrieff, an irrigation engineer who had worked on the vast canal system in northern India, comprehensively reorganised the irrigation system of Egypt. He divided Egypt into five circles of irrigation, two in the Nile Valley, three in the Delta, and he rebuilt Mohammed Ali's 1830s Delta Barrage and extensively recanalised the Delta, with the result that crop production, particularly cotton, increased phenomenally during the 1890s. The headquarters of the Irrigation Department was in Cairo, with the offices of the Third Circle of Irrigation devolved to Alexandria, which was immediately responsible for the western Delta, including El Beheira province, that is the 'lake province' (for Beheirat Mariut, Lake Mariut) lying west of the Rosetta arm of the Nile. The level of Lake Mariut was (and still is) controlled by a sluice opening onto the Mediterranean at Mex on the western outskirts of Alexandria.

22 The building once containing the offices of the Third Circle of Irrigation is now the Metropole Hotel near the Ramleh tram terminus. At street level is the Grand Trianon restaurant, café and patisserie, established during or just after the First World War.

23 The title has recently been restyled 'of Alexandria and all Africa', both forms recalling the title of the Roman 'Prefect of Alexandria and all Egypt' and the remark of Dio of Prusa, when visiting the city in the AD 70s, that Egypt was merely an 'appendage' of Alexandria (*Orations*, 32.36).

24 St Saba's was rebuilt in 1975, but the new church partly incorporates the old.

25 Liddell, *Cavafy*, 129.

26 *Cavafy: Collected Poems*, 34.

27 The Rue Missalla is now Sharia Safiya Zaghloul. The Café Al Salam is long gone. The Billiards Palace, on the west side of the street and towards its northern end, closed only in the early 1980s and was demolished in 1995. A shopping mall has been built in its place.

28 *Cavafy: Collected Poems*, 68.

29 'The Poetry of C. P. Cavafy', 91, 92.

30 The allusion is to the opening line of Cavafy's 'Exiles' written in 1914: 'It goes on being Alexandria still.' See *Cavafy: Collected Poems*, 146.

31 *Cavafy: Collected Poems*, 145. The title of the poem in Greek is 'Επάνοδος από τιν Ελλάδα', where 'επάνοδος' means not so much 'return' as 'going home', giving emphasis to the paradox that Hermippos and his friend, though Greek, are returning home from Greece.

32 Liddell, *Cavafy*, 30f.

33 Ibid., 99f.

34 The house in which Cavafy was born in the Rue Chérif Pasha was let to his family by the Zoghebs.

35 Liddell, *Cavafy*, 41.

36 Ibid., 123.

37 Ibid., 128.

38 To provide some flavour of the poems as Forster knew them, the translations of 'The God Abandons Antony' and 'Alexandrian Kings' in the previous chapter are by Valassopoulos.

39 George Valassopoulos to EMF, 2 February 1944. KCC.

40 Liddell, *Cavafy*, 168.

41 Ibid., 191.

42 *Cavafy: Collected Poems*, 59. 'Understanding', 'Tomb of Lanis' and 'Body, Remember . . .' were previously thought to have been published in January 1918 (see, for example, *Cavafy: Collected Poems* and Keeley, *Cavafy's Alexandria*). This was based on misinformation provided by George Savidis. But the author has been fortunate in seeing a copy of the October 1917 issue of *Grammata*.

43 For that matter Forster never told Cavafy about *Maurice*, writing to him in 1929, 'I quite forgot to tell you that I have written a novel . . . which cannot be published, and which I should like you to have seen.' See EMF to Constantine Cavafy, September 1929, in Pinchin, *Alexandria Still*, 141.

44 Keeley, *Cavafy's Alexandria*, 19.

45 *Cavafy: Collected Poems*, 22.

46 Ibid., 105.

47 Keeley, *Cavafy's Alexandria*, 18.

48 Ibid., 17.

49 *Cavafy: Collected Poems*, 122.

50 Ibid., 53.

51 'The Complete Poetry of C. P. Cavafy', 237.

52 EMF to Christopher Isherwood, 16 July 1933, *Letters*, vol. 2, 117.

53 E. M. Forster, 'T. S. Eliot', in *Abinger Harvest*, Harmondsworth 1967, 102.

54 *Letters*, vol. 1, xi.

55 *AHG*/1982, 35, 37.

56 EMF to Siegfried Sassoon, 2 May 1918, *Letters*, vol. 1, 289.

57 EMF to SS, 3 August 1918, *Letters*, vol. 1, 292.

58 Liddell, *Cavafy*, 186.

59 Alexander Kitroeff, *The Greeks in Egypt, 1919–1937: Ethnicity and Class*, Oxford 1989, 50.

60 EMF to Robert Trevelyan, 6 August 1917, *Letters*, vol. 1, 266.

61 E. M. Forster, 'Cnidus', in *Abinger Harvest*, 192.

62 EMF to FB, 31 July 1917, *Letters*, vol. 1, 264.

CHAPTER 3

If Love is Eternal

1 Private collection.

2 *AHG*/1982, 204f.

3 E. M. Forster, 'Alexandria Vignettes: The Solitary Place', *Egyptian Mail*, 10 March 1918; republished as 'The Solitary Place', in *Pharos and Pharillon*, 82.

4 Horace, *Odes*, I.37.

5 *AHG*/1982, 29.

6 Ibid., 30.

7 F. E. Adcock, *Greek and Macedonian Kingship*, London 1953, 171.

8 *AHG*/1982, 16.

9 EMF to FB, 18 February 1918, *Letters*, vol. 1, 286.

10 Quoted by Forster in EMF to FB, 23 March 1918, *Letters*, vol. 1, 288.

11 EMF to FB, 23 March 1918, *Letters*, vol. 1, 288.

12 Ibid.

13 EMF to FB, 11 October 1917, *Letters*, vol. 1, 274.

14 EMF to FB, 18 February 1918, *Letters*, vol. 1, 286.

15 EMF to FB, 14 May 1918, in Furbank, *E. M. Forster*, vol. 2, 49.

16 *AHG*/1982, xxxii.

17 EMF to his mother, 30 March 1918, *Letters*, vol. 1, 306.

18 D. H. Lawrence to EMF, 11 April 1923, in Pinchin, *Alexandria Still*, 153.

19 EMF to Robert Trevelyan, 23 August 1918, *Letters*, vol. 1, 294.

20 EMF to his mother, 4 November 1918, in Stape, *Chronology*, 65.

21 *AHG*/1982, xv.

22 Ibid., xxvi.

23 Ibid., 28.

24 *Clea*, AQ, 832.

25 EMF to FB, 16 July 1918, *Letters*, vol. 1, 290.

26 Ibid.

27 EMF to SS, 3 August 1918, *Letters*, vol. 1, 292.

28 EMF to Bertrand Russell, 12 February 1918, in Bertrand Russell, *Autobiography*, London 1968, vol. 2, 82.

29 EMF to SS, 2 May 1918, *Letters*, vol. 1, 289.

30 EMF to SS, 3 August 1918, *Letters*, vol. 1, 292. For Timothy the Cat, see E. M. Forster, 'Timothy the Cat and Timothy Whitebonnet', in *Pharos and Pharillon*. Each in turn was a fifth-century patriarch of Alexandria but the two held opposing views on the nature of Christ in the quarrel between monophysites and diophysites. For Plotinus, see below.

31 *AHG*/1982, 141.

32 Sir David Waley, *Edwin Montagu*, London 1964, 145.

33 *AHG*/1982, xxv.

34 Ibid., 64.

35 *Howards End*, 58f.

36 Ibid., 337.

37 *AHG*/1982, 84.

38 Ibid., 69.

39 Plotinus, in *AHG*/1982, 71f., translation by Stephen MacKenna.

40 *AHG*/1982, 204.

41 'Historia Monachorum', in *The Desert Fathers*, trans. Helen Waddell, London 1936, 79f.

42 Eusebius, *The History of the Church*, trans. G. A. Williamson, Harmondsworth 1965, 9.4, 338.

43 *AHG*/1982, 56.

44 Ibid., 79.

45 Ibid., 235.

46 Ibid., 79.

47 E. M. Forster, 'St Athanasius', in *Pharos and Pharillon*, 48.

48 Arius, a priest at St Mark's, had argued that as Christ was the Son of God, so there must have been a time when Christ was not. This endangered the unity of the godhead – the Father, the Son and the Holy Ghost – and opened the way to regarding Christ's nature as being not of the same substance as God's and, indeed, of his being inferior to God. Therefore in 325 the Council of Nicaea anathematised 'those who say that there was a time when the Son of God was not, and that he was not before he was begotten, and that he was made from that which did not exist; or who assert that he is of other substance or essence than the Father, or is susceptible of change'. Today Arianism survives among Unitarians.

49 *AHG*/1982, 61.

50 Ibid., 84.

51 Ibid., 61. Forster is quoting from Butler's *Arab Conquest of Egypt*; see note 52 below.

52 Forster read of Amr's letter to the caliph in Butler's *The Arab Conquest of Egypt*, where the point is made that the figures would be more accurate if divided by ten, and that their exaggeration indicates amazement rather than indifference. See Alfred J. Butler, *The Arab Conquest of Egypt*, Oxford 1978, 368.

53 *AHG*/1982, 62.

54 Mohammed el Adl to EMF, in Furbank, *E. M. Forster*, vol. 2, 50.

55 Mohammed el Adl to EMF, 2 October 1918, *Letters*, vol. 1, 298.

56 Forster, 'The Lost Guide'.

57 EMF to Jasper Y. Brinton, 5 February 1936. Private collection. Copyright, instead of remaining Forster's, was vested in Whitehead Morris. In exchange he would receive a royalty of 25 per cent of the cover price of the first thousand copies sold, yielding Forster LE62.50 (LE = *livre égyptienne*, or Egyptian pound, worth £1.05 sterling), some at least paid in advance of the sale of the books. On subsequent printings or revised editions he was to receive a royalty of 20 per cent, and this again was unusual as royalties normally start at about 10 per cent and increase with sales. The agreement would have made it hard for Whitehead Morris to show a profit on the first thousand copies and probably goes some way to explaining the subsequent curious history of Forster's *Alexandria*.

58 EMF to Laura Forster, 28 October 1918, in Stape, *Chronology*, 65.

59 EMF to Forrest Reid, 10 January 1919, *Letters*, vol. 1, 298.

60 Mohammed el Adl to EMF, in Furbank, *E. M. Forster*, vol. 2, 51.

61 Ibid.

62 EMF to FB, November 1918, *Letters*, vol. 1, 296.

63 EMF to FB, January 1919, *Letters*, vol. 1, 299.

64 The title of khedive was replaced by that of sultan in 1914, when Egypt's nominal subjection to the Ottoman Empire was abrogated and Britain established its Protectorate. Fuad, the son of the deposed Khedive Ismail, came to the throne as sultan in 1917.

65 Lord Cromer's farewell speech of 1907, in Hanna Wissa, *Assiout: The Saga of an Egyptian Family*, Lewes 1994, 200.

66 Grafftey-Smith, *Bright Levant*, 59.

67 *Manchester Guardian*, 29 March 1919, in Furbank, *E. M. Forster*, vol. 2, 58.

68 Quoted by Malcolm Darling to EMF, 11 July 1919, in Furbank, *E. M. Forster*, vol. 2, 61.

69 *Daily Herald*, 30 May 1919, in Furbank, *E. M. Forster*, vol. 2, 59. Winston Churchill, then secretary of state at the War Office, was giving British support to the White Russians in their attempt to overthrow Lenin's Bolshevik government. One of the few to favour a lenient peace with Germany, his policy was to 'Feed Germany; fight Bolshevism; make Germany fight Bolshevism'. Previously, as first lord of the admiralty, he had urged the Dardenelles campaign. Forster saw him as a cynical dealer in death and forever detested him above all politicians.

70 EMF to SS, May or June 1919, *Letters*, vol. 1, 302.

71 EMF to SRM, 29 December 1915, *Letters*, vol. 1, 232.

72 *AHG*/1982, 134.

73 Ibid., 177.

74 Forster's remark does a great injustice to St Mark's, which was built in 1845–54 by James Wild, who had already built the richly eclectic Christ Church, Brixton Hill, London (1839–41). Of his church in Alexandria, Wild said that though it 'agrees in plan and mass

with the style of art used by the early church
architects, it carries out a general sentiment
of Arabian detail' (Mark Crinson, 'Leading
into Captivity: James Wild and His Work in
Egypt', *Georgian Group Journal*, 1993, 62).
Forster seems to have had little appreciation
of Islamic or Eastern Christian architecture
and decoration, his own taste running to the
Renaissance, so that 'the finest building in
the city' (*AHG*/1982, 111), he said, was the
Banco di Roma in the Rue Chérif Pasha, a
modified copy of Rome's Palazzo Farnese
built by Michelangelo.

75 *AHG*/1982, 110.

76 EMF to G. H. Ludolf, 16 July 1919, *Letters*,
vol. 1, 304.

77 EMF to GHL, 10 October 1919, *Letters*, vol. 1,
306.

78 EMF to GHL, 16 July 1919, *Letters*, vol. 1, 304.

79 Mohammed el Adl to EMF, in Furbank,
E. M. Forster, vol. 2, 62.

80 Furbank, *E. M. Forster*, vol. 2, 63.

81 EMF to GHL, 10 October 1919, *Letters*, vol. 1,
306.

82 Ibid.

83 *AHG*/1982, 125f.

84 Peter Fraser, *Ptolemaic Alexandria*, Oxford
1972, vol. 1, 730.

85 *AHG*/1982, 32.

86 Ibid., 103f.

87 J. C. B. Richmond, *Egypt 1798–1952: Her
Advance towards a Modern Identity*, London
1977, 182f.

88 EMF to FB, 6 November 1919, *Letters*, vol. 1,
312.

89 EMF to FB, 10 November 1920, *Letters*, vol. 1,
317.

90 Labour Research Department, *The Government of Egypt*, London 1920.

91 Grafftey-Smith, *Bright Levant*, 76.

92 EMF to FB, 10 November 1920, *Letters*, vol. 1,
317.

93 EMF to Cavafy, 15 March 1921, in Pinchin,
Alexandria Still, 107.

94 EMF to FB, 20 May 1921, *Letters*, vol. 2, 6.

95 'Letter to Mohammed el Adl.'

96 EMF to FB, 17 March 1921, *Letters*, vol. 2, 2.

97 EMF to SRM, 16 May 1920, in Beauman,
Morgan, 311.

98 Lily Forster (mother) to EMF, *c.* 3 March
1921, in Furbank, *E. M. Forster*, vol. 2, 67.

99 E. M. Forster, 'Kanaya', unpublished MS, in

100 EMF to GLD, 6 August 1921, *Letters*, vol. 2,
10.

101 'Kanaya', in Beauman, *Morgan*, 315.

102 E. M. Forster, 'Reflections in India, 1: Too
Late?', *Nation and Athenaeum*, 21 January
1922.

103 Mohammed el Adl to EMF, *c.* September
1921, in Furbank, *E. M. Forster*, vol. 2, 85f.

104 'Letter to Mohammed el Adl'. Also in
Beauman, *Morgan*, 320.

105 EMF to his mother, 22 January 1922 (continuation of 19 January 1922), *Letters*, vol. 2,
18.

106 EMF to FB, 28 January 1922, *Letters*, vol. 2,
21.

107 EMF to GLD, 28 January 1922, in Furbank,
E. M. Forster, vol. 2, 103.

108 *AHG*/1982, 136.

109 Ibid., 209f. The assumption that Forster
visited Jennings Bramly's Burg el Arab in
1922 is based on the following. Jennings
Bramly himself said that the idea for a
carpet industry there came only in 1919
and that it was some months before the
first women were at work, which would
date the construction of the carpet factory
to some time after Forster's departure from
Egypt (*Wilfred Jennings Bramly, 1871–1960:
Memorabilia*, Cairo 1970, 17; see also 27).
From the description of Burg el Arab in
Forster's *Alexandria*, Anthony de Cosson,
who knew the settlement's history well,
assumed that Forster had been there in
1920, not before; also prior to its removal
to Burg el Arab there had been a small
carpet industry at Amriya, run by Nina
Baird until her death there in 1919 (see
Anthony de Cosson, *Mareotis*, London 1935,
129 and 146).

110 E. M. Forster, 'A Birth in the Desert', *Nation
and Athenaeum*, 8 November 1924.

111 'Letter to Mohammed el Adl.'

112 EMF to FB, 25 February 1922, *Letters*, vol. 2,
23.

113 *AHG*/1982, 103.

114 Ibid., xix.

115 EMF to Hilton Young, 15 February 1940,
Letters, vol. 2, 171.

116 Virginia Woolf, *Diary*, London 1977, vol. 2,
171.

117 Mohammed el Adl to EMF, March 1922, in

Furbank, *E. M. Forster*, vol. 2, 107.

118 Furbank, *E. M. Forster*, vol. 2, 108. See also *A Passage to India*, London 1924, 256, where later Forster, describing Fielding's thoughts at the death of Mrs Moore, wrote, 'It struck him that people are not really dead until they are felt to be dead. As long as there is some misunderstanding about them, they possess a sort of immortality. An experience of his own confirmed this. Many years ago he had lost a great friend, a woman, who believed in the Christian heaven, and assured him that after the changes and chances of this mortal life they would meet in it again. Fielding was a black, frank atheist, but he respected every opinion his friend held: to do this is essential in friendship. And it seemed to him for a time that the dead awaited him, and when the illusion faded it left behind it an emptiness that was almost guilt: "This is really the end", he thought, "and I gave her the final blow." '

119 EMF to GLD, 8 May 1922, *Letters*, vol. 2, 25.

120 Mohammed el Adl to EMF, 6 May 1922, in Furbank, *E. M. Forster*, vol. 2, 108.

121 Mohammed el Adl to EMF, 8 May 1922, in Furbank, *E. M. Forster*, vol. 2, 108.

122 EMF to his mother, 29 May 1922, *Letters*, vol. 2, 27.

123 Furbank, *E. M. Forster*, vol. 2, 109.

124 EMF to GHL, 13 July 1922, *Letters*, vol. 2, 42.

125 'Letter to Mohammed el Adl'.

126 *Cavafy: Collected Poems*, 86.

127 Egypt inherited the Capitulations (from the Latin 'capitula', meaning the heads or chapters of agreement) from the Ottoman Empire, where the system was introduced in the sixteenth century to encourage trade with Europe by exempting resident foreigners from the rigours of Islamic law and from local taxes, making them subject instead to their own consular authorities. In nineteenth- and twentieth-century Egypt there were fourteen Capitulatory powers: Belgium, Britain, Denmark, France, Greece, Holland, Italy, Portugal, Spain, Sweden, the United States, Austria, Germany and Russia – the last three losing their rights after the First World War. The system was reformed in 1875 by the creation of the Mixed Courts, in which foreign and Egyptian judges, following the Napoleonic Code, presided over civil cases involving foreigners of different nationalities or foreigners and Egyptians. In 1937 the Mixed Courts also assumed jurisdiction in criminal cases.

128 *Tachidromos*, 24 May 1921, in Kitroeff, *The Greeks in Egypt*, 45f.

129 Michael Salvagos to Allenby, 28 May 1921, in Kitroeff, *The Greeks in Egypt*, 46.

130 Grafftey-Smith, *Bright Levant*, 84.

131 EMF to Gerald Brenan, 27 March 1923, *Letters*, vol. 2, 36.

132 EMF to GHL, 27 January 1924, *Letters*, vol. 2, 46.

133 *The Times Literary Supplement*, 31 May 1923.

134 EMF to Cavafy, 5 July 1923, *Letters*, vol. 2, 40.

135 EMF to Christopher Plomer, 2 July 1945, *Letters*, vol. 2, 46.

136 'Letter to Mohammed el Adl'.

137 EMF to SS, 1 August 1923, *Letters*, vol. 2, 45.

138 EMF to Malcolm Darling, 10 May 1923, in Beauman, *Morgan*, 333f.

139 EMF to SS, 31 December 1923, in Furbank, *E. M. Forster*, vol. 2, 120.

140 *A Passage to India*, 324.

141 Virginia Woolf, *Diary*, 23 January 1924, vol. 2, 289.

142 EMF to Malcolm Darling, 15 September 1924, *Letters*, vol. 2, 63.

143 Stape, *Chronology*, 99, states that in mid-February 1928 Forster received £23 13s 10d for the destruction of 246 copies by fire. In 'The Lost Guide' Forster says that the first edition, printed in December 1922, amounted to a thousand copies. This appears to be corroborated by a letter from Whitehead Morris to Judge Jasper Brinton dated 29 February 1936, which refers to the first edition: 'Previously we used to get rid of these books at the rate of about 100 copies a year, and to re-print less than 1,000 copies would be obviously uneconomical.' Of the original thousand copies printed in December 1922, several hundred were probably sold in the first year, and if a hundred or so were sold in each following year that would account for the 246 remaining copies destroyed early in 1928.

144 'The Lost Guide'.

145 Furbank, *E. M. Forster*, vol. 2, 159.

146 EMF to Sebastian Sprott, 8 August 1929, *Letters*, vol. 2, 76.

147 EMF to FB, 26 December 1926, *Letters*, vol. 2, 74.

148 EMF interviewed by Rika Singopoulos in *Tachidromos*, 26 September 1929, in *Forster in Egypt*, ed. Hilda Spem and Abdel Moneim Aly, London 1987.

149 EMF to Joe Ackerley, 9 September 1929, in Furbank, *E. M. Forster*, vol. 2, 161.

150 EMF to Joe Ackerley, September 1929, in Furbank, *E. M. Forster*, vol. 2, 161.

151 Cavafy to EMF, 15 October 1929, in Pinchin, *Alexandria Still*, 140f.

152 'Letter to Mohammed el Adl'.

153 EMF to P. N. Furbank, 16 July 1958, *Letters*, vol. 2, 271.

154 EMF to William Plomer, 20 November 1963, *Letters*, vol. 2, 287. Presumably the exception was Bob Buckingham.

155 EMF to Leonard Woolf, 24 May 1936, *Letters*, vol. 2, 140.

CHAPTER 4
High Society: A History and a Guide

1 Typescript of an article written in 1972 by Nancy B. Turck for the *Philadelphia Bulletin*, based on an interview with Jasper Yeates Brinton; the article was presumably published in that same year. Private collection.

2 Jasper Yeates Brinton, 'East and Near East: Memoirs of a Philadelphia Lawyer', unpublished manuscript, XIV, 2. Private collection.

3 Whitehead Morris to JYB, 9 February 1936. Private collection.

4 Bob Buckingham to JYB, 13 March 1936. Private collection.

5 EMF to JYB, 24 March 1936. Private collection.

6 EMF to Leonard Woolf, 27 March 1936, *Letters*, vol. 2, 139.

7 E. M. Forster, 'The Menace to Freedom', in *Two Cheers*, 10f.

8 JYB to EMF, 28 April 1938. Private collection.

9 These and the following remarks are from J. M. Marshall's typed notes 'E. M. Forster: Alexandria, A History and a Guide', where Forster's comments are written in the margins. Private collection.

10 *AHG*/1982, 112.

11 EMF to JYB, 11 June 1936. Private collection.

12 *AHG*/1982, 61.

13 Marshall first refers to *The Arab Conquest of Egypt* by A. J. Butler, listed by Forster among his authorities in his *Alexandria*, and then quotes from Breccia's *Alexandrea ad Aegyptum*, 29f., and from Forster's *Alexandria*, *AHG*/1982, 62.

14 *AHG*/1982, 32.

15 *AHG*/1938, 69, repeated from *AHG*/1982, 84.

16 *AHG*/1982, 84.

17 Ibid., 33.

18 Ibid., 103.

19 JYB, 'Memoirs', IX, 2.

20 Ibid.

21 JYB, 'Memoirs', II, 13.

22 Ibid., VI, 17.

23 Ibid.

24 Turck, typescript for *Philadelphia Bulletin* article.

25 Jasper Yeates Brinton, diary, 22 November 1926. Private collection.

26 John Brinton, 'Stanley Bay', unpublished memoir. Private collection.

27 JYB, 'Memoirs', XII, 16ff.

28 Ibid., XI, 22.

29 JYB to his mother, 11 February 1922. Private collection.

30 JYB, diary, 4 December 1926.

31 Grafftey-Smith, *Bright Levant*, 80.

32 JYB, 'Memoirs', XIV, 24.

33 JYB, diary, 14 November 1926.

34 Ibid., 13 November 1926.

35 Ibid., 17 November 1926.

36 Jasper Yeates Brinton, untitled notebook containing notes for 'Memoirs', 42. Private collection.

37 JYB, diary, 30 October 1926.

38 Ibid., 11 January 1927.

39 Ibid., 18 October 1926.

40 Ibid., 22 November 1926.

41 The Royal Institute of International Affairs, Information Department Papers No. 19, *Great Britain and Egypt 1914–1936*, London 1936, 14.

42 Grafftey-Smith, *Bright Levant*, 104.

43 JYB, 'Memoirs', XI, 21.

44 JYB, diary, 3 November 1926, 21 December 1926, 4 November 1926.

45 Ibid., 9 January 1927.

46 Ibid., 21 November 1926.

47 JYB, untitled notebook, 30.

48 Ibid.

49 JYB, diary, 18 November 1926.

50 Ibid., 30 January 1927.

51 Ibid., 18 November 1926.

52 Ibid.

53 JYB, diary, 29 November 1926.

54 Kitroeff, *The Greeks in Egypt*, 171.

55 Liddell, *Cavafy*, 184.

56 Ibid., 203.

57 Photograph. Marta Loria Fuller collection.

58 JYB, diary, 29 December 1926.

59 Ibid., 21 January 1927.

60 Grafftey-Smith, *Bright Levant*, 15.

61 LD to Alan Thomas, postmark 21 May 1957. British Library.

62 JYB, untitled notebook, 30.

63 JYB, 'Memoirs', XI, 8.

64 T. S. Eliot to Jean de Menasce, 11 November 1942. Private collection.

65 Obituary of Felix de Menasce, *Jewish Chronicle*, 3 September 1943.

66 Gudrun Krämer, *The Jews in Modern Egypt, 1914–1952*, Seattle 1989, 190.

67 Fernand Braudel, *The Mediterranean and the Mediterranean World in the Age of Philip II*, London 1973, vol. 2, 819.

68 Virtually the whole of Egypt's railway system was financed by four Sephardi families, the Menasces, the Rolos, the Suareses and the Cattaouis, the first two associated with Alexandria, the third with both Alexandria and Cairo, the last mostly with Cairo. The one significant exception was the line between Alexandria and Cairo, which was paid for by the Khedive Abbas. The first railway line in the Middle East, it was constructed in 1851–4 (as was the Alexandria railway station, still standing in Forster's time) by Robert Stephenson, son of George Stephenson, the inventor of the Rocket, the world's first steam locomotive.

69 Krämer, *The Jews in Modern Egypt*, 79.

70 Jehuda Reinharz, *Chaim Weizmann: The Making of a Statesman*, Oxford 1993, 19.

71 Benjamin Disraeli's background was similar to that of many Alexandrian Jews: his grandfather, Benjamin D'Israeli, was born at Cento, near Ferrara, but instead of going to Egypt he left Italy for London in 1748, where he became a successful businessman and member of the Stock Exchange.

72 Reinharz, *Weizmann*, 19.

73 Ibid., 30.

74 Krämer, *The Jews in Modern Egypt*, 279.

75 Reinharz, *Weizmann*, 252.

76 Ibid.

77 Ibid., 257.

78 Ronald Storrs, *Orientations*, London 1945, 366.

79 Samir Raafat, *Maadi 1904–1962: Society and History in a Cairo Suburb*, Cairo 1994, 65.

80 In 1924–5 Jean de Menasce was employed by Chaim Weizmann at the Zionist Organisation's Geneva bureau.

81 Jacques Mawas, son of Denise and grandson of Rosette de Menasce, in conversation with the author.

82 Chaim Weizmann, *The Letters and Papers of Chaim Weizmann*, ed. Barnet Litvinoff, Jerusalem 1977, vol. 12, series A, 240.

83 Weizmann, *Letters*, vol. 16, series A, 448. In addition to his political activities, Chaim Weizmann was a noted chemist and the driving force behind the founding in 1934 of what since 1949 has been called the Weizmann Institute of Science at Rehovot, fourteen miles south of Tel Aviv.

84 Letter from Eric Vincendon, brother of Claude Vincendon, to the author, 10 July 1995.

85 Claude (Vincendon), *Mrs O'*, London 1957. Claude wrote under her first name only.

86 London's Hotel Cecil, larger even than the Savoy, was built in the Strand in the 1890s on land that had recently been sold by Lord Salisbury, the prime minister, whose family name was Cecil.

87 LD in Paul Hogarth, *The Mediterranean Shore: Travels in Lawrence Durrell Country*, London 1988, 58.

88 *Mountolive*, AQ, 550.

89 *Justine*, AQ, 31f.

90 Gaston Zananiri, *Rythmes disperses*, Cairo 1932. These lines are translated from the French by Hala Halim in her article on Zananiri, 'In the Absence of Regret', in *Al Ahram Weekly* 265, 21–7 March 1996, ii.

91 Nagui's *School of Alexandria* now hangs in the main meeting hall of the Governorate of Alexandria on Sharia Mohafza at the corner of Sharia Abu el Dardaa.

92 Taha Hussein, the first Egyptian to be nominated for the Nobel Prize, was head of the faculty of arts at Fuad University in Cairo when Robin Furness was professor of English there.

93 The Atelier opened in 1935 in the Rue Missalla, on the site of the present-day Metro cinema in the renamed Sharia Safiya Zaghloul, but very soon moved to 2 Rue St Saba, on the east side of the street at the corner of the Rue Fuad, so that its façade along the Rue Fuad stood directly opposite Pastroudis. After the war it migrated east along the Rue Fuad to the corner of the Rue du Musée (the street of the Graeco-Roman Museum). Since 1956 it has occupied the 'Palais Karam', once the home of the Syro-Lebanese Karam family at the corner of the Rue des Pharaons and the Rue de Corinthe (the latter now called the Rue Victor Bassili) in the Quartier Grec.

94 John Brinton, 'Burg el Arab', unpublished memoir. Private collection.

95 Forster, 'A Birth in the Desert'.

96 JYB, 'Memoirs', XI, 33.

97 'A Birth in the Desert'.

98 *AHG*/1938, iv.

99 JYB, 'Memoirs', XI, 36.

100 Vivien Jennings Bramly to Geneva Brinton, undated except for 'Tuesday', but *c.* early 1937. This and Vivien Jennings Bramly's following letters are from a private collection.

101 *Mountolive, AQ*, 599.

102 Krämer, *The Jews in Modern Egypt*, 125.

103 Ibid., 231.

104 Lord Killearn (Miles Lampson), *The Killearn Diaries 1934–1946*, ed. Trefor E. Evans, London 1972, 6 May 1936.

105 Grafftey-Smith, *Bright Levant*, 138.

106 JYB, 'Memoirs', XI, 17f.

107 VJB to Geneva Brinton, undated except for 'Wednesday', but *c.* early 1937.

108 *AHG*/1982, 115.

109 VJB to Geneva Brinton, undated except for 'Monday – no Tuesday!', but *c.* first half of 1937.

110 VJB to JYB, undated except for 'Monday', but *c.* first half of 1937.

111 VJB to Geneva Brinton, undated except for 'Wednesday', but *c.* first half of 1937.

112 VJB to John Brinton, 21 July 1937.

113 John Brinton, 'Stanley Bay'.

114 Josie Brinton to her mother, 27 February 1937. This and Josie Brinton's following letters are from a private collection.

115 Josie Brinton to her mother, 3 March 1937.

116 Josie Brinton to her mother, 8 March 1937.

117 Josie Brinton to her mother, 20 March 1937.

118 Josie Brinton to her mother, 8 March 1937.

119 Josie Brinton to her mother, 21 May 1937.

120 Josie Brinton to her mother, 12 April 1937.

121 JYB, 'Memoirs', XI, 5.

122 Josie Brinton to her mother, 3 March 1937. Finney's Marlborough tapestries are now in the Victoria and Albert Museum, London.

123 Count Patrice de Zogheb, *Alexandria Memories*, Alexandria 1949, 39.

124 Josie Brinton to her mother, 3 December 1937.

125 Daphne du Maurier, *The Rebecca Notebook and Other Memories*, London 1981, 12f.

126 Josie Brinton to her mother, 8 March 1937.

127 Josie Brinton to her grandmother, 10 April 1937.

128 Draft letter from John Brinton to EMF, *c.* 1961. Private collection.

129 William Walker of Whitehead Morris to JYB, 26 November 1936. Private collection.

130 EMF to JYB, 5 March 1937. Private collection.

131 Draft letter from JYB to William Walker, 8 April 1937. Private collection.

132 EMF to JYB, 23 April 1937. Private collection.

133 EMF to William Walker, 23 April 1937 (carbon). Private collection.

134 JYB to EMF, 28 April 1938. Private collection.

135 Evelyn Waugh, *Officers and Gentlemen*, Harmondsworth 1964, 126f.

CHAPTER 5
Mixed Doubles as Usual

1 Undated article clipped from the *Egyptian Gazette* and held in the Forster archives at KCC. It is probably from December 1938, when the second edition of *Alexandria* was published, but as no archive copies of the newspaper have been found for late 1938 or early 1939, it has not been possible to date the article precisely.

2 Rudolf Hess to his mother, 1951, in Peter Padfield, *Hess: Flight for the Führer*, London 1991, 3.

3 JYB, 'Memoirs', XIII, 3f.

4 Josie Brinton to her mother, 14 June 1940.

5 Josie Brinton, diary, 14 June 1940.

6 JYB, 'Memoirs', alternative version of chapter XIII (marked 'not for publication'), 4f.

7 JYB, diary, 20 June 1940.

8 Josie Brinton, diary, 16 June 1940.

9 Ibid., 14 February 1940.

10 Ibid., 16 June 1940.

11 Ibid., 21 August 1940.

12 *A Bank in Battledress: Being the Story of Barclays Bank (Dominion, Colonial and Overseas) during the Second World War 1939-45*, no author, 'for private circulation', [London] 1948, 117.

13 Josie Brinton, diary, 8 June 1940.

14 JYB, diary, 18 June 1940.

15 Ibid., 30 June 1940.

16 In fact one battleship, four cruisers and three destroyers.

17 *Clea, AQ*, 677.

18 JYB, diary, 23 June 1940.

19 Ibid., 27 June 1940.

20 Martin Gilbert, *Churchill: A Life*, London 1991, 667.

21 *Clea, AQ*, 817.

22 Artemis Cooper, *Cairo in the War, 1939-1945*, London 1989, 53.

23 JYB, 'Memoirs', alternative XIII, 1.

24 Josie Brinton, diary, 13 July 1940.

25 Josie Brinton to her mother, 5 September 1940.

26 Josie Brinton, diary, 8 September 1940.

27 Ibid., 11 September 1940.

28 Gilbert, *Churchill*, 675–7.

29 JYB, diary, 13 September 1940.

30 Josie Brinton to her mother, 2 October 1940.

31 JYB, diary, 23 October 1940.

32 Eden was Churchill's secretary of state for war at this time; he soon after became foreign secretary again.

33 Gilbert, *Churchill*, 692.

34 Ibid., 646.

35 EMF to Christopher Isherwood, 16 July 1933, *Letters*, vol. 2, 117.

36 Josie Brinton, diary, 11 November 1940.

37 Ibid., 22 November 1940.

38 Ibid., 7 December 1940.

39 Jean Lugol, *Egypt and World War II*, Cairo 1945, 136f.

40 JYB, 'Memoirs', alternative XIII, 13.

41 Ibid., 6.

42 *Egyptian Gazette*, 11 June 1942.

43 The Karam 'palace' is now the home of the Atelier; the Rue de Corinthe has been renamed the Rue Victor Bassili.

44 Josie Brinton, diary, 20 November 1940.

45 JYB, 'Memoirs', alternative XIII, 7.

46 JYB, diary, 10 November 1940.

47 JYB, 'Memoirs', alternative XIII, 7.

48 Claude (Vincendon), *The Rum Go*, London 1958, 56.

49 Jacqueline Carol (Jacqueline Klat), *Cocktails and Camels*, New York 1960, 36.

50 Josie Brinton to her mother, 2 October 1940.

51 JYB, 'Memoirs', alternative XIII, 9.

52 Josie Brinton, diary, 14 December 1940.

53 Inscription by an unidentified serviceman in Geneva Brinton's 'War Chronicles', her Alexandria guest book cum diary, 27 January 1941. Private collection.

54 Rowland Langmaid, *'The Med': The Royal Navy in the Mediterranean, 1939-45*, London 1948, 49. Churchill addressed the Commons on 9 April 1941.

55 *Schindler's Guide to Alexandria*, Cairo 1943, 91.

56 Robert Crisp, *The Gods Were Neutral*, London 1960, 17ff.

57 *Schindler's Guide*, 88.

58 *Justine, AQ*, 47.

59 *The Guinness Book of Records*, London 1997, describes Robert Crisp as 'the only cricketer to have taken four wickets with consecutive balls more than once'. For his part in Operation Crusader against Rommel in November–December 1941 Crisp was decorated with the Military Cross.

60 Crisp, *The Gods Were Neutral*, 15ff.

61 Langmaid, *'The Med'*, 51f.

62 Crisp, *The Gods Were Neutral*, 209.

63 Fuller, *Decisive Battles*, vol. 2, 457.

64 'List of Personalities in Egypt', from Sir Miles Lampson to Anthony Eden, 22 July 1941, 65, Foreign Office file 1941: J2624/18/16: FO 371 27432. Public Record Office.

65 JYB, 'Memoirs', alternative XIII, 25f.

66 Ibid., 24ff.

67 John Cromer Braun, 'Lawrence Durrell's Arrival at Alexandria', in *Return to Oasis*, ed. Victor Selwyn et al., London 1980, xxviiiff.

68 Lawrence Durrell, *Spirit of Place*, ed. Alan G. Thomas, London 1971, 28.

69 This and John Cromer Braun's following remarks are from a conversation with the author.

70 LD interviewed by Ahmed Loutfi in *Le Progrès égyptien*, 1 November 1977.

71 Gerald Durrell, *My Family and Other Animals*, Harmondsworth 1959, 74.

72 George Seferis to HM, 25 December 1941, *Labrys* 5, July 1979, 83.

73 Theodore Stephanides, memoir of meetings with LD at Corfu, Athens, Cairo and Alexandria. British Library.

74 Marc Alyn, *The Big Supposer: Lawrence Durrell, a Dialogue with Marc Alyn*, London 1973, 55.

75 Stephanides, memoir.

76 Ibid.

77 LD to HM, 13 March 1941, in *DML*, 147.

78 LD to HM, before 13 February 1941, in *DML*, 144.

CHAPTER 6
Personal Landscape

1 Open letter from LD to George Seferis, *La Semaine égyptienne*, 28 October 1941, quoted in a letter from Seferis to HM, 25 December 1941, *Labrys* 5, July 1979, 82.

2 Lawrence Durrell, *Prospero's Cell*, London 1962, 131.

3 Rommel to his wife, 30 June 1942, in Erwin Rommel, *The Rommel Papers*, ed. Basil Liddell Hart, London 1953, 241.

4 Gilbert, *Churchill*, 709.

5 Killearn, *Diaries*, 27 January 1942.

6 *A Bank in Battledress*, 120f.

7 Ibid., 118f.

8 Countess Mary de Zogheb, unpublished diary, 29 June 1942. Private collection. Wrens: members of the Women's Royal Navy Service.

9 Ibid., 30 June 1942.

10 Cecil Beaton, *Near East*, London 1943, 133.

11 Ibid., 127.

12 JYB, diary, 30 June 1942.

13 JYB, 'Memoirs', alternative XIII, 35.

14 Jasper Yeates Brinton, 'Some Recent Discoveries at el-Alamein', *Bulletin de la Société Royale d'Archéologie d'Alexandrie* 35, 1942.

15 JYB, diary, 30 June 1942.

16 Lawrence Durrell, *Blue Thirst*, Santa Barbara 1975, 50.

17 Rommel to his wife, 4 and 5 July 1942, in *The Rommel Papers*, 249f.

18 Mary de Zogheb, diary, 5 July 1942.

19 *Justine, AQ*, 87.

20 Letter from Mary Bentley Honor to the author, 16 October 2003.

21 Grafftey-Smith, *Bright Levant*, 228.

22 LD to Anne Ridler, 1942, in *Spirit of Place*, 75.

23 Lawrence Durrell, *Collected Poems, 1931–1974*, London 1985, 103.

24 Basil Liddell Hart, *History of the Second World War*, London 1970, 290.

25 Gilbert, *Churchill*, 726.

26 The minister of state for the Middle East, based in Cairo, was appointed by the war cabinet in London, his function to regulate the often conflicting priorities of the various British ambassadors and military commanders in the region.

27 The above account has been assembled from the *Egyptian Gazette*, 28 August 1942, Geneva Brinton's 'War Chronicles' and JYB's 'Memoirs', alternative XIII, 33f.

28 Rommel to his wife, 30 August 1942, in *The Rommel Papers*, 275.

29 *AHG*/1982, xix.

30 *Mountolive, AQ*, 482.

31 *Balthazar, AQ*, 314.

32 *AHG*/1982, xvi.

33 Ibid., xix.

34 Penelope Durrell Hope recalling her mother's memories in *Lawrence Durrell*, a BBC2 *Bookmark* programme, 15 August 1998.

35 *Collected Poems*, 25.

36 Lawrence Durrell, untitled 'Bloomsbury' notebook dated 1938. British Library.

37 Margaret Bourke-White, *Interview with India*, London 1950, 81.

38 Lawrence Durrell, *Pied Piper of Lovers*, London 1935, 230.

39 *The Big Supposer*, 24.

40 A 'letter' sent in booklet form from LD to Alan Thomas, 31 January 1957, 'Alan Thomas, Hys Booke from Larry Durrell 1957'. British Library.

41 Ibid.

42 'Cities, Plains and People', in *Collected Poems*, 158.

43 *The Big Supposer*, 25.

44 *Spirit of Place*, 15.

45 'Alan Thomas, Hys Booke from Larry Durrell'.

46 *The Big Supposer*, 25f.

47 Observation made by Eve Durrell to the author; see also Douglas Botting, *Gerald Durrell: The Authorised Biography*, London 1999, 6.

48 LD quoted in Botting, *Gerald Durrell*, 73.
49 *Blue Thirst*, 22.
50 Ibid., 34.
51 Ibid.
52 LD to Anne Ridler, late October 1939, in *Spirit of Place*, 61.
53 The exception is Durrell's first and highly autobiographical novel, *Pied Piper of Lovers*, published in 1935 and written before he had gone to Corfu, in which Indians are reduced to caricatures while India itself serves largely as the landscape of childhood's idyll. Durrell felt it had no literary merit and never allowed its republication; instead he regarded *The Black Book* as his true beginning as a novelist.
54 *The Big Supposer*, 125.
55 Gwyn Williams, *ABC of (D)GW*, Llandysul 1981, 86.
56 *AHG*/1982, xix.
57 Ibid., xviii.
58 Stephanides, memoir.
59 Letter from LD to the author, 17 February 1982.
60 Quoted in an article from an unidentified French magazine sent by LD to the author, 17 February 1982, with the remark 'The vulgar press has started to stir up the Alexandrian puddle with romantic articles – three this month of which I enclose the latest. Actually the most accurate.'
61 Killearn, *Diaries*, 24 October 1942.
62 W. E. Benyon-Tinker, *Dust upon the Sea*, London 1947, 202.
63 *Clea, AQ*, 732.
64 Williams, *ABC*, 62.
65 *Clea, AQ*, 732.
66 Rommel to his wife, 3 November 1942, in *The Rommel Papers*, 320.
67 *Egyptian Gazette*, 5 November 1942.
68 *The Rommel Papers*, 302.
69 Gilbert, *Churchill*, 734.
70 *The Big Supposer*, 60.
71 HM to LD, 1 September 1935, *DML*, 3.
72 *Blue Thirst*, 16f.
73 Lawrence Durrell, *The Black Book*, London 1977, 21.
74 HM to LD, 8 March 1937, *DML*, 56.
75 HM to LD, 13 March 1937, *DML*, 58.
76 HM to LD, 15 September 1942, *DML*, 153.
77 George Seferiades, who wrote under the name George Seferis, was awarded the Nobel Prize for Literature in 1963.
78 George Seferis, *On the Greek Style*, London 1967, 126.
79 Liddell, *Cavafy*, 204.
80 LD in conversation with the author.
81 Philip Sherrard, *The Marble Threshing Floor: Studies in Modern Greek Poetry*, London 1956, 73.
82 Ibid.
83 Ibid., 40.
84 *The Black Book*, 9.
85 LD to HM, late March 1937, *DML*, 63.
86 LD to HM, 21 July 1937, *DML*, 80. The Book of Miracles, later called the Book of Time, would eventually emerge between 1974 and 1985 as *The Avignon Quintet*.
87 HM to LD, 21 November 1942, *DML*, 156.
88 *AHG*/1982, xvii.
89 Williams, *ABC*, 86.
90 Ibid., 83.
91 Ibid., 87.
92 Ibid., 31.
93 *AHG*/1982, xvii.
94 Grafftey-Smith, *Bright Levant*, 134.
95 Thus Robert Liddell in *Cavafy*, 180, records the visit of '"an important English Sir" (unidentified)'; in a letter to the author dated 10 February 1987 Liddell wrote, 'I have since been told (I forget by whom) that this was my old friend Sir Walter Smart. This is most likely.'
96 Liddell, *Cavafy*, 210.
97 Seferis, *On the Greek Style*, 127.
98 Ibid., 130.
99 Liddell, *Cavafy*, 118.
100 Ibid., 211.
101 Ibid., 205.
102 Robert Liddell, 'Cavafy', essay first published in *Personal Landscape* magazine, reprinted in *Personal Landscape: An Anthology of Exile*, ed. Robin Fedden et al., London 1945, 106. *Balthazar, AQ*, 338.
103 *AHG*/1982, xvif. Durrell wrote 'Petrides' but meant 'Perides'. Paul Petrides was a doctor and indeed another friend of Cavafy's but not one who wrote a book about him. This is clearly an error for 'Michael Perides', whose book on Cavafy was published in Athens in 1948.
104 Letter from Bernard de Zogheb to the author, 1 March 1999: 'Robert Liddell told me that Durrell at one point lived at

Anfouchy – on the sea front – but when? and for how long? – God only knows.' Liddell and Zogheb were very close friends; Liddell dedicated his *Cavafy: A Critical Biography* 'à Bernard de Zogheb et aux autres amis alexandrins'.

105 *Justine, AQ*, 41ff.

106 *Mountolive, AQ*, 623ff.

107 *Balthazar, AQ*, 226.

108 LD in *Bimbashi McPherson: A Life in Egypt*, ed. Barry Carman and John McPherson, London 1983, 7.

109 *Justine, AQ*, 104.

110 Ibid., 105.

111 Ian MacNiven, *Lawrence Durrell: A Biography*, London 1998, 269.

112 *Collected Poems*, 154.

113 *Egyptian Gazette*, 8 April 1943.

114 *Justine, AQ*, 84f.

115 Open letter from LD to George Seferis, *La Semaine égyptienne*, 28 October 1941, quoted in a letter from Seferis to HM, 25 December 1941, *Labrys* 5, July 1979, 82.

116 George Seferis, 'The Greek Poems of Lawrence Durrell', *Labrys* 5, July 1979, 85.

117 George Seferis to HM, 25 December 1941, *Labrys* 5, July 1979, 82.

118 Seferis, 'The Greek Poems of Lawrence Durrell', 88.

119 *Collected Poems*, 99.

120 Seferis, 'The Greek Poems of Lawrence Durrell', 88.

121 Neither Anfushi nor 40 Rue Fuad are mentioned by Durrell's biographer, Ian Mac-Niven, who instead has him living at 11 bis (now 14) Rue des Pharaons in the Quartier Grec, a building then and now of expensive and enormous apartments, eight rooms or more. But MacNiven is uncertain from whom he obtained his information, while the evidence for 40 Rue Fuad is incontrovertible: Eve Durrell took the author to the place, and Paul Gotch, who together with his wife lived there with Durrell and Eve, has a captioned photograph of the building. Neither Gotch nor Eve knows anything about Durrell living in the Rue des Pharaons, nor for that matter about him living in Anfushi, which would have been before they knew him in Alexandria. The sole source for Anfushi is Liddell, who told Bernard de Zogheb; both are now dead.

CHAPTER 7
Mirrors

1 *Justine, AQ*, 82.

2 Baudrot stood at 2 Rue Fuad on the corner of the Rue Chérif Pasha, directly opposite the Mohammed Ali Club; it has since been converted to an office, and renumbered and renamed 1 Sharia Horreya.

3 The entrance to the Atelier was at 2 Rue St Saba, but the building (since replaced by another) flanked the Rue Fuad.

4 *Schindler's Guide*, 17.

5 Rosie Israel, 'Histoire de la famille de Maman', unpublished genealogy of the Cohen-Arazi and Palacci-Miram families, 1996. Private collection. Rosie Israel, née Cohen, is the daughter of Nessim Cohen-Arazi and Ventura Palacci-Miram, and is a cousin of Eve Durrell.

6 Ibid.

7 *Justine, AQ*, 57.

8 Lawrence Durrell, 'Notes for Alex', 9. British Library. A notebook begun in 1944, possibly incorporating notes from 1943. British Library pagination.

9 Ibid., 6.

10 Melanie's niece, Naomi 'Moughee' Athanassian, in conversation with the author and Eve Durrell.

11 Archives of the Greek Community of Alexandria, biographies file, quoted in Kitroeff, *The Greeks in Egypt*, 153.

12 *Justine, AQ*, 186.

13 Ibid., 188.

14 Ibid., 54f.

15 JYB, 'Memoirs', XI, 14ff.

16 Alice Brinton, daughter of John and Josie Brinton, in conversation with the author.

17 Cooper, *Cairo in the War*, 243.

18 Killearn, *Diaries*, 4 February 1942.

19 Draft of telegram sent on 24 October 1941 from the war cabinet, London, to Sir Miles Lampson, Cairo, signed 'AE' (i.e. Anthony Eden), Foreign Office files. Public Record Office.

20 Sir Miles Lampson to Lancelot Oliphant, deputy under-secretary of state, Foreign Office, 6 January 1939, in Janice J. Terry, *The Wafd: 1919–1952*, London 1982, 242.

21 Unpublished diary entry, 30 May 1940, in Cooper, *Cairo in the War*, 296.

22 Richmond, *Egypt 1798–1952*, 218.

23 The Gotches moved from Tanta to Alexandria on 28 June 1943 according to the caption accompanying a photograph of 40 Rue Fuad in Paul Gotch's photograph album of that time.

24 Lawrence Durrell, 'Imbecility File – This Egypt', scrapbook. British Library.

25 T. S. Eliot, *The Waste Land*, London 1922, lines 43 and 46; lines 372–7.

26 *Justine*, *AQ*, 126.

27 *Clea*, *AQ*, 700.

28 Ibid., 702.

29 LD to HM, probably mid-July 1944, *DML*, 167. The letter is undated and in *DML* is dated by the editor as mid-May, continued late May 1944, but this second half of the letter may well date from as late as 11–25 July.

30 Ibid.

31 *Collected Poems*, 115.

32 *Justine*, *AQ*, 197.

33 Sir John Pentland Mahaffy (1839–1919) of Trinity College, Dublin, was author of *The Empire of the Ptolemies*, 1895. This was among the works Cavafy kept in his personal library.

34 *Justine*, *AQ*, 79.

35 Ibid., 80.

36 Ibid., 18.

37 Krämer, *The Jews in Modern Egypt*, 146.

38 B. L. Carter, *The Copts in Egyptian Politics 1918–1952*, Cairo 1988, 109.

39 Michael M. Laskier, *The Jews of Egypt, 1920–1970*, New York 1992, 48.

40 George Antonius to Walter Rogers, 24 August 1938. Archives of the Institute for Current World Affairs, Hanover, New Hampshire. Quoted in an unpublished paper by Professor William Cleveland of Simon Fraser University, British Columbia, 'George Antonius and the Making of *The Arab Awakening*', 26.

41 *Mountolive*, *AQ*, 553.

42 Sir Miles Lampson was made a baron in the New Year's Honours List of 1 January 1943, largely in reward for his Abdin Palace coup, and took the title Lord Killearn of Killearn after his birthplace in Scotland.

43 Killearn, *Diaries*, 26 January 1943.

44 Churchill's address to the Joint Session of Congress in Washington, 19 May 1943, in Langmaid, 'The Med', 79.

45 Langmaid, 'The Med', 101.

46 Williams, *ABC*, 31. Williams is wrong about George de Menasce's 'Wednesday afternoons', which were actually on Sundays and Tuesdays. See following chapter.

47 Gwyn Williams, 'Durrell in Egypt', *Twentieth Century Literature* 33:3, fall 1987, 301. Williams is referring to Gaston Zananiri, Clea Badaro, George de Menasce, Count Patrice de Zogheb and Michael Perides, who have already been identified in these pages. Carlo ('Joe') Suares appears later. Of the others less is known. Clement Barber, manager of the British Government Cotton Buying Commission, and his wife Margot promoted madrigal singing. Naguib (better known as Costa) Baladi was a philosopher; for him and his French wife jazz was a religion. Marcel Salinas was artistically linked with Paris; his wife Wanda later became a novelist. Jacques Fumaroli, a Corsican, was a director of financial and textile companies. Papassinessiou, if Emmanuel, was a *commerçant*. Sachs, if Freddy, was a *rentier*; if David, a banker; David died during the war and was married to Linda, a beautiful and cultured woman. Ivan Oumoff was the White Russian consul and was known as a dreamer with the heart of a child; he married an ugly but very rich Syro-Lebanese and raised a musical family. Barukh is known only to have been an *homme d'affaires*. Of Kerekreti nothing is known; he may be Bereketi who moved in Greek circles and whose daughter married first Cyril Sursock and then Prince Sadruddin Aga Khan.

CHAPTER 8
Prospero's Tower

1 LD to Diana Gould in Naples, postmark 27 April 1944. British Library.

2 Noël Coward, *Middle East Diary*, London 1944, 57.

3 *Blue Thirst*, 41.

4 Killearn, *Diaries*, 18 August 1943.

5 John Simpson, 'Noel Coward Was a Spy, Too', *Spectator*, 17–24 December 1994.

6 Coward, *Middle East Diary*, 92f.

7 Ibid., 91f.

8 By the summer of 1943 the British and American governments were well aware of the Nazis' 'final solution' but believed that their best course was to win the war as quickly as possible and meanwhile not to arouse public criticism for failing to take specific and probably impracticable action against the genocide. The suppression of information ceased only in 1944.

9 In Paul Gotch's photograph album of the time, the caption reads: 'Move from 40 Fouad-el-Awal [Fuad the First] to 17 Maamoun – Moharrem Bey October 1st 1943.'

10 LD to HM, *c.* 25 December 1943, *DML*, 159.

11 LD to HM, 23 May 1944, *DML*, 171.

12 *Balthazar, AQ*, 234 and 365.

13 Ibid., 365.

14 Ibid., 234f.

15 JYB, diary, 30 October 1926.

16 MacNiven, *Lawrence Durrell*, 283.

17 *Justine, AQ*, 107.

18 Much of the biographical information on Clea Badaro is taken from the book by her sister, Jeanne Engalytcheff-Badaro, *Clea Badaro, 1913–1968: Sa vie, son oeuvre*, Alexandria 1978.

19 *Justine, AQ*, 197.

20 *Balthazar, AQ*, 371.

21 *Justine, AQ*, 199.

22 'Notes for Alex', 37.

23 LD to HM, mid-January 1937, *DML*, 42.

24 *Justine, AQ*, 108.

25 Charles Gibson Cowan, *The Voyage of the Evelyn Hope*, London 1946, 83.

26 Artemis Cooper, *Writing at the Kitchen Table: The Authorised Biography of Elizabeth David*, London 1999, 87.

27 LD in conversation with the author.

28 Henry Romilly (Robin) Fedden, 'A Study of the Monastery of St Anthony in the Eastern Desert', *University of Egypt, Faculty of Arts Bulletin* 5, 1937.

29 Henry Romilly (Robin) Fedden, *Suicide: A Social and Historical Study*, London 1938.

30 Robin Fedden, *Personal Landscape* (an account of the genesis of the wartime magazine *Personal Landscape*), London 1966, 5.

31 Fedden, *Personal Landscape*, 7.

32 Josie Brinton, diary, 8 February 1942.

33 Robin Fedden, 'Personal Landscape', *Personal Landscape* 1, January 1942, 8.

34 Lisa Chaney, *Elizabeth David: A Biography*, London 1998, 163.

35 Chaney, *Elizabeth David*, 165.

36 Cooper, *Writing at the Kitchen Table*, 89.

37 Caroline Lassalle, widow of George Lassalle, in conversation with the author.

38 Cooper, *Writing at the Kitchen Table*, 106f.

39 LD in conversation with the author.

40 Eve Durrell interviewed by Paul Gotch, 22 August 1996, corroborated by Eve Durrell's conversations with the author.

41 Chaney, *Elizabeth David*, 171.

42 Reported to the author by Lisa Chaney, who was told by George Lassalle's ex-wife Judith.

43 *Justine, AQ*, 69.

44 Eve Durrell interviewed by Paul Gotch, 10 May 1992.

45 Hugh Shire, 'George de Menasce OBE, 1890–1967', in *The George de Menasce Collection*, part 1, Spink, London 1971, 5.

46 Laskier, *The Jews of Egypt*, 104.

47 Cooper, *Cairo in the War*, 33 and 191, mistakenly reports that George de Menasce played the piano behind a screen owing to a phobia about showing his hands; in fact that was Count Patrice de Zogheb.

48 *Justine, AQ*, 148f.

49 *Mountolive, AQ*, 395.

50 LD to Tambimuttu, in Victor Selwyn, 'Preface', *Return to Oasis*, xx.

51 Gwyn Williams, 'To Robin Furness', in Gwyn Williams, *Flyting in Egypt: The Story of a Verse War, 1943–45*, Port Talbot 1991, 15.

52 Bernard Spencer, 'From Cairo', in Williams, *Flyting*, 14.

53 Lawrence Durrell, 'Against Cairo: An Ode', in Williams, *Flyting*, 19.

54 Gwyn Williams, 'Lines Written upon Contemplation of the Mystery of the Sex Life of Mr Terence Rogers Tiller', in Williams, *Flyting*, 20.

55 Robin Furness, 'Upon Tease: Epig.', in Williams, *Flyting*, 21.

56 Lawrence Durrell, 'Premature Epitaphs and All', unpublished typescript, six bound copies produced for friends, 1944. British Library.

57 Liddell, 'From Cleopatra', in Williams, *Flyting*, 26.

58 *Justine, AQ*, 49.

59 *Collected Poems*, 158.

60 HM to LD, 12 November 1943, *DML*, 158.

61 LD to HM, *c.* 25 December 1943, *DML*, 159.

62 LD to T. S. Eliot, 3 November 1943, in Mac-Niven, *Lawrence Durrell*, 273.

63 LD to T. S. Eliot, 8 February 1944, second letter of this date, in MacNiven, *Lawrence Durrell*, 285.

64 LD to HM, *c.* 1 March 1945, *DML*, 179.

65 LD to HM, 10 November 1940, *DML*, 144.

66 Henry Miller, *Colossus of Maroussi*, Harmondsworth 1950, 28.

67 LD to HM, 13 March 1941, *DML*, 147.

68 LD to T. S. Eliot, 8 February 1944, first letter of this date, in MacNiven, *Lawrence Durrell*, 285.

69 LD to George Seferis, *c.* October 1943, *Labrys* 5, July 1979, 88f, apparently the earliest indication that Durrell is writing an Alexandrian novel, though he put it aside and did not resume until the following year, first mentioning it to Miller in the summer of 1944. The letter is undated, but Seferis himself dated it to 'around October 1943' rather than later, which seems supported by internal evidence. Moreover, Durrell later wrote on the inside cover of 'Justine Rough Draft', begun in 1955, that the duck shoot on Mareotis, which would become the climactic scene in *Justine*, was based on notes made in 1943.

70 LD to HM, July 1940, *DML*, 139.

71 Shakespeare, *The Tempest*, IV.i.59.

72 *Prospero's Cell*, 16.

73 Ibid., 11.

74 Ibid., 47.

75 Ibid., 59.

76 Ibid., 113.

77 Ibid., 131.

78 Ibid., 133.

79 LD to HM, 21 July 1937, *DML*, 80.

80 Lawrence Durrell, 'Ideas about Poems', *Personal Landscape* 1, January 1942, 3; reprinted in *Personal Landscape: An Anthology of Exile*, 72f.

81 *Justine*, *AQ*, 15.

82 *Prospero's Cell*, 108.

83 *The Black Book*, 223.

84 Molly Tuby in conversation with the author.

85 Among four sheets of notes for *Prospero's Cell* written in red ink on blue air-mail paper. British Library.

86 According to Alan Thomas, Durrell's friend and a collector of his writings, Eve kept various items given her as well as notes that Durrell discarded, often selling them on to Thomas. Alan Thomas in conversation with the author.

87 The correct French is 'il faut avoir confiance en soi-même', i.e. 'you have to have confidence in yourself'.

88 Lawrence Durrell, 'A Little Letter to Eve – Alexandria 1944'. British Library.

89 'Notes for Alex', 9.

90 *Justine*, *AQ*, 26.

91 Lawrence Durrell, notes for *Prospero's Cell*. British Library.

92 LD to HM, 8 February 1944, *DML*, 159.

93 LD to DG, no date. British Library.

94 Diana Menuhin, 'Lawrence Durrell in Alexandria and Sommières', *Twentieth Century Literature* 33:3, fall 1987, 309.

95 Cooper, *Cairo in the War*, 257.

96 Diana Menuhin to Alan Thomas, no date, but probably 1966. British Library.

97 LD to DG ('Dearest Frou Frou'), no date. British Library.

98 Diana Menuhin, *Fiddler's Moll: Life with Yehudi*, London 1984, 25f.

99 Menuhin, 'Lawrence Durrell in Alexandria and Sommières', 310.

100 This is from the version first given by Durrell to Diana Menuhin; the final version is in *Collected Poems*, 130.

101 Lawrence Durrell, 'The Caballi', 32. British Library. A notebook begun in 1953. British Library pagination.

102 *Justine*, *AQ*, 177f.

103 LD to DG in Naples, postmark 27 April 1944. British Library.

104 Mary de Zogheb, diary, 17 April 1944.

105 Williams, *ABC*, 33.

106 *Balthazar*, *AQ*, 235.

107 Ibid., 314.

108 Ibid., 318.

109 Stratis Tsirkas, *Drifting Cities*, New York 1974, 708.

110 MacNiven, *Lawrence Durrell*, 288.

111 HM to LD, 5 May 1944, *DML*, 165.

112 LD to HM, mid-May 1944, *DML*, 167.

113 LD to HM, 23 May 1944, *DML*, 171.

114 Ibid.

115 LD to HM, probably mid-July 1944, *DML*, 167. The letter is undated and in *DML* is dated by the editor as mid-May, continued late May 1944, but this second half of the letter may well date from as late as 11–25 July.

CHAPTER 9 *The Unburied City*

1 LD to HM, 23 May 1944, *DML*, 171.

2 Ibid.

3 Ibid.

4 *Justine, AQ*, 132.

5 Ibid., 135.

6 Derwas Chitty, *The Desert a City*, Oxford 1964, 61. Scetis was the original name for the Wadi Natrun.

7 Robin Fedden, 'Introduction: An Anatomy of Exile', in *Personal Landscape: An Anthology of Exile*, 13.

8 Fedden, 'Introduction: An Anatomy of Exile', 7.

9 Eve Durrell in conversation with the author.

10 Fedden, 'Introduction: An Anatomy of Exile', 10.

11 *Balthazar, AQ*, 280.

12 LD to DG, postmark 29 March 1944. British Library.

13 LD to DG, postmark 27 April 1944. British Library.

14 LD to DG, airgraph, 7 August 1944. British Library. Emile Coué (1857–1926), was a French doctor who devised a system of cures by autosuggestion (Couéism).

15 Killearn, *Diaries*, 3 January 1944.

16 Ibid., 6 February 1944.

17 Josie Brinton to her mother, 1 May 1944.

18 Killearn, *Diaries*, 3 January 1944.

19 Cooper, *Cairo in the War*, 296.

20 William Sholto Douglas, *Years of Command*, London 1966, 198.

21 Cooper, *Cairo in the War*, 172.

22 The foregoing account is drawn from JYB, 'Memoirs', alternative XIII, 23f.

23 LD to HM, 22 August 1944, *DML*, 173.

24 LD to HM, 22 August 1944, a portion of the letter not published in *DML*, 173; see Mac-Niven, *Lawrence Durrell*, 297.

25 LD to HM, 22 August 1944, a portion of the letter not published in *DML*, 173; see Mac-Niven, *Lawrence Durrell*, 296.

26 LD to HM, *c.* September 1944, in MacNiven, *Lawrence Durrell*, 295. Durrell frequently failed to date his letters, so that postmarks have to be deciphered, or failing that, the sequence of letters has to be determined from internal evidence.

27 LD to HM, September 1944, *DML*, 175.

28 LD to HM, October 1944. Southern Illinois University at Carbondale.

29 LD to HM, spring 1945, in *Lawrence Durrell and Henry Miller: A Private Correspondence*, ed. George Wickes, London 1963, 200.

30 *AHG*/1982, xvi.

31 *Justine, AQ*, 81.

32 Ibid., 171.

33 'Notes for Alex' (i.e. 'The Book of the Dead, Manuscript I, Lawrence Durrell Underworld: Notes for Alex'), begun 1944 or possibly 1943. British Library.

34 'Notes for Alex', 6 left. Throughout 'Notes for Alex' Durrell generally wrote out scenes, ideas and extended notes on the right-hand pages, leaving the left-hand pages blank or filling them with doodles or using them to jot down signposts for himself. The pagination system imposed by the British Library is followed throughout: the cover is 1, the first spread (i.e. the inside cover and the first right-hand page) is 2, the second spread (i.e. the following left- and right-hand pages) is 3, and so on. In the example above, the page referred to is thus on the left-hand side of the sixth spread. Where Durrell identifies Melissa as 'Cohen', he also identifies her as 'Teresa Epstein'. Tessa, as he called her, was an American Jewish journalist with whom he had a brief but marking affair while visiting Paris with Nancy towards the end of 1938. Four years later in Palestine he told Nancy, who knew him well enough to believe him, that he had been unfaithful only twice; Tessa was one, and he never forgot her, writing her into his poem 'Cities, Plains and People'. '. . . Tessa was here whose dark / Quickened hair had brushed back rivers, / Trembling with stars by Buda, / In whose inconstant arms he waited' (*Collected Poems*, 158). A few pages further on in 'Notes for Alex' she appears briefly as a character under her own name before being dropped from the MS.

35 'Notes for Alex', 4 right.

36 As Durrell would have known, the publishing firm began as Faber and Gwyer; when the Gwyer family withdrew, Geoffrey Faber decided that his name was insufficient on its own, so he doubled it to Faber and Faber.

37 'Notes for Alex', 4 left.

38 Ibid., 5 left.

39 Lawrence Durrell, untitled 'Bloomsbury' notebook dated 1938. British Library.

40 *AHG*/1982, 70.

41 'Notes for Alex', 15 left.

42 *Justine*, *AQ*, 28.

43 Plotinus, *Enneads*, trans. Stephen MacKenna, London 1991, I.1.8, 10.

44 'Notes for Alex', 14 left.

45 Ibid., 5 right.

46 *Justine*, *AQ*, 18.

47 *AHG*/1982, xv.

48 Ibid., xvf.

49 Sigmund Freud, *The Interpretation of Dreams*, London 1991, 214, where Freud makes reference to Plotinus' *Enneads*, IV.4.17.

50 Plotinus, *Enneads*, IV.4.4.

51 'Notes for Alex', 6 left.

52 Freud, *The Interpretation of Dreams*, 44.

53 'Notes for Alex', 23 right.

54 *Justine*, *AQ*, 143.

55 Ibid., 144.

56 Ibid., 156.

57 Ibid., 143.

58 LD to HM, *c.* September 1944, in MacNiven, *Lawrence Durrell*, 298.

59 Georg Groddeck, *The Book of the It*, London 1949, xxiv. *The Book of the It* was first published in 1923 by the Internationaler Psychoanalytischer Verlag in Vienna, whose founding directors were Sigmund Freud, Sandor Ferenczi and Otto Rank.

60 *Justine*, *AQ*, 17.

61 LD to HM, September 1944, *DML*, 175.

62 *Prospero's Cell*, 9.

63 Killearn, *Diaries*, 14 November 1944.

64 The Stern Gang, named after its founder Avraham Stern, was run from 1940 to 1945 by Yitzhak Shamir, the future leader of the right-wing Likud party, who from 1983 to 1984 and again from 1986 to 1992 was prime minister of Israel.

65 Gilbert, *Churchill*, 803.

66 Ibid.

67 LD to HM, *c.* 1 March 1945, *DML*, 179.

68 LD to HM, spring 1945, in *A Private Correspondence*, 200.

69 LD to HM, *c.* 1 March 1945, *DML*, 179.

70 LD to HM, spring 1945, in *A Private Correspondence*, 200.

71 LD to HM, *c.* 1 March 1945, *DML*, 179.

72 LD to HM, spring 1945, in *A Private Correspondence*, 200.

73 Ibid.

74 Jack Sarfatti to the author, 5 January 2001.

    The remark was made by Carlo Suares to Jack Sarfatti in Paris in 1973; Sarfatti also says he heard it repeated by 'the Krishnamurti/Theosophists when I was in Ojai'.

75 Gabriel Josipovici in conversation with the author.

76 HM to LD, 5 April 1937, *DML*, 68.

77 Summary of *La Procession enchaînée* in *Fondation Carlo Suarès*, 1, Paris 1978, 8.

78 LD to DG, 2 April 1945. British Library.

79 'Notes for Alex', 19 left, 20 left and right.

80 *Justine*, *AQ*, 85.

81 Psalms, 33:6.

82 'Notes for Alex', 26 right.

83 Throughout all Durrell's notes and drafts and throughout *Justine* itself, this character is identified as 'I'. Only towards the end of *Balthazar* is he named as Darley – see *AQ*, 356.

84 *Justine*, *AQ*, 96.

85 Ibid., 97.

86 Ibid., 33.

87 Gilbert, *Churchill*, 816.

88 Josie Brinton to her mother, 22 February 1945.

89 JYB, 'Memoirs', alternative XIII, 10.

90 LD to DG, 2 April 1945. British Library.

91 MacNiven, *Lawrence Durrell*, 300.

92 LD to T. S. Eliot, 17 November 1945, *Twentieth Century Literature* 33:3, fall 1987, 356.

93 LD to T. S. Eliot, early summer 1945, *Twentieth Century Literature* 33:3, fall 1987, 355.

94 LD to HM, 22 June 1945, *DML*, 181.

95 LD to Gwyn Williams, summer 1945, *Flyting*, 10; also *Spirit of Place*, 78.

96 LD to HM, 28 February 1946, *DML*, 194.

97 LD to HM, *c.* October 1945, *DML*, 186.

98 'Notes for Alex', 29 left.

99 *AHG*/1982, xix.

100 *Justine*, *AQ*, 201.

101 *Spirit of Place*, 79.

102 *Collected Poetry*, 99.

103 Lawrence Durrell, *The Greek Islands*, London 1978, 128.

104 Gwyn Williams to LD, 7 November 1945, in MacNiven, *Lawrence Durrell*, 320.

105 Williams, 'Durrell in Egypt', 301.

106 Williams, *ABC*, 32.

107 Elizabeth French, daughter of Alan Wace, in conversation with the author. It is not certain by what route Wace found out about

Menasce, but the embassy was following Zionist activities in Egypt and reports were being sent to Smart.

108 The palace scene was translated by M. E. F. Maxwell; J. S. Blake-Reed translated the hymn of Adonis and M. S. A. Wright translated the street scene. All three men were members of the Royal Archaeological Society; the first two were judges at the Mixed Courts.

109 *AHG*/1982, 37f.

110 Victor Emmanuel later moved to a villa in Smouha, a development built in the 1930s on the drained lake-bed of Hadra, between Moharrem Bey and Abou el Nawatir. In his final illness, however, he returned to the Ambron villa; he died there on 28 December 1947 and is buried behind the altar in St Catherine's, Alexandria's Roman Catholic cathedral. But Gilda Ambron's name is not among those 'which the passer-by may one day read upon the tombs in the cemetery'; her body, if it was found, seems to have been taken to Italy: there is no record of her burial in the registers of either the Italian or the Jewish communities in Alexandria.

EPILOGUE
A Passage from Alexandria

1 See Fraser, *Ptolemaic Alexandria*, vol. 1, 681ff, and Alan K. Bowman, *Egypt after the Pharaohs*, London 1986, 31.

2 'The Caballi', 3 right. In 'The Caballi' the text runs continuously over left- and right-hand pages. See *Justine, AQ*, 17.

3 Memorandum signed by Captain D. Sherret, RAMC, psychiatrist, Psychiatric Division, British Military Hospital, Hanover, BAOR, 5 [January 1953]. Eve Durrell collection.

4 H. Pozner, psychiatrist, British Military Hospital, Hanover, to LD, 5 January 1953. Eve Durrell collection.

5 LD to Alan Thomas, [spring 1953]. British Library.

6 LD to HM, May (?) 1953, *DML*, 269.

7 LD to HM, postmark 24 October 1953, *DML*, 272. In referring to a '4-dimensional' novel which is 'taut and very short', Durrell clearly means the book in hand; the remark does not indicate that he had any intention of writing a quartet.

8 *Justine, AQ*, 165.

9 Ibid., 21. A year or two later Durrell would read Sigmund Freud's letter to Wilhelm Fliess, 1 August 1899, in Sigmund Freud, *The Origins of Psychoanalysis*, London 1954. 'Now for bisexuality!' wrote Freud, and Durrell would quote what followed (above the quotation from the Marquis de Sade) as a preface to *Justine*: 'I am accustoming myself to the idea of regarding every sexual act as a process in which four persons are involved. We shall have a lot to discuss about that.' The four persons are the female and male aspects of the man and the male and female aspects of the woman, a theme Freud addressed in many of his writings and which Durrell also made part of the 'four-dimensional' nature of his novel *Justine*.

10 'The Caballi', last pages.

11 LD to Theodore Stephanides, [April 1954]. British Library.

12 Lawrence Durrell, 'Justine Rough Draft', cover. British Library. Inside the front cover of this blue notebook Durrell at some later point wrote, 'Draft begun in Venice 21st Jan 1954 on notes from '46–'47 – some passages – shoot Mareotis – in 1943. Kyrenia 6 months with S. alone. Terribly happy – dog tired –'. His dating is confusing and can be misleading unless one examines the matter carefully. January 1954 does not indicate when Durrell began writing in this notebook; rather the inscription was written some time later and is meant as a summary of his work in 'Notes for Alex', 'The Caballi' and now in 'Justine Rough Draft'. In fact Durrell sailed from Venice in January 1953, and indeed he did first write 1953 but changed it to 1954, both the inscription and his correction probably being written in 1955, for immediately below it there is an outline of a hand which he has inscribed as 'Sapphy's hand March 1955'. Durrell offered a similar sort of summary when at some time he wrote on the back cover of 'The Caballi' '1944–1954', which does not mean he began the notebook in 1944, as it was apparently manufactured by the government only in 1949; rather he is taking into account his earlier work in 'Notes for Alex'. To summarise

the chronology, then: in 'Notes for Alex', begun in 1944, Durrell works out his ideas and characters; in 'The Caballi', begun in 1953, he begins telling the story as it would more or less appear in the published version of *Justine*; and in 'Justine Rough Draft', begun in 1954, he continues that same story. Whatever notes he had from 1943 of his experience at a duck shoot were not after all put to use in 'Justine Rough Draft', as he abandoned writing in this notebook just as he was approaching the climactic duck shoot scene.

13 'Justine Rough Draft', 2. British Library pagination. The ellipsis represents about a dozen lines that Durrell copied out of Forster's quotation from Plotinus. See *Justine, AQ*, 147f.

14 MacNiven, *Lawrence Durrell*, 419.

15 LD to Alan Thomas, [1955]. British Library.

16 First written in 'Justine Rough Draft', these lines appear in *Justine, AQ*, 153.

17 Lawrence Durrell, poetry notebook. British Library.

18 LD to HM, *c.* January (?) 1956, *DML*, 279.

19 LD to HM, *c.* November 1955, *DML*, 278.

20 LD to HM, *c.* January (?) 1956, *DML*, 279.

21 LD to Richard Aldington, after 11 October 1957, in *Literary Lifelines*, ed. Ian S. Mac-Niven and Harry T. Moore, New York 1981, 31.

22 Ibid.

23 LD to HM, *c.* January (?) 1956, *DML*, 279.

24 *Clea, AQ*, 832.

25 LD to Alan Thomas, postmark 13 June 1956. British Library.

26 Lawrence Durrell, *Bitter Lemons*, London 1959, 214.

27 Ibid., 216.

28 Ibid., 163f.

29 *Balthazar, AQ*, 235.

30 *Bitter Lemons*, 164.

31 LD to Alan Pringle, editor at Faber and Faber, received 24 July 1956.

32 LD interviewed by Edwin Newman on *Speaking Freely*, WNBC TV, 6 April 1970, broadcast a week later. After telling Faber in July 1956 that he wanted to write 'a series, I don't know how many', Durrell was still undecided about their number a month before the publication of *Justine*, writing to Miller in December 1955 that he was thinking of writing *five* Alexandrian novels.

33 *Balthazar, AQ*, 209f.

34 EMF to FB, 25 August 1917, *Letters*, vol. 1, 267.

35 Jasper Yeates Brinton, 'A Philadelphian Describes the Mass Evacuation from Egypt', *Philadelphia Sunday Bulletin*, 25 November 1956.

36 Hugh Thomas, *The Suez Affair*, London 1967, 164.

INDEX